The Project Management Answer Book

The Project Management Answer Book

Jeff Furman, PMP

MANAGEMENTCONCEPTS

MANAGEMENTCONCEPTS

8230 Leesburg Pike, Suite 800
Vienna, VA 22182
(703) 790-9595
Fax: (703) 790-1371
www.managementconcepts.com

PMI, PMP, Program Management Professional (PgMP), CAPM, OPM3, OPM3 Product-Suite, PMI Certified OPM3 Assessor, PMI Certified OPM3 Consultant, PMI global standards, and PMI-ISSIG are registered marks of the Project Management Institute, Inc.

Printed in the United States of America

Library of Congress Cataloging-in-Publication Data
Furman, Jeffrey L.
  The project management answer book / Jeff Furman.
      p. cm.
   ISBN 978-1-56726-297-1
1. Project management. 2. Project management--Standards. I. Title.
HD69.P75.F87 2010

658.4'04--dc22

2010041564

10 9 8 7 6 5 4 3 2 1

About the Author

Jeff Furman, PMP, has extensive experience as both a PMP® instructor/corporate technical trainer and an IT project manager. He has managed many large IT projects for Fortune 500 companies in the New York metropolitan area, including new product evaluations and installations, quality assurance testing, and infrastructure upgrades. He also led the implementation and management of a major change management system for a large brokerage firm, used continuously by more than 1,000 developers to move their new code into production.

As an instructor, Jeff has helped many project managers, as well as IT developers and trainers, through his award-winning classes. For the last four years he has specialized in teaching PMP® certification exam preparation classes, conducting more than 75 five-day sessions in New York and around the United States and helping hundreds of project managers attain certification. He also teaches advanced presentation skills, helping many technical trainers become certified by Microsoft, CompTIA, and Adobe. Jeff himself is a Comp TIA CTT+ Certified Technical Trainer and CompTIP Project+ Certifieed Project Manager.

Jeff has published technical articles on a broad range of topics, from IT software tools to Y2K to PMP® exam preparation to risk management, and has interviewed singer/songwriters for the *Bergen Record*. He lives in Hoboken, New Jersey, with his wife Martha and their shelter rescue dog, Faith.

Contents

Foreword

Many years ago I began my career working as a software developer, until one momentous day I was pulled aside by the department director and asked if I wanted to make the transition to project manager. I readily accepted without any inkling that this would change the direction of my entire career.

The following Monday, I found myself in charge of my first real project. The team consisted of six developers, one business analyst, and a quality assurance manager. Our combined annual burn rate was almost $1,000,000, and as I stared at my computer monitor, it slowly dawned on me that I did not have a very good idea of what I was supposed to do. Worse yet, I found that answers were not as readily available as I had hoped. Project management at this organization, and indeed in much of the business world, was largely a vague concept.

I had to look outside of the company for ideas on how to lead and manage a real project. One of the best resources, I discovered, was to simply sit down and talk with other project managers who were facing the same problems I was. This process really was the proverbial school of hard knocks, and I look back at the first few projects I managed with a mixture of pride and embarrassment. I didn't understand the best way to build, track, and communicate a schedule. I wasn't aware that there were techniques to help me estimate costs. I had never heard of a work breakdown structure. Worst of all, I didn't know how to organize, motivate, and lead a team. There were better ways to do most of the things I was doing; I just didn't know what they were.

My turning point came when a senior manager came by my desk gushing over a project management plan that a new colleague had developed for him.

From the moment I saw this comprehensive plan, I realized there was a better way to manage projects after all. This colleague took time to mentor me in this process, showing me best practices, connecting me with resources, and helping me to move beyond some of the mistakes I was making. At the same time I was learning about process, it became clear to me that projects are accomplished through people. Managing projects is more about leading, motivating, and managing the right people than it is about defining tasks and schedules. Process is important, but good process without capable, trained, and motivated people is worthless.

So it is no shock that my first reaction when I picked up this book was to exclaim, "If only Jeff had written this book 25 years ago!" *The Project Management Answer Book* covers an amazing breadth of topics. The advice it includes is concise and straightforward. It is brimming with wisdom from someone who faced these questions in the real world and has sifted through the various theories and practices to find what works.

If you are just starting out as a project manager, Furman's book is the perfect place to begin. It is a rich resource of concepts and practical help. The questions that are asked throughout the book are ones that every project manager has asked at some point in his or her career.

If you have been practicing project management for some time, this will earn a place on your desk as an excellent field reference. How many times have you wished you had a particular template, example, or a guide to walk you through a process?

Whatever path you've taken to get here, this book will prove to be a valuable resource in taking you further.

With you on the journey,
Andy Crowe, PMP, PgMP

Author of *The PMP Exam: How To Pass On Your First Try* and
*Alpha Project Managers: What The Top 2% Know
That Everyone Else Does Not*

Preface

In spite of the ongoing parade of amazing technological advances, the vast majority of projects do not come in on time, on budget, or completely to specifications. Modern projects are ever larger and more complex, and project managers (PMs) often are not hands-on experts in the content areas of their projects' deliverables. On top of scheduling and management issues, they have to grapple with software bugs, engineering issues, and all kinds of personnel-related curveballs.

From a human resources standpoint, projects are frequently understaffed to keep costs down. Additional difficulties arise when PMs are brought in as consultants, often mid-project, and are expected to manage team members who hold permanent positions. Managing virtual teams, often dispersed across the country or the world, puts PMs at an even bigger disadvantage.

With all of these factors making the PM's job harder, I wrote this book to make your life easier. In 15 years of managing IT projects for Fortune 500 financial firms, I led a wide array of new product evaluations, implementations, and support initiatives. As a PMP® instructor for the last four years, I have logged many frequent flier miles teaching project management across the United States, from Carlyss, Louisiana, and Houston on the Gulf Coast, to northeastern cities including Bethesda, Maryland; Washington, D.C.; and Philadelphia, and, frequently, in the Empire State Building back home in New York.

I wrote this book to take the most valuable PM best practices known today and break them down into quick, easy-to-read questions and answers that all levels of PM can relate to. The intended audience for this book includes everyone from beginners looking to break into managing projects to PMs looking for new skills to help them out on a current project to more senior managers interested in updating their knowledge or preparing for PM certification.

In developing this book, I was able to draw on thousands of hours of teaching time and distill the many PM concepts into easy-to-understand, bite-size Q&As. The book covers all the fundamentals covered in the Project Management Institute's (PMI) A Guide to the Project Management Body of Knowledge (*PMBOK® Guide*), plus many techniques and best practices I've picked up in the companies where I worked and those shared in class by my PM students. As an added bonus, I have devoted a full chapter, plus several appendices, to the various PM certifications. These sections of the book offer many little-known tricks of the trade about applying, preparing for, and passing the exams, plus networking resources that my students have found useful.

My goal with this book is to help as many PMs as I can become more productive and efficient on their projects and, also, help them toward obtaining the PMP® and related certifications—which make a huge difference in today's job market.

The Project Management Answer Book introduces the reader to the key principles of project management that every private- or public-sector PM needs to know. It also does double duty as a primer for anyone considering formal project management certification as a PMP, CAPM, PgMP, CompTIA Project+, Microsoft MCSE, and others. The book carefully ties all the content to PMI's accumulated knowledge base, the *PMBOK® Guide*, which is the official knowledge source not only for the PMI certifications but for certifications from other vendors as well.

The book covers the following critical topics and more:

- Bringing projects in on time, on budget, and on scope
- Controlling risks that can threaten a project
- Building quality into a project
- Using key project management tools and best practices and following current standards
- Effectively integrating soft skills into your projects
- Navigating the ethical challenges that PMs face in today's business world.

The Project Management Answer Book consists of 13 chapters. We begin with questions about what constitutes a project, the role of a PM, and the fundamentals of project planning and end with a chapter full of tips about the PM certification process and exams. Each chapter opens with a short intro/overview to orient the reader to the questions covered in that chapter and ends with a "Top Ten Pitfalls" list, which serves as a handy quick reference as well as a summary of key points in the chapter. All the questions are listed in the table of contents at the front of the book, allowing for quick access and future follow-up review of all the questions and content.

Throughout the 13 chapters, sidebars cover the following topic areas:

- **Worldwide best practices** (in accordance with PMI's *PMBOK® Guide*): practical ways to implement the core PM concepts, artifacts, and tools to improve project performance and achieve high-quality, low-risk results.
- **Real-world tips for successful project management** based on my 15 years of PM experience in IT for leading financial firms.
- **Hints and tips to demystify the PM certification exams** based on my experience teaching PM prep courses.

Three appendices also are included:

- **Appendix A. Networking Tips and Social Media For PMs:** The best professional organizations, virtual groups, and webcast sources for PMs.
- **Appendix B. The Formulas PMs Need to Know for Certification Exams:** A list of the key formulas PMs need to know for the PM exams (PMP, CAPM, PgMP, Project+, and more). A companion fill-in-the-blanks version of this list is provided to help you study and self-test in preparation for the PM certification exams.
- **Appendix C. Quick Study Sheet for the Processes Covered on the PMP® Exam:** A sheet highlighting the PMP® processes, mapped to the *PMBOK® Guide* knowledge areas and process groups. A fill-in-the-blanks version also is provided, which will be helpful for memorizing the key processes for the exam and testing your learning as you go.

Wishing all my students and readers much continued success...

Jeff Furman
December 2010

Acknowledgments

I would like to thank the following authors and experts: Scott Berkun, Randy Cohen ("The Ethicist"), Andy Crowe, Dr. Gary Evans, Dr. David Hillson ("The Risk Doctor"), the late Rita Mulcahy, and the writing team of Jennifer Greene and Andrew Stellman.

Special thanks also to Mark Morrow, editor and book packager, who helped make this book happen, Courtney Chiaparas, my editor at Management Concepts, and Myra Strauss, editorial director at Management Concepts. I would also like to thank Lisa Snyder, my web-designer, Michelle Wild, my photographer, Dylan Lorenz, my video editor, Jack Davis, my PMP® instructor, Joseph Furman, my father, and Martha Garvey, my wife.

CHAPTER 1

Project Management Basics

Before we dive into the many facets of planning and managing projects, there are several key concepts, definitions, and resources that PMs need to know about. Here are a few quick Q&As to give you the basics.

PROJECTS, PMs, PROJECT MANAGEMENT, AND PROGRAMS

Q1. What is the formal definition of a project?

A1. A project is defined as a temporary and unique work effort with a beginning date and an end date that creates a product, service, or result. Here's a little more detail on each of the key pieces of this definition:

- **Unique work effort:** A team is assembled and commits to work on a specific goal, often under a contract.
- **Temporary, with a beginning date and an end date:** A project is planned to start on a certain date and complete on a deadline (unlike maintenance or operations work, which is ongoing or perpetual).
- **Creates a product, service, or result:** The purpose of the project is to create something that didn't exist before, often called the deliverable, which is turned over at completion to the customer who initiated the project.

Q2. How would you define the terms *project management* and *project manager*?

A2. Project management, performed by a project manager, is planning, organizing, and supervising a project (a work effort that fulfills the definition in Q&A 1), and proactively doing everything possible to make it succeed.

Project managers (PMs) often are either consultants or full-time employees of the company executing the project for the client (the providing organization or service provider). Often, there is a project manager on the client side as well; the client's PM is a counterpart to the PM running the project on behalf of the providing organization.

It is assumed that a PM is, to some extent, following the formal discipline of leading a project and working from a project plan.

Q3. What are a few good examples of projects?

A3. Here are six examples of projects in the business world:

In IT:

- Creating a new software application or system
- Assembling a help desk from scratch to support such an application.

In a pharmaceutical company:

- Creating a new drug
- Putting together a marketing plan and rolling out the new drug on the world marketplace.

In construction:

- Building a house
- Building a new stretch of road.

Q4. What's the difference between a project and a program?

A4. Constructing a single house is a basic example of a project. By contrast, designing an entire housing complex and building all the houses, plus all of the peripherals that might be part of the complex (for example, a parking garage or health club) would be an example of a program, which is defined as a group of related projects.

PROJECT KICKOFF DOCUMENTS

Q5. What is the document that starts off a project called?

A5. The charter is the first document created on a project. It is typically created by the project sponsor, who is the manager on the client side requesting and financing the project. But in many cases, the charter can also be created by the PM at the request and direction of the sponsor.

Note that from the PM's point of view, it might seem as if the first documents kicking off a project are legal documents, such as a contract or a statement of work (SOW). This is because PMs are often brought in after the client has already written a project charter and sometimes after it has created additional planning documents, such as the schedule.

Q6. What are the main elements of a charter?

A6. The charter provides a clear statement of what the project is supposed to accomplish, including a high-level description of its goals and intended deliverables. This lays the groundwork for effective requirements gathering and, later, for properly defining the scope of the project, from which the schedule will ultimately be created.

Usually the name of the PM assigned to the project appears in the charter, along with the sponsor's name and sometimes his or her signature. The sponsor's signature is very valuable because it authorizes the project and officially permits people in the performing organization to work on the project, and it also empowers the PM, helping him or her obtain the resources needed to succeed in leading the project's activities.

Top Ten Most Important Elements in the Project Charter

1. A high-level description of the project.
2. The goals and expected deliverables of the project.
3. The name of the PM, making it official who'll be running the project, and the name and (optionally) the signature of the project sponsor.
4. Time constraints, such as hard deadlines for the project or for any of the project's individual milestones.
5. Cost constraints, if a budget cap is known at charter creation time.
6. Other constraints—for example, a new car being created by the project must average 32 mpg, must surpass certain quality metrics, or must comply with a certain law or regulation.
7. The names of the key stakeholders who will be part of the project.

8. Risks that could jeopardize the project's success, e.g., "If this project is not completed before our competitor's product hits the market, our efforts may be in vain."

9. Assumptions about the project—for example, "We are assuming that roughly ten technicians will be provided for this project, and that level of staffing will enable us to come in on deadline."

10. Dependencies—on other projects being completed, as well as on market conditions, pending rules or legislation, and other external factors.

Q7. Why do PMs need a formal project charter?

A7. The project charter is more than a recommendation—it's considered a necessity. Many projects have a policy: "If there's no charter, there's no project." This is because when projects are launched without a charter, serious problems can (and often do) arise. For example:

• Did you ever work on a project for which the PM had trouble getting resources or claiming his or her authority? Having your name on the charter as the PM empowers you and helps you get the resources and respect you need, which is especially helpful in situations in which the power of the PM is limited.

• Were you ever on a project that you thought was a go but that was never actually green-lighted? Making a project official by documenting it in an authorized charter and getting the required sign-offs is a way of putting the pedal to the metal and forcing attention to be paid to the project.

• Did you ever work on a project for which the goals (or the scope, deadlines, budget cap, or risks) were not all clearly communicated to the project manager or team? Getting the key elements of the project down in writing in the charter clarifies and communicates them for all of the many people who will need to know about them.

PROCESSES AND PHASES

Q8. What is meant by the terms *project management processes* and *process groups?*

A8. An easy way to think of PM processes is to think of them as steps, meaning a set of sequential actions to accomplish a specific piece of the project.

Within the PMI methodology, anything a PM or project team member may be working on at any given time falls into one of the 42 PMI processes, such as developing the schedule, developing the project management plan, or closing the project or phase. The processes, in turn, fall into five categories, which PMI calls process groups. These include:

- *Initiating processes:* These are the early steps that start off a project, including the initial request from the client and the sponsor's and (later) the PM's early efforts to respond. They include developing the project charter, identifying stakeholders, and collecting requirements.

- *Planning processes:* The PM executes these processes to plan the project. Planning is initially based on the request to begin the project and, later, on the requirements collected from the client. The process of developing the schedule and the planning steps, including planning quality, procurements, communications, risk management, and other aspects of planning, fall into this group.

- *Executing processes:* This, in a nutshell, is the "git 'er done!" work of the project. The PM oversees production of the deliverables the project is contracted to create and manages the employees performing this work. Processes in this group include directing and managing the project, developing the project team, and conducting procurements.

- *Monitoring and controlling processes:* Referred to in some companies as "check and correct," this is the group of processes in which the PM constantly observes and measures progress against the plan and makes corrections where needed to keep the project under control. Processes include controlling the scope, controlling the schedule, and controlling the budget.

- *Closing processes:* These are the final steps a PM completes to wrap up a project. There are only two closing processes in the PMI model: closing procurements and closing the project or phase.

Q9. What is the difference between a *process* and a *phase*?

A9. Think of processes as specifically tied to artifacts that the PM is working on *internally* to help the team run the project. These include the processes of developing the charter, the document that defines and authorizes the project, and developing the schedule, the document that will guide all the project's activities.

Phases are broader, like subprojects within a project. Like a project, each phase usually consists of many processes from the five process groups listed in the previous Q&A. Phases are tied to both external deliverables and time milestones that the client is watching for, as in the following example:

- Phase 1 could be completion of the beta version of a new software application.
- Phase 2 could be completion of initial testing of the beta version.
- Phase 3 could be completion of the rollout of the application to a pilot team of users.
- Phase 4 could be completion of the first production rollout to customers.

THE *PMBOK® GUIDE* AND PMI

Q10. What is the *PMBOK® Guide*, and how can it help me as a project manager?

A10. The *PMBOK® Guide* is formally titled *A Guide to the Project Management Body of Knowledge*. It's the go-to reference guide for standards and best practices for many project managers around the world. The certification exams for project managers given by PMI, and other certifying bodies are officially based largely (but not exclusively) on the content in the *PMBOK® Guide*.

If you have never used the *PMBOK® Guide*, you may have the impression that it's a dusty old manual of little practical value. But it's actually a vital book for all PM practitioners, filled with valuable PM best practices, concepts, and standards. And it is updated every three years like clockwork by expert project management practitioners from all around the world. The current edition is version 4, released January 1, 2009.

The *PMBOK® Guide*: Body or Book?

Though it is issued in book form by PMI, the *B* in *PMBOK® Guide* stands for *body* (not *book*) because it refers to the entire body of worldwide project management knowledge currently available (which is something of a moving target because PM best practices are always being added to and updated).

Q11. How can PMI help me in my career?

A11. Project managers are fortunate to have a large and robust support organization behind them in the Project Management Institute. PMI is a nonprofit, member-driven organization made up of project managers helping other project managers. It is a truly global organization with hundreds of local chapters in places from Rio de Janeiro to New York to Nova Scotia in the Americas to exotic locales around the world, including Porto Salvo, San Isidro, Moscow, and Mumbai. This is good news for job seekers: The certification process and exams are identical in every location, so certification by PMI makes PMs marketable for positions all over the globe.

Other benefits of PMI membership:

- PMI is very well known as the publisher of the authoritative *PMBOK® Guide*. All members of the organization receive a free downloadable version of the *PMBOK® Guide*.
- PMI is the industry-leading certifying body for PMs, offering the Project Management Professional® (PMP®) certification and several other much-sought-after credentials. (Certification is covered in detail in Chapter 13).

Additional career benefits for PMs include:

- Chapter meetings for networking
- Leading-edge educational seminars and magazines on the latest PM tools and techniques
- SIGs (specific interest groups) for specialized areas of PM knowledge, including risk management, IT, energy, human resources, and many more
- Volunteer project management opportunities and chapter officerships
- Annual conferences (one in the U.S. and one international conference each year) offering many educational seminars and excellent networking opportunities
- Career websites—for instance, most local PMI chapters will offer members free access to job postings in that area and allow PMs to post their resumes and any work they have published on career websites
- One-on-one mentoring programs
- Free study groups for the PMP® and other PMI certification exams.

THE WORK OF PROJECT MANAGEMENT

Q12. What is a project management office, and how can it help PMs?

A12. A project management office (PMO) is typically a team made up of some of the highly experienced PMs and senior managers at a company, who often split their PMO duties with their primary management responsibilities. Not every company is large enough for a PMO or decides to have a formal office for project management. But many companies create PMOs to help keep track of key projects and to help their PMs successfully face the many challenges that come with the job.

Most PMOs can be classified as one of three types (or a blend of the three):

- *PM assistance:* This common type of PMO provides assistance to PMs, acting as a go-to resource where PMs can find project management templates, documentation, training, and other needed support.
- *PM oversight:* These PMOs play a strong oversight role. The company's projects are all under the high-level jurisdiction of the PMO, and the PMs often have an informal or dotted-line reporting relationship and some accountability to the PMO on their projects.
- *The PMs are a part of the PMO:* In some companies, PMs are direct reports to senior managers in the PMO. The PMO is the department for which the PMs work on projects.

Q13. What job titles might I have as a project manager?

A13. A project manager is usually in charge of managing a single project or several projects concurrently. In some companies, PMs may be called "junior" or "senior" PMs, based on experience and seniority. In addition, a PM's title might have one of three "flavors," based on his or her decision-making authority, as follows:

| 1. Project expeditor → 2. Project coordinator → 3. Project manager → |

This is what I call a "three bears" example, because each position provides a different degree of decision-making authority relative to the other two. You can think of it as a power continuum from left to right, where:

- A project expeditor has the least power
- A project coordinator is in the middle in terms of power
- A full PM has the most decision-making authority of the three.

A program manager is more highly ranked than a project manager. He or she is usually a former PM who manages multiple related projects—in other words, programs—and may also manage several project managers.

Q14. What is a *project portfolio*, and what is the role of a project portfolio manager?

A14. A project portfolio is broader than a program; it usually refers to all of the projects in a company (or all of the projects in a large division of a company). And so:

- Several *projects* make up a *program*
- Multiple *programs* comprise a company's *portfolio*
- In companies in which a senior PM is in charge of the project portfolio, he or she is called a *portfolio manager*.

PM Vocabulary Mash-Up		
A *project*	Can be part of a *program*	And all of a company's projects and programs make up its *portfolio.*
A *project manager*	Reports up to a *program manager*	And several program managers can report up to a *portfolio manager.*

Q15. What is the project sponsor's role?

A15. Every project must have a sponsor, who you can think of as the "money person" who green-lights your project. Often, a sponsor is a senior manager on the client side. He or she initiates the project, secures the funding for it, and continues to fund and support the project throughout its life cycle.

During the project, the sponsor often acts as the go-to person in disputes between the client and the performing organization, regarding issues that cannot be resolved by the PM, or on other issues requiring an executive decision. The sponsor also has a key role at the end of the project: He or she accepts the project's final deliverables, often signing off at that time to verify that the project's goals, scope, and quality requirements have all been met.

The sponsor isn't always on the client side. For example, in an IT department such as the one in which I worked for many years, the chief information officer (CIO) on the performing organization side could be considered the sponsor by the project team, whose projects the CIO green-lights. Meanwhile, the CIO answers to senior management on the client side.

Q16. What are the key differences between project management in the past and in the present?

A16. It's an understatement to say that projects in the past were much smaller and much less complex than today's projects are. For example, people have been building houses for thousands of years. In the last century, wiring homes for electricity became standard, followed by modern conveniences such as central heat and air. New houses built in the last decade or two are often equipped with cable and satellite TV wiring, computer-controlled security and appliances, and wireless internet. As high-tech equipment has become more prevalent in new homes, residential construction projects have become ever more demanding, which has dramatically raised the bar for the level of expertise required of PMs.

Q17. How can software assist PMs?

A17. There is a wide array of amazingly powerful project management software. To paraphrase William Shakespeare, these days there are products undreamt of in the philosophy of people who managed projects before software toolkits began making their way to PMs' desktops. See Figure 1-1 for a list of just some of the types of tools that PMs can use to lighten their workloads.

A FEW MORE KEY MANAGEMENT FUNDAMENTALS

Q18. If all projects have a start point and an end point, why is project management called an iterative process?

A18. It would be a lot easier if project management consisted of simply leading a team, once, through a number of linear processes. But as experienced PMs know, it's inevitable that on any project, some important information will change between day 1 and project close. Perhaps the client will request a new feature or there will be an unexpected personnel change or a funding cut—you name it! And this is why project management is usually *not* linear but instead is iterative. As critical info affecting the project changes, the project plans need to be adjusted accordingly to comply with the changes. This requires at least one additional pass (and often more than one) through the key planning processes. For instance, change requests often result in schedule changes, so the process of developing the schedule must be re-executed. And according to the PMI model, this also means revisiting additional processes that are heavily tied in to the schedule, such as creating the work breakdown structure and estimating activity duration (covered in detail in Chapter 4).

Automated software tools that can help project managers include:

- Project schedule creation tools
- Work breakdown structure creation tools
- Blueprint generation tools
- Computer-aided design (CAD) software
- Graphic design tools
- Modeling tools
- Estimating tools
- Earned value calculation tools
- Human resources management tools
- Risk probability and analysis tools
- Presentation-building software
- Screen-capture and script-building software
- Website prototyping tools
- Idea-map generators
- Change management systems
- Configuration management systems
- Monte Carlo tools
- Testing and debugging tools
- System performance measurement tools
- Inventory tools
- Social networking tools
- Online survey/questionnaire tools
- Modeling tools
- Smartphone PM applications

…and more.

Figure 1-1: Types of Automated Software Tools that Can Make Project
Management Faster and More Efficient

In a ripple effect, changes to the schedule can heavily impact other aspects of the project, such as the project scope. For instance, if management needs to move a deadline up, the change often necessitates a reduction in the project's scope to help meet that deadline. In process terms, this means re-executing the process of defining the scope and other interrelated processes. The result is that project processes in the real world often are iterative, meaning that they are done as many times as needed—and this leads us to the Deming cycle.

Q19. What is the *Deming cycle?*

A19. The Deming cycle, also called the plan-do-check-act cycle, is a best practice for managing projects. It gets its name from well-known management consultant W. Edwards Deming, who popularized this concept (following the work of quality-control pioneer Walter Shewhart). The Deming cycle (shown in Figure 1-2) represents project management as a repeated-as-needed series of the following four steps:

1. *Plan:* Create the project plan.
2. *Do:* Execute the plan created in step 1.
3. *Check:* Verify that the action you took in step 2 yielded the correct results.
4. *Act:* If any issues, errors, or corrections came up when you checked in step 3, go back to step 1 and proceed again through steps 2, 3, and 4.

This is a *feedback loop* in which the four sequential steps are repeated as necessary until the performing organization and the client are satisfied with the way the project deliverables are being created.

Figure 1-2: The Deming Cycle

We can make a helpful analogy between the Deming cycle and a board game like *Chutes and Ladders*. The objective of the game is to move from start to finish, but problems often come up along the way that send you back up to a spot higher on the board. You then have to proceed back down again from there. The difference is that in project management, on a second pass through a process, you build on the prior work you have already done in that process, as well as everything you and your team have learned on the project since you initiated the process the first time.

Q20. What is *agile project management,* and how does it compare to or replace more traditional approaches, such as PMI's?

A20. Agile is a new project management method that is now in vogue. It's thought of as a faster, leaner way to manage projects. It follows in the footsteps of agile programming, based on the principles outlined in *The Agile Manifesto,* available as an authorized free download at http://agilemanifesto.org.

Agile project management is intended to be quicker, cheaper, less process driven, and more results driven. It promotes taking shortcuts such as the following:

- *Plan less thoroughly, and focus on the short term.* Because requirements are likely to change in mid-project anyway, too much planning can often be counterproductive. For example, instead of using PM software to create extremely detailed schedules, use old-fashioned, simple tools like a whiteboard or yellow sticky notes put up on a corkboard. Each team member can then quickly update the status of his or her tasks in a central, easily accessible location.

- *Collocate as much as possible.* Locate your people together whenever you can to foster cooperation, cut through red tape, and discourage turf battles and indirect communication such as memos and emails. For example, if developers and testers share an office, they can talk face-to-face about bugs instead of sending long emails back and forth.

- *Anticipate that clients will frequently change their requirements, and be ready to adapt.* Have your team come in to work each day ready to come up with solutions to client requests, instead of reluctant to deviate from the existing game plan.

- Hold fewer and shorter meetings.
- Instead of holding weekly status meetings, ask team members to update their status via email.
- Only assemble the team when there are major problems to be solved that require the presence and expertise of all team members.
- Hold stand-up meetings—at which all team members literally have to stand. Standing up has been proven to shorten meetings in itself (people want to avoid foot pain). But this format also encourages team members to walk directly up to the stakeholders they have current issues with and iron things out right away, further cutting down on the length of the meeting.

Q21. What does the Japanese term *kaizen* mean, and why is it a central tenet of project management around the world?

A21. *Kaizen* is the philosophy of proactively making continuous, small improvements on a project. It's the idea that every process, even when it's running well, can always be improved—a PM can always find some part that can be tweaked, automated, or even eliminated, improving the project's chance of success.

In *kaizen*, there is an emphasis on the word *small*. Many people are, by nature averse to change, so small positive changes are often more likely to be accepted than are large, disruptive changes. By starting small, a PM can more easily manage the implementation of the change. Once the change is accepted on a small scale, it stands a much better chance of catching on because the stakeholders who have accepted the change and seen its benefits have bought into it. You can tap into this buy-in to help spread the change further and on a larger scale.

TOP TEN PITFALLS TO AVOID WHEN STARTING A PROJECT

1. Trying to add an extra project to your team's current workload without allocating additional time or resources.
2. Beginning a project with very loose time and cost estimates or no specific estimates. This happens a lot in start-up companies, where there can be a great deal of optimism without enough oversight and corporate structure to keep things realistic.

3. Working outside PMI standards.

4. Doing it your way, ignoring company protocol, company templates, and other established guidelines.

5. Failing to look for pertinent lessons learned and general historical data.

6. Jumping into a project without clarifying your customer's specifications.

7. Not specifying which costs will be covered by the client and which by the performing organization—for example, who will cover the cost of a license for software the project team needs but that it is not yet licensed to use.

8. Failing to clearly establish the metrics by which the project will be evaluated, especially quality, risk, and customer satisfaction metrics.

9. Not clarifying the team reporting structure and stakeholders' roles early on, causing conflict and making it difficult for the PM to foster teamwork and good morale.

10. Beginning a project without a formal project charter. Some companies use similar documents with other names, such as a kickoff document, which is fine as long as it includes the same essentials, such as the sponsor's signature. Working without such a document, however, can be a recipe for disaster!

CHAPTER 2

Project Planning Essentials

Give me six hours to chop down a tree and I will spend the first four sharpening the axe.

—Abraham Lincoln

With projects under ever-shrinking budgets and deadlines, many PM environments have become a madhouse of multitasking. Unfortunately, the PM equivalent of texting while driving does *not* double efficiency, and cutting corners to speed up projects often hurts more than it helps. The good news is that, like chopping wood with a well-sharpened axe, many projects today run extremely efficiently when care is taken to plan them properly. This chapter covers a number of key planning skills, including using historical information, studying the performing organization's environmental factors, and pre-planning (a.k.a. "planning the planning"). Pre-planning is up-front planning with a purpose: to start the project off right.

PLANNING BASICS

Q1. What are some general tips about project planning that help build in success?

A1. Begin with these three tips:

- All planning documents distributed to the team should always be as short and concise as possible. If plans get too lengthy, no one will want to read them.

- Not all planning methods and steps are right for all projects. For smaller projects, be careful not to go overboard, using methods and steps more appropriate for large-scale projects.

- Before jumping into planning, first make sure you have assembled a planning toolkit.

Q2. What should be part of a modern PM's planning toolkit?

A2. When you sit down to plan a project, you should have three key types of tools at hand:

- *PMI's* **PMBOK® Guide**, plus other books and manuals specific to the subject of your project. You'll find that the *PMBOK® Guide* touches on most things you will do as a PM, so you'll find it to be a handy desk reference.

- *Project templates.* Using templates is the fastest way to ramp up a project and a good way to avoid reinventing the wheel. There are two types of templates: old plans and project artifacts that you can use as models, and commercial fill-in-the-blanks templates, which are readily available.

- *The PM software*, such as MS Project, Oracle Primavera, or other program, that you'll use to create your schedule and other project artifacts.

Top Ten Features of Automated Project Scheduling Software

1. Lets you quickly key in (and later update) all of the tasks on a project, in a standard format that all PM professionals can easily understand and work from.

2. Displays the schedule in a variety of useful visual formats, including Gantt charts, network diagrams, task sheet lists, milestone views, and many more.

3. Represents the logical paths through your project, with an emphasis on the critical path and critical-path-related information, such as float (covered in detail in Chapter 4).

4. Auto-numbering of tasks. In one keystroke, you can number all of the tasks on your project, including auto-generated subordinate numbering for child-relationship tasks, among other features.

5. Shows dependencies between tasks along with the type of dependency relationship, such as finish-to-start or start-to-start.

6. Tracks the current progress of the tasks on your project by percentage of completion.

7. Automatically calculates earned value (EV) for your project. (EV is covered in depth in Chapter 5.)

8. Prints your schedule with all current changes and in many views and reports.

9. Allows you to assign resources to your project and document essential information about them—including names, pay rates, and overtime rates—and keeps a running total of each resource's hours and pay.

10. Has many additional capabilities: lets you merge schedules from different files, link to other software artifacts, connect your schedule with other schedule management software on your network, and more.

HISTORICAL INFORMATION AND LESSONS LEARNED

Q3. What is *historical information*, and how does it help a PM with planning?

A3. Historical information is any information a PM can gather from past projects that can help the current project. It includes methods, tips, tools, techniques, best practices, old plans, and reports from prior projects. The information can either come from past projects at the company where you are currently working or from all sources at your disposal, such as projects documented by other PMs in magazine articles, websites, blogs, and online discussion groups. Good information is readily available and easy to access. It is a highly recommended best practice to take advantage of historical information when planning any project.

To their own detriment, many PMs fail to take the time at the onset of a project to look for historical information that might help make a big difference in its success. There is always pressure to get a project started "yesterday" and to try and save time and money by hitting the ground running without first taking the time to find useful historical information and lessons learned. Of course, the point of using such information is to avoid reinventing the wheel by taking advantage of the wealth of knowledge that can be used to inform any new project, thus saving time and money and improving the quality of the project by doing things the best way possible.

Q4. What are the two kinds of lessons learned that are used in planning?

A4. Lessons learned are a specific type of historical information that is derived from analyzing past projects. As a huge fan of Bill Murray, who starred in the movie *Groundhog Day*, I call this the "Groundhog Day approach" because looking at lessons learned allows you to think about mistakes that were made in the past, consider what you would do if you could go back in time and fix them, and apply those solutions to the future by planning them into your current projects.

There are two kinds of lessons learned: negative and positive. Each is equally valuable for PMs.

- ***Negative lessons: What went wrong on past projects?*** PMs should consciously try to avoid making the same mistakes on a current project that were made in the past and should strive to use workarounds or fixes that were developed to solve problems other PMs previously encountered.

- ***Positive lessons: What went right on past projects?*** Savvy PMs also allow time for researching the wealth of wisdom that can be drawn from past projects and choosing best practices to make their projects as successful as possible.

The key with both kinds of lessons is to pay attention to not just the "whats" but also the "whys" and "hows." Unlike more general historical information, which might just be a straight narrative of what took place without conclusions or recommendations, a good lessons-learned document might include the following kind of details:

- A description of a bug that occurred
- Why it was believed to have occurred
- How the team proved that it discovered why the bug occurred—for example, a list of steps the team took to reproduce the bug
- A description of the fix that was put in place to solve the bug
- Documentation of the tests that showed that the solution worked
- Proof that the solution was implemented in the production system after testing
- Documentation showing that more tests were run after the fix was implemented under conditions that could have provoked the same bug but that the bug did not recur because the fix was effective
- Other good post-mortem data from the project team's analysis after the project was completed.

Q5. Where can a PM find good historical information and lessons learned that he or she can apply to the current project?

A5. Today there are more great information sources than ever, both internal and external.

- *Internal:* Some companies have become very proficient at leveraging their own lessons learned. They encourage their PMs to capture lessons learned as part of the PM life cycle and to make the information available for the company's future projects. Often, this data is documented in a company's internal database or on an intranet site. A famous example is the *Boeing Black Book*; the aircraft giant pioneered the process of writing up its lessons learned with the goal of never making the same manufacturing mistake twice.[1] By putting a strong lessons-learned process and mindset in place, as at Boeing, every project at a company can benefit from all the projects that came before it.

- *External:* It's very easy to search online to find many lessons learned that could potentially help your project. You have at your fingertips a wealth of websites and electronic content originating from newspapers, magazines, and other media. You can even set up RSS feeds to have relevant content emailed to you.

PMI is another great source for lessons learned, a topic that is often covered in local chapter meetings, conferences, magazines for members, and special interest group (SIG) discussions and newsletters.

For more lessons-learned resources, see Appendix A.

Starting a Lessons-Learned Database

You can help your company (and your career!) by initiating an effort to put the lessons learned from your company's projects on an enterprise-wide intranet site or in a lessons-learned database. This will make the information available to all of the firm's PMs for future projects, and this small investment in time can pay large dividends in improved performance and project success for your company.

HOW ORGANIZATIONAL FACTORS AFFECT PLANNING

Q6. What are *organizational process assets*, and what are some examples that can help a PM in the planning stages?

A6. Organizational process assets are tangible resources available at a company that can help PMs on projects. They include:

- Lessons-learned databases and other documentation databases
- Company-specific templates, such as collections of the company's project plans, which PMs can use as starting points for many PM documents
- Standard operating procedure (SOP) manuals: guides written specifically to be used as standards for a company's projects
- Training materials and resources
- Company intranet sites with resources that can inform a project (e.g., project plans and related documentation from completed projects, how-to guides, preferred vendor lists, online org charts).

Q7. What are *enterprise environmental factors*, and how can analyzing them help a PM make the right decisions?

A7. *Enterprise environmental factors* is a catchall term for the internal characteristics of a company that can affect its projects. It is highly recommended that a PM allocate some time to analyzing these factors as part of pre-project planning because they can play a major role in the success or failure of a project.

PMs should do their homework to understand their company's environment before making decisions or proposing ideas to the client or senior management. Otherwise, their ideas can easily be shot down by stakeholders who argue that "this is not how things are done around here." This can weaken a PM's credibility and authority on the project. Questions PMs should research as part of enterprise environmental factors on projects include:

- **Buy or build:** Does your company prefer to create its own software systems or buy them from a vendor?
- **Does your company favor outsourcing or oppose it?** For example, be careful about proposing an overseas outsourcing initiative to reduce costs if your company favors hiring locally.
- **Virtual teams:** Before proposing a virtual team solution, determine whether the company has been successful with virtual teams in recent

history and has good infrastructure and processes in place to support virtual teams.

- *Preferred vendor lists:* Does your company require them, or are you not obligated to use vendor or headhunter lists in your current project environment? (If you are not sure, it's best to look before you leap to avoid making a costly sourcing error.)

- *Corporate culture:* Is your company risk friendly or risk averse? This can be subtle and easy to overlook. For instance, you might want to use a product that worked well for you at another company. But your current company might see the product as high risk if it involves a sole source procurement. (*Sole source procurement* is defined in Chapter 8.)

- *PMs' extracurricular activities:* Does your company prohibit PMs from doing speaking engagements or writing articles out of fear of losing competitive advantage, or does it encourage such activities as good for morale and good for attracting talented people to work for your company?

THE BASELINE

Q8. What is the *baseline*, and how does it help prevent team members from working off of different versions of the plan?

A8. The baseline specifies the current, approved version of the project plan. Calling it the baseline means that:

- The PM is designating it as the official version of the project plan, superseding all other versions. This helps ensure that all team members and stakeholders are on the same page, with the same version, preventing miscommunications and errors.

- By implication, the PM has gained management's approval of this version and sometimes even obtained senior management's signature on the document, formalizing the approval.

Q9. When does the term *baseline not* refer to the entire project plan?

A9. When you hear the term *baseline* used by itself, it refers to the latest approved version of the full plan by the *PMBOK® Guide* standard. But *baseline* is also sometimes used to refer to subcomponents of the plan. A term such as *schedule baseline* refers to one specific piece of the project plan, but it also implies that the document is the current, approved version (in this case, of the schedule).

The *scope baseline* is a unique case; the baseline refers to three related documents:

1. The scope statement
2. The WBS (work breakdown structure)
3. The WBS dictionary.

The concept behind the scope baseline is that a change to any one of the three artifacts requires an update to the other two so that all three remain in sync. This protects the integrity of the scope statement on the project, which is critical for project success, and it also directly prevents scope creep, universally considered a very destructive force on any project.

Q10. How do changes in plans affect the baseline?

A10. Critical to the baseline concept is the requirement that all proposed changes be approved before they are enacted. Once approved, those changes need to be incorporated into the baseline, creating a new baseline.

An important corollary is that if a change request is *not* added to the baseline, the team should not work on that request. It shouldn't be treated as a valid change request unless or until it makes it into the baseline.

Q11. I've heard that MS Project stores baselines for you. Is that the same kind of baseline?

A11. Yes and no. MS Project is a scheduling tool, so it stores the current version of the project schedule, a.k.a. the schedule baseline. MS Project also saves old versions of schedule baselines and automatically assigns version numbers to them so that you can easily keep track of them all in chronological order. But MS Project does *not* store all the other project artifacts that could also be considered baselines by the PMI definition, including project plan subcomponents such as the quality baseline or risk baseline. The PM is responsible for storing those planning documents separately and keeping them all in sync.

THE PROJECT PLAN

Q12. What exactly is meant by the term *project plan*, and what's the most important part of a project plan?

A12. PMs are usually expected to do a thorough job of writing up all plans and activities on behalf of the project, using a style and format and including content that all project stakeholders can understand. The cornerstone of the project plan is the project schedule, in which the PM, often with the input of the project team, itemizes all the specific work tasks through which the project's goals will be accomplished and its deliverables created.

Q13. Besides the schedule, what are other key components of the project plan?

A13. There are many steps and earlier documents to help get the PM ready to build the schedule. Along with the schedule, there also will be companion documents, such as the schedule management plan, as well as other important subcomponents, such as the quality management plan and risk management plan, that will help make sure the project succeeds.

Figure 2-1 lists the many key subcomponents that can compose a project plan for a large and complex project. The italicized documents are standard components of the PM plan. The non-italicized documents are popular supplemental components of the plan. TIP: The distinction between *standard* and *supplemental* components is something PM certification exams like to test on.

Many of the components in Figure 2-1 are discussed in detail in subsequent chapters; for instance, we discuss the risk register and risk management plan in Chapter 7. Note that for smaller projects, it may not be advisable to create all the subcomponents shown in the figure (see planning pitfall #7 at the end of the chapter).

Q14. What is *rolling wave planning*, and why is it necessary for more complex projects?

A14. We can make an analogy between watching an ocean wave roll in and planning a long project. When you're standing on the shore, a faraway wave may look small at first. But gradually, as it comes closer to shore, it begins to look bigger, and it changes: It curls, crests, and ultimately breaks on the

- Project charter
- Stakeholder register
- *Change management plan*
- *Configuration management plan*
- Project requirements document
- Requirements traceability matrix
- *Requirements management plan*
- *Scope management plan*
- *Scope baseline* (which consists of the three following components)
- *Scope statement*
- *Work breakdown structure*
- *WBS dictionary*
- Activity list
- Activity attributes
- Network diagram
- *Schedule management plan*
- *Project schedule (schedule baseline)*

- Resource breakdown structure
- Resource histogram
- *Cost management plan*
- *Project budget (cost performance baseline)*
- *Quality management plan*
- *Process improvement plan*
- Political management plan
- *Human resources plan*
- Staffing management plan
- Project org chart
- RAM/RACI charts
- *Communications management plan*
- Release plan
- *Risk management plan*
- Risk breakdown structure

- Risk register
- Risk response plan
- *Procurement management plan*
- Request for proposal
- Statement of work
- Contract
- Lessons learned documentation
- Performance reports
- Procurement performance review documentation
- Team performance assessment
- Project-specific glossary of terms

Figure 2-1:   Key Components of the Project Management Plan and Related Artifacts

shoreline. Similarly, a project may at first look deceptively simple, but all kinds of complexities may emerge once the full requirements are agreed upon with the client and the project is fully planned out.

Rolling wave planning takes into account that the requirements, and even the project plans themselves, can be something of a moving target, and it acknowledges that it's impossible to sit down and crank out a complete plan on day 1 of a project (though managers sometimes request this, and PMs sometimes attempt it). No one has enough information initially to develop a full project plan, and the information you do have will change over time as you and your team learn more through meetings and research over the course of the project.

Rolling wave planning has two key elements:

- The PM thoroughly plans for the activities that will come up in the near future
- The PM does less detailed, more high-level planning on the activities that are not scheduled to be performed until later in the project life cycle.

Q15. How does progressive elaboration help a PM plan as thoroughly as necessary?

A15. Like rolling wave planning, progressive elaboration is also about planning as a process over time. Central to progressive elaboration is the idea that the PM will get the best results by creating an early version of the planning documents initially, with the intention of coming back to those plans again later when more information is known, possibly in several passes (*progressively*). With each pass, the PM updates the plan (*elaborates* on it) as the project progresses and as the team acquires more information and possibly feedback. An example is the project's budget, for which a rough estimate is frequently done early on that is later revised into a finalized budget.

Another important aspect of progressive elaboration is that some of the planning outputs (subcomponents) will themselves become inputs to subsequent planning documents created later in the planning process. For example, some elements of the charter, such as early identified risks, can be elaborated on when the team creates the risk response plan later during the formal risk planning processes.

PRE-PLANNING

Q16. What is meant by pre-planning, or "planning the planning"?

A16. PMs create a number of early, high-level planning documents to lay a foundation before they drill down into the detailed planning that will map out the project. This pre-planning can be very high level. It describes how the detailed planning will later be done. PMs find pre-planning very useful because it gives them a chance to make the best early decisions regarding the detailed project plans they will create later.

Questions PMs can ask to help with pre-planning include:

- What are the most critical constraints on this project, and how can we best address them?
- What is most important to the client on this project?
- Which methodologies will be used in the planning processes? For example, will we use a PMP® approach (document-driven and iterative), an agile approach (less formal, less bureaucratic), or some mix of these?
- Which planning tools—in particular, which software—will we use?
- Which planning documents will we create?
- Which templates will we use to create the plans, and where will we get them?
- How can we streamline the planning process to facilitate maximum efficiency and success on this project?

Q17. What are the six early planning documents?

A17. After writing the project charter (covered in Chapter 1), PMs typically create six early planning documents. To document constraints around schedule, budget, requirements, and scope, PMs do advance planning, producing four outputs: the schedule management plan, cost management plan, requirements management plan, and scope management plan. Each document contains the PM's early plans on how these constraints will be managed and describes the planning the team will do in the future to ensure project success.

In addition, the PM must create and distribute a change management plan and configuration management plan as early in the project as possible. The change management plan establishes ground rules for change requests—for example, how enhancement requests from the customer will be submitted, approved, and processed. The configuration management plan covers procedures for tasks like ordering new software and hardware for the project and rolling out installations and upgrades.

Both documents are intended to help get the project off on the right foot and avoid problems associated with change requests once activity is in full swing. Putting these management procedures in writing allows stakeholders to know the protocol in advance, so they will know how to submit requests properly when the time comes. These documents also help stakeholders understand that it benefits the project as a whole to accept change requests only after proper procedures occur and reviews are followed.

Figure 2-2 describes the six early planning documents and the detailed documents that typically follow.

What Makes a Good Change Control System?

- These tips are based on my experience managing an automated change system for many years for a major brokerage company.
- The key is to establish a ground rule early on that *all* change requests on the project must go through your formal change control system (with no exceptions, even for the CEO!).
- Also key is that this system, whether it is a people-driven, paper-driven, or automated solution, has clearly defined approvers with formal power to approve or reject any change request. The approvers can be individuals or a change control board.
- The PM can be a member of the project's change control board, but for best results, he or she should not be the only approver.
- Some of the best change control systems use automated change-control vendor packages that have many powerful features for controlling project changes, especially approver lists, version control, and automated change back-out capability.

Q18. What "planning the planning" documents are used later in the planning process?

A18. Figure 2-3 details additional high-level planning documents that, like the documents used earlier in planning, address particular project elements such as risk, quality, and procurement.

Document	Description
Schedule management plan	Lists whatever date milestones are known early in the project, along with high-level plans for how the PM intends to meet them. These could include which documents, templates, and software will be used, as well as historical info and lessons learned from prior projects. → This document will guide the project schedule, to follow later.
Cost management plan	Similar to the schedule management plan, lists budget caps that may be known early on and describes how the PM will estimate, manage, and control the budget (for example, how will earned value reporting be done?). → This document will guide the project budget or cost baseline, to follow later.
Requirements management plan	Documents the plans for how the project team will prioritize the client's requirements and convert them into a scope statement and ultimately into deliverables. Also can specify how the team will conduct requirements gathering (if not already done by the time this document is created). → This document will guide the requirements document, to follow later.
Scope management plan	Describes how the scope statement will be created, which templates will be used, how the scope will be controlled (how creep will be prevented), and how the deliverables will fulfill the required scope. → This document will guide the scope statement and WBS, to follow later.
Change management plan	Specifies a mechanism (paper forms, change control software, a change control board, or a mix) for controlling how all change requests will be submitted, approved/denied, and implemented on the project. → This document will guide the project's change management system, to follow later.
Configuration management plan	Specifies how the team will decide upon, acquire, install, update, and replace software/hardware/other equipment on the project. → This document will guide the project's configuration management system, to follow later.

Figure 2-2: The Six Early High-Level Planning Documents

Quality management plan	Describes the standards and metrics you will use for achieving quality on your project and how you plan to implement them, which tools will be used, and which templates you will use for the tools.
HR management plan	High-level plans regarding the personnel you will need for the project and how you will recruit and manage them.
Communications management plan	Documents how communications will be handled for maximum effectiveness on the project, e.g., frequency of meetings and status updates, who should speak directly to the client, and which communication software, devices, and protocols will be used.
Risk management plan	High-level plans for how risks will be identified and addressed on the project, e.g., which templates will be used for the RBS and risk register, team members' risk-related roles and responsibilities, which subject matter experts should be consulted, and which tools will be used for risk management.
Procurement management plan	Documents the products or services the performing organization plans to purchase, how it will choose a vendor, what contract type is desired, and which legal services will be used.
Integration management plan	Details how the PM will weave the many aspects of the project together.

Figure 2-3:   The Later "Planning the Planning" Documents

TOP TEN PITFALLS TO AVOID WHEN PLANNING A PROJECT

1. Creating a schedule in a software product (like MS Project or Primavera) without first creating the predecessor documents (especially the WBS) that would help yield a more complete and more accurate schedule.

2. Using a software product not designed for schedule management, such as Excel, to build your schedule. These products may work well for other applications, but not for managing PM schedules. A quick look at the sidebar "Top Ten Features of Automated Project Scheduling Software" should convince you that you don't want your team, yourself, or your clients to miss out on the many powerful features of products specifically designed for schedule management.

3. Confusion about what is considered part of the project plan; calling the schedule the project plan is particularly problematic. While this may seem like a "you say potato, I say potah-to" matter, trouble ensues every time a client expects a full plan and gets only a schedule. Conversely, if the client only wants a schedule, it won't like receiving all kinds of documents that it will think you developed on its dime without authorization. When in doubt, the PM should confirm which document the client wants. To avoid this pitfall, it's helpful to think of the schedule as just one of many parts of the project plan. (See Figure 2-1, which shows the schedule as one of many planning artifacts.)

4. Not taking the time to find relevant historical information/lessons learned.

5. Failing to do the necessary pre-planning, including assessing constraints and priorities and choosing appropriate planning methods and tools.

6. Not creating all of the needed planning subcomponents, such as the planning documents listed in Figures 2-2 and 2-3. For example, the *PMBOK® Guide* stresses the importance of having, among other documents, a schedule management plan to help guide execution of the schedule, and a communications management plan to specify how project communications with the client and other stakeholders will occur.

7. Going overboard—creating too many planning documents! If your project is small, it can be counterproductive to spend too much time creating a lot of documents that are not really needed and may dilute the impact and value of the planning documents that *are* essential to your project.

8. Taking on a project without a charter.

9. Rushing into the project activities without taking time to do proper planning.

10. Having an antiplanning attitude: "Who needs planning? We know how to just git 'er done!" or "We're *agile*—planning is for wimps, or worse, bureaucrats, or even worse, PMPs!"

Note

1. Scott Berkun, *The Art of Project Management* (Sebastopol, CA: O'Reilly Media, 2005).

CHAPTER 3

From Requirements to Scope to the WBS

This chapter will show you how to give your customers what they want by capturing their requirements in writing and translating them into documents your team will use to create your project's deliverables. The widely accepted PM best practice is to create three main documents in order: the requirements document, the scope statement, and the work breakdown structure (WBS), along with their corresponding supporting documents. The WBS becomes the precursor to the project schedule, the document that will drive the execution of your project and that is at the center of Chapter 4.

The following Q&As detail how to create these three key outputs as well as the supporting documents that will help you manage them effectively.

PRELIMINARY PM DOCUMENTS

Q1. Once I have a charter authorizing my project, am I ready to create the schedule and start assigning the work?

A1. The PM typically creates a number of documents after the charter is written to build a smooth bridge from the charter to the schedule. Most important of these are the requirements and scope documents and the WBS. Figure 3-1 shows the significant documents typically created along the way. It is intended to help you see the big picture of how a PM ultimately translates the project charter into the project schedule. In this chapter, we'll cover the stakeholder register through the WBS dictionary.

| => Project charter |
| => => Stakeholder register |
| => => => Requirements documentation |
| => => => => Requirements management plan |
| => => => => => Requirements traceability matrix |
| => => => => => => Scope management plan |
| => => => => => => => Scope statement |
| => => => => => => => => WBS |
| => => => => => => => => => WBS dictionary |
| => => => => => => => => => => Activity list and activity attributes |
| => => => => => => => => => => => Schedule management plan |
| => => => => => => => => => => => => Activity resource estimates and activity duration estimates |
| => => => => => => => => => => => => => Network diagram and project schedule |

Figure 3-1: Document Flow from the Charter to the Schedule

Q2. Why are all of these documents necessary?

A2. Creating these artifacts sequentially is a proven recipe for project management success. Each document is the logical outgrowth of the one that preceded it. In many cases, one document functions as a companion or supporting document to the next; for example, the scope management plan will be the supporting document for the scope statement.

The PM should take the time to create all of the listed documents in this order instead of rushing his or her team into insufficiently defined or poorly estimated tasks.

Q3. How does the charter help the PM create the subsequent documents?

A3. The charter often contains elements that are the "seeds" for subsequent documents. For instance, a charter contains high-level descriptions of the project's deliverables, which will drive the creation of the requirements document and that will later be fleshed out in the scope statement.

Q4. What is the purpose of a stakeholder register?

A4. The charter names some of the key stakeholders known to the project early on. The stakeholder register is a more complete follow-up document. (This is an example of progressive elaboration, discussed in Chapter 2, Q&A 15.) Here, the idea is to name all of the key players on your project and add whatever information you have about each that will help you manage them throughout the project, including each person's role and responsibilities, title, and department (see Figure 3-2).

Some PMs also document their assessment of each stakeholder's influence/power on the project and whether the stakeholder is for or against the project. This kind of information should be kept confidential. Addressing the politics of the project can be helpful and necessary in some situations—especially when there are stakeholders who are difficult or even opposed to your project and you need to find ways to work with them, or at least, around them. Some PMs take this a step further and create a document called a political management plan, which is a strategy for maximizing the chances of a project's success by focusing some planning effort on overcoming the political obstacles surrounding the project.

REQUIREMENTS GATHERING

Q5. What does a requirements document contain?

A5. The requirements document also expands upon information in the charter. It is a summary of the needs and wants of the client. The PM or someone he or she assigns captures all requests from your stakeholders and details them here. Certain requirements are given high priority; others may be given low priority or even removed from the list at this time. The requirements that remain and are documented in the requirements document will be translated later into the scope statement and ultimately brought to life as deliverables.

Q6. If I already have a requirements document, why is a requirements management plan necessary?

A6. The requirements themselves detail exactly what the client wants. The requirements management plan details the strategy for meeting those requirements. It is a place for the PM to put the how's of the project in writing, specifically *how* the team will capture and document the requirements and

Stakeholder Name	Role and Responsibility on Project	Title	Client or Performing Organization	Department	Manager	Influence/ Power on Project (On a 1–5 scale; confidential)	For or Against Project? (confidential)

Figure 3-2: The Stakeholder Register
(This is a template that you can modify to suit your organization.)

Requirement #	Summary of Requirement	Requested by	Role/Power of Requester (optional and confidential)	Description	Priority/ Criticality	Weighting Factor (optional)	Assigned to	Issues/Risks/ Dependencies/ Assumptions
001								
002								
003								

Figure 3-3: The Requirements Traceability Matrix
(This is a template that you can modify to suit your organization.)

how it intends to fulfill those requirements by turning them into deliverables that will satisfy the customer.

Q7. What is a *requirements traceability matrix*, and how can it help a PM fulfill the project's requirements?

A7. After the team has gathered the requirements and written them up, it is a best practice for the PM to create a matrix to document the details of each requirement (see Figure 3-3). Using the stakeholder register, the PM creates a spreadsheet matching up stakeholders with the requirements they requested. The matrix can contain related data, including confidential (for the PM's eyes only) notes—for example, on which stakeholders have the most power on the project. This matrix is a great way to protect your client's best interests on a project because it helps you keep track of and manage competing requirements from many stakeholders.

Q8. What are recommended methods for effective requirements gathering?

A8. There are many methods to choose from, and choosing one (or more) is a key decision. Without solid requirements, it's next to impossible to have a successful project. The requirements gathering process often brings some very tough challenges—for example, prioritizing competing requirements from opposing stakeholders. So before you collect your requirements, you'll want to determine the best way to solicit the requirements from your customers based on your best determination about which method will work best for the project at hand.

You can gather requirements by phone or email, in person, at meetings or workshops, and in focus groups.

- *Interviews* are generally held with one or two key stakeholders at a time.
- In *focus groups*, several stakeholders meet to discuss their needs and expectations for the project. The discussion can be general, in advance of more specific requirements gathering later. The group facilitator is usually the PM or whoever the PM feels is best qualified to effectively lead it. In some cases an outside facilitator is brought in for this purpose. Benefits of this method include the group member interaction and the generation of ideas. Drawbacks can include the lack of confidentiality and the lack of honesty a focus group setting can bring (see the Delphi technique, below).

- *Facilitated workshops* are conducted by a leader who meets with key stakeholders. The group generates specific requirements that the leader records in a somewhat formal and structured process. For example, a specific kind of workshop commonly used on IT projects is called a joint application development, or JAD, session, which generally follows a set agenda and includes documentation templates. The best method for your project depends on the personalities involved. You might even mix and match methods if, for example, you work best with some people in person and others by email.

Q9. Which specific skills come into play for effective requirements gathering?

A9. Choosing the right team member to lead the requirements gathering is crucial. Not everyone is good at this, so the PM should choose someone who has an overall skill set that will help him or her successfully elicit the best set of working requirements.

- Strong listening skills are key.
- A positive, cooperative attitude is essential.
- Also required is an ability to keep your eye on the ball and keep driving forward toward the common goal: the project's success. The ideal person to lead the requirements-gathering effort is a driver who keeps things going, not the kind of person who pushes his or her own agenda too strongly. A facilitator who already knows where he or she want to go and marches the team in that direction impedes effective requirements gathering.

Chapter 10 offers more guidance on communication skills.

Q10. What are the most effective group creativity techniques for eliciting requirements?

A10.

- *Brainstorming:* Brainstorming helps teams cast a wide net to capture as many good ideas as possible. Participants are encouraged to freely share all kinds of out-of-the-box ideas. For this process to work, the facilitator must have a positive attitude, creating an atmosphere in which all ideas are considered good ideas. The best of the ideas will be selected later through a vote. Ideas that are not feasible will be discarded, and those that remain will be whittled down to the requirements that will drive the project.

- *Idea-mapping/mind-mapping:* The facilitator records participants' ideas so that everyone can see them, perhaps using a big whiteboard and colorful markers and drawing clouds or other fun shapes or pictures to represent categories of requirements. Alternatively, there are mind-mapping software products that facilitate gathering and recording ideas. Whatever method works best with your people is fine. The goal is to maximize mental stimulation in the stakeholders and to spark more and better ideas and ideas that will build off the initial suggestions. Idea- or mind-mapping often goes hand in hand with brainstorming.

- *Delphi technique:* This method acknowledges that people are often less forthcoming or honest about ideas when their managers or competitors are in the same room. It is named after the legendary blind, invisible oracle on the mountaintop in ancient Greece. The key to the Delphi technique is anonymity; the PM will keep the identity of the contributor of each proposed requirement confidential so that participants will not have cause to worry about being criticized (or worse, punished) for their ideas. The PM, of course, will know who suggested each requirement, but no one else will. This is one way of getting the most honest, and therefore the most useful, input. Using this technique can be as simple as asking your people to email requirements to you, which you can then compile into a list, no names attached.

Options for Using the Delphi Technique

Wide-band Delphi technique: The Delphi technique is often done repetitively, in stages. This process is called wide-band. In each pass, contributors' collective input to date is shared anonymously with participants. Participants can keep reassessing their contributions in light of the input from the other stakeholders as a reality check.

Google Docs: You can easily automate the capture of requirements and other feedback without having to send a lot of emails back and forth or manually track or compile the data. Free products like Google Docs have built-in capabilities for creating unique electronic forms your people can use to send out surveys and capture, compile, and even tally the responses, while keeping all survey answers anonymous.

QII. How does a PM decide how to prioritize competing requirements?

A11. Many projects have key stakeholders, and it's often necessary to give their requirements greater consideration. But this should be as transparent and well-communicated a process as feasible so that there will be maximum buy-in later from as many stakeholders as possible once the deliverables are created and turned over. (Secrecy and the feeling that the requirements process is unfair can undermine morale on a project).

The requirements traceability matrix shown in Figure 3-3 can help PMs track and prioritize requirements. After the PM lists the requirements and the stakeholders who requested them, he or she can rank each suggested requirement. It's common to use a 1-to-10 priority scale, but the PM can devise another system as well. Sometimes a weighting factor, or multiplier, is used to indicate the importance of the request (which is sometimes based on who the requestor is). Using numbers to rank proposed requirements can make the prioritization and decision-making process quick, easy, and objective.

SCOPE

Q12. What is a *scope statement*, and how does it differ from the requirements document?

A12. Once created, the scope statement becomes the primary document that will guide the project's deliverables (superseding both the charter and the requirements document). After the requirements doc is finalized, the PM, often with help from technical specialists, design architects, or other SMEs, translates the requirements into detailed descriptions of each required deliverable, which together become the scope statement.

An effective scope statement is written as clearly and concisely as possible, in a way that can be best understood by the people who will be doing the work of the project as well as the other team members and stakeholders on the project. The team will frequently refer to the scope statement while performing the project to make sure that the project's deliverables are being created properly and that the project is still on scope.

It is a particularly critical document when there are problems with change requests or enhancement requests or if legal issues arise between the client and the providing organization. A meeting is typically held, often including higher-ups such as the sponsor, to examine the request against the scope statement and reach a consensus about whether the change is within project scope or not. The scope statement is also the key input when creating the WBS, WBS dictionary, and ultimately the project schedule, which will direct all of the work activities of the project.

Q13. What is the difference between *product* scope and *project* scope?

A13. They go hand in hand but are different.

- *Product scope* is all about the details of the deliverables of the project. For instance, if the project is about building cars, the product scope would be comprised of all of the design parameters for the cars: miles per gallon, the look of the car, and what kind of stereo and GPS systems the cars would offer.

- *Project scope* is about the aspects and constraints of the project itself. The scope of the car-building project would include the intended time frame for the project, its budget, how many cars must be built, and how many employees the team will require to produce the cars.

Q14. How can a PM use a scope management plan to help deliver the scope of the project?

A14. In the scope management plan, the PM puts his or her thoughts in writing about *how* the scope will be delivered (the *what* is documented in the scope statement itself). A scope management plan:

- Lists the inputs that will be used to build the scope statement, such as the project charter, the requirements document, and specific historical information, lessons learned, and templates that will be used to create the scope statement for the project

- Describes how the PM plans to create the scope statement, including methods he or she will use and where templates and pertinent historical information or lessons learned can be found

- Lists SMEs by name who will be consulted in the process of creating the scope statement

- Documents the project's change control system, which will help keep the project on scope.

Q15. What is *scope creep*, and why is it so destructive (and yet so common) on projects?

A15. Scope creep is considered by a great many PMs to be the single biggest problem in all of project management. In the course of a typical project, customers ask for more deliverables or more features than were originally agreed upon. The PM thinks that he or she can't say no, because the customer is paying the bills. Accommodating those additional requests and adding them into the project adds to the scope of the project, which affects the triple constraint. Typically, each request adds to the length of the schedule and increases the budget just a little at a time (hence the term scope *creep*). But usually the customer did not agree to change the schedule or budget—it just asked to have the changes added. And so a messy situation develops because the same customer who asked you to add the extras will be the guy who is mad at you if the project runs over schedule or over budget.

Adding to scope affects the other elements of the triple constraint as well. To try to keep the new requests from increasing the schedule and budget, PMs sometimes try to cut corners in other ways, often resulting in a decrease in quality, an increase in project risk, and ironically, a drop in customer satisfaction, when the whole point of adding the extras was to keep the customer happy. Therefore, proactively doing everything possible to prevent scope creep is one of the best things a PM can do for his or her project.

Q16. What is *gold-plating* in relation to scope creep?

A16. Gold-plating is a subset of scope creep: It means the project team—not the customer—has added features beyond project scope. Team members, usually with good intentions, add features to improve the deliverable. Often the motivation to do this comes from specialists such as designers, engineers, technicians, and even PMs who feel that they know what the client needs better than the clients themselves, who, in the end, will be pleased by such "improvements" to the plan. This is a very common cause of project schedule slippage and cost overruns and must be prevented by the PM.

Q17. What are the best ways to avoid scope creep?

A17. There are several standard, recommended approaches:

- Documenting the requirements well to avoid misunderstandings
- Creating a clear, actionable scope statement from the requirements, a WBS from the scope statement, and a project schedule from the WBS

- Taking the time to create the supporting documents, including the requirements management plan, scope management plan, schedule management plan, and WBS dictionary
- Communicating the scope and related documentation to the team
- Setting up strong change controls for the project
- Managing proactively, with the triple constraint and customer's best interest always in mind
- Having frequent check-ins with the customer and other stakeholders. This is also called the process of verifying scope, the subject of the next Q&A.

Q18. What is the process of verifying scope?

A18. This is one of the few PMI process names that only half-sounds like what it means. It's really about stakeholders on the customer side verifying the scope and, more important verifying the deliverables *against* the scope. The point of the process is for the PM to give the customer opportunities to inspect the results, then officially weigh in on whether the deliverables being created on the customer's behalf are in fact what it intended back when it first gave its requirements to the project team.

Q19. What are examples of the process of verifying scope?

A19. Scope verification can take place several times before the end of a project. Early on, the customer can meet with the project team to look at whatever early outputs have been created at that point and compare them with the scope statement. For example, before a full-fledged computer application is created, the customer can look at a beta version. Or before a house or boat is built, the customer can come in to view a prototype or mock-up built by the team to show what the final product will look like. (If you want to impress friends at parties, use the term *maquette*, the French word that architects favor!)

Whatever you call it, the customer inspects an early version of the final deliverable against the scope statement to make sure the project team is on the right track to meet the scope. If it is not on track, the customer can make change requests. It is considered a best practice to purposely plan in such early verifications to help ensure that any problems will be nipped in the bud before too much time and effort have been invested in doing work that would not ultimately satisfy the customer and while there is still time to make corrections.

Verifying scope can also be done toward the end of the project, when a customer inspects what are intended to be the final deliverables before signing off on them to make sure they are on scope.

Another example of scope verification is called an on-site customer review or buyer-conducted performance review (discussed in Chapter 8, Q&A 48). The customer formally schedules dates with the vendor to meet with the project team to review project progress and verify the deliverables against the scope. If customers want to mandate such reviews, they must make sure to include specific language saying so in the contract; otherwise, the vendor would not be obligated to participate in such formal reviews and would not necessarily have an incentive to do so.

THE WORK BREAKDOWN STRUCTURE

Q20. What exactly is a *work breakdown structure*, and how does the scope statement get translated into the WBS?

A20. The WBS is one of the most important outputs on a project. It is usually a pyramid-shaped graphic, created with software like MS Visio or Word or with products specifically designed for this purpose, such as WBS Chart Pro. The PM and the project team look at all of the expected deliverables outlined in the scope statement, split them up into the pieces of work that will get the project done, and group them into graphic format.

As shown in Figure 3-4, the name of the project itself is represented as a node at the top; below that are the main segments of the project (in this example, there are three main areas: Design, Code, and Test). Below each segment are what are called work packages. These represent the work that the team will perform—e.g., nodes 3.1, 3.2, and 3.3. The process of taking larger pieces of work and breaking them down into smaller and smaller pieces is called scope decomposition.

Note that the nodes of the WBS may sometimes contain just the numbers and names of the work packages, as shown in Figure 3-4. But often, teams revisit the WBS from time to time and update the work packages as more information becomes known. For instance, when the time, resource, and cost estimates are created for a work package, the node for the work package may be filled in with that info. As change requests are approved and the scope of the project changes, new work packages may be added.

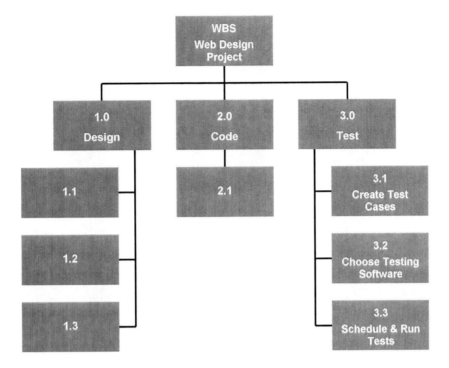

Figure 3-4: The Work Breakdown Structure

Tips for Creating a Good WBS

- A clear, straightforward numbering scheme as shown in Figure 3-4 is generally ideal. The higher-level nodes are numbered 1, 2, and 3, and each node that is subordinate to a higher-level node takes the higher-level node's number as a prefix (e.g., 1.1, 1.2, 1.3).

- Many PMs find it helpful for the project team to participate in the scope decomposition process so that the team members, who will be the ultimate owners of each work package, will feel that their knowledge and expertise were taken into consideration and will then buy in to the project. Building the foundation of the project as a team can also strengthen team unity.

Q21. What are the key differences between a WBS and a project schedule?

A21. The WBS is the early precursor of the schedule. The key purpose of developing the WBS is to identify and plan, on a somewhat high level, each work package that will make up the project. Take care in creating the WBS to ensure it is very thorough and that no project components are left out.

Later, the PM and team will further break down the work packages as necessary into the individual activities that will make up the project. They will arrange the activities in the sequence in which they will be performed and estimate the time duration of each activity. Once the individual activities have been estimated and arranged in sequence, usually in a Gantt chart or network diagram using a product such as MS Project or Primavera, the team has arrived at the project schedule.

Note that an early WBS, like the one shown in Figure 3-4, can be further elaborated. Initially, the nodes for work packages can simply note the names and numbers of the work packages, as shown. But later, after the work packages have been broken down further into activities, and the team has developed estimates for time, human resources, and cost for those activities, those additional details are often added to each corresponding node.

OTHER DOCUMENTS: THE WBS DICTIONARY AND SCOPE BASELINE

Q22. What role does a WBS dictionary play in support of the WBS?

A22. The WBS should be as short and sweet as possible; team members should be able to see the big picture at a glance and instantly understand where their work packages fit into the big picture from the groupings shown in the graphic.

The WBS dictionary is a companion artifact to the WBS. It is often created as a spreadsheet in a product like MS Excel or Word. Each work package from the WBS is given an entire row in the dictionary; the PM can create as many columns of information about the work package as needed. Though brevity is key in the WBS, the opposite is true of the dictionary, which can be as descriptive as desired. The dictionary should include all of the important details of each work package, such as the package's number and name, a detailed description, its estimated time duration and cost, the associated accounting code, who it is assigned to, and sometimes many more categories of information. Figure 3-5 shows a sample excerpt from a WBS dictionary, showing partially completed records for three of the project's work packages.

Work Package #	Name of Work Package	Detailed Description	Estimated Time	Estimated Cost	Department/ Account Code	Assigned to
3.1	Create test cases	Design comprehensive test cases. Cover month-end, year-end. Comply with all pertinent Sarbanes-Oxley considerations.	5 days	$2,000	Dept. 10	D. Vitale
3.2	Choose testing software		10 days	$5,000	Dept. 10	H. Cohen
3.3	Schedule and run tests		15 days	$14,000	Dept. 12	G. King

Figure 3-5: WBS Dictionary: A Companion Artifact for the WBS

Q23. What are the three components of the scope baseline, and why are the three taken together considered to be one artifact?

A23. The *PMBOK Guide* refers to three documents—the scope statement, the WBS, and the WBS dictionary—by the term *scope baseline*. A thorough PM strives to keep all three documents updated and in sync with each other. When a new requirement is added to the project through a change request or enhancement request, all three documents must be revised.

- The scope of the project must be changed in the scope statement.
- A new work package must be created for this item in the WBS.
- A new entry should be added in the WBS dictionary to describe the work package.

PMI calls these related artifacts the scope baseline because they are closely connected—and to encourage PMs to make all three updates.

Top Ten Pitfalls to Avoid in Going from Requirements to Scope to the WBS

1. Creating a schedule without taking the time to create a WBS first. Many PMs do this, partly because of the irresistible lure of products like MS Project that allow the schedule to be typed up directly. It is worth taking the time to do it the right way and create a WBS first.

2. Not putting sufficient effort into getting proper requirements from the customer. PMs and other technical people on the team sometimes get carried away and think that they already know what the user wants. This can be a big mistake! Even if the team has correctly anticipated the user's needs, this approach is wrong even when the team is right—the customer likes to be asked!

3. Being too much of a yes-man with the customer—for example, accepting requests that are not part of the agreed-upon scope, leading to scope creep.

4. Not being flexible and open to change, such as changes in the business need that can come up as the project evolves or even changes in client management, which can alter project benchmarks and success metrics.

5. Failing to implement a strong change management system, which is possibly the single best way to prevent scope creep.

6. Failing to adequately prioritize and manage competing requirements, which is very common when a PM tries to accommodate a client who "wants it all," but inevitably bumps up against the deadline with incomplete results. A requirements traceability matrix and following PMI's core ethical principles of honesty and responsibility can help (for more on ethics, see Chapter 9).

7. Allowing some people (especially high-powered stakeholders) to bypass the change management system.

8. Creating the scope statement and WBS without doing an adequate job of gathering the requirements from the customer or without fully understanding the customer's requirements.

9. Not scheduling scope verification meetings early enough between the customer side and the performing organization. Teams are often very busy, and things seem to be going well—but by the time the customer gets to take a look at the project's progress, he or she can be disappointed with the results, and it may be too late to quickly, cheaply, or easily rectify the situation.

10. Allowing the addition of a new work package without updating the complete scope baseline. This can seem like a good idea at the time but can later come back to bite the PM (right in the WBS!). The problem is that if a change is not fully documented, it can fall through the cracks and cause trouble in resource allocation or billing, among other areas. These problems can delay the project or cause it to run over budget.

CHAPTER 4

Time Management: Estimating and Coming in on Schedule

On-schedule delivery is the single most common yardstick for measuring a project's success, but in spite of PMs' best intentions and efforts, a great many projects come in late. Late delivery is very visible to the client and the PM's own management and can wipe out the positive results of an otherwise successful project. Project teams are more likely to bring projects in on time and successfully overall if they first build the WBS and scope statement, then generate the activity list, and from there build a solid schedule, which is covered fully in this chapter.

Accurate estimating is also key, and this chapter explores the many estimating techniques regarded as best practices today. Also covered are various best practices for protecting a schedule by building in time reserves, including Eliyahu Goldratt's critical chain buffers. There are also tried-and-true key tactics for keeping on schedule once a project is underway, including the widely used critical path method.

Schedule slippage often goes hand in hand with running over budget. This close relationship between schedule and cost is expressed by the triple constraint, a powerful concept for helping PMs keep on plan.

THE TRIPLE CONSTRAINT

Q1. What is the triple constraint, and how do PMs use it to complete their projects successfully?

A1. The term *triple constraint* usually refers to the three primary constraints, or limiting factors, on a project: scope, time, and cost. Each of these factors can tie down (constrain) the project, which has a set budget (cost), a fixed deadline (time), and a mandatory list of requirements that the final deliverables must achieve (scope). Because scope, time, and cost are considered immutable in the sense that a change to any of these constraints can drastically change the project, the triple-constraint concept is also known as the *iron triangle*. The three parameters are often represented as the three sides of a triangle (see Figure 4-1). Scope, considered the foundation of the project, is shown on the bottom, and time and cost face each other on the left and right, underscoring the closely linked relationship between schedule and budget (time = money).

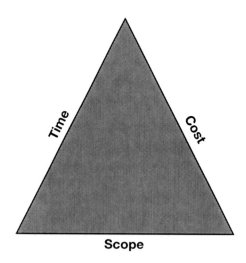

Figure 4-1:   Classic Representation of the Triple Constraint

The key to understanding this concept is that each constraint can greatly influence the others in a ripple effect—in other words, there can be unintended consequences. This influence can be negative or positive. For instance, an overly heavy emphasis on one constraint, usually cost, can cause unintended problems for the project: If not enough money is spent on personnel, for instance, the schedule may be delayed, or the scope might need to be reduced to complete the project on time. Projects generally cannot be delivered "good, fast, and cheap"—something has to give if you overemphasize any of the constraints.

Figure 4-2 shows examples of negative and positive results of manipulating one of the three project constraints.

The Constraint and the Situation	The Effects on the Project	Negative or Positive Result?
Cost: The staffing budget is reduced to cut costs.	**Time:** The schedule is drawn out because fewer workers, or less-experienced/less-qualified workers, can't deliver the same results as quickly as the original team.	Negative
Cost: The client cuts back on the total budget for the project.	**Scope:** The number of features or the quality of the features of the project's deliverables decrease.	Negative
Cost: The budget is increased because hiring more workers might get the job done faster.	**Time:** The project is completed successfully, ahead of schedule.	Positive
Time: The schedule is lengthened so that the deliverable can be enhanced to accommodate additional customers.	**Scope/Quality:** The original plan was to build an application to accommodate one department, but the longer schedule allowed the team to expand the application to support multiple departments, yielding broader benefits than originally planned.	Positive

Figure 4-2: What Happens When You Change One of the Three Constraints?

Q2. Are there other accepted variations of the triple constraint?

A2. Yes, and knowing the other versions helps in more fully understanding the concept. Other popular versions include:

- **A three-component version with *quality* substituted for *scope*:** This version places the emphasis on quality as the key outcome (Figure 4-3). Time and cost are the main driving influences, but the successful outcome of the project is expressed by its quality. In other words, the better the PM utilizes his or her resources and delivers on time, the higher quality the project. Scope is not explicitly shown in this model, but it is behind the scenes: Schedule and budget are manipulated to deliver the scope the client wants. The client will judge the project's quality based on his or her perception of how well the project team satisfied the desired scope.

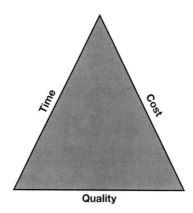

Figure 4-3:   Time, Cost, Quality Representation of the Triple Constraint

- *A six-component version:* Another commonly accepted version shows six constraints, usually prioritized in order of scope, time, cost, quality, risk, and customer satisfaction. This model is commonly represented as either a hexagon with one constraint per six sides or as two triangles—an outer triangle with scope, time, and cost as the primary elements and an additional inner triangle with quality, risk, and customer satisfaction as secondary elements (Figure 4-4). Again, like the three-constraint models, changing any one element can affect any or all of the other elements.

- *Value triple constraint (ValueTripleC):* This new model, developed by consultant Angelo Baratta, features *value* as the key, meaning the overall worth a project ultimately brings to a customer. It factors in the losses in profitability attributable to opportunity costs and also nets out what Baratta calls *schedule opportunity costs,* meaning the time lost during project

Figure 4-4:   Six-Component Representation of the Triple Constraint

selection and implementation, before the project begins bringing in profits to the customer (see Chapter 12 for more details on VTripleC).[1]

Q3. What is a practical way PMs can apply the triple constraint to promote project success?

A3. It is helpful for PMs to consciously keep the triple constraint in mind while making decisions on a project. Whenever a change request comes in, it is good to not only consider the request on face value, but to hold it up to the triple constraint and judge how the change might impact the scope, schedule, and budget; whether it will raise risk, reduce quality, and decrease customer satisfaction; and how much real value it will yield relative to the associated effort and cost, in light of Baratta's VTripleC model. When a request is held up to all of the angles of the triple constraint prism, the chance of adding a change or feature just because someone thinks it's cool or because an aggressive stakeholder is pushing his or her own agenda is greatly reduced.

ESTIMATION

Q4. What estimating techniques are recommended?

A4. Accurately estimating a project's schedule is central to effective project management. Successful PMs analyze which estimation method would be best for the project at hand, then devote time to estimating the length of the schedule to the best of their abilities. They know rushing an estimate is not worth the time savings, as it might turn out to be inaccurate and hurt the project.

Figure 4-5 details the best-practice schedule estimation methods currently used in project management.

Q5. There are so many estimating methods—how can a PM choose the best one?

A5. The best estimating method for a specific project can vary depending on the constraints the PM is working under. For example:

- Does your boss need an estimate ten minutes before her meeting? If so, the *top-down* or *heuristic* method might be best.
- Do you have plenty of time to allocate to the estimating process? If so, that might make the *bottom-up* method the way to go.

Estimating Method	Description	Pros, Cons, and Tips
Analogous	Often the best way to estimate is to look for a similar project and use the estimates made for that project as a starting point.	Success here rests on finding as analogous a project as possible and on accurately analyzing how the new project differs from the model.
Bottom-up	This is the nose-to-the-grindstone approach. The PM and team first estimate all the work packages in the WBS, then add them all together.	While this may sound like the best way to determine a schedule estimate, it often is not recommended, because: • It's very time consuming • It's hard to take interdependencies between tasks into account • The more individual estimates, the more room for estimating errors.
Top-down	This is high-level estimating. The PM and team work from the WBS, as in bottom-up estimating, but they only estimate the top nodes (the groups of work) and add those together.	This is a much faster process than bottom-up, and it can be very accurate, depending on the degree of skill and experience of the estimator.
Delphi technique	Keeping estimators' numbers anonymous to elicit the most honest estimates possible. (This method is covered in detail in Chapter 3; it can also be used as a requirements-gathering technique.)	This method has proven highly effective in cases in which people are reluctant to give honest numbers—perhaps they feel intimidated or afraid of other people knowing who gave which estimate. A common scenario is when a senior manager who is strongly attached to a project has high expectations, and no one wants to tell him or her that they think the project will take longer or cost more or be less successful than the manager expects.

(Continued on next page)

Expert opinion	The PM recognizes that an expert can provide a better estimate than he or she or the team can come up with, so a SME is hired to provide an estimate.	It takes money to make money, so if a SME can give you a better estimate, sometimes this can translate to many dollars saved on a better-planned, more successful project. Many consulting companies provide estimating as one of their service offerings. You might be pleasantly surprised how much an outside consultant may already know about a project that is new to you!
Parametric	In some industries, there are published figures (parameters) that can be used as bases for estimation. For example, in construction, there might be a parameter for the length of time it typically takes to build a mini-mall with seven retail outlets.	If your project is in an industry supported by parametric estimates, this is usually the way to go. A PM can heavily rely on estimates based on numerous similar projects.
Heuristics	Devising rules of thumb based on your own personal experience and trial and error, e.g., "Our team typically takes about three months to do this kind of work."	Although it sounds loose, this kind of estimating can be very accurate if you know your team's capabilities well and have hands-on experience with the kind of work involved.
Monte Carlo method	Using computer software tools to help with estimating as well as look for risks in the schedule. The tools are based on the traditional Monte Carlo method, which uses proven algorithms designed for working with many variables, such as those inherent in a project plan.	Some companies have full-time estimators who often use Monte Carlo software every day as their tool of choice. If you find a Monte Carlo tool specific to your industry, you may discover that it is extremely useful. The tools have a great deal of knowledge built in over years of customer use, and they can crunch numbers and analyze multiple logic paths much faster than the humans who designed them!

(Continued on next page)

Estimating Method	Description	Pros, Cons, and Tips
Program Evaluation and Review Technique (PERT) formula (a.k.a. three-point estimate)	The PM takes three estimates, (referred to as P, O, and M) and averages them using what is called a *weighted average* (see the formula below). "P" is for *pessimistic* (the longest estimate), "O" is for *optimistic* (the shortest estimate), and "M" is for *most likely*, the estimate the PM feels is most likely to be correct. The three are added up and averaged, but with a weighting factor of four applied to the most likely estimate. PERT estimate = (P + 4M + O) / 6.	This method can easily be combined with the other estimating methods shown. It is also known as a three-point estimate because you are averaging three individual estimates, P, O, and M. Note that some estimators take a straight average of P, M, and O, but many estimators prefer the classic weighted average as shown. Note also that the sum of the numbers is divided by six and not three, because the estimate M is counted four times.

Figure 4-5:   Best-Practice Schedule Estimation Techniques

- Is the project being performed within an industry, such as construction, that works from published, common-standard estimating guidelines? That makes *parametric* estimating best.

- Is this project similar to another project, and do you have good historical information about that project? If so, that would make *analogous* estimating a very good starting point.

- Do you have several competing estimates from different sources and aren't sure which one you trust the most? You might want to use some variation of the *PERT* or possibly enlist the professional aid of a SME (the *expert opinion* method).

Note that it's very common to mix and match techniques to your best advantage. For instance, a PM could solicit several estimates from the team using the Delphi technique, then seek out a SME's estimate as a reality check (expert opinion), then take those numbers and apply some variation of the PERT three-point formula to reconcile them.

Q6. What if you have to develop an estimate by working backwards from a predetermined date?

A6. PMs very often are not given a chance to estimate first and come up with a time frame, but, rather, are tasked with working backwards from a predetermined date from the client or from their senior management. This is sometimes referred to as *backing into a date*; the expected completion date of the project is documented from the get-go in the project charter, SOW, or contract.

This doesn't mean, however, PMs do not need good estimating skills. Good PMs are skillful at taking a deadline in these situations and planning out the activities so they can bring the project in on time, on scope, and on budget. Even if a PM is given a completion date ahead of time, he or she can still use the estimating techniques discussed above. As he or she plans each activity, the PM will still need to estimate its resource requirements and duration, just as if there were no external deadline. Here he or she will use the hard deadline as a constraint, keeping it constantly in mind while estimating the individual activities and making sure they fit into the project's required timeline.

DEVELOPING THE SCHEDULE

Q7. How does a PM turn a WBS into a project schedule, and what are the differences between the two documents?

A7. The schedule is a further drill-down (progressive elaboration) from the WBS. Once the schedule has been constructed, there are three key differences between a WBS and schedule:

- *The activities in the schedule may be at a lower level of decomposition.* The lowest level of the WBS is the work package, but work packages often can be further broken down into smaller pieces, called activities, which make up an activity list. The activity list feeds the schedule. For example, there may be 20 work packages in the WBS, but those 20 can be further decomposed into 35 activities, and each of the 35 activities would be represented as nodes on the schedule.

- *The activities in the schedule are sequential.* A WBS does not necessarily appear in sequential order. A key differentiator is that all of the activities in a schedule are, by definition, in sequential order.

- *The WBS has a shape.* A WBS is usually pyramidal to show the hierarchy and grouping of related tasks. In contrast, the schedule represents the sequence, timing, and duration of the activities, and can be visually represented in many different ways. Project network diagrams showing the linear progression of the activities and Gantt charts emphasizing the relative durations of the activities are among the most popular representations of schedules.

Q8. Are intermediate steps taken or documents developed in between the WBS and the schedule?

A8. Yes. Before the PM or project scheduler develops the schedule, he or she goes through a process that PMI calls *define activities*, producing two outputs:

- *Activity list.* The PM or project scheduler takes the work packages from the WBS, decomposes them further as necessary down to the activity level, and puts the activities into a list called an activity list. This is usually a vertical list and is often built using scheduling software like MS Project, but it can be created using any word processing software.

- ***Activity attributes.*** This document is like a second version of the WBS dictionary, but instead of detailing work packages, it covers all of the activities that are now part of the activity list. It's a best practice to keep the WBS synchronized with the dictionary and the activity list synchronized with the activity attributes.

Figure 4-6 shows a portion of a sample activity list based on three of the work packages (3.1, 3.2, and 3.3) in the WBS shown in Figure 3-4. The original codes from the WBS are shown in the left-most column of the figure.

WBS Code	Activity	Estimated Time	Predecessor Activity	Successor Activity
3.1	**Create test cases**	0 days		Analyze old tests
3.1.1	Analyze old tests	4 days	Create test cases	Analyze new business cases
3.1.2	Analyze new business cases	4 days	Analyze old tests	Create the cases
3.1.3	Create the cases	6 days	Analyze new business cases	Choose testing software
3.2	**Choose testing software**	0 days	Create the cases	Analyze test tool vendors
3.2.1	Analyze test tool vendors	3 days	Choose testing software	Select vendor
3.2.2	Select vendor	5 days	Analyze test tool vendors	Contract process for test tool
3.2.3	Contract process for test tool	10 days	Select vendor	Install test tool
3.2.4	Install test tool	3 days	Contract process for test tool	Schedule and run tests
3.3	**Schedule and run tests**	5 days	Contract process for test tool	

Figure 4-6: Activity List

When new activities are added, new codes also are added that reflect the child-parent relationship per the original work packages. When a work package is further subdivided into smaller activities, as with 3.1 and 3.2 (but not 3.3) below, a time duration of 0 is specified for the work package itself, indicating that the work packages are parent activities and also designating them as milestones.

Q9. What does a Gantt chart show, and why does it offer a better view of a project schedule than an activity list?

A9. The Gantt chart is a very popular view that comes up by default in MS Project. As soon as the PM or scheduler starts keying in the activity list, MS Project pops up a Gantt chart in split-screen mode to the right of the activity list based on all the key details about each task as detailed in the activity list. For each activity identified in words in the activity list (on the left-hand screen in MS Project), the Gantt chart shows a horizontal bar representing the same task (on the right-hand screen in MS Project, adjacent to the corresponding activity in the list; see Figure 4-7).

The beauty of the Gantt chart is that it instantly communicates visually several key facts about each task:

- The task names
- Whether they are subordinate to a parent task, which is indicated by indentation, as shown in Figure 4-7 (tasks 3.1.1, 3.1.2, and 3.1.3 are all subordinate to 3.1)
- The relative lengths of each task (the longer the horizontal blue bar, as shown in Figure 4-7, the longer the duration).

Also shown are:

- Whether the tasks are linked (as indicated in the figure by the downward arrows, tasks 3.1.1, 3.1.2, and 3.1.3 are linked to each other, making them consecutive)
- The names of each task (e.g., *Analyze new business cases* in the figure)
- The start date of each task (e.g., *Tuesday, 4/6/10* in the figure)
- The finish date of each task (e.g., *Friday, 4/9/10* in the figure)
- The time duration of each task (e.g., *4 days* in the figure)
- The predecessor task (e.g., *Task 2, Analyze old tests* in the figure).

Figure 4-7:   Activity List and Gantt Chart from MS Project

Q10. What does the network diagram show that is different from the Gantt view, and when is a network diagram helpful?

A10. Many PMs and team members like the network diagram best of all the schedule views because it shows the logic flow clearly at a glance. As shown in Figure 4-8, the network diagram displays each activity as a rectangular box with horizontal lines (arrows) connecting dependent activities, meaning tasks that are scheduled to occur sequentially. In the example below, *Analyze old tests* (far left) must take place before *Analyze new business cases*, which in turn must take place before *Create the cases*.

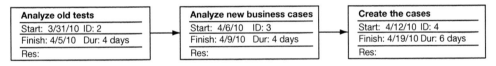

Figure 4-8:   Network Diagram from MS Project

Note that in Figure 4-8, each node (box) clearly indicates the following key pieces of information about each activity:

- The task name
- The start date
- The end date
- The ID number of each task
- The duration of the activity.

Q11. Is standard software available for building Gantt charts and network diagrams?

A11. Yes, several programs are available. As noted, Figures 4-7 and 4-8 were created in MS Project, which has been the industry-leading product for many years. It offers Gantt charts, network diagrams, and many other schedule views, plus a robust set of features that can help PMs and scheduling specialists. The latest version, MS Project 2010, is much more user-friendly than prior versions.

But there are also many competing scheduling products, including Primavera from Oracle, Base Camp from 37 Signals, and even new smartphone applications. WBS Chart Pro from Critical Tools does a very good job building a WBS that can easily be imported into MS Project and converted to a schedule. It's up to the PM to determine which tool set is best for his or her project and environment.

DEPENDENCIES

Q12. What is it called when one activity on a schedule must be done before another activity?

A12. This is called a dependency relationship. The task that is scheduled to go first is called the predecessor activity, and the task that must wait for it to take place and then follows after it is called the successor activity.

Three types of dependencies—mandatory, discretionary, and external—and four types of dependency relationships can exist between two successive activities. It can be very useful for planning purposes to analyze which type is involved, to help the PM better plan the schedule. Q&As 13–16 detail the three types of dependencies and dependency relationships.

Q13. When does a mandatory dependency exist between activities?

A13. A mandatory dependency exists when a predecessor activity absolutely must take place before its successor for the successor to succeed. For example, suppose that construction workers had to perform the following three tasks:

1. Remove the old carpeting from all the rooms in a house
2. Prepare the floor surface for new carpeting
3. Lay down the new rug.

It would not make sense to consider doing these three tasks in any order other than this 1, 2, 3 sequence.

Q14. When is a dependency considered discretionary?

A14. When there is a discretionary dependency, the PM may have an opinion about the order in which tasks should be performed, but he or she recognizes that reasonable people can disagree on the sequence.

For example, let's say that you are managing a dual project: installing a new operating system (OS) on all of your customers' desktops as well as installing new applications to run under that OS. Many PMs with an IT background might think that it is typically wiser to install the OS first and then the apps. But some customers might prefer receiving the new apps first and trying them out without having to deal with the additional disruption of a new OS at the same time. As long as the vendors of the application software support either order of installation, it's up to the PM to decide how best to do it. This is considered a discretionary dependency because it's up to the *discretion* of the PM.

Q15. What is the difference between a mandatory dependency and an external dependency?

A15. An external dependency is not inherently mandatory, but it involves an outside factor, such as a rule, law, holiday, deadline, or even possible weather conditions, that imposes a sequence on the tasks of a project. An example would be an end-of-year deadline—a company must have certain tasks completed before December 31 for tax purposes. An external dependency can force some of a project's activities to be completed ahead of others, but it differs from a mandatory dependency because without the deadline, the tasks would not have to be completed in that sequence.

Q16. What are the four types of dependency relationships that can exist between two tasks?

A16. Many people look at a network diagram and assume there is only one kind of dependency relationship: finish-to-start, described below, but there are actually four kinds. Identifying which one best describes the relationships between your project's tasks is a best practice for improving the effectiveness of your schedule.

- *Finish-to-start:* This is the classic dependency relationship. Two tasks are connected on a path, and Task 1 (the predecessor) must start and finish before the next successor activity, Task 2, can start.

- *Start-to-start:* Sometimes a predecessor needs to start before the next task can start, but it doesn't have to finish before the next one can start. Imagine an IT project with three sequential activities: (a) design, (b) code, and (c) test. The PM wants to allow the testers (performing task c) to get started a little early, before the time allocated for the coding (task b) is completed. This gives the testers a chance to get a jump on learning the new system and possibly catching some bugs and fixing them early.

- *Finish-to-finish:* Sometimes a successor activity cannot complete until the predecessor completes, but it can start before or after the other activity starts (i.e., the successor activity does not depend upon the start of the predecessor activity). For example, a vendor might in some cases allow a customer to install, test, and implement a software product (successor task) before contracting and purchasing it (predecessor task). This means the customer can use a temporary password supplied by the vendor to install the product and do complete testing. But only when the customer has contracted for and bought the product (finished the predecessor task) will the vendor give the customer a permanent password to install the software, letting him or her finish the successor activity.

- *Start-to-finish:* Here the successor activity cannot finish until the predecessor activity starts. In a similar example to the finish-to-finish scenario, suppose the seller has a great deal of trust in the buyer because they have done a lot of business together before. The seller lets the buyer work with the product initially without any legal document whatsoever. The buyer's PM installs and tests the product and then asks the buyer's attorney to send a signed letter of intent (see Chapter 8, Q&A 41) to the seller. As soon as the seller receives the letter, he or she considers the contract-and-purchase activity (predecessor) to have officially started, and in good faith, gives the buyer the permanent password (even though there still is no signed contract), letting the successor activity (install-test-and-implement) complete.

SCHEDULE COMPRESSION AND RESOURCE LEVELING

Q17. What is duration compression, and how can a PM accomplish it?

A17. Duration compression, also called schedule compression, means speeding up a project without reducing its scope by compressing the schedule.

Usually, this is done out of necessity, when the schedule is running late and needs to be brought back in line or there is an external driver forcing, what Maverick in *Top Gun* called "the need for speed." The need is typically triggered by an updated deadline from the client, pressure from senior management, a conflict with another project or resource, a newly pending merger, or any such event.

The two standard ways of compressing a project's schedule are crashing and fast tracking, discussed in Q&As 18–21.

Q18. What is crashing the schedule?

A18. Crashing is adding more resources to a project with the goal of getting the work done faster. This usually means hiring more workers, but there are other approaches as well: the existing team can work overtime, time can be borrowed from workers on other projects, or the PM can roll up his or her sleeves to pitch in on some of the technical work.

Q19. What are the main drawbacks of crashing?

A19. There are two main drawbacks. The obvious one is that the additional resources cost more money. Another drawback is that crashing doesn't always work, particularly for the following reasons:

- The chemistry of a team changes when new people are added, and original team members may resent new people, especially when they are paid more money for the same work.

- The new people added aren't always qualified to do the work or ready to go on day 1. This is especially common if they have been outsourced from another company or country and quickly thrown into the team. Compounding this problem is that in situations that require crashing, there usually aren't spare resources to train the new people or add extra supervision or oversight.

- Too many cooks can spoil the broth, and adding workers often does not increase productivity as much hoped for. The degree to which crashing works can depend on the type of work being performed, the experience and quality of the team members, and especially the PM's ability to quickly and effectively incorporate and manage more people.

- Managing the new resources can tie up a PM's time, which might be better spent managing the other areas of the project and the original team members.

Q20. What is fast-tracking a schedule, and how does it differ from crashing?

A20. Fast-tracking is taking activities that were planned to run sequentially (one after another), and instead running them in parallel (starting at the same time), again with the express goal of speeding things up. Unlike crashing, this is a way of compressing a schedule without spending additional money or hiring more resources.

For example, suppose that in the original project schedule, four tasks are arranged to run in 1, 2, 3, 4 order, as shown in Figure 4-9, a much-abbreviated version of a network diagram.

Original Version (four sequential tasks, no fast-tracking)
Task 1 → Task 2 → Task 3 → Task 4

Figure 4-9: Project Schedule before Fast-Tracking

To speed up the project, the four tasks on the single serial path might be split up into two parallel paths with two tasks each. In this example, Task 3 has been moved up to start on the same day as Task 1, as shown in Figure 4-10.

Fast-Tracked Version (The four tasks are split into two paths, both starting on the same day.)
Task 1 → Task 2
Task 3 → Task 4

Figure 4-10: Fast-Tracked Schedule

Q21. What are the drawbacks of fast-tracking?

A21. Juggling the schedule in this way carries an inherent high risk, especially for the following reasons:

- Usually, the PM had good reasons for planning the tasks sequentially in the first place—if, for instance, the successor tasks are dependent upon the predecessor tasks, even if the dependencies are not absolutely rigid. The dependencies and the reasons they were important can become painfully evident after the tasks are fast-tracked, to the project's detriment.

- PMs cannot be in two places at the same time. Their effectiveness as a resource can be compromised by their having to manage twice as many tasks at the same time.

- Sometimes team members wind up over-allocated and over-stretched because of fast-tracking. They may have been originally assigned to perform several sequential tasks that were easy enough to handle. But if those tasks become parallel, they will either need to be replaced on one or the other task (and their replacement might not be as good a fit for those tasks), or else they may wind up doing double duty, working on both tasks at once, which often is counterproductive (see the discussion of multitasking in Chapter 10, Q&A 29).

Q22. Is resource leveling a form of schedule compression?

A22. No. The terms sound similar, and this is a source of some confusion, but resource leveling is *not necessarily* about trying to shrink the schedule (although sometimes the schedule does shrink as a result). Resource leveling is the process a PM undertakes when he or she needs to adjust the project schedule to accommodate a decrease or increase in resources.

Imagine that a PM plans to have six testers conducting tests and assumes the testing will be completed in two days. If the number of available testers gets cut down to three, it's up to the PM to recalibrate how much longer he or she thinks the testing will take and to adjust the schedule accordingly. In this example, the PM might decide that with this reduction in resources, it might take four days to do the same testing (half of the people might take twice as long).

It's also considered resource leveling when a PM is given *more* resources than originally expected and needs to adjust the schedule accordingly. Returning to the example above, suppose that two teams merged, and an additional tester became available for the PM's testing phase. Seven testers might now be able to complete the work in a day and a half, and after this analysis, the PM would update the schedule accordingly.

A good way to differentiate between duration compression and resource leveling is to remember that duration compression is *proactive*—the PM is consciously trying to shorten the project's time frame—whereas resource leveling is *reactive*; the PM is dealing with a change in resources and recalibrating the schedule based on the new numbers.

THE CRITICAL PATH METHOD

Q23. What is the critical path method (CPM), and why is it considered so important for project management?

A23. At the heart of the critical path method is analyzing which logic path in the schedule is the most critical to the project and using that knowledge to manage the schedule and make sure that the project comes in on time. For example, determining which activity path is the critical path can enable the PM to adjust resources accordingly, such as moving more senior or more skilled team members from less critical activities onto critical path activities.

In addition to determining which is the critical path, CPM also involves several other key concepts (float, free float, early start/late start, and forward pass/backward pass), detailed in Q&As 27–32.

Q24. How do you determine the critical path on a project?

A24. By definition, the critical path is the longest path on a project. This is because the length of the critical path is the same as the duration of the entire project, and if the critical path winds up taking longer than planned, this automatically makes the entire project late (and there is no getting around that fact!). But if the critical path is managed well and finishes on schedule, the project will come in on time, unless another path that was planned to be shorter ends up taking longer than the critical path.

For example, suppose a project has eight individual activities: A, B, C, D, E, X, Y, and Z. Activities A, B, and C are on one sequential path; D and E are on a second path, and X, Y, and Z are on a third, as follows:

Path 1: Start, A, B, C, finish →→ 10 days

Path 2: Start, D, E, finish →→ 20 days

Path 3: Start, X, Y, Z, finish →→ 19 days.

The critical path would be Path 2 (activities D and E) because this is the longest path of the three, at 20 days. This also means that the total planned length of the project is 20 days because that's the duration of the critical path.

Q25. Can there be more than one critical path?

A25. On some projects, there is more than one critical path; two or more paths are in a tie for the longest path on the project. But in the example in

Q&A 24, there is only one critical path, simply because neither of the other paths is as long as the path comprising activities D and E.

Whenever there is more than one critical path, the PM, as a resource, may be greatly stretched: He or she must pay equal attention to two paths, either of which could slip slightly and delay the project. A project with more than one critical path inherently carries high risk, called *schedule risk* in PM parlance.

Q26. What if there is a path that is almost as long as the critical path?

A26. In our example, the X, Y, Z path lasts 19 days, almost as long as the critical path lasting 20 days. The slightly shorter path is referred to as a near-critical path. Because it is almost as long as the critical path, it also could cause a delay in project completion if it is not closely monitored. Designating a path as near-critical is useful for the PM as well as for the stakeholders because putting it in this category focuses awareness on its potential schedule risk, which might not otherwise appear on the team's radar.

FLOAT

Q27. What is *float*?

A27. Float is a key concept for helping PMs manage schedules effectively. There are two types of float: total float (also simply called float or slack), which we'll cover first, and free float, which we'll explore in Q&A 29.

Total float is the amount of extra time an activity can take to complete without making the entire project late. You can think of it as the amount of wiggle room a task has in your schedule. If an activity is on the critical path, by definition it has no float, because if any activity on the critical path takes even one day longer than planned, the project, by definition, immediately becomes one day late.

Total float is a core tool of the critical path method that is helpful to PMs in two important ways:

1. *On the critical path:* The PM places extra focus on every activity on the critical path because these activities have no float; slippage is not allowed. If an employee working on an activity on the critical path wants to take

vacation time, the PM either has to say no or find a way to replace the resource and get the activity done with no slippage.

2. **On non-critical paths:** The PM calculates the amount of total float on each activity that is *not* on the critical path. This exercise is useful because it gives the PM an idea of which activities he or she should focus on or, alternatively, devote less time to supervising, and it helps him or her determine which activities he or she can borrow resources from to augment resources on the critical path.

The PM also can monitor the progress of each activity against its float. For example, if a non-critical task gets delayed by a day, the PM can note that this activity now has one less day of float. By keeping an eye on float in this way, all team members can understand the individual tasks in the big picture and can help make sure that their tasks don't jeopardize the deadline for the project.

Q28. How is float calculated?

A28. Recall our sample project with three paths (1, 2, and 3) introduced in Q&A 24. Let's calculate the total float for all the activities on Path 1.

We said earlier that Path 2 was the critical path, so all activities on Path 2 have no float. But because Path 1 is not the critical path, all of its activities do have float. The critical path is 20 days long, and Path 1 has a total length of ten days. To calculate the total float for Activity A on this path, see Figure 4-11.

Note that for Path 1, all three activities (A, B, and C) have ten days of float before any of the activities are started. But this does *not* mean that each activity on Path 1 can use ten days of float. The total float of the *entire path* is ten days (not 30!). As soon as any activity on Path 1 uses up some of its float, the float for the other two activities on this path is reduced by the same amount. For example, if Activity A runs over by three days, the remaining float for all

Total float of Activity A = Length of critical path – length of Path 1
Total float of Activity A = 20 days – 10 days
Total float of Activity A = 10 days

Figure 4-11: Calculating Total Float

three activities in Path 1 is reduced to seven days: 10 days total float – 3 days of delay = 7 days remaining float.

Quick Synonym Review for Float-Related Terms	
Float is the same as...	*Slack*
Total float is used interchangeably with...	*Float*
Total float is the same as...	*Total slack*
No float is used interchangeably with...	*Zero float* or *zero slack*

Q29. What is *free float*, and how does it differ from *total float*?

A29. Free float is like total float but on a micro level—it's simply the float between two successive tasks. It indicates how late an activity can be without delaying its successor activity.

Free float, along with total float, are both very valuable numbers to PMs: The more aware the PM is of how much wiggle room each activity has, the more control he or she gains over the schedule and the greater the likelihood of bringing the project in on time.

Free float is easier to calculate than total float because it does not depend on the critical path. But the calculation for free float requires understanding the concept of early start (ES) and early finish (EF), which we explain in the next few Q&As.

Q30. How are early start and early finish derived?

A30. To calculate free float, you first need to know the definitions of early start and early finish and how to determine them.

- *Early start* is simply the planned start date of an activity on a project schedule.
- *Early finish* is the date you plan for an activity to complete, based on the early start date and the estimated duration (ED) of the activity.

For example, suppose you have two activities: Activity 1 (the predecessor) and Activity 2 (the successor), as shown in Figure 4-12.

January 1 is the planned start date of Activity 1, so it is considered Activity 1's early start. The early start of Activity 2 is January 14, its planned start date.

Activity	Estimated Duration	Early Start (planned start date)	Early Finish (planned finish date)	Free Float
Activity 1 (predecessor)	10 days	January 1	January 10	3 days
Activity 2 (successor)	5 days	January 14	January 18	

Figure 4-12:   Calculating Early Start

The next two values from our example, the early finish of Activity 1 and Activity 2, require a calculation, using the early finish formula.

Early finish of Activity 1: If Activity 1 is planned to start on January 1, and we expect it to take ten days to complete, the activity should complete on January 10, which is considered its early finish, as shown in Figure 4-13.

EF of Activity 1 = ES of Activity 1 + ED of Activity 1 – 1 day

EF = January 1 + 10 days – 1 day

EF = January 10

Figure 4-13:   Calculating Early Finish for Activity 1

Early finish of Activity 2: If Activity 2 is planned to start on January 14, and its estimated duration is five days, the activity should complete on January 18, as shown in Figure 4-14.

EF of Activity 2 = ES of Activity 2 + ED of Activity 2 – 1 day

EF = January 14 + 5 days – 1 day

EF = January 18

Figure 4-14:   Calculating Early Finish for Activity 2

Q31. How is free float calculated?

A31. Once you have a good idea of when your current activity will finish (early finish) and when its successor will start (early start), there's a formula that makes it easy to calculate free float. To calculate the free float of Activity 1, we simply need to plug the early finish date of Activity 1 and the early start date of Activity 2 into the formula for free float shown in Figure 4-15.

Free float = early start (of successor) − early finish (of predecessor) − 1 day

FF (of Activity 1) = ES (of Activity 2) − EF (of Activity 1) − 1 day

FF (of Activity 1) = January 14 − January 10 − 1

Free float of Activity 1 = 3 days

Figure 4-15: Calculating Free Float for Activity 1

Q32. Why are early finish and the free float calculation considered a forward pass, while deriving the total float is considered a backward pass?

A32. Determining how long an activity will take from the time it starts to its completion date (early finish) and how much extra time there will be before its successor activity can get started (free float) are examples of forward thinking and therefore are considered part of a forward pass.

By contrast, to calculate total float, it's necessary to first look forward to the end of the schedule, then do critical path analysis, and then circle back to see how much slack exists in various parts of the schedule, always with the end in mind. For this reason, calculating total float is considered a backward pass (even though it has elements of *both* looking forward and backward).

Q33. When are the dates for late start and late finish useful?

A33. For planning purposes, it is very handy to know the latest date an activity can start—its late start. Knowing the late start date can give the PM options for juggling resources on other activities, in addition to the activity he or she is analyzing for late start. Similarly, it is important for a PM to know the latest date an activity can safely end without jeopardizing the project's completion date. That date is called late finish.

Late start and late finish can be determined by a lot of factors. For example, there could be an external dependency driving the dates; the project charter could list as a milestone that beta testing of the new system will be done by a certain date. That would force a late-finish date onto the tasks behind the testing and would also determine the latest possible date the beta testing activities could start. For instance, suppose the late finish for testing is mandated to be June 20, and the task has an expected duration of five days. Working backwards in this case, the late start would have to be no later than June 16, and the testing would run June 16, 17, 18, 19, 20. So in this example, the milestone date for completing the beta testing would also drive the late-start date.

Q34. How do early start, early finish, late start, and late finish fit in with critical path analysis?

A34. Late start and late finish are both derived by the critical path method.

- *If on the critical path:* All critical path activities have zero float, and this means they each have only one allowable end date: the planned end date for that task. So for these activities, their planned end date is not only their early finish, but it's also their late finish, driven by the end date of the critical path.

- *If not on the critical path:* For an activity on a non-critical path, it's common to calculate its late finish by thinking about how late it could complete without making its path longer than the critical path. Then, working backwards, its early finish can be calculated by subtracting its float from its late finish. This gives its early finish.

CONVERGENT PATHS

Q35. What is meant by the term *convergent paths* on a schedule?

A35. All paths on a project end at the finish line (or, in a network diagram view, they all converge in the finish box at the far right). But activities on different paths also can sometimes converge at points along the way, before the finish point.

Consider an example of a project with two parallel paths:

Path 1: A→B→C
Path 2: X→Y→Z

Activity A on Path 1 has Activity B as its successor activity. But sometimes activities on one logic path also have a dependency on tasks on other paths.

For example, suppose Activity A on Path 1 also has a dependency relationship with Activity Y on Path 2, where Activity Y cannot start until Activity A completes. Here, Activity A is the predecessor for two successor activities: B and Y. In other words, there is convergence between the two paths. This is emphasized in Figure 4-16, where the connector arrow from Activity A to Y indicates that Y and Z also must wait for A and then sequentially follow A.

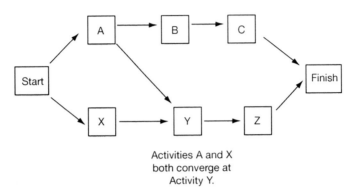

Activities A and X
both converge at
Activity Y.

Figure 4-16: Showing Convergence on a Network Diagram

Path convergence adds to the risk of a project by complicating the schedule with interdependencies between paths. If A in our example is delayed for any reason, *both* paths 1 and 2 will be delayed because A will hold up B on Path 1 and Y on Path 2. This will also push back all tasks following B on Path 1 and Y on Path 2. Path convergence in this example also shows that no matter what, a delay to Activity A will inevitably hold up the critical path, because a delay to Activity A will hold up either path. It could be said that Activity A is part of three paths: Path 1, Path 2, and a third path consisting of activities A, Y, and Z, as indicated in Figure 4-16. Scheduling tools like MS Project make it easy for the PM to represent the convergent activities across different pathways.

Looking for path convergence is one of the specific ways PMs proactively analyze schedule risk. In the above example, a PM might decide to add additional resources to Activity A because A is a linchpin in paths 1 and 2. One of the key features of Monte Carlo software for risk analysis is that it can take large, complex schedules and calculate all path convergences and their resulting ripple effects, including some that might not be evident even to a trained PM.

Q36. Are dummy activities the same as convergent activities?

A36. Dummy activities are similar to convergent activities, but the difference is that they are not true activities, as their name implies. A dummy activity is created and added to a network diagram simply to visually emphasize a dependency relationship between two activities. It does not officially take up time or resources, and so it said to have a zero duration.

An example might be an activity called BetaTestCompleted/Notify Vendor. This might entail nothing more than sending off a quick email to a vendor, taking almost no time. While this is not an activity in the true sense because it will not require significant work requiring resources, it might nevertheless be a very important action. It might, for example, give a green light to the start a subsequent activity, which would make it worth indicating in the project schedule as a dummy activity to avoid confusion.

There is another type of network diagram, activity on arrow (AOA), that has a feature specifically geared for indicating dummy activities: It uses broken-line connector arrows only for the dummy relationships and solid arrows for all others. This is called the arrow diagramming method (ADM).

BUILDING SAFEGUARDS INTO THE SCHEDULE: CONTINGENCY, DELAYS, AND LEADS

Q37. What can PMs do to build extra time into a schedule in case unforeseen delays arise?

A37. It is crucial on any project for PMs to perform reserve analysis, which is adding extra time into the schedule (as well as extra money to the budget) so that when delays come up, the team is positioned to handle them and make the project succeed.

Risk management—analyzing the potential events that could cause delays and overruns—is covered in detail in Chapter 7, but it is also discussed here as a schedule management tool to help the PM bring projects in on time. The extra time built into a schedule to handle delays is called contingency reserve. It is time (or money) set aside for the "known unknowns," in other words, for the events that the PM and team can predict in advance that might possibly delay the project.

For instance, on a project to print and sell books, it is fairly obvious that it's possible the printer could break down. It would make sense to plan for this as a possibility. But many PMs are overly optimistic in these situations: They ignore the potential for serious problems and get caught flat-footed—along with their project sponsor and customers—when something goes wrong. Planning in extra time, money, or both to deal with a potential problem (e.g., to fix or replace the printer if needed) is an example of setting aside contingency reserve. Clients are generally comfortable with the reserve concept as long as the reserve allocations are clearly communicated to them in advance. Clients understand that the PM is protecting their interests, and they also know that the extra time or money will not be spent if the risk event does not happen.

Q38. How is contingency reserve added into the schedule?

A38. There are four general ways it can be added to a schedule:

- *Adding a lump sum of time to all activities.* For example, adding two days to each task as contingency reserve. This approach does not take into account the specific risks that each activity potentially faces, so it does not require the PM to spend a lot of time on analysis. It is a very fast way to allocate the reserve. Though it sounds like a scattershot approach, it can work fairly well and is widely used. Many PMs think this approach is more efficient than trying to analyze every activity to determine the ideal amount of reserve for each, which is difficult, time consuming, and not necessarily accurate anyway, as risk is based on unknowns that are not known until after the project is over.

- *Adding a percentage of time to each activity.* This approach is based on the idea that the longer the activity, the more reserve time it might need. If the PM decides to allow 10 percent reserve time for every activity, longer activities will automatically receive more reserve time than shorter activities.

- *Adding a lump sum of time to the entire project length.* Based on risk analysis, the PM estimates the amount of potential risk and accordingly allocates a reserve as a lump sum. The PM does not have to worry about determining appropriate reserve time for individual activities and can use the time allocated to the entire project as needed.

- *Adding a percentage of time to the entire project length.* Similar to adding a percentage of time to each activity, the larger the project, the larger the reserve added automatically by percentage. If a PM is managing five projects of different lengths but uses the same percentage allocation for all five, each will get a different amount of contingency reserve, corresponding directly to that project's total duration.

Note that for all four of these methods, the PM sometimes works with risk analysts or other SMEs to best determine the reserve allocation.

Q39. Contingency reserve sounds like padding. How are they different?

A39. Padding has a negative connotation from the customer's point of view. While contingency reserves are added to the schedule and budget in an up-front manner, clearly to protect the project and the customer, padding has a secretive, behind-the-client's-back quality.

For example, a project team might arrive at an estimate of nine months, but a PM might pad the estimate by telling the client that the team estimates the work will take ten months. One big problem with this is that the customer might feel as if it were being deceived, or even cheated, if it found out that the estimate was padded. At the very least, it might feel uneasy because the PM was not confident in the team's original nine-month estimate and added a month without giving any specific reasons or risks for needing the extra month as a contingency reserve.

Padding also can create a multiplier effect: If the team members pad their individual activity estimates, and then the PM adds up the individual estimates and pads them again, the result can be a doubly padded estimate.

It's best for the PM to lead by example by always giving his or her most accurate and professional estimate to the customer. This will encourage team members to provide the most honest estimates possible to the PM. If the PM thinks that a one-month contingency reserve may be necessary, it's better to add the month as a line item and tie it to the potential risks it's intended to mitigate, than to bury it by padding it into the estimate. The line-item method is a best practice for two reasons: The customer likes feeling that the PM is being honest and forthright, and the customer can feel more confident that it will have to pay for only a nine-month project, not a ten-month project, if things go as planned.

Q40. What if you need to build a delay into the schedule?

A40. There are many scenarios in which it's necessary to build in wait time between activities—the classic example is that after pouring concrete, you must wait for the concrete to dry, or cure, before beginning construction. A delay that is deliberately built into the schedule in cases like this is called a lag. Adding this time as a lag, not as an activity, benefits the PM because a lag is recognized as non-chargeable. (As the old saying goes, "You don't want to pay your people to watch the cement dry.")

As with contingency reserves, a lag can be added in as a lump sum or as a percentage, whichever makes the best sense for the project.

- *Lag as a lump sum:* Adding a lag as lump sum clearly makes the most sense in the concrete scenario. An engineer would analyze the optimum amount of time needed for the concrete to dry, based on pertinent factors such as the thickness of the concrete and the mixture of cement to stone, and would come up with an accurate estimate for the lag time, such as three days.

- *Lag as a percentage:* Sometimes it makes more sense to schedule lag time in proportion to the size of the task. For instance, the PM may schedule lag time to follow the completion of a task so the PM and the team can review the outcomes of a task before moving forward. The larger and more complex the task, the more lag time the PM might want to allocate because there may be more issues to analyze and solve.

Support for Lags in Scheduling Software

Because it is often necessary to build in lag time, some software scheduling tools, such as MS Project, offer a lag feature expressly for this purpose. The PM goes to the screen where the task relationship between two activities is detailed, enters the desired time, and designates it as lag time. Both the lump sum and percentage options are supported by the software. A helpful feature of the software is that it understands that a lag is not a chargeable task but rather is non-working time. This makes the delay very clear in the schedule without complicating the billing.

If a lag feature is important to you, it can be a key criterion to look for when choosing a scheduling product. Note that this feature, for instance in MS Project, can support adding leads as well as lags.

Q41. What if you want to allow an activity to start early, if possible?

A41. You can specify lead time for the activity, which is the opposite of lag time. Lags *add* time between tasks, and leads *decrease* the time by giving the PM a way to build in a possible early start between a predecessor and its successor task. Specifying lead time is common in coding and testing on IT projects, where it can be advantageous for the testers to get an early jump on kicking the tires of a new system before it's ready to be formally turned over for testing.

The PM can formally plan in a possible early start by creating a lead in the schedule between the two tasks. As with lags, the lead time can either be added as a lump sum—for example, a one-day lead—or as a percentage of the predecessor task's duration. Both choices are well-supported by some of the software scheduling products.

The Two Main Benefits of Building in Leads

- A lead formalizes an early start in the schedule. All team members get a heads-up about the possible lead, making it more likely that the team will gear up to it and begin the successor activity early.
- Leads are optionally taken, which allows flexibility: If the predecessor task is going quickly and well, the team can start the successor task early, per the scheduled lead; but if not, the team can begin the successor on its planned start date, with no change order needed to modify the schedule.

CRITICAL CHAIN THEORY AND THE THEORY OF CONSTRAINTS

Q42. Is there a more precise way to build safeguards into the schedule than the methods we've discussed?

A42. Yes. Eliyahu Goldratt's *critical chain theory* can go hand in hand with the critical path method, but it's a departure from the traditional use of reserve time on a project.[2] Instead, it suggests using reserve time in a very specific and proactive way. After the PM conducts a traditional critical path analysis, he or she further analyzes the schedule, drilling down and looking for specific tasks that pose the greatest schedule risk, based on such factors as the experience level of personnel, the availability of materials, and so on. These tasks would usually be on the critical path, but they could also be on other paths that, if delayed, could influence the critical path. The PM then determines where best to carve out small pieces of the reserve time, which Goldratt calls *buffers*, and strategically places them in between high-risk activities, giving the team a little extra time as needed. The name *critical chain* comes from the way two sequential tasks on a network diagram look when they have a time buffer depicted in between them: like two connecting links on a chain.

The key to using the critical chain method effectively is to perform it iteratively, constantly monitoring the schedule to see if the buffers are still needed where they were originally assigned. If they are no longer needed between certain activities, they can be "given back," and the PM might move them to another link in the chain where he or she determines they might do the most good.

The critical chain method is part of the schedule control process, but it also touches on the process of monitoring and controlling risks, because looking for schedule issues and reacting accordingly is part of risk management. (For more about risk processes, see Chapter 7.)

Q43. How does Goldratt's theory of constraints further help PMs manage the schedule?

A43.   Per Goldratt's theory of constraints (TOC), the PM drills down into the network diagram beyond the critical path, looking for the few key constraints that pose the greatest threats to the project.[3] Goldratt refers to key constraints in a schedule as *bottlenecks*. These are often at the heart of slowdowns, so PMs need to find, analyze, and solve all bottlenecks as best they can.

Goldratt points out, however, that not all bottlenecks can or must be eliminated. Rather, some bottlenecks can be exploited to maximize productivity. For instance, a PM might identify a bottleneck in a critical gateway in a manufacturing process—a point at which work often slows or even stops. This bottleneck can't be completely eliminated, however, because the gateway activity is essential and needs to remain fundamentally the way it is in the schedule. Using the theory of constraints, the PM could find creative ways to improve this part of the system. For example, he or she might strategize to find ways to speed up the delivery of raw materials to this gateway, boosting throughput. By adjusting the *constraints*, in this case, the quantities and delivery of materials, the PM can increase project efficiency.

Note that TOC, like Goldratt's critical chain theory, must be an iterative process. Even once a PM solves a key bottleneck, he or she should continually seek to determine whether any other bottlenecks remain at that point or new bottlenecks have emerged since the solution was implemented.

TOP TEN TIME MANAGEMENT PITFALLS TO AVOID

1. Neglecting risk planning. Failing to anticipate and plan responses for risks can do tremendous damage to an otherwise well-planned project and is probably the most common cause of project failure.

2. Underestimating or overestimating. Underestimating often results from not putting enough time or effort into the estimating process. It can hamstring the entire project and lead to failure. At best, overestimating means you will finish early, but finishing early is considered a variance, too, because it can mean you either estimated badly or padded the schedule or, at worst, neglected quality considerations in the interest of saving time or money.

3. Not providing adequate contingency reserves in your schedule, and, therefore, not having enough time to handle unforeseen problems or events when they come up on a project.

4. Accepting an inadequate deadline from the client or upper management without registering your concerns.

5. Not assigning sufficient resources to the critical path.

6. Over-focusing on the critical path, and therefore not paying sufficient attention to the risks or demands of a non-critical path.

7. Putting too much focus on the schedule itself (e.g., spending a lot of time playing with PM software) and not spending enough time working directly with your team members and stakeholders.

8. Rigidly sticking to the deadlines without enough flexibility to adapt to changes.

9. Taking shortcuts to try to come in on deadline at the expense of other equally important measures of success, such as making sure your customer is happy with the quality of your deliverables.

10. Doing things the way your company has always done them—for example, not embracing modern tools like scheduling software, ignoring historical information and lessons learned, and succumbing to not-invented-here syndrome (discussed in Chapter 12).

Notes

1. Angelo Baratta, "Value Triple Constraint: How To Evaluate Project Value Delivered," *Executive Brief, Technology Management Resource for Business Leaders* (February 2010).

2. Eliyahu M. Goldratt, *Critical Chain* (Great Barrington, MA: North River Press, 1997).

3. Eliyahu M. Goldratt, *Theory of Constraints* (Great Barrington, MA: North River Press, 1990).

CHAPTER 5

Cost Management: Controlling Costs and Coming in on Budget

Coming in on budget is a crucial measure of project success, and this chapter presents the key cost-related formulas and strategic concepts used by PMs, such as sunk costs and opportunity costs, with an emphasis on making strong long-term decisions.

The truism "time is money" is nowhere more evident than in cost management, as schedule slippage often leads directly to going over budget. This chapter covers earned value management (EVM) formulas, a set of interrelated formulas that PMs use to capture and correct schedule and budget variances. These formulas not only help PMs control costs but also manage multiple, concurrent projects. In addition, by using them, PMs add trend analysis, performance reporting, and forecasting skills to their bag of tricks, so they become more promotable and marketable. To help make these formulas easy to learn and apply, I present them around one central example: a simplified web page creation project.

When looking for cost savings, it is important to keep in mind that projects can be greatly harmed by improperly applying cost-cutting measures. Common mistakes range from cutting planning to save time, to sacrificing quality for cost, to outsourcing without adding sufficient oversight.

Cost management breaks down into three processes by the PMI model. First is a two-step planning approach: the process of estimating costs followed by the process of determining the budget. The third process is controlling costs, during which the PM proactively works to keep the project on budget, without allowing its mission or any of its performance metrics to be compromised.

FOUNDATIONAL COST CONCEPTS

Q1. Where are the biggest opportunities for managing costs on projects?

A1. PMs can do many things to control costs, specifically:

- Estimating time and costs well
- Putting sufficient time into planning
- Making sure to create a good contract (see Chapter 8, particularly Q&A 6, for more on good contracts)
- Communicating well with the customer and other stakeholders (misunderstandings often spawn rework and waste, driving up costs)
- Building sufficient risk mitigation into the budget and schedule (to avoid unforeseen charges)
- Preventing scope creep by following a strong change-control process
- Continuously measuring time and cost performance (e.g., by using the earned value formulas) and nipping any problems in the bud
- Training team members (spending a little on training often pays big dividends in increased efficiencies)
- Managing the project team effectively.

Q2. What's the key difference between cost efficiency and cost savings?

A2. Cost efficiency means getting the same—or better—results for less. But many PMs and senior managers make the mistake of trying to cut costs without making sure they have improved processes (or at least not hurt them). It is essential to make sure you will achieve the same or better results *before* implementing any cost reductions. This means doing your homework. Before you reduce resources or switch to a less expensive software tool, put in the time to analyze whether the replacement really will be as good as, or better than, what you currently have. The problem is that cheaper always sounds better (especially in a tough economy). But it's the PM's responsibility to stand up for the solution that will deliver the project successfully and not simply cave to demands to choose a cheaper option.

Q3. Why do long-term results beat short-term ones?

A3. When you as the PM are faced with decisions, a good approach is to ask, "Which choice is good for the project right now, and which is better long-term?" Aligning short-term goals with long-term goals whenever possible is a winning strategy. Focusing on long-term results can create a positive ripple effect, resulting in greater profits in the end. For example, a PM whose decisions take the customer's long-term interests into effect will often see that same customer return for future business, and he or she may even refer new clients to the PM's company. This boosts the company's profits beyond the original project.

In contrast, short-sighted decisions can bring "here today, gone tomorrow" results. For example, hiring less-experienced staff may increase the profit margin in the short run, but the project results may be poor (and customers will be more likely to complain than give referrals).

Q4. What are ways to achieve long-term results?

A4. The key is to follow two rules:

- Always weigh all the components of the triple constraint when making a decision, and resist the urge to be unduly swayed by any one constraint, especially time or cost.
- Never allow yourself to be pressured by any one stakeholder into doing something that is not best for the body of key stakeholders.

Any time you are pressured to go the cheap route, rush a deadline, or make a debatable change, you need to resist the knee-jerk reaction of going for a short-term accomplishment (usually to gain stakeholder approval) without making sure it's the best decision. Doing something that will only help in the short term may make your customer or manager happy with you at the time (instant gratification!), but it might have a negative overall effect on the project.

Q5. Is it ever OK to prioritize short-term over long-term results?

A5. It's never a great idea to comply with any request that you don't feel is best over the long term. In cases where a stakeholder is insistent, always ask them make their requests using the project's change management system, in which case you can hope the approvers will do what's best to balance short-term and long-term interests. Beware of any stakeholder who asks you to bypass proper change management channels.

For instance, suppose your PM counterpart on the customer side tells you: "We need to lower the project's budget by 10 percent, which means you'll need to get it done with two fewer application developers. We are willing to accept a few less of the fancy features we had asked for." In this scenario, the customer seems to understand that he or she is likely to see a trade-off in scope or quality in return for reduced costs and manpower. And this might tempt you to comply with their request. But you should not do so unless the following are both also true:

- The customer has made his or her request through the project's integrated change control process. Ensure all key stakeholders understand the change and are on board with it.

- You have carefully analyzed the potential impact of the change on the project. Are you sure you will you really be able to deliver on the main requirements if constrained by a 10 percent budget cut? (Just because the customer says it can be done doesn't make it true). And if the 10 percent cut would introduce too many risks, could it do more harm than good to say yes? (Saying no to a customer can be the hardest part of the PM's job; this is covered further in Chapter 9, Q&As 14 and 15.)

Q6. Where do PMs often go wrong trying to implement cost savings?

A6. Some very common and very damaging mistakes include:

- *Using cheaper resources.* This is extremely common. PMs often choose to have fewer team members or select less-qualified staff to reduce costs. But this often causes the opposite of the desired result—the project takes longer to achieve and under-delivers on quality or even scope.

- *Outsourcing without proper oversight.* Outsourcing is often implemented to cut costs, but the results are very often less than satisfactory. To make it work, additional care must be taken to manage the outsourced components. (For more about this, see Chapter 11.)

- *Under-planning.* Often, planning time gets short shrift ("Quit planning and do the real work!"). But insufficient planning can hurt project execution big time, leading to unsatisfactory results and costly rework.

- *Cutting so-called red-ink expenses.* In a cost-cutting atmosphere, expenses such as productivity tools, training, and investment in new equipment are often cut. This is counterproductive if the purpose of funding them in the first place was ultimately cost reduction. It's important to keep the big picture in mind and not cut overzealously, which can be shortsighted.

MANAGING COSTS

Q7. What are sunk costs, and how do they sometimes influence PMs to make the wrong decisions?

A7. Imagine that a sales rep has put a lot of money into keeping his old car going. The car often breaks down, causing him to miss appointments. He doesn't want to replace the car, because he likes thinking of the money he has put into the car as a wise investment in his job. But if he could step back, he would see that his beloved old Buick is hurting him in lost sales and that he would make more money this year and in the future by biting the bullet and buying a new car. He wouldn't miss any more appointments, he'd make more sales, and his reputation for dependability would increase, leading to more customer referrals.

The important thing for the salesman to realize is that the money he spent on the purchase and maintenance of the old car is not the point. That money is gone and is never coming back. It's a sunk cost. You can think of it as water under the bridge. What *is* crucial is making the best decision for his business today.

Poor decisions linked to sunk costs are very common in the business world. For example, a computer system that was state-of-the-art a few years ago and was useful on many projects is now outdated and slow, but the engineer who brought it in to the PM firm where he or she works is afraid of looking bad by suggesting that at this point it should be replaced. This may be a bad decision because the system is already a sunk cost.

To make the best decisions regarding sunk costs, there is a wrong question and a right question to ask yourself.

- *Wrong question:* Considering how much money I spent so far on my old car/laptop/office system, what's the optimum amount of money to spend to keep it going for another year so we can still get some use out of it?
- *Right question:* How much more money will we make in the next three years overall if we upgrade now, compared to what we'll make if we keep the old product?

Q8. What are opportunity costs, and how can you use this concept to make the best long-term choices?

A8. You can think of opportunity costs as the cost of not pursuing a certain path. Let's say you have a choice between two job offers: Cool PM Job 1 for

$70K per year, and an even cooler PM job, Job 2, for $80K per year. Obviously Job 2 offers a higher salary, but is it the better choice overall? Taking a long-term view, which position will wind up paying off better for you, years down the road? And what would be the real cost of giving up the other opportunity?

The key here is considering which one is more likely to pay off for you over time, in various ways. Is Job 2 as secure as Job 1? Are there similar chances for advancement in both positions? Would one of the two jobs probably make you more marketable for future positions down the road?

In our example, if you take Cool PM Job 2 for $80K, but the company goes out of business, you could end up making a not-so-cool $0K! A simple way to look at it is that here, the opportunity cost for taking Job 2 would be $70K the first year (the salary you would have been making at Job 1), $140K over two years ($70K * 2), and $210,000 over three years ($70K * 3). Figure 5-1 shows the opportunity costs for either choice, Job 1 or Job 2, broken down over one year, two years, and three years. A more complex calculation would be to try to think ahead to where you would be in five years, in a totally new position, while factoring in your market value based on the position you select today, either Job 1 or Job 2.

The concept of opportunity costs can help you with any decision for which you are able to analyze the dollar impact of the choices—for instance, when you are trying to select one of two possible projects. It helps you quantify what you are giving up and gets you to focus more than you otherwise might have on all of the important pros and cons of each choice.

Job Offer	Annual Salary	Opp. Cost: Year 1	Opp. Cost: Year 2	Opp. Cost: Year 3
Cool PM Job 1	$70K	$80K	$160K	$240K
Cool PM Job 2	$80K	$70K	$140K	$210K

Figure 5-1:   Making the Best Decisions Considering Opportunity Costs

Q9. What are variable costs versus fixed costs on projects, and how can understanding both kinds help PMs keep their costs down?

A9. When you're putting together a budget, variable costs are the ones that can change, based (literally) on variables. Personnel expenses are a good example. They are dependent on many factors—for example, how many team members you hire, their level of experience, and whether you will be paying recruiter fees for them.

The opposite of variable costs are fixed costs, for which you know in advance exactly what the charge will be. If you are going to be working with an internal (HR) recruiter to help you staff up your team, your company will be paying a fixed cost for the recruiter's salary, and your project budget will not be hit with a fee for each hiring.

It's often useful to lock in fixed costs as much as possible, to avoid surprises—variances—between the planned budget and what you actually wind up spending. In our staffing example, we have a blend of variable and fixed costs. The internal recruiter's salary is fixed, and there are no hiring fees, but the number of staff hired will usually be variable, as will the individual salaries of the new employees.

Choosing variable over fixed costs when possible is one way of keeping costs down. For instance, hiring temporary workers instead of permanent ones keeps HR costs variable. If the budget for the project remains healthy, the personnel can all be kept on the project, but if cuts become necessary, some companies may choose to downsize the temporary workers, eliminating the variable costs on the project (while protecting the permanent staff).

Q10. How do direct versus indirect costs relate to a project's budget?

A10. It's essential when creating a budget to know which charges can be directly billed to the project. Some costs are clearly direct to the project, such as the billable hours of the team members creating the deliverables or the laptops or software licenses you need to purchase to help your staff build the deliverables.

Indirect charges are ones that are not tied to one particular project but are shared over multiple projects. An example would be the salary of the director of projects for the performing organization, or a chargeback of some kind for the company's PMO.

Training can be an example of a gray area. Let's say your company has an initiative to provide ethics training for all employees. This would clearly be an indirect cost, even though the training might help your people do a better job for your current customer. But if you are leading a project to build a website using Java language and your staff of in-house developers will require advanced Java training to produce the results at the skill level and speed you need, you would probably be able to classify these training costs as direct. The training does have an indirect element in that once the employees learn the skills, they will be able to use them on future projects. But the costs are primarily direct because they must have the training to do the project.

PMI COST PROCESS 1: ESTIMATING COSTS

Q11. How is the process of estimating costs connected to the various time-estimating and planning processes?

A11. The process of estimating costs is the crucial step in which a dollar value is calculated for all of the individual parts of the project, and these costs are accumulated into a single figure, simply called the cost estimate or, more formally, the activity cost estimates. Another useful output of this process is the documentation of the justification for the estimates, which is called the basis of estimates.

This process is a close cousin of the earlier process of estimating activity durations. As in that process, cost estimating can be done on the work package level (bottom-up estimating), at the activity level, or on a larger level (e.g., top-down, analogous, heuristics).

The process of estimating costs is closely linked to the time-planning steps in several ways:

- Estimating costs immediately follows the five sequential time-management planning steps.
- The primary output of the time processes (the schedule) is the primary input here (although artifacts from other PM knowledge areas, such as the scope baseline and risk register, can also be used as inputs).
- When estimating costs, PMs can use any or all of the set of nine estimating methods used to estimate time.

Once the cost estimates for the activities are finalized, they will be passed on to the second consecutive cost process, determining the budget. But cost estimating can be done over several passes, per the next Q&A.

Q12. Why is cost estimating done as an iterative process, over several passes?

A12. Estimating dollars is a crucial and complex part of project managing. Accuracy is difficult, even for experts, because so many variables and risks come into the mix. Cost estimating involves compiling multiple inputs, including the requirements, scope, WBS, and schedule, along with factoring in other variables, such as contract issues, personnel problems, market conditions, and even the economy itself. On top of all that is the added pressure to be especially accurate with this process since errors around dollars can have serious consequences and also tend to stand out very visibly to stakeholders. And so for all these reasons, it is considered a best practice for estimation to be done iteratively.

For example, if you are going through a five-week planning phase on a large project, you might ask your designated estimator to bring an initial estimate, called a *rough order of magnitude estimate* (ROM), to the first meeting. This rough estimate is only expected to fall within a very broad range of accuracy, from −50 percent (on the low end) to +100 percent (on the high end). For example, if an estimate is $1 million, the ROM estimate would still be considered accurate as long as the variance fell within the following numbers:

- If your estimator overestimated, his or her figure would still be considered accurate as long as the project wound up coming in no lower than $500,000.

- If your estimator underestimated, the ROM would still be considered accurate if the project came in no higher than $2,000,000.

Over the course of the next few weeks, as more is learned about the project, your estimator can keep sharpening her pencils and may present a revised, more refined estimate at each meeting. Each successive estimate should be more accurate and should be a higher-quality estimate than the prior number.

The PMI model supports five kinds of estimate in total (see the next Q&A). It is not always necessary to go through five estimates every time; this is a judgment call that depends on the size and complexity of the project and on how similar it is to others you have worked on. But the iterative approach takes some of the pressure off the estimator and typically produces a more accurate result.

Q13. What are the five kinds of cost estimates and the expected accuracy ranges for each?

A13. Figure 5-2 lists the five kinds of cost estimates in ascending order of expected accuracy, along with the desired ranges for each. These are standard percentages, commonly accepted and cited in many sources. The ROM (earliest estimate) has the widest range of expected accuracy. The control estimate (final estimate) is expected to be the most accurate—in other words, it should have the narrowest range of error (−10 percent on the low end to +15 percent on the high end).

Level of Estimate	Expected Level of Accuracy, Low Range (you *overestimated*, and the final budget came in *lower* than expected)	Expected Level of Accuracy, High Range (you *underestimated*, and the costs came in *higher* than expected)
5. Rough order of magnitude: ROM (this one is expected to be the *least* accurate)	− 50%	+100%
4. Conceptual estimate	−30%	+50%
3. Preliminary estimate	−20%	+30%
2. Definitive estimate	−15%	+20%
1. Control estimate (this one is expected to be the *most* accurate)	−10%	+15%

Figure 5-2:   The Five Kinds of Sequential Estimates
(from least accurate to most accurate)

PMI COST PROCESS II: DETERMINING THE BUDGET

Q14. Why are the processes of estimating costs and determining the budget considered two separate processes?

A14. Producing a finalized budget really takes several steps. After estimating the individual activities, there are three more important techniques that each create their own outputs, and all are part of the process of determining the budget:

- Cost aggregation
- Reserve analysis
- Funding limit reconciliation.

Each is discussed in its own Q&A below.

Q15. What is *cost aggregation*, and how is it used in the process of determining the budget?

A15. Cost aggregation is simply adding up the individual finalized estimates on the project and summing them into a grand total estimate. This may sound a little like bottom-up estimating. But here, the activities have already been estimated and finalized, and you are not necessarily working from the lowest-level work packages.

Q16. What is reserve analysis as it relates to cost?

A16. It's essential for the PM to figure out how much extra money needs to be added to the budget for emergencies, unforeseen problems, or schedule slippages. The technique used to do this is called reserve analysis. Though it is part of the process of determining the budget, it touches on two other knowledge areas: risk management and time management. Analyzing the problems that could impact your budget is part of risk analysis, and the same problems that could affect your budget can usually impact your schedule, too. (That's why reserve analysis is also addressed in Chapter 4, on time management, and Chapter 7, on risk management.) But it's here, during the process of determining the budget, that the dollar number for your project's cash reserve must be quantified.

You can think of reserve analysis as several skills in one—it's risk management combined with estimating and capped off with aggregation. The PM identifies and analyzes the potential risks, sizes up the costs for each potential threat, and then puts all these costs together and adds them up. This sum is called the contingency reserves.

As a best practice, it is recommended to keep your contingency reserve figure as a line item (separate from the main budget). This provides two important benefits. First, it keeps the reserve money clearly set apart and specific, so the stakeholders can see what it's for and that it's not part of the regular budget. (In some companies I've worked with, this is taken a step further—separate line items are kept for each individual risk, creating even greater transparency.) Also, keeping these funds separate reassures the customer that the team does not intend to charge them for those funds (unless the risks actually occur, and the contingency actions need to be taken).

Q17. What are the outputs of the process to determine the budget?

A17. There are actually two key outputs, and surprisingly, neither is called the budget.

The primary output is the cost baseline, which *is* the budget, but with a nuance: it's the current, approved budget. This means that, like any baseline artifact in the PMI model, it has been carefully created; has benefited from the input of all necessary stakeholders; and has gotten the required approvals, authorizations, and even signatures. This eliminates confusion about which budget is the correct one. Such confusion is common because there are often a number of figures floating around on a project (for example, the original cap documented in the charter versus the first formal estimate submitted by the team versus the number your senior management is remembering from an early meeting). It is derived by simply summing activity estimates and the contingency reserves.

The project funding requirements are the other output of this process.

Q18. What is the technique of funding limit reconciliation?

A18. In many PM environments, much work must be done behind the scenes to make sure that after the project is budgeted for, all of the funds are allocated correctly for the project. The funds also have to be secured, scheduled, and disbursed. Planning and finalizing the payment disbursement schedule on a project is known as *funding limit reconciliation*. Many challenges can arise here. Often, the funding is not distributed evenly over the project life cycle; for instance, there is great activity at development time but a steep drop-off later. This can make payment schedules tricky, and they will be all-the-more complicated if unforeseen circumstances arise (e.g., if funds allocated to handle emergencies are depleted, if priorities change, if other projects are suddenly competing for the same funds).

The output of funding limit reconciliation is the *project funding requirements*, which indicate that money has been designated to the project, free and clear, and a schedule has been approved for disbursing the funds.

PMI COST PROCESS III: CONTROLLING COSTS

Q19. What is *earned value management*, and how does it help PMs keep their projects on time and on budget?

A19. Earned value is a concept that helps many managers keep their projects both on schedule and on budget. There are 11 main earned value formulas, which together make up earned value management, or EVM, a popular technique used in the process of controlling costs. Each formula will be described in detail in its own Q&A.

Without EVM, a PM can try to generally gauge the health of a project. But the formulas provide a very detailed drill-down, revealing how much value the project has created so far and pointing out the variances between planned work versus actual.

Each formula offers a unique perspective on the project's health. Some focus on schedule, some on budget, and some on both. Taken together, they provide a multidimensional picture, giving the PM powerful information that can boost the chances of project success.

Q20. What are the specific benefits of EVM for PMs?

A20. Earned value management offers a number of concrete benefits:

- *Performance reports:* EVM offers unique project data that the PM can use to show stakeholders exactly how well the project is going. The data identify variances and trends.

- *Problem-solving/corrective action:* Even better than identifying variances and trends is catching and fixing problems before they worsen. The EVM calculations pinpoint the problem areas you as the PM need to focus on.

- *Analyzing schedule and budget together:* Time is money, but without EVM, it can be very difficult to track both at once and to see the linkages. Many of the EVM formulas tie schedule and budget together and provide very useful metrics for both.

- *Forecasting:* If you've ever wanted your own magic crystal ball, several of the EVM formulas may suffice. They can help you make predictions about where your project will be at points in the future.

- *Communication benefits:* The EVM formulas arm you with highly specific data that you can use to spur your team to take action on a variance or trend and share high-quality information with your stakeholders.

Q21. What are the six things you need to know before you can use the EVM formulas?

A21. There are six key pieces of information you'll use as input to the earned value calculations:

- *Budget at completion (BAC).* This is your finalized dollar estimate for the project. For example, suppose your project is to create four web pages, at a cost of $5,000 each, over the course of four weeks. This would total up to a BAC of $20,000. ($5,000 * 4 = $20,000.) Note that once you identify a BAC, it can't be changed. This is because you'll need to use a consistent benchmark for all the EVM formulas. Think of the BAC as your final answer.

- *Actual costs (AC).* This is how much money you have spent on the project to date. For instance, in our example above, after two weeks, how much money did you spend out of your budget? Was it $10,000? Or more, if unexpected charges came up? Or less, if you overestimated? Whatever the number, that's your AC.

- *Total time estimate for the project.* Just as with the BAC, you need to lock in a time benchmark. In our example, we are using four weeks. (The numbers aren't always as round as four weeks, but the formulas always work—just plug in your numbers.)

- *The moment in time you want to base your calculation on.* You can think of calculating earned value as taking a snapshot of a project's financial health at a given point in time. To use the formulas correctly, you just need to be aware of how far into the project you are, and, also, what percentage this represents of the total schedule. In our example, two weeks out of four weeks total is 50 percent.

- *The number of planned deliverables.* Our sample project is to build four web pages. But some projects are to build 20 miles of highway, or five houses on a piece of land. You need to nail down the output of the project as a number, because your EVM metrics will be calculated based on the quantity of deliverables built so far.

- *How many deliverables (or how much of the deliverable) you have created so far.* This is the key number that tells you, at any moment in time, how much value you have created so far. If the project is to build five houses, but you've only built three so far, you can translate that to 60 percent complete or whatever you can best determine is the percent complete for the goods and services of your project.

THE EARNED VALUE FORMULAS

Q22. What is planned value?

A22. Planned value is the dollar amount associated with a work effort that you plan to complete during a specific time period.

Formula: Planned value = planned percentage complete * budget at completion
Abbreviated: PV = planned % complete * BAC

Planned value lies at the heart of EVM in two important ways: First, it is key to the entire EVM concept because earned value is defined and measured against planned value. Second, once PV is calculated, it is used as an input into some of the other EVM formulas. In turn, those values (with planned value factored in) are used in additional EVM formulas.

In our sample web pages project, since we are planning to build four pages in four weeks at $5,000 per page, the entire project is estimated at a cost of $20,000 (4 * $5,000). This means that the planned value of the work effort, once completed, will be $20,000, because that's the dollar value of the resources you are estimating it will take to produce that deliverable.

Figure 5-3 shows the web page project's planned value after two weeks.

Scenario: We plan to build two out of a total of four web pages in the next two weeks at a cost of $5,000 per page. What's the planned value after two weeks?

PV = planned % complete * BAC
PV = 50% * $20,000
PV = $10,000

What this answer tells the PM: Ten thousand dollars is exactly half of the total estimated budget for the project, which makes sense because two weeks into a four-week project, we expect to have completed two of four (half) the deliverables.

Figure 5-3:   Planned Value after Two Weeks

Q23. Why is planned value expressed in dollars?

A23. Most of the EVM variables are expressed in monetary terms because in using EVM, you are really talking about the economic value of the project to the customer or performing organization. In our example above, you could not necessarily sell those two web pages to a buyer for $10,000. But in calculating planned value, you assign a dollar value to the effort you believe will be required *to produce* those deliverables.

Putting these variables in terms of dollars also enables apples-to-apples comparisons of any kind of deliverable on any project.

Q24. What is the difference between planned value and earned value?

A24. Earned value is the other side of the value coin. When you calculate planned value, you haven't done the work yet, so you are looking ahead. Earned value is a backward look. It tells you how much the work your team has completed so far is worth, in the same monetary terms as planned value.

> **Formula:** Earned value = actual percentage complete * budget at completion
> **Abbreviated:** EV = actual % complete * BAC

Figure 5-4 shows the web page project's earned value after two weeks.

It's important to realize that the fact that you are two weeks into the project is irrelevant to the EV calculation. The $5,000 value for EV is based solely on

Scenario: Suppose unforeseen issues arise, and the team was only able to get one web page built in the first two weeks, instead of the expected two pages. What's the earned value?
EV = actual % complete * BAC EV = 25% * $20,000 EV = $5,000
What this answer tells the PM: Here, the EV ($5,000) works out to exactly half the PV ($10,000) because we accomplished exactly half as much as planned for that time period (one web page built instead of two). The PM would want to determine the reason behind the lack of productivity and correct the situation ASAP.

Figure 5-4: Earned Value after Two Weeks

how much of the deliverable has been created so far, as a percentage of the whole. One page out of four total pages equals 25 percent. (In contrast, when we calculated PV, the fact that two weeks had elapsed *was* key because we were estimating how far along we would be and were using two weeks as a yardstick.)

Q25. Which earned value formulas use PV and EV as inputs, and what additional information do they provide about a project's status?

A25. There are four EVM formulas that use PV and EV as input variables. These are the most popular and most useful formulas for many PMs first starting to use EVM. Two tell you specifically about the status of your schedule, and two report on budget.

These four are easy to learn as a set of two pairs because they have similar names as well as similar-looking formulas and outputs. They can be conveniently paired as follows:

- The two EV formulas for *schedule* status are schedule performance index (SPI) and schedule variance (SV).
- The two EV formulas for *cost* status are cost performance index (CPI) and cost variance (CV).

Each of these four formulas is covered in its own Q&A below.

Q26. How is schedule performance index calculated, and what does it tell you?

A26. As its name implies, schedule performance index (SPI) tells you how your project is performing against its target dates. It measures performance by how far along the project's deliverables are at that point. How does it do that? EV is one of the two inputs into the equation, and the actual percentage complete of the deliverables is already factored into the formula for EV.

Schedule performance index is expressed as a mathematical ratio of earned value divided by planned value.

Formula: Schedule performance index = earned value/planned value

Abbreviated: SPI = EV/PV

Figure 5-5 shows the web page project's SPI after two weeks.

Scenario: Same as earlier for EV.
SPI = EV/PV SPI = $5,000/$10,000 SPI = 0.5
What this answer tells the PM: Again, as we saw with EV, we have accomplished just half what we had planned to accomplish in this time period, and 0.5 means exactly that. The PM would want to see what could be done to speed up the team's output going forward. (A ratio of 1.0 would indicate that we are performing perfectly on schedule, because the performance would exactly match the plan.)

Figure 5-5: Schedule Performance Index after Two Weeks

Q27. How is schedule variance calculated, and how does it differ from schedule performance index?

A27. Like SPI, schedule variance (SV) is also a status of your project's schedule as measured by the completion to date of its deliverables. It is very similar to SPI and uses the same input variables, EV and PV, but there are two differences. First, because SV is a variance (as opposed to an index), it is calculated by subtracting PV from EV, not dividing EV by PV. Second, for SV, the output of the formula is in dollars (because we are subtracting dollars from dollars).

> **Formula:** Schedule variance = earned value − planned value
>
> **Abbreviated:** SV = EV − PV

Figure 5-6 shows the web page project's schedule variance after two weeks.

Scenario: Same as earlier EV and SPI examples.
SV = EV − PV SV = $5,000 − $10,000 SV = -$5,000
What this answer tells the PM: We are $5,000 in the red relative to where we wanted our deliverables to be at this point in time. Note, however, that this does not necessarily mean we are in the red money-wise, because here we are talking about schedule, not cost. (For the formulas that do address money actually spent, see the next two Q&As.)

Figure 5-6: Schedule Variance after Two Weeks

Q28. How is cost performance index calculated, and what does it tell you?

A28. Cost performance index (CPI) tells us how our project is performing against two factors: money spent and deliverables created so far. So to determine CPI, we will need one more piece of data: actual cost (AC), the real amount of money spent to date on the project. Cost performance index is expressed as a ratio of earned value divided by actual cost.

Formula: Cost performance index = earned value / actual cost

Abbreviated: CPI = EV / AC

Figure 5-7 shows the web page project's CPI after two weeks.

Scenario: Same as earlier, but adding in the actual cost of $7,500.
CPI = EV/AC CPI = $5,000/$7,500 CPI = 0.667
What this answer tells the PM: Because the ratio is less than 1.0, we are underperforming on cost. But notice that our CPI of 0.667 is higher than our SPI of 0.5. We are underperforming on that index, too, and more so. This is because while we created much less than we planned (50 percent less, which is bad), we also spent somewhat less than planned. Note that if we had spent only $5,000, our CPI would be 1.0 because we would have spent the amount we had planned to spend to create one page. But if we had spent the full $10,000 as planned, our CPI would be 0.5 (matching our SPI).   The PM should ask why the team has spent less than planned. The answer may be at the heart of the problem: Underperforming is sometimes linked to underspending. Is one of the project's hourly workers not putting in the needed time on the critical path because he or she is distracted by other priorities? Did we not hire enough resources? Did we hire less-expensive resources to save money, and they are not delivering the way we hoped they would? These are the kind of questions CPI can help draw out and address.

Figure 5-7: Cost Performance Index after Two Weeks

Q29. How is cost variance calculated, and what does it tell you?

A29. Like CPI, cost variance (CV) is another measure of how well a project is performing based on deliverables created versus the funds spent to create them. But as a variance, it is expressed as the mathematical difference between earned value and actual cost—we subtract to get the variance. Cost variance is to CPI as schedule variance is to SPI. And like SV, CV is expressed in dollars.

Formula: Cost variance = earned value – actual cost

Abbreviated: CV = EV – AC

Figure 5-8 shows the web page project's cost variance after two weeks.

Scenario: Same as earlier for CPI.
CV = EV – AC CV = $5,000 – $7,500 CV = -$2,500
What this answer tells the PM: As with CPI, we see again that we are underperforming, indicated here by the negative dollar amount. The dollar figure can be very useful, but it must be understood in the context of the specific planned value for this project. Here, our CV is −$2,500, which is half the planned cost of building one full page ($5,000). Why is the CV only half the cost of a page and not the full cost, when we've only built one page instead of two? Remember that in our scenario, while we built *much* less than planned, we also spent *somewhat* less than planned. Had we spent the full $10K for the two-week time period, our cost variance would have been −$5K ($5K – $10K), or exactly in the red by the cost of one page.

Figure 5-8:   Cost Variance after Two Weeks

Q30. Which are more valuable for PMs, the indexes (SPI and CPI) or the variances (SV and CV)?

A30. There are pros and cons to both metrics. The answer can depend on such things as the scale of the numbers, how well you know the dollar figures of the inputs into the formulas, and any other performance information you may already have.

- *Indexes:* The great thing about the indexes is that they are so *portable*. A schedule performance index of 1.2 can tell any PM anywhere in the world that a project is performing 20% better than planned on schedule (EV/ PV). But while a cost performance index of 1.2 is also somewhat portable, it is not as clear-cut. With CPI, derived by EV/AC, you could get a 1.2 *either* by having a higher EV than expected or by having a lower AC than expected. In other words, with CPI, both EV and AC are variable, and each can make a big difference. But with SPI, EV is variable and measured against PV, which is a fixed number.

- **Variances:** The dollar values on the variances have the advantage of being *specific*. Figure 5-8 reveals a CV of –$2,500. But as we've seen, for a specific variance to be fully understood, you need to know what that dollar amount means for that project. For example, $5,000 could be equal to the entire planned value of one of four deliverables, as on our sample web-pages project, or it could be just a small fraction of the deliverable—the number out of context doesn't tell you which. So by itself, a dollar amount may not be very meaningful; you have to understand the significance of that dollar amount to the project as a whole.

The more EVM values you have to work with, the more you can see the big picture regarding your project's health. So let's forge ahead to the five more advanced formulas, beginning with cost performance index cumulative.

Q31. What is the cumulative cost performance index formula, and what does it tell a PM that the regular CPI doesn't?

A31. The cumulative cost performance index, represented as CPI^c, is CPI with a difference. Its calculation is based on several pieces of data, taken over time (instead of from just one static set of inputs), so it may be more accurate than CPI. For example, if you have four months' worth of project data (EV and AC for January, February, March, and April), your results will likely be more meaningful than if you used April's numbers only.

The formula is $CPI^c = EV^c/AC^c$. It looks just like the CPI formula, except you are using multiple, cumulative numbers. If you have four months of data, you would add up the earned value from each of those months and sum them into what's called the cumulative EV, or EV^c. Then you would add up the four ACs from the same time period, yielding AC^c. Finally, you would simply plug the EV^c and AC^c into the CPI^c formula and get a CPI directly tied to all four months' worth of numbers.

Q32. When is cumulative CPI better than CPI? How do you know which one to use?

A32. More is usually better, and so it is often better to use the cumulative version of the cost performance index formula. CPI^c will *generally* be more accurate than CPI because its calculation is based on *sets* of EV and AC data over time, not just one pair of numbers. So it's likely to be more accurate for identifying trends.

However, data compiled over time is not *always* more useful. Think about the stock market. When there is an event like a market crash, the stock price the day after the crash can be much more useful as a future performance indicator than the cumulative prices from the days immediately before the crash. For example, if a stock drops from $90 per share to $50 overnight, the $50 price may be a much more accurate indicator of how it will do in the near future. What counts most right now about that stock's future performance might be how strong the company's fundamentals are today. If you give too much consideration to the fact that the stock recently was $90, you might wind up looking in vain for an upward trend that is not going to happen.

Because cost performance index is used as an input in several EVM formulas (as seen in upcoming Q&As), one way to increase the accuracy of your data is to use CPI^c, when appropriate, instead of CPI. But while cumulative CPI is *usually* better, the PM needs to make a judgment call in each case to determine which data are more useful before deciding between CPI and CPI^c.

Note that for the next three formulas, CPI is an input. It's a *direct* input into estimate at completion (EAC), and it's an *indirect* input into estimate to complete (ETC) and variance at completion (VAC) because both of those formulas use EAC as an input, which already factors in CPI.

Q33. What is the estimate at completion formula, and how can it help me forecast my final budget more accurately?

A33. Here you get to take out your crystal ball and predict the future. Estimate at completion, or EAC, takes your original budget estimate, ties it to your calculated CPI (or CPI^c is sometimes used) and extrapolates your spending in the future. It is a revised cost estimate based on the current cost performance index.

EAC has a twofold purpose: First, it's always good to know where you're going, especially on budget matters. Also—and even better—if you're heading for an overrun, EAC helps you nip it in the bud.

Formula: Estimate at completion = budget at completion/cost performance index (or cumulative cost performance index)

Abbreviated: $EAC = BAC/CPI$, or $EAC = BAC/CPI^c$

Figure 5-9 shows the web page project's estimate at completion after two weeks.

Scenario: Same as earlier.
EAC = BAC/CPI EAC = $20,000/0.667 (rounded) EAC = $30,000 (rounded)
What this answer tells the PM: Our original budget was $20,000, but we are under-performing at 66.667% (two-thirds) on how much product we are creating, as a function of funds spent. EAC tells us that at the current rate, we are on track to spend $30,000 (1/3 more) to create our final three web pages.   The PM should realize that for this project to succeed, he or she will either need to get the needed $10,000 in additional funding, or else take some other action, such as fast-tracking, to try to improve the project's CPI. The EAC is not good news in this case, but it *is* good information for the PM.

Figure 5-9: Estimate at Completion after Two Weeks

Q34. How does estimate to complete complement estimate at completion, and what information does it add for PMs?

A34. This formula can do more than Rogaine for senior management's hair! If you have ever been in the position of trying to ask someone below you how much more money it will take to complete a rogue project, you know how tough it can be to get a straight answer. Estimate to complete (ETC) is the formula that can make things easy for both the asker and the askee.

Very simply, estimate to complete is how much more money a project will cost, derived by subtracting the amount of money already spent (AC) from the latest revised forecast (EAC).

Formula: Estimate to complete = estimate at completion − actual cost

Abbreviated: ETC = EAC − AC

Figure 5-10 shows the web page project's estimate to complete after two weeks.

Q35. What does variance at completion, as opposed to estimate to complete, tell you?

A35. Variance at completion (VAC) indicates how far apart the new estimate (EAC) is from the original estimate (BAC). In other words, it is the difference between the original budget and the current revised budget, designating the

Scenario: Same as earlier.
ETC = EAC – AC
ETC = $30,000 – $7,500
ETC = $22,500
What this answer tells the PM: At the current rate of spending and progress, the project will need a total budget of $30,000; $7,500 has already been spent. Estimate to complete, the difference between those two numbers, tells you exactly how much more money is needed.   It's important to note that the original estimate of $20,000 (the BAC) is no longer relevant to determining how much more money it will take to finish the project, and that's why EAC is used here and not BAC.

Figure 5-10:   Estimate to Complete after Two Weeks

project as either in the black or in the red and by how much. This is a critical piece of information for senior management, the customer, and the sponsor as well as a key variance to keep track of lessons learned regarding the accuracy of your estimation process and any improvements for next time. It is derived simply by subtracting the revised estimate (EAC) from the original estimate (BAC). This is very different than estimate to complete, which is how much more money is needed to complete the project (using EAC and AC, not EAC and BAC).

> **Formula:** Variance at completion = budget at completion – estimate at completion
> **Abbreviated:** VAC = BAC – EAC

Figure 5-11 shows the web page project's variance at completion after two weeks.

Q36. What is the to-complete performance index, and how does it differ from the cost performance index?

A36. The to-complete performance index (TCPI) is a very valuable metric because it quantifies the rate at which the project work must be performed to complete the remaining work on budget. It's based on how much work remains versus how much budget remains. It takes CPI a step further; TCPI is not just the current rate, but the required future rate needed—a kind of forecast.

Scenario: Same as earlier.
VAC = BAC − EAC VAC = \$20,000 − \$30,000 VAC = −\$10,000
What this answer tells the PM: With a VAC of −\$10,000, this project is on a path to costing \$10,000 more than was originally budgeted. This is a huge red flag that might prompt action toward improving efficiencies to try to get the project back on track toward finishing on the original budget of \$20,000. If that can't be done, the PM has to either come up with the needed increase in funding or else take drastic action—perhaps getting approval to cut back on scope or even terminating the project if the additional money cannot be allocated.

Figure 5-11: Variance at Completion after Two Weeks

The calculation is the value of the amount of work remaining (BAC − EV) divided by the funds remaining, which is usually BAC − AC, although not always. Other factors could determine how much funding remains on a project, such as a change in priorities by the client or the performing organization.

Formula: To-complete performance index = (budget at completion −
earned value)/remaining funds

Abbreviated: TCPI = (BAC − EV) / remaining funds

Figure 5-12 shows the web page project's to-complete performance index after two weeks.

Q37. How do the earned value formulas make a positive difference communications-wise on a project?

A37. Sometimes a PM has a strong gut feeling that a project is heading the wrong way, but without hard numbers, no one may pay attention to unsupported comments such as, "Guys, we might be facing a possible overrun here."

But armed with solid EVM data, PMs are much more likely to get a response if they deliver an update along these lines: "According to today's EVM reports, we are currently heading toward spending \$1.85 million on our project—that's our estimate at completion. And remember, we had a cap of \$900K originally; that represents a variance at completion of \$950,000! This is a major concern: Let's put this on the agenda for tomorrow's morning meeting."

Scenario: Same as earlier, but note that to calculate TCPI, we need to first calculate one more input variable: remaining funds, which sometimes can be calculated by subtracting funds already spent (actual cost) from our original funds (budget at completion). In our running scenario, this would mean doing the following quick arithmetic:

Remaining funds = BAC − AC
Remaining funds = $20,000 − $7,500
Remaining funds = $12,500
Now that we know our remaining funds, we can plug this value into the TCPI formula.

TCPI = (BAC − EV)/remaining funds
TCPI = ($20,000 − $5,000)/$12,500
TCPI = $15,000/$12,500
TCPI = 1.2

What this answer tells the PM: Notice that even though this project is not very healthy, our TCPI is greater than 1.0. TCPI is different from all of our other EV formulas because here, *smaller* is better: A TCPI greater than 1.0 is bad; less than 1.0 is good. As with our other indexes, 1.0 would be right on plan because the dollar value of the work remaining would be equal to the funds remaining to do that work. But a TCPI greater than 1.0, as in our scenario, means we have less money left to do the work than we had planned for. It's aptly called a performance index because the more money you have left, the easier it will be to perform the remaining work, and, ideally, you want to have a cushion of more money than you need. A 1.2 (as above) tells the PM that to finish on budget, he or she might need to fast-track the schedule, reduce scope (with the client's permission), or take some other corrective measure.

Figure 5-12:   To-Complete Performance Index after Two Weeks

Q38. When is the best time to communicate EV figures, is there a recommended format, and how often should they be reported?

A38. While there is no specific format for reporting them, PMI considers the EVM numbers important enough that there is an output called *performance reports*, and there is a specific communications process called *report performance.* This is one of the monitoring and controlling processes because the purpose of the reports is to track progress against the plan, identify variances, and use this information to bring the project under control.

The numbers should be reported as often as necessary to get the job done. On many projects, EVM metrics are included with each weekly status report. On others, they are included on an as-needed basis, per the PM's judgment. The key is to give the stakeholders just the right amount of information they want and need. (You can use a communications management plan to govern your interactions with stakeholders. See Q&A 11 and 13 in Chapter 10 for details.)

Q39. Is there a shortcut to doing all of this EV math?

A39. Yes. (Hooray!) If you like what EVM can do for you but don't want to do a lot of math, a very pleasant surprise is that the electronic scheduling products, like MS Project and others, can do the EVM math for you. (MS Project, for one, does not require any special extras or installs to do this.) But a word of caution: The first time you let a software tool do the EVM math for you, it's always good to try the calculations manually to make sure you get the same results. A little tweaking may be needed if you discover, for instance, that you're not supplying all the inputs properly. But once the scheduler's numbers match yours, you should be good to go from there. Many PMs rely on programs that calculate EVM numbers for them in this way.

A FEW KEY COST AND ACCOUNTING CONCEPTS USED IN SELECTING PROJECTS

Q40. What is the benefit cost ratio (BCR), and when is it used?

A40. This simple formula is a classic way to evaluate whether a project is a worthwhile undertaking or not. It compares the expected benefits the project will bring against the costs of gaining those benefits. And the math is very easy—it is expressed as a pure ratio of benefits to costs, as follows: BCR = benefits/costs.

In a nutshell, the greater the benefits and the lower the costs, the higher the BCR and the more reason to select the project. Another way to put it is that the higher the BCR, the sooner the project will begin to pay for itself and then start to bring a profit (as long as the benefits come through as forecasted and the costs remain as low as estimated).

For example, if a project will bring in $5,000,000 in benefits and will cost $3,000,000, the BCR could be calculated as shown in Figure 5-13.

> BCR = benefits/costs
> BCR = $5,000,000/$3,000,000
> BCR = 1.67 (rounded)

Figure 5-13:   Example of Benefit Cost Ratio

Q41. How does benefit cost ratio compare with return on investment?

A41. The return on investment (ROI) formula looks very similar to BCR: ROI = (return − investment)/investment. But while the input variables are basically the same with different names (*investment = cost*, and *return = benefit*), there are two key differences:

- After it's calculated, ROI is converted to a percentage.
- ROI factors cost into the equation twice: First, investment is subtracted from return. The difference obtained is then divided by investment.

Figure 5-14 shows how ROI is computed. As you follow this calculation, notice how the double use of the investment quantity adds a layer of complexity to the math and causes the quotient to come out much lower (0.667, or 67%, in this scenario, compared with 1.67).

> ROI = (return − investment)/investment
> ROI = ($5,000,000 − $3,000,000)/$3,000,000
> ROI = $2,000,000/$3,000,000
> ROI = 0.667
> ROI = 67% (rounded)

Figure 5-14:   Example of Return on Investment

Q42. How does payoff period come into play on project selection?

A42. When considering a revenue-creating project, it's key to try to forecast how long the payoff period will be, meaning how soon the investment will return the expected profit. An early payoff period can bring both short-term and long-term benefits.

- **Short-term benefits:** The sooner the money comes in, the better, especially if the company is in need of short-term income for cash-flow purposes.

- ***Long-term benefits:*** The sooner the company receives the payoff, the sooner it can gain interest on the money, turning it into more money; also, the sooner it can invest the money in future opportunities.

Q43. When is a short payoff period not advantageous?

A43. Short-term gains can also *hurt* in the long term. Suppose that you are a vendor, and you need an early payoff for cash-flow purposes. But suppose your client is also strapped for cash, and as a concession on the contract, the client asks you to lower your price (for more on concessions, see Chapter 8). To induce the client to pay you sooner (short payoff period), you might agree to come down in price. For instance, instead of paying you $1 million over the two-year payoff period you might normally charge, you could offer to reduce the payoff to $850,000 on the condition that the client must pay within one month of signing the contract.

On one hand, this is a win-win compromise (lower charge to the customer; good cash-flow for the seller). But it also means less income for the seller, both in the short term and even more so in the long term, factoring in the money the seller will be missing out on and that it could have invested. Many companies make this exact mistake in their eagerness to rack up sales and grow their business. And another negative is that by lowering your price, you could be lowering the value of your brand—you could become defined by the lower price as a lower-quality provider, even though this may not be accurate or fair. By pushing their prices too far down to force sales, companies sometimes destroy their own business model.

Q44. When is a longer payoff period not advantageous?

A44. Slightly changing the above scenario, your customer might tell you it has cash-flow problems and ask you as a concession to lengthen the payoff period. Instead of paying you $1,000,000 in one lump sum up front, the customer might ask if the payment can be split into four quarterly payments of $250,000 each.

This also can be considered a win-win compromise because the customer gets to hold on to more of its money longer, and you, as the seller, get the full payment of $1,000,000. But in the long term, you would be losing out—had you gotten the $1,000,000 as a lump sum, you could have immediately invested the money to further grow your business.

To make things more fair for your own company and still help the customer's cash-flow situation, you could offer the customer a longer payoff period but higher payments—for instance, four quarterly payments of $275,000 each (instead of $250K). The customer benefits in the short run, and you would eventually end up with $1,100,000 (10 percent more in the end than the original $1 million).

An arrangement like this is not ideal for the seller's cash flow, and it also increases the risk that the customer might somehow default on the full payment. A seller should make sure to do its homework before agreeing to a longer payoff arrangement. But sometimes compromises are necessary to close a deal, and being flexible on payoff period can give you leeway in negotiating, whichever side of the table you are on.

Figure 5-15 breaks down four possible payment scenarios to help you remember them for future PM decisions.

Q45. How does the law of diminishing returns come into play on project selection?

A45. This concept helps PMs identify the point at which a drop-off in profits is to be expected over the life cycle of a revenue stream. The typical profit pattern often looks something like this: A project generates some profit initially, then more and more, at an increasing rate. But eventually the increase hits a peak. From that point on, though there will still be profit for some time, the amount of profit begins to drop. The moment in time at which it begins to fall is called the point of diminishing returns.

For example, imagine that the latest and greatest PDA device has just been released. If it's been well hyped in advance, people might start buying it the minute it hits the market. Over the first few weeks, sales may continue to grow, and they may snowball by Christmas gift-buying season. And if the product takes on industry dominance, like the iPod did, its sales may continue to swell for a long time. But eventually, the device may reach a saturation point among available customers or a competitor may come along or its patent may expire, opening the door to cheaper alternatives. And at that time, its sales rate will begin to drop off.

The law of diminishing returns can be used as a factor in a project selection decision. When choosing between two projects, if the numbers appear similar

Payoff Scenario	Description	Payment Amount	Who Benefits?
Scenario #1	Normal fee, short payoff period, one lump-sum, immediate payment.	$1,000,000 (lump sum)	***Seller*** gets full payoff right away.
Scenario #2	Immediate payoff, but reduced payment amount.	$850,000 (lump sum)	***Both parties benefit, but especially buyer:*** • Buyer gets reduced charge. • Can be good for the seller's cash flow, but the seller is taking a loss on its usual fee.
Scenario #3	Long payoff period, with the full original cost split out evenly into four quarterly payments, paid over one year.	$250,000 each quarter for four quarters (total $1,000,000)	***Both, but especially buyer:*** • Buyer still pays full amount, but less in the short term. • Seller still gets full amount, but less in the short term (which also equates to less in the long term, factoring in loss of interest/investment opportunity). • Seller also takes on greater risk of not receiving full payment.
Scenario #4	Long payoff period, but payoff adds up to more than the original cost.	$275,000 each quarter for four quarters (total $1,100,000)	***Both, more balanced than scenario #3 above:*** • Buyer gets the cash-flow benefit of forestalling payment. • Seller gets a higher total fee (but again, seller is taking on more risk of receiving full payment).

Figure 5-15: Payoff Periods and Their Effects on Buyers and Sellers

over the same time frame, identifying and factoring in different points of diminishing returns can help you decide which one to pursue.

Q46. What does economic value add bring to the table when you are evaluating the worth of a project?

A46. Opportunity costs are associated with every business decision. Funds spent on one project are money that could have been spent on a different project or invested for profit in other ways. Part of the challenge of project selection, then, is to think from an investment point of view.

In the web page project example, the PM thinks of the $10,000 he's been given to perform the work as money that is free and clear for the project. But from senior management's point of view, this money could, for example, have gone into an investment yielding a payout of 6.5 percent. The economic value add (EVA) formula takes this into consideration. Our $10,000 investment is called capital expenditures, and the potential 6.5 percent interest rate is called the cost of capital. We'll assume that our profit is going to be $10,000 ($20,000 payment – $10,000 expenditure). But the economic value added will be somewhat less, factoring in the interest rate applied to our capital, as follows:

Economic value add = after tax profit – (capital expenditures * cost of capital)

Economic value add = $10,000 – ($10,000 * 6.5%)

Economic value add = $10,000 – ($650)

Economic value add = $9,350

And so our EVA for the $20,000 project drops down by $650 when we consider the opportunity cost for one specific investment possibility. Note that this is a simplified example; we are not considering taxes on our profit or on the interest of $650, which might be taxed at a different rate.

Q47. What is value add as opposed to economic value add?

A47. Value add is the true value a project adds to an organization. There is no formula to calculate it because value add takes into account many intangibles that are hard to measure but that can be very important considerations for your organization's overall long-term success.

For example, suppose that the customer for whom we built the web pages was very happy with the results and recommended our company to a new client. The new client contracted our company to do a much larger project, further increasing our profits. This enhanced our reputation, and we were then able to attract higher-caliber personnel, leading to greater quality in our work. Ultimately, we grew enough to be able to buy out a smaller competitor, picking up more market share and further expanding our business.

None of these possible side benefits can be plugged into the formulas discussed in this chapter, but the factors that go into value add *can* be analyzed and projected. And creativity and open-mindedness can be important inputs when making decisions about which projects to choose and how best to accomplish them. Adding value, which is an intangible, can be more important over the long term for your company than calculations that can easily be plugged into a spreadsheet. (The value triple constraint discussed in Chapters 4 and 12 is related to value add.)

Q48. When you have to pick one, which wins: delivering a project on time or on budget?

A48. Sometimes this decision depends on enterprise environmental factors, first discussed in Chapter 2. If you're a PM in a pharmaceutical company and your project involves creating a new drug and getting it patented before a competitor company brings out a similar drug, your company may have a spare-no-expenses attitude about the project, and that may be a very good business decision. If two pharmaceutical companies are both working on a patentable formula, the one who comes out with it first is going to win all the marbles. It will take home *all* the revenue once its drug hits the market. Its competitor will take home *none* and will also have mostly wasted the R&D money it put into a race that it wound up losing.

But there are many times when budget is the number-one priority—for example, in a down economy or when the performing organization is strapped for cash or when the client makes very clear that the agreed-upon budget must be treated as if it is set in stone (and usually backing that position with a fixed-price contract; for more about contract types, see Chapter 8).

A Classic Case of Time over Money

Do you know how much the U.S. spent to put its first astronauts on the moon?

Most Americans have no idea how much the country spent to send Neil Armstrong and Buzz Aldrin, the first astronauts to walk on the moon, into space in 1969. More than 40 years later, many Americans still remember key details of this mission, but almost no one you meet will be able to tell you what the cost was. Tom Wolfe, author of *The Right Stuff*, revealed in a 2009 *New York Times* article that the mission cost some $150 billion.[1]

On this project, time was the top consideration. The driving force behind it was to claim technological supremacy in the midst of the Cold War and to fulfill a national vision. President John F. Kennedy passionately conveyed this vision in a well-known speech in 1961: The United States would accomplish this goal in ten years. Clearly, cost was considered secondary to this mission's purposes because coming in on deadline (and ahead of the Russians) was the primary yardstick that Kennedy set for this project. All funds necessary were to be spent to ensure that this goal was accomplished on time because achieving the deliverable late would have been considered a partial failure.

TOP TEN PITFALLS TO AVOID IN COST MANAGEMENT

1. Going overboard on cost-cutting as a general priority, resulting in a penny-wise, pound-foolish mentality that does more harm than good.
2. Skimping on resources, especially on salaries for staff (this can lead to the wrong hires, as well as problems retaining good employees).
3. Focusing on short-term gain at the expense of long-term goals, which can result in poor quality and alienate customers and ultimately hurt a company's bottom line.
4. Skimping on training and new technology that could bring efficiencies that would decrease costs later.

5. Accepting a project that sounds good but would result in less of a profit margin than what you want because the contract is not favorable to your company (perhaps because you skimped on legal resources).

6. Taking a contract as offered because you are in a hurry to get the business or don't want to alienate clients, instead of reconciling it to make sure the contract will fulfill your business needs.

7. Failing to proactively monitor for slippages in schedule, which can forecast cost overruns so they can be caught early.

8. Failing to put enough effort or resources into planning, leading to errors in execution and underestimation of time and costs.

9. Planning insufficiently for risks. Unforeseen threats can emerge, affecting your deadlines and budget.

10. Communication errors, which can lead to wrong work and rework.

Note

1. Tom Wolfe, "One Giant Leap To Nowhere," *New York Times*, July 19, 2009.

CHAPTER 6

Building in Quality

We pursued growth over the speed at which we were able to develop our people and our organization... And I am deeply sorry for any accident that Toyota drivers have experienced.
—Akio Toyoda, president and CEO of Toyota Motor Corporation

The world has seen so many success stories in quality management that it's always a little surprising when products *don't* work properly. But as each year brings many new innovations and advances, there are always a few dramatic failures, often directly traceable to poor quality control.

How is it possible that the world's largest automaker, renowned for quality, sent millions of cars out to customers with bugs in its braking systems? Or that lead paint got past inspectors at Mattel? Or that the chemical melamine was used as an additive in pet foods when it's poisonous to pets?

The question for PMs is, if quality control failures can happen to giant companies with big budgets for quality assurance (QA), what can all of us do to better ensure quality on our projects?

Based on my experience, the hard part is not figuring out how to build quality into projects. The hard part is convincing management that it's worth allocating the resources for thorough testing, redundant systems, and contingency plans strong enough to maintain quality when something goes wrong (hello, BP oil spill!).

Quality management according to the PMI model comes down to three fundamental processes. There are many tried-and-true techniques for executing these processes. These best practices have brought successful results on a great many projects and are covered in detail in this chapter. They have evolved over the years, and many are now software-based and very fast and easy to use.

Also discussed in this chapter are several organizations that evaluate the quality of a company's project office. They can help you measure the quality of your own firm's structure and standards and, in the process, raise the bar.

FUNDAMENTAL QUALITY CONCEPTS

Q1. Where does quality management fit in on the triple constraint?

A1. Quality management is an extremely important component. In Chapter 4, where three variations of the triple constraint are diagrammed, quality is shown as an element in the six-component representation (time/cost/scope/ quality/risk/customer satisfaction). It is also one of the three elements in the second version, time/cost/quality. This second version emphasizes the particular importance of quality in projects. While time and cost are the primary constraints limiting a project team's efforts, many customers primarily judge and remember the perceived quality of the end result.

In the time/cost/quality version of the triple constraint, scope, customer satisfaction, and risk are not explicitly listed, but all three of these elements are to an extent implicitly represented by quality, as follows:

- *Customer satisfaction (custsat):* The better the quality of the deliverables and of the customer service provided by the team, the higher the customer's satisfaction level will be. Many customers use quality as their yardstick for measuring their satisfaction with a project.
- *Risk:* The lower the risk level of the deliverables and the project itself, the more likely the customer will be to perceive the project as high quality.
- *Scope:* If a customer has to choose between two similar products, it may judge the one with more features as having superior quality. Each piece of scope has the potential to raise a project's perceived quality level.

Q2. How is quality management defined?

A2. There are two classic definitions of quality that still hold up today as part of the PMI framework. They were put forward by Philip Crosby and Joseph

Juran, two of the developers of the core principles on which PMI later founded its standards.

- Crosby defines quality as "conformance to specifications." When a customer asks for five key requirements, they will not be happy if they don't get all five or if those five don't precisely satisfy their specifications. As Crosby points out, "The *nonconformance* added is the absence of quality."[1]

- Crosby also emphasizes that quality is *not* some elusive thing, such as "goodness" or "luxury" or "shininess" or "goldplating." (*Goldplating* is defined in A16 in Chapter 3.) It is simply a matter of aggressively satisfying customer specifications.

- Crosby directly ties profits to conforming to specifications. He writes, "If you concentrate on making quality certain, you can probably increase your profit by 5 to 10 percent of your sales."

- Joseph Juran's defines quality as "fitness for use." Every new car, even the cheapest, conforms to its unique specifications. But while the Nano, the least expensive car in the world right now, might satisfy Crosby's definition of quality as conforming to the requirements set out for it, that doesn't mean all customers would perceive it as a high-quality product. Juran's definition factors in the way a customer would judge the quality of a product. The customer would determine the quality of the product according to his own preferences—in other words, whether he sees it as fit for his use, e.g., the car he would choose out of all the models on the market.

Q3. What else did Crosby contribute to quality management that PMs still study today?

A3. Crosby had several more key contributions, all still considered current today[2]:

- Crosby is credited with the expression "***zero defects***." The phrase does not suggest that perfection is possible—it promotes the idea of shooting for zero defects as a way of striving for very high quality.

- ***The philosophy of prevention, not inspection.*** Crosby advocated the idea of building quality into a project. The idea was to do things right up front, by planning properly and doing sufficient advance testing, rather than tolerating a certain number of defects and worrying about them later. "It is always cheaper to do things right the first time."

- ***The calculation of cost of quality,*** which is detailed in the next Q&A.

Q4. How did Crosby express cost of quality as something that can be calculated, and how is this calculation useful to PMs today?

A4. Crosby came up with an out-of-the-box calculation for quality, and if more people followed the principle on which it is based, we might have fewer accidents and scandals today. He wrote in *Quality Is Free* that the cost of quality is "the expense of nonconformance—the cost of doing things wrong." And he said you could calculate these costs as follows:

$$\text{Cost of quality} = \text{prevention costs} + \text{appraisal costs} + \text{failure costs}$$

A little more about the three components of nonconformance:

- *Prevention costs:* The resources a company intends to spend for project quality management, including design and specification reviews, acceptance planning, quality audits, and preventive maintenance.

- *Appraisal costs:* All the areas where appraisal and testing will be done, including prototype inspection and testing, packaging inspection, and status measurement and reporting.

- *Failure costs:* The money a company spends to fix unexpected quality issues, including dealing with waste and scrap, creating fixes, replanning, rework, and service after service. In extreme cases, failure costs may also include huge legal fees, damages awarded to victims, and new advertising and marketing campaigns launched in attempts to regain public trust. When problems of this magnitude occur, it is painfully obvious that failure costs greatly outweigh prevention costs. PMs should keep this in mind when planning for quality and risk management. Pay now, or pay more later.

Q5. How is the cost of quality (COQ) used as a planning tool?

A5. Let's apply these calculations to an example based on a fictional company called, say, English Oil 'R' Us. Suppose this fictional company under-spent on prevention—things were done on-the-cheap, safety procedures were given short shrift—and maybe this led to a huge offshore oil-drilling accident. Suppose that poor quality was also evidenced in insufficient risk management planning—the plans to cap a ruptured well had never been fully tested under a mile deep of water, and this mitigation strategy turned out not to work under such high water pressure. The company then had to pay an enormous amount of money for damage repair, damage control, cleanup, and victim compensation.

The numbers below are made up, but you could plug in similar real numbers for *several* recent scandals:

Cost of quality = prevention costs + appraisal costs + failure costs

Cost of quality = $3,000,000 + $4,000,000 + $800,000,000 (spent to fix
problems after the disaster)

Cost of quality = $807,000,000!

Again, these are fictional numbers, but they are not far off from what sometimes happens. Projecting failure costs as accurately as possible in advance of any disaster can help PMs justify the spending necessary for effective quality control. The goal is to make the cost of quality equal to the cost of prevention and appraisal, ideally without needing to spend any money on failure costs. Failure costs are also often referred to as the cost of *poor* quality (CoPQ).

Q6. What other contributions is Joseph Juran known for?

A6. Juran also made major contributions to quality management with Pareto's law and the Pareto chart based on that law.

- *Pareto's law (the 80/20 rule, a.k.a., the law of the vital few).* The original Pareto's law was devised by Vilfredo Pareto in nineteenth-century Italy. He said that 80 percent of the land was owned by 20 percent of the citizens. Juran took this and applied it to project management, stating that 80 percent of the problems on a project, such as bugs in a new product, can usually be attributed to 20 percent of the causes. This rule is extremely useful for managing quality issues in an efficient way. Any given project may have many kinds of quality issues, such as slow systems or faulty equipment. A proven approach is to step back, analyze, and identify the few causes behind the greatest number of issues. By prioritizing those few causes and resolving them, you can solve the majority of open issues quickly and also prevent many more issues from reoccurring.

- *Pareto chart.* Juran also came up with the Pareto chart, described later in this chapter as one of the basic tools of quality. It is used during the process of performing quality control.

Q7. What is W. Edwards Deming best known for, and which of his ideas are still in use today?

A7. Considered the father of the modern quality movement, Deming is one of several American business leaders who spent considerable time in war-torn Japan after World War II helping the Japanese modernize with American mass-production methods. In return, he learned best practice methods from the Japanese that he brought back to the West.

He is especially well known among PMs and business students for the Deming cycle, the project management cycle that bears his name. Also known as the plan-do-check-act cycle, this cycle encapsulates the iterative nature of how a PM runs a project. From a quality perspective, the cycle protects quality on the project as follows:

- *Plan:* The PM plans as best as possible from the information known to her at the time.

- *Do:* She then takes initial action toward implementing the plan.

- *Check:* As soon as she takes that action, she immediately monitors her results to see if the action is working as planned or if any corrective action is needed.

- *Act:* If corrective action is needed, she is ready to quickly jump back to planning, where she will replan as necessary and go through the cycle again. She does all this with her eyes on the prize: delivering quality results to her customer.

See Chapter 1, Q&A 19, for more about the Deming cycle.

Q8. Besides the Deming cycle, what other major contributions did Deming make to quality management?

A8. Deming is credited for pioneering, introducing, and implementing *kaizen* in Japan. *Kaizen* is a Japanese word meaning continuous small improvement, and it is a driving philosophy for running projects. The *kaizen* way is not only about improving the quality of the deliverables but also the processes that create them. This emphasis on proactively building in quality became a central tenet of the PMI knowledge area of quality management. (See Chapter 1, Q&A 21, for more on *kaizen*.)

Other Deming innovations include the following:

- *Only 85%?* For as long as there have been workers and bosses, management has tended to blame lower-level workers for problems. Deming gets credit for pointing out that the reverse is usually true: 85 percent of all problems, such as quality issues in manufacturing, are actually management's fault, and management needs to take ownership of them.

- *Total quality management (TQM).* This was Deming's overall strategy for achieving quality. It involves reducing errors in production by conforming to customer specifications/requirements, thereby increasing customer satisfaction, and by emphasizing that *all* employees, especially the manager and on down, are ultimately responsible for quality.

- *Statistical process control (SPC).* This is the process, now ubiquitous, of applying objective statistics to measure quality results, especially by analyzing and reporting on variations and defects. Today it's a given that statistics will be used to measure quality on any large project, and software tools are commonly used, such as the popular Mercury tool suite. But before Deming, quality determination was largely subjective. He first utilized SPC to improve quality results in America's mass production efforts during World War II, with great success.

Lessons Learned From A Real-World Example of *Kaizen* at Toyota

Here are some of the key improvements Toyota successfully implemented in a joint effort with the General Motors (GM) auto manufacturing plant in Fremont, California.[3] This was the first case of successfully implementing *kaizen* in an American auto factory.

- In 1970, GM invited experts from Toyota to bring their version of *kaizen* to an American auto manufacturing plant called NUMMI (New United Motor Manufacturing, Inc.). The results were historic improvements in efficiency, morale, and productivity.

- GM modeled its plant and operations on the Toyota factories in Japan, where whenever a problem arises, management asks every worker for their suggestions on how to fix the problem and prevent it from happening again.

- At Toyota, every time a worker suggests an improvement that saves the company money, he or she is given a bonus of several hundred dollars.

> • Another key element of Toyota management was teamwork and equality among workers. Instead of a foreman managing a large team and keeping his or her distance, Toyota uses small teams, and when a problem occurs, a team leader comes over and asks if he or she can jump in and help out.
>
> (See Figure 6-2 for more on the differences between mass production and lean production.)

Q9. What do today's PMs still take from Walter Shewhart?

A9. Deming was heavily influenced by a quality pioneer who came before him, Walter Shewhart. Shewhart was responsible for two of the major innovations that Deming later brought into widespread use:

- The plan→ do→ check→ act→ cycle originated with Shewhart and was known early on as the Shewhart cycle.
- Statistical process control also began with Shewhart many years before Deming implemented it on a large scale.

Shewhart also originated the control chart, one of the important tools PMs still use frequently to help them control quality. It is discussed in detail later in this chapter, as one of the basic tools of quality, in the discussion of the process of performing quality control.

Q10. Which of Genichi Taguchi's contributions are still in use today?

A10. Genichi Taguchi's body of work was primarily done in his native Japan; later in his career, he helped several U.S. companies. His work strongly influenced what later became known as *lean production*, which helped propel the Japanese auto industry's rise to supremacy. His three primary contributions include:

- *Quality loss function.* When a product has defects, the loss goes beyond the immediate costs of repair or replacement of the specific problem.

It carries over to a loss in total value of the product. The depreciation of a car's value after a major repairs is an example: Even after repairs are made, the car's value is permanently reduced. Taguchi also said that a specific product's loss of quality can ripple outward in various ways. For example, as a house drops in value due to poor quality in construction, surrounding houses drop in value also.

- **Statistical design of experiments.** Taguchi contributed to quality testing by improving the design of experiments. When creating tests for new products, he built an outer array into the test cases, meaning that he would include random factors likely to be found in the real world but that were outside the bounds of traditional laboratory-only testing.

- **Offline quality control.** Quality used to be managed by building a product, testing it, capturing variances, and trying to correct and eliminate them. Taguchi pioneered a new approach, putting more effort up front into planning for the proper results and estimating results better in advance, thereby eliminating variation at the design stage.

Q11. What contributions did Kaoru Ishikawa make?

A11. A quality innovator in his native Japan, Ishikawa remains well known today for several key contributions:

- **The Ishikawa diagram.** This is Ishikawa's most long-lasting contribution. Ishikawa diagrams are still used frequently today, very much the same way he first used them. The diagram is described in detail in Q&A 46 later in this chapter as one of the basic tools of quality.

- **TQM.** Ishikawa built upon some of the earlier work of Deming and Juran and gets credited with translating TQM from English into Japanese, helping integrate it into Japanese business, and expanding on it.

- **Quality circles.** Ishikawa initiated the idea of assembling workers at companies into groups called *quality circles*, in which they join forces, brainstorm, solve problems, and then report their findings to management. The problem-solving part of this method raises quality directly, and quality circles also have the positive benefits of increasing morale and motivation by fostering a quality-focused environment. The concept of quality circles ties into the basic tenet of TQM that all employees can contribute to quality.

ANATOMY OF A FEW RECENT QUALITY SCANDALS: WHAT WENT WRONG AND LESSONS LEARNED

Q12. What are the most useful lessons in quality control we can take from some of the biggest recent scandals in the business world?

A12. Figure 6-1 shows several of the biggest corporate scandals in the last few years along with some of their key root causes. While describing major business failings in this limited space is obviously an oversimplification, some general lessons learned jump out of each scenario; these are summarized at the bottom of the figure.

Scandal	Root Causes
Toyota brake and accelerator failures These failures have caused numerous car accidents, leading to injuries and some deaths, and millions of cars have been recalled.	Several probable causes include: • Possibly faulty brake pedals, accelerator pedals, ill-fitting floor mats, and electronics • A drop in quality control that accompanied Toyota's *rise* in size and sales • Heavy denial by Toyota, which, for a long time, insisted that the reported problems would only impact drivers in Japan.
Poison added to U.S. pet food formula When a number of leading pet food companies in the United States outsourced production to China, a toxic chemical, melamine, was added to the product to artificially boost the protein count. A great many cats and dogs suffered serious illnesses as a result, and some died.	Direct tests for melamine in the pet food were not conducted as part of quality control because it had not been an issue in the past. Changes in the pet food production process also were not detected.
Cranes falling down in Manhattan New York City has seen several accidents in recent years involving cranes toppling over on construction sites, causing damage, injury, and some deaths.	One word: bribery! In at least one of the cases, someone at the construction company pled guilty to giving bribes to the inspectors, who consequently overlooked the deficiencies and potential safety risks instead of doing the inspections. Quality control was insufficient compensation for this breach.

(Continued on next page)

Key Lessons Learned about Quality Management

- *Don't rest on your laurels.* Even in companies with long-established product lines and great successes, rigorous quality assurance must *always* be conducted. Toyota helped put the concept of *kaizen* on the map. But by Toyota President Akio Toyoda's own admission, his company lost sight of the continuous improvement ideology when the goal of becoming bigger than General Motors came true.
- ***When outsourcing to save a lot of money, splurge a little on quality control.*** Poor quality can have severe, even lethal consequences, and the risks are multiplied when the outsourcer is thousands of miles away, with different rules, regulations, laws, and languages.
- *Short-term profit can equal long-term loss.* Any money the major American pet food companies saved by outsourcing production to China was a drop in the bucket compared to what they later lost in the aftermath of the scandal, including recalls, rework, and lost customers. Added to the money directly lost were the vast sums the companies needed to spend on damage control. This was a dramatic example of Crosby's cost of quality formula at work.
- *Audit the process, not just the product.* In the pet food scandal, it wasn't enough to test the product using the same tests as before because the deadly component melamine was not among those tested for, and no one would have thought to add it. Carefully auditing the processes might have made the difference.
- *Trust, but verify.* When an inspector's signature is not sufficient, additional safeguards must be added.

Figure 6-1: A Few Recent Major Scandals and Their Root Causes

Q13. What is redundancy design, and why is it critically important for quality?

A13. Redundancy design is the idea of building duplication into a design so that even if one part fails, the product will still work. Common examples are a computer network designed to keep users logged in, even if some components crash, or a spaceship designed with an extra rocket that will function as a backup in case the main rocket fails.

The drawback is that redundancy adds cost and complicates design. For example, an additional rocket on a spaceship would add an enormous amount of extra weight, affecting flight, performance, and fuel needs; to compensate for the weight, many more design requirements would have to be engineered. But if you're the cosmonaut out in space after your rocket just died, you will appreciate that extra power under the hood! Redundancy can add reliability and safety, which contribute to overall quality.

Q14. What is redundancy testing, as opposed to redundancy design?

A14. Redundancy in testing also contributes to quality. In many situations, one test alone may seem to indicate a certain result, but multiple tests more conclusively prove the answer. For example, thorough testing of a car's braking systems can be done in a lab setting. But additional testing should also be done in real road conditions, such as on badly paved highway and in bad weather.

With any product, instead of just testing by professional testers, it's also good to have additional tests done by customers who are not familiar with the deliverable or test procedures. It's very common on IT projects, for example, that an application will work for expert system testers, but then the minute customers access the new application, they immediately find bugs. By asking someone on the customer side to do duplicate testing, you will get a fresh perspective and possibly uncover flaws that might otherwise go overlooked. This redundancy adds quality to your test process because it increases the likelihood of finding and fixing more errors. It also provides a kind of audit of the testing being done by your quality experts.

Q15. What is just-in-time (JIT), and how does it translate to quality?

A15. Just-in-time, usually called JIT, is a phrase used to describe business models in which inventory is deliberately kept low by only ordering product replacements when needed.

JIT helped propel Dell Computers to great success in the 1980s, following Toyota's pioneering of this method in the 1960s. Instead of keeping thousands of PCs on their shelves, as its competitors were doing, Dell instituted a "roll-your-own" model: Customers could call in the exact specs of the PC they wanted, and Dell would build the customized machines and ship them directly to the customers.

Customers associated this business model with superior quality. They could get their own PC tailor-made to their liking, they liked the delivery to their door, and they loved the convenience of being able to purchase a computer over the phone (this was long before Internet shopping became commonplace).

JIT is usually more about costs than quality because the lower the inventory on hand, the greater the profit margin. But increased quality is also often a result: In the case of Dell, customers appreciated the quality of the custom-built PCs, as well as of the JIT process itself. And in a ripple effect demonstrating the triple constraint, greater profits for Dell from its PC sales also meant that the company had more money to spend on increasing quality further, by hiring more skilled workers, adding more features to its PCs, and increasing its product line.

Q16. How did Walmart's single-point-of-sale system take JIT to a new level?

A16. It may look to the customer as if Walmart's superstores keep huge inventories, but the company is really practicing JIT on steroids. The "steroids" are actually radio frequency identifier (RFI) waves. The split second a product is pulled from the shelf, a wireless signal tells the Walmart database to send a replacement. This saves Walmart tons of money, as the radio waves replace the legwork of human beings doing the reordering.

Similar to the Dell example, by cornering the market on this exclusive method, Walmart's profits rose dramatically. And its RFI system was perceived in itself as an indicator of quality; it helped turn the image of a retail giant, known for some not-so-employee–friendly ways into a technology leader as well as an industry leader.

PLANNING HOW YOU WILL DESIGN AND CONDUCT YOUR TESTING

Q17. What are some ways to build better quality into your test planning?

A17. In addition to the core concepts of the quality pioneers outlined above, some specific methods test-planners use to help them create test cases and plan solid testing are:

- Design of experiments
- Mutual exclusivity
- Statistical independence
- Benchmarking.

See the Q&As on these four methods below.

Q18. What are some recommendations for design of experiments?

A18.   It's important to put a lot of thought and planning into design of experiments (DOE) on your projects.

- *Tests need to be thorough and comprehensive.* The most important thing is to try to analyze all the main criteria you want to test for.

- *Do the right tests.* There may be many possible tests to choose from; you want to concentrate on the most important tests for your product.

- *Tests must be repeatable.* Often testers rush to get results but forget what they did to get them, calling the outcome into question. Requiring your people to be meticulous and to document what they are testing and all their steps is key here. Any test result should be quickly reproducible.

- *Create a variety of conditions.* It's not enough, for example, to test car brakes at different speeds. You also need to test the brakes on different surfaces, such as wet roads, asphalt, concrete, smooth roads, roads with potholes, and even cobblestone and dirt roads, all of which are used by car owners.

- *Establish real-world (not just lab) conditions.* A common mistake is to test under factory conditions, not real-world conditions. This happens a lot in IT, where testers traditionally work on the weekend so as not to impact the customers. Too often, though, the product works for the tester but not for the real customers. Sometimes this is due to insufficient test volume; and very often this is due to interdependencies that are not present when a tester is at home on the weekend doing standalone tests but that do come into play in the production environment. Test design must take all relevant interdependencies into account.

- *Beware of assumptions.* A lot of test designers neglect to run a needed test because of an incorrect assumption—for example, they assume that a new release corrected a known bug from an old release. If you haven't verified that the fix was added and that it works, make sure to add the test to your test bed.

Q19. How does the concept of mutual exclusivity help with doing proper DOE?

A19.   A key question to keep in mind when designing quality testing is whether variables you will be testing for will be mutually exclusive or not, meaning if one of two conditions is true, the other condition would be impossible.

Mutual exclusivity can be trickier to test for than it sounds. Let's say that a team is writing tests for a computer program designed to handle insurance data. The question of whether an insured person is married or single is less straightforward than it would appear. The two conditions are, of course, mutually exclusive. But there can be data dependencies that make this question less binary than meets the eye. A test designer might make the assumption that a married person has his or her spouse as a beneficiary on his or her insurance policy while someone who is single does not. But what about a woman who was formerly married but still wants her ex-husband provided for as a beneficiary on her policy? What about a married man whose wife does not want to be listed because she has her own insurance and the couple doesn't want to pay double for coverage? What about the scenario of a policy that lapsed and was reinstated, where the policy holder is married and his beneficiary could either be re-added, changed, or lost? (This actually happened to one of my policies and had to be corrected!)

In short, because of dependencies on many criteria, test designers often need to take into account some of the same complexities as the developers writing the computer applications.

Q20. How does statistical independence figure into building test cases?

A20. Some test criteria are independent of others, but this is not always obvious, leading to errors. For example, before you flip a quarter, the chance of seeing George Washington is 1 in 2, or 50 percent. After you flip heads on your first coin toss, what are the odds of getting heads a second time? The answer is 50 percent again because this is an example of statistical independence: The coin does not remember that it landed on heads earlier. (This is different from asking what the odds are of getting heads two times in a row, which would be approximately 25 percent [50% * 50% = 0.25].)

Therefore, when designing tests, it's key to consider whether two separate testing criteria are truly independent or not. For instance, software bugs often seem to be independent of each other but turn out to be linked. To avoid this when building test cases, keep tests separate that need to be separate. Don't combine them to save time. Be sure to link tests that *do* need to be linked. Don't let your testers tell you it's too difficult to arrange the double test. You'll pay for relenting later if the software fails in production and you're asked to explain why you didn't see the need for the linked test.

Q21. How is benchmarking valuable for achieving quality testing and results?

A21. Possibly the most important decision you as the PM will make on a project is choosing how you will measure its success. Often, you will compare your test results to tests from projects that preceded your current effort. Benchmarking, then, means choosing the earlier metrics you will compare your new numbers against (i.e., the numbers you will use as a benchmark).

For instance, if your project is to create a lunch restaurant that will compete with the falafel place down the block, which averages 100 customers per night, you might use that figure of 100 customers as a benchmark for volume. Your project goal might be to open the restaurant and bring your clientele up to 100 lunch patrons per afternoon within six months of opening. Or if you're designing a car to compete with the Toyota Prius, which averages approximately 50 mpg, there are several ways you could use that number as a benchmark. For example, you would conduct tests in which you measured your car against the 50 mpg benchmark as follows:

- If the Prius gets 50 mpg, you might shoot for 53 mpg so that you will be able to use your car's superior mpg as a selling point.

- If your car is somewhat less expensive than your competitor's, you might shoot for 48 mpg in your design and testing, hoping that your combination of lower price, superior features, plus comparable (though slightly lower) mpg will appeal to your customer base.

BEST PRACTICES FOR QUALITY TESTING

Q22. What are some best practices for quality testing itself?

A22. After your tests have been designed and planned, there are several key concepts and best practice methods for the testing.

- Automated testing
- Creating "super tests"
- Statistical sampling
- Striving for zero defects (versus setting a tolerance number)
- Six Sigma accuracy
- Attribute sampling versus variance sampling
- Assignable cause versus random cause

- Quality versus grade
- Rule of sevens.

Q23. What exactly is automated testing?

A23. Automated testing, as the name suggests, means that workers don't have to manually perform individual tests; rather, a number of tests are programmed to run automatically. This can be incredibly powerful, letting you perform much more testing with much less effort.

Automated testing boosts the quality of testing by standardizing it. The computer always runs the testing in the same sequence and with the same input data. Another benefit is automation in creating the tests. For instance, using a computer application, a tester can first run through the sequence of operations he or she wants to test and then program the computer to capture the sequence as a script. The tester can then run the recorded script against various sets of data, with the guarantee that he or she is testing all desired features and actions. This can bring remarkable efficiency and results.

The main danger to watch out for is that the more automated testing is used, the more likely we are to take it for granted and sometimes miss some of the results. For instance, I've seen testers use the same automated tests many times with good results, but then they fall into a practice of repeatedly accepting the status quo and neglecting to add new tests to keep up with changes in the product or the product's environment.

I've also seen tests run automatically every night for many months, and eventually people get complacent without looking closely at the outputs of the testing. Reports are delivered properly to all the managers' desks, and everyone assumes things are fine. Instead, it's best to treat automated testing as diligently as you would if you were running all the tests manually, focusing on each individual test case and on your results.

Case Study: How Automated "Super Tests" Improved Quality

I once was brought in to manage QA testing on infrastructure development tools in a mainframe environment in which users had been complaining about quality results.

At the time, only scattered quality tests were being done, and they were being run manually as individual one-offs.

We pooled all of the various tests and created one comprehensive test bed for each product so that all the tests could be submitted in one keystroke. We also added hundreds more tests, creating "super tests" for each product that could all be run in just a few minutes.

These tests were saved and documented on a company database so they wouldn't get lost with future versions of the products. And we made the scripts portable, so they could be used to test the products in varying environments, as well as on new hardware and future versions of operating systems. This greatly improved the quality of the product releases for our customers.

Q24. When is statistical sampling recommended over full-blown testing?

A24. Statistical sampling is partial testing, done instead of full testing to save resources. When possible, it is almost always better to do full testing because there is always a higher risk of missing a bug when only partial testing is done. But full testing can sometimes be cost prohibitive and therefore not feasible. When resource constraints mandate statistical sampling, the goal is to make the sampling reflect as true a picture of a full test as possible.

Sometimes a hybrid of statistical sampling and full testing is possible. Suppose you were leading QA on a project to create a new design for a baseball glove. Each glove needs to have a very strong double-knot or it will be considered defective. Ideally, you'd like to do full inspections on every piece, but 1,000 gloves will be produced every day, and testing each of them will be too expensive. So you might decide to run full tests on a random sampling of 50 gloves each day. But to be safe, and to boost the quality of the testing, you might initially bring in extra testers and test every piece during the first two days of production (all 1,000 gloves) before cutting over to statistical sampling (50 gloves). To further safeguard your testing, you might add x-raying to the process. It might prove much cheaper to x-ray 1,000 gloves than to manually inspect each glove. So as a compromise, on top of the hands-on statistical sampling of 50 pieces per day, you might decide to x-ray all 1,000 gloves in each production cycle, but be sure to have your inspectors verify every x-ray image.

Q25. How do you decide whether to go for zero defects in your testing or build in tolerance for a certain number of defects?

A25. This decision partly depends on what you're testing. If you're building pacemakers, you truly *must* aim for zero defects; you can't tolerate *any* failures. But on most projects, shooting for zero defects as an aspirational goal is a way of achieving high quality. When you aim for no defects, you are more likely to end up with high-caliber results than if you are planning in advance to allow some defective products with the hope of fixing them later.

Tolerating defects vs. striving for zero defects also reflects a difference in philosophy between mass production and lean production. Going back to the 1930s, when mass production was becoming predominant in the United States, tolerance for a certain number of defects was considered a cost of doing business. If you were going to mass-produce a product, you would expect your testing to capture x number of defects. The defective products would then either be discarded or sent back for rework. But in hindsight, there was an element of sloppiness to this approach because it tolerated a certain failure percentage, or in other words, a lack of quality.

In the 1960s came quality pioneers like Philip Crosby, who championed the concept of zero defects as an aspirational goal. The idea was that companies should strive to do things right in the first place by planning for—and thereby building in—quality. They should not just assume that defects are inevitable. The fewer defects, the greater the efficiency, the less waste, and the *leaner* the company could be. Lean production helped Japan catch and eventually surpass the West in a number of industries, most dramatically in car production, where America's mass-production model had once achieved world-wide domination.[4]

Figure 6-2 outlines some of the differences in attitudes toward quality in mass production and in lean production.

Q26. What is Six Sigma quality, and how does it apply to testing?

A26. The term Six Sigma has become synonymous with quality. It is even the name of an organization and certifying body in quality management (discussed later in this chapter and in Chapter 13). It comes from the Greek term used to designate an extremely high percentage, specifically 99.999% (rounded up from 99.99966667). It is loosely called the *five nines*.

Mass Production (old way)	Lean Production (new way; "the Toyota way")
Never stop the production line, no matter what.	Any worker on Toyota's production line can stop production when he or she determines there's a problem by pulling on a nylon line called an *andon cord*.
Emphasize quantity.	Quality, not quantity.
Tolerate a number of defects, which will be fixed later (known today as a "run it, break it, fix it" mentality).	Build in quality; shoot for zero defects. If you see a defect, fix it now, and make sure you also fix the *process* so the same defect doesn't reoccur again later.
Keep large inventory on hand; production should never stop due to parts shortage.	Only keep enough materials on hand as needed (lean!) and keep them as close by as possible, reducing waste and expenses in transportation and storage. This became known as JIT (just in time) because the resources are there just in time to use them.
Workers should do what they're told.	Workers should constantly think of ways to improve production, and they receive cash bonuses every time they suggest an idea that saves the company money.
Management: • Separate manager and employees • Place one manager in charge of large group of workers • Give special privileges to managers, e.g., executive cafeteria and parking spaces.	Management: • Create small groups of workers, and if there's a problem, ask a team leader to jump in help out. • Foster a spirit of equality; don't give special privileges to managers.
Labor mentality: • Master one function and stick with it. • Treat workers as expendable; in a recession economy, lay off excess employees. • Organize labor into unions.	Labor mentality: • Help workers learn many different skills and roles and rotate job functions, building an efficient, lean workforce. • Foster *reciprocal obligation*—provide permanent, secure jobs to workers, and in return, ask for strong loyalty and commitment to the company.

Figure 6-2: Mass Production versus Lean Production

At first glance, you might think that Six Sigma means zero defects because the number does look close to perfect. And Three Sigma (which equates to approximately 99.73 percent) doesn't look too shabby either—if your child gets either score on his or her test at school, that's a gold star. But in quality management, these numbers can represent a world of difference. If you're conducting quality tests for aircraft reliability, Six Sigma results could mean that out of 1 million tests, on average, only 3.4 planes fell out of the sky. That's pretty good math-wise, but not so good as a record to advertise to customers. Meanwhile, Three Sigma quality would mean that roughly 2,700 planes out of one million had problems! (Note that Two Sigma and One Sigma are also used as quality markers. Two Sigma means that 95.46 percent of your tests meet your standards, and One Sigma means 68.25 percent of all tests hit the mark.)

Coming up with the right sigma target depends on what you're testing. If you're producing M&Ms instead of aircraft, you might allow a Three-Sigma tolerance for how many times one of the letter *m*'s can be a little smudged on the famous candy shell. But when human life is concerned, even Six Sigma is not always good enough; there are projects on which the PM needs to lead the testing literally toward zero defects.

Q27. What is the difference between attribute sampling and variance sampling?

A27. In addition to decisions about metrics (such as an allowable number or percentage of defects), it is sometimes important to decide if your quality testing will include attribute versus variance testing.

- *Attribute sampling* is binary and rigid—either an attribute is present in your test or it isn't. Regarding the example of poisoned pet food, there should *never* be *any* melamine found in cat food. A test revealing even a small amount would represent a severe quality problem requiring immediate action.

  But there are situations in which attribute sampling can get tricky. For example, you wouldn't want anyone slipping any arsenic into your water. But it's a naturally occurring element, and it's likely that it would show up in trace amounts in quality tests of tap water. In a case like this, you would need to do variance sampling, because attribute sampling of arsenic in water is inevitably going to be positive.

- *Variance sampling* is less rigid; a certain level of imperfection is tolerated. In the case of arsenic, you would test for a specific number of parts per million that is considered safe. Or suppose your customer's spec for high-quality dog food specifies primarily choice beef, but a certain amount of gristle is allowed. You might design tests that would capture the percentage of gristle, and 2 percent, for example, might represent an allowable variance from 100 percent pure meat. Per your client's specs, this would be an allowable variance, agreed upon up front.

Q28. In testing, what is meant by *assignable cause* versus *random cause*?

A28. Imagine that your project is to create a new line of products for one of the high-end cookie emporiums in Manhattan, where they literally pump the aroma of their irresistible product out onto the fabled sidewalks of Broadway, pulling customers in. Suppose one of the criteria your quality manager must monitor is how many cookies have slight burn marks when they come out of the oven.

How do you decide if slight burning indicates a problem with the oven or if it is just a minor, random defect that you can ignore? Sometimes you can just make a judgment call based on how burned the cookie was or how many burned cookies there were.

- If just one cookie is burned, and the next 20 are all OK, you can usually chalk it up to *random cause*. Maybe the burnt cookie was too thin, so it baked too fast. This is also called common cause because it's common for anomalies to occasionally appear in a process.

- But suppose that as you baked several batches of cookies, more and more cookies came out too dark, and they became darker and drier with each successive batch. Now you have a problem that must be solved, or in other words, you must assign cause. *Assignable cause* is also called *special cause* because something special, or out of the ordinary, is going on, and your process is no longer functioning as it should be. Properly assigning cause entails all the following:
  o Deciding that there *is* a problem
  o Getting at the root cause
  o Coming up with a solution
  o Testing the solution

o Proving that the solution works

o Making sure to incorporate the solution into the production process

o Documenting the problem and the solution.

Q29. How can grade factor into quality testing?

A29. This is a choice you would usually make at the design stage but is something you can sometimes also test for after creating your deliverables. Suppose your project is manufacturing high-end canoes, and there is a high expectation of quality. One element contributing to the quality of the final product might be the grade of wood, so the quality of the wood itself will ultimately figure into the quality of the final product. While you might need a raging river to do some of the quality testing, part of your testing regimen might include testing for grade, with an expert physically examining the boats. You might determine that you do not need to inspect every canoe for wood grade—a random study might suffice. You could choose one of two types of statistical sampling:

- *Attribute sampling:* If all of the wood used was supposed to be of a certain high grade, call it grade 7, you would want to do attribute sampling because you would be checking to ensure 100 percent of the wood sampled tests as grade 7.

- *Variance sampling:* If your specifications required 70 percent of the wood to be grade 7, but 30 percent did not have to be as high a grade, then variance sampling would be appropriate. You would design tests that would measure how much of the wood used in the construction of your deliverable met the grade-7 criteria and report on it as a percentage of the total wood tested.

Q30. What is the rule of sevens, and how is it applied in quality testing?

A30. The rule of sevens is often used with a tool of quality control testing called the *control chart*, discussed later in this chapter. But before we get there, let's look at a very simplified example: once again, those delicious, aromatic chocolate chip cookies fresh out of the oven. One slightly burned cookie can often be chalked up to random cause, and maybe a couple in a row could still possibly be caused by random factors. But at some point you have to draw the line, determine there's a problem, and solve for it.

By the rule of sevens, it would be extremely unlikely for seven burned cookies in a row to come out of the oven at random. In fact, it would be close to statistically impossible, because the probability of getting seven burned cookies at random would be the chance of one burned cookie, multiplied to the seventh power.

Seven burned cookies in a row would be a red flag signaling a problem in your process: Perhaps your oven is too hot, or your batter is too dry, or a new baker might be spreading the dough too thin. And so the rule of sevens is that seven consecutive cases (even if they may be minor in themselves) add up to an issue that needs to be investigated. One application of this rule is to help you decide when to bite the bullet (or cookie) and decide that there is a real problem. And of course, you don't have to wait for seven variances—that's your judgment call. Three slightly defective products in a row might instinctively make you feel that something is up.

Q31. What's an example of a test case too complicated to be decided by simple attribute sampling versus variance sampling?

A31. In 2010, expert science reporter Gina Kolata wrote an article for the *New York Times* about research and testing to cure a specific type of breast cancer, detectable by high levels of a protein called HER2 in tumors.[5] Among the challenges doctors are facing in testing for the protein is that both false positives and false negatives frequently occur, and some tumors are partially positive and also partially negative for the protein. Dr. Linda Griffith, director of the Center for Gynepathology Research at MIT and a source Kolata interviewed for the article, is one such patient who tested positive for HER2 but whose test results were considered ambiguous.

Q32. Why is it important to have a fully redundant test environment?

A32. People tend to take shortcuts, but this can diminish the quality of your testing. It is crucially important that a separate testing environment be created and maintained that fully matches the real environment in which the deliverable will be used.

For instance, if you are testing software that will be running on certain servers in your production environment, it is important to create a test environment that uses the same model of server and has all the same software installed on it as in production. Unfortunately, teams often neglect to create a fully redundant test environment. For example, they might use a different vendor's server for testing because that's the extra server they have available. And they might neglect to install some of the ancillary products on the test server that could indirectly affect how the main product being tested will behave. The PM needs to make sure that the test environment is fully redundant. This means that it should be as close to a mirror image of production as possible, from hardware to software to data files.

Another danger to watch out for is sharing products concurrently between the production and test sites. Often, to save money or time, the technicians setting up test environments will try to share product licenses across various platforms to avoid new licensing and new installations. But this can lead to poor quality results because the test product is not really a unique copy, installed from scratch in the test environment. For instance, a product ported over from a different system might have been altered in its default settings. Or there could be issues about running the product concurrently in multiple environments. PMs need to watch out for this for the sake of test quality (as well as to prevent licensing and legal issues).

THE THREE PMI QUALITY MANAGEMENT PROCESSES

Q33. What are the three PMI quality management processes, and how are they interrelated?

A33. There are three quality management processes per the standard in version 4 of the *PMBOK® Guide:*

- Planning quality (part of the planning process group)
- Performing quality assurance (part of the executing processes group)
- Performing quality control (part of the monitoring and controlling process group).

Each process is explored in detail in Q&As 33–39.

Q34. What does the PM do as part of the process of planning quality?

A34. In a nutshell, the PM determines what the criteria, standards, and metrics will be for measuring quality success on the project and comes up with a plan to deliver those metrics.

For example, if the deliverable is going to be a new kind of hybrid car, you as the PM might shoot for a fuel efficiency standard of 52 mpg as part of the product scope for this project. You might choose a quality testing metric of Six Sigma level performance accuracy if you think you have the budget, resources, and expertise to accommodate such a high quality level. You will plan what kind of testing your team will do, who will do the testing, and what equipment the testers will do. Finally, you'll plan how the test results will be measured, collected, analyzed, and reported.

Q35. What are the key inputs, tools, and outputs commonly used in the process of planning quality?

A35. The key inputs, tools and outputs are as follows.

- *Inputs:* Of the project artifacts, you would especially use the scope statement and requirements doc, as well the contract, the SOW, or both, when available. You might refer to the project charter to make sure you stay on track with the major quality goals of the project. Company standards and quality policies also are important to have on hand. For instance, your company might have a broad quality policy document, and you might research historical information to find appropriate benchmarks to compare your project's test results against.

- *Tools/techniques:* Key to quality planning is having expert knowledge. If the PM lacks some of the necessary technical expertise, he or she may need to bring in an outside expert to provide guidance on the quality plan.

- *Outputs:*

    The *quality management plan* will be the key output. This is where the PM or your designee will put in writing all the strategies, test plans, intended software products, and the specific action items you intend to use to deliver quality on the project. Once finalized, this will also be known as the *quality baseline*, a key part of the overall project plan/baseline.

Other outputs that also drive the quality management plan are:

- o *The quality standards* that will be used for this project.
- o *Checklists,* which will be used as part of the quality control process.
- o *Metrics*—for example, how many defects will be allowed.
- o *The process improvement plan.*

Q36. What is the process improvement plan, and why is it a separate output from the quality management plan?

A36. A process improvement plan applies not just to the specific quality of the deliverables; rather, it's a place for the PM to document ideas and suggestions the team develops on an ongoing basis for improving all of the processes of the project.

In keeping with the spirit of continuous improvement, the PM and the team should always be on the lookout for ways to make projects faster, cheaper, and better. At team meetings, the PM should ask for improvements team members have come up with that can be added to the process improvement plan. These will also be useable as lessons learned to improve future projects.

Many PMs I talk to are not aware of this output as a requirement, probably because it's not directly linked to the project deliverables (which the customer sees). But having a process improvement plan as a separate artifact helps the PM encourage a *kaizen* attitude, and teams can use it to their advantage to improve the quality of their projects.

Q37. What is the difference between quality assurance and quality control?

A37. These terms are a source of confusion for PM test takers because they sound similar, and at a networking party, they might be used interchangeably. But per the *PMBOK® Guide*, they are two distinct processes:

- *Quality assurance* is about the PM doing due diligence to make sure the processes and procedures are being followed correctly, as specified in the quality management plan.

- *Quality control* is the measurement and analysis of the test results on your deliverables to make sure the planned quality metrics are being met.

Q38. What is the specific purpose of the process of performing quality assurance?

A38. The key to understanding the quality assurance process is that it is like an audit. You are auditing your project to make sure you are on plan for quality. A PM, along with her manager or project sponsor, can sometimes audit her own project for quality. This involves looking closely at all the processes of the project with an eye toward quality, as well as looking for compliance and areas for improvement.

But often, QA is done by an auditor. The auditor may be internal, if you work for a large company that has that kind of resource, and sometimes an external auditor is brought in from an outside company to perform a quality audit. The benefit of doing it yourself, or to a lesser extent, using an internal auditor, is that you or the auditor has preexisting (and hands-on) knowledge of your project and the company's goals, processes, standards, and mission. But an outside auditor is by definition more objective and will be more willing to suggest needed changes and point out flaws in your process (even if that means ruffling feathers).

Q39. What is a quality audit looking for?

A39. Whether you do a quality audit yourself or with the help of an auditor, there are three key questions that must be asked:

1. Did the PM choose the right standards and metrics for achieving quality results on the project? (If not, questions 2 and 3 below are largely pointless.)
2. Did you create a quality management plan that would, if executed, achieve the desired level of quality?
3. Are you following the plan?

If the answer is yes to all three of the above, your project is on track for quality. If not, you will need to make changes to your quality plan and possibly to other parts of your project plan, such as your WBS and project schedule.

Q40. How is quality control performed?

A40. Quality control is a look at the actual results of your quality testing. If you were testing a new car model, you would take all the data from the prior week's safety tests, such as how many airbags deployed in 1,000 test drives, summarize the figures in a spreadsheet, and analyze the results to see exactly how the deliverable performed on quality for that week. Instead of auditing your *process,* here you are literally inspecting and measuring the quality of your results.

To help PMs with quality control, there are a number of methods, collectively called the basic tools of quality, covered in Q&As 41–49.

THE BASIC TOOLS OF QUALITY

Q41. What are the basic tools of quality, and how do they help PMs control quality on their projects?

A41. Central to quality management is the idea that any two deliverables will show a difference if you measure them to a fine enough level. Much of quality control is making sense of the numbers after quality testing has been done and the data have been collected. The basic tools of quality are reporting tools for helping PMs do this. Each tool is very different, and each one is ideal for certain tasks. Knowing them all gives you a robust tool kit and prepares you for any kind of quality data you ever need to analyze.

A nice thing about these tools is that many of them are basically free. You can create them with just pen and paper, or up on a whiteboard in a meeting, or with software you already might own, such as Word or Excel.

The basic tools of quality are also often called the *seven tools of quality*, but different sources offer slightly different lists of the seven. Forgive the math— Figure 6-3 shows the *eight* most commonly listed of the *seven* tools of quality. Each is then detailed in its own Q&A.

1.	Checklists
2.	Bar charts (histograms)
3.	Pareto charts
4.	Flow charts
5.	Cause-and-effect diagrams (a.k.a., fishbone or Ishikawa diagrams)
6.	Scatter diagrams
7.	Run charts
8.	Control charts

Figure 6-3:   The *Eight* Most Popular of The Seven Tools of Quality

Q42. Why are checklists the most basic and yet in some ways the most important of the tools of quality?

A42. Checklists are a great way to verify that quality control work has been done. Creating them is easy; it's a simple matter of listing your key action items and providing space for confirmation that they've been done, such as a check mark, or better yet, a signature, both of which are often done electronically nowadays.

But the hard part is getting people to honor what they check off on. Unfortunately, problems, such as the NYC falling-cranes scandal, can emerge even if at first glance, all of the necessary check marks and signatures appear to be in place.

So while checklists can be valuable, they are often not sufficient in themselves, and it is the responsibility of the PM or quality engineer to make double sure when using a checklist that the work has actually been done. As the old saying goes, it's important to trust but verify—meaning that we have to do whatever it takes to ensure that all of the necessary quality control tasks have in fact been done and that there are verifiable results, not just signoffs.

Q43. What are histograms, and how are they used in quality control?

A43. Histograms, also called bar charts, or column charts, are very commonly used nowadays, thanks to products like Excel. They are charts that show data as a series of parallel bars; the longer the bar, the bigger the corresponding number.

Suppose as part of quality control, a PM wanted to monitor incoming help desk calls on the system her team was supporting. She planned to compile the information each week over a four-week period. Eighteen calls came in the first week, 25 the second week, 16 the third week, and 20 the fourth week. A software tool like Excel can easily turn those four numbers into a bar chart in a matter of seconds. The result would be four parallel vertical bars, representing from left to right the number of calls from weeks 1, 2, 3, and 4. Here, the tallest bar would represent week 2's 25 calls, and the shortest bar would be for the 16 calls handled during week 3. (Note that a bar chart can be horizontal instead of vertical.)

The value of a bar chart is that it instantly makes your numbers visual. Anyone looking at the chart can immediately see the biggest and smallest bars and can see each bar's size relative to the others. And anyone with a PC can easily convert a bar chart into many other formats, from pie charts to pyramids, whatever format you think would best help your stakeholders understand your data.

Q44. What are Pareto charts, and when do PMs use them instead of traditional bar charts?

A44. Pareto charts are a form of bar chart, but the bars appear in either ascending or descending order, meaning that the longest bar comes first, then the next-longest, then the one after that. The order can start from left to right, right to left, top to bottom, or bottom to top. Creating Pareto charts is as easy as creating any bar chart. You just sort your data first so the bars wind up in the same order as your numbers.

Pareto charts are better than regular bar charts when you have data that are best viewed in size order. For instance, in the example in the previous Q&A, we talked about a bar chart depicting the number of help desk calls coming in each week. Depicting the number in chronological order by week makes sense, especially for only four weeks worth of figures, which are easy to view and analyze. But suppose we had data for 52 weeks instead of four, and we wanted to quickly be able to see which weeks in the year had the most problems or greatest activity. By simply sorting the data, we can easily create a Pareto chart, which would show at a glance data from all the weeks in order of volume of activity. Compared to a Pareto chart, a chronological bar chart would be a much more cumbersome tool.

Q45. How are flow charts used in quality control?

A45. Much of quality control involves tracing through the sequence of activities of a project, either to verify that things are going as planned or to track down the source of a defect or bug. Project network diagrams are one example of a type of flow chart, popularized by software products like MS Project and Primavera. But there are many types of flowcharts/flow diagrams to choose from, and some still use the same set of geometric shapes that you may find familiar if you've ever created flow charts on paper. Each shape, by convention, has a unique, standardized purpose: parallelograms represent inputs/outputs, boxes represent activities, circles between activities represent connectors, and diamond shapes represent decision points or branches. By representing processes as pictures, flow charts make problem-solving for quality control much easier and faster, when compared with working from a text-based schedule.

Q46. When is a cause-and-effect diagram superior to a traditional flow chart?

A46. The cause-and-effect diagram is a very specific type of flow chart, and it has two main purposes in quality control: for product design and to analyze the root causes of defects, problems, or variations.

Like the traditional flow chart, it offers a bird's eye view and represents your processes visually, in sequence. But while the traditional flow chart is somewhat neutral and shows all the activities in pure chronological order, a cause-and-effect diagram is intentionally *not* neutral. Its purpose is not just to show sequence, but to get at the root of a problem, so activities are grouped as they are best related logically. For instance, you might design the diagram with an emphasis on grouping the tasks around which teams performed them or by the equipment used to create certain deliverables. Focusing on those factors one group at a time often helps bring out a solution for the problem in question.

Note that this diagram also goes by two other names: *Ishikawa diagram*, named after its inventor, Kaoru Ishikawa, and *fishbone diagram*, because it visually resembles a fish skeleton. Cause-and-effect diagrams have a heavy horizontal line running through the center from left to right, which looks like a fish's backbone. And at the far right of this horizontal line is what looks like the head of a fish: a small box representing the end result of the design path or process, what you are trying to analyze.

Q47. When would a PM use a scatter diagram, and what are its characteristics?

A47. Another tool used for cause-and-effect analysis is the scatter diagram. The scatter diagram takes a data-driven approach. A PM or quality engineer starts with a theory about the cause of a problem or condition and then designs tests based on two sets of data: one representing the *results* they are going for, and the other representing the single factor he or she believes might *cause* those results. After testing, the PM plots both sets of data on a graph to see if they line up in a meaningful way. If they do, the single factor is probably the cause of the results. As a fun example, imagine that your client company owns a vineyard, where three varieties of champagne are created in three different price ranges. As part of quality control, you run taste tests. Ten testers try each of the three wines. You are looking for data showing that the testers will give the highest ratings to the most expensive of your three champagnes.

For the scatter diagram, you would create a graph with an *x*-axis (horizontal) representing the price of each glass of wine. The price is called the *dependent variable* because that's the factor you think your results will depend on. Your *y*-axis (vertical) would represent each tester's rating—that's your independent variable. After each tester tastes a glass of wine, you would plot two data points. One would be for the price, plotted with dollar signs ($) on the *x*-axis (prices would be plotted from left to right, least to most expensive). And for the taste results, each test would be represented on the *y*-axis, perhaps with a letter "A" for the best taste (on the highest point on the vertical axis), a "B" near the midpoint for a moderately good taste, and a "C" low on the vertical scale for a low-rated taste.

You would hope that your diagram would wind up showing a lot of A's at the far upper right, B's in the middle, and C's in the lower left. This would be a positive linear correlation, as shown in Figure 6-4, and would perfectly confirm your desired results. Tests don't always go perfectly according to plan, however, but even less-than-ideal results are useful because they would send you back to do more testing, possibly with a different dependent variable.

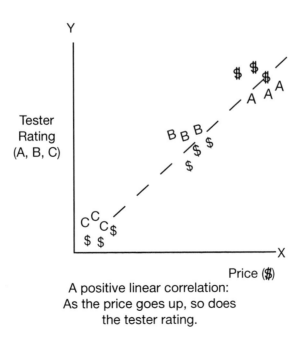

A positive linear correlation:
As the price goes up, so does
the tester rating.

Figure 6-4: Scatter Diagram

Q48. When are run charts used?

A48. Run charts are the ideal tool for examining results over time and using those results to spot trends. We return to our example of incoming help desk calls, but now it's not the sheer numbers we are interested in. We want to focus on whether the quality of our process is trending in the right direction.

Like the scatter diagram, our graph will have an *x*-axis and *y*-axis, and again, we'll look at two variables. But this time we will plot them on a single line, with each point representing both variables. Here, our *x*-axis will represent time, showing four demarcations from left to right for weeks 1, 2, 3, and 4. And our *y*-axis will simply show the number of calls for each week:

- Week 1: 37 support calls
- Week 2: 33 support calls
- Week 3: 35 support calls
- Week 4: 29 support calls.

The run chart for this data appears in Figure 6-5. It shows a line that starts in the top left corner and slopes downward toward the bottom right corner of our graph, indicating a general downward trend in calls over time. Indeed, there were fewer support calls in each successive week, except for in week 3, where the number went up slightly from week 2.

The angle and direction of the line instantly shows us that we are basically trending toward improved quality, using the number of customers needing

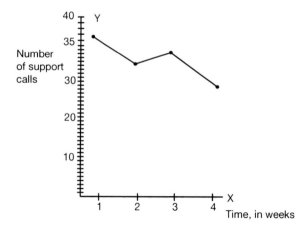

Figure 6-5: Run Chart

support over the four-week period as a metric. But it also clearly points out the blip between week 2 and week 3, where the number went up slightly. This directs us to explore that anomaly further, perhaps by creating an Ishikawa diagram. We would want to review and analyze the conditions that might have been different between week 2 and week 3 and why the trend went in the wrong direction for that time period, as opposed to the greater positive trend over the one-month period.

Q49. What kind of data is best represented on a control chart, and why are control charts usually drawn with five parallel horizontal lines?

A49. Control charts are a tool of choice for comparing many similar data points to show how close they come to a desired value and to make sure they do not exceed the allowable high and low ranges, which are called the *control limits*.

Suppose that you are leading a project to create a new pill for a pharmaceutical company, and the customer gives you the following quality specifications:

- The ideal amount of the drug that should be absorbed into each patient's bloodstream is 4 parts per million (commonly represented as *ppm*).
- The highest allowable amount of absorption is 5 ppm.
- The lowest allowable amount is 3 ppm.

Your control chart, represented in Figure 6-6, will look like a rectangular box containing five parallel horizontal lines as follows:

1. *Customer specification limit (upper).* This will be the first line down from the top, representing 5 ppm in our scenario.
2. *Customer specification limit (lower).* This will be the first line up from the bottom, representing 3 ppm in this example.
3. *The mean.* You would be correct to guess that the mean will be shown as a line right in the middle of the chart. *However*, you might assume that in our scenario, the mean would be 4 ppm, falling perfectly between the lower and upper limits of 3 and 5 ppm. But that assumption would not necessarily be correct; the mean is actually calculated *after* initial testing has been done. Let's say that the mean in our example might average out to 4.1 ppm.

Note that to increase quality, a PM or quality engineer usually shoots for tighter limits than the customer specs demand (and those tighter limits will be the control limits, explored below). Why would you impose tighter limits, and make your job harder? For good reason: Suppose the pill your team is developing will test fine for a 200-pound man living in Manhattan. He can safely absorb 5 ppm. But what if the patient is a 105-pound woman living in the Swiss Alps, at a much higher altitude and with a much lower oxygen level? Different people, under different real-world conditions, may absorb the same pill differently. Therefore, the actual range you will want to use in your testing will be somewhat narrower for best results in the real world. Two more lines representing your own tighter limits will appear in the control chart:

4. **Upper control limit (UCL).** Between the mean and the upper customer specification limit will be the highest allowable limit you will allow for your testing. In our example, our self-imposed UCL might be 4.5.

5. **Lower control limit (LCL).** This limit, the lowest level your test will tolerate, will be below the mean, but above the lower customer specification limit. Our LCL might be 3.5.

Q50. When is a quality process considered out of control?

A50.   One of the benefits of a control chart is that it allows you to see at a glance when a data point is not behaving the way you want it to—in other words, when the data is out of control. And a rule of control charts is that any data point outside the control limits means that your quality process is considered out of control and that assignable cause must be found for the outlying data.

In our medication scenario, there might be a test case in which a subject took a pill and absorbed 5.3 ppm into her bloodstream, which is well above both the upper control limit and the customer specification limit (upper) discussed in our scenario. This case is represented by the top-most asterisk (*) in Figure 6-6. Depending on the drug, absorbing 5.3 ppm could potentially be extremely dangerous. Even if it is not, this data point near the top of our control chart shows that the process for that test case is out of control.

As a challenge, take a look at Figure 6-6, and then answer the three questions below. This will reinforce the concept of control charts and will help you learn to determine which data points are considered out of control. The answers to these questions are given at the end of this chapter.

- Based on our control chart scenario, are the three data points 4.6, 4.8, and 4.9 ppm out of control?
- What about points 3.3 and 3.2 ppm?
- What if in our control chart scenario, there were seven consecutive tests yielding the following data: 4.4, 4.3, 4.2, 4.3, 4.4, 4.2, and 4.3 ppm. Is this in control or out of control?

5.5 ppm	
5 ppm	Customer specification limit (upper)
4.5 ppm	Upper control limit (UCL)
4.1 ppm	← Rule of sevens Mean
3.5 ppm	Lower control limit (LCL)
3 ppm	Customer specification limit (lower)
2.5 ppm	

Figure 6-6:   Control Chart

QUALITY CERTIFICATIONS

Q51. Is there a certification for PMs specifically in quality management?

A51. Yes, in addition to the general PM certifications, such as CAPM, PMP, and Project+, which all test knowledge of quality management as one of the nine knowledge areas, there is a family of certifications specific to quality management called Six Sigma that validates your knowledge as a quality management practitioner. Each level is represented by its own different karate belt color to signify the certification holder's level of mastery (the black belt is at the top of the ladder). Going through the certification process validates your knowledge, boosts your resume, and improves your skill level in quality management.

Q52. Are there ways to measure and certify quality on a company level?

A52. Yes, there are three well-known and very different certification processes your company can benefit from on an organizational level:

- International Organization for Standardization (ISO)
- Capability Maturity Model® Integration (CMMI®)
- Organizational Project Management Maturity Model (OPM3®).

All three of the above share the common goals of:

- *Evaluating* your PM environment for adherence to quality standards appropriate to the industry
- *Certifying/ranking* your company based on the quality of your PM processes
- *Improving the quality of your organization.* Going through the process of earning any of these certifications focuses project teams on quality, which in itself helps raise the bar. The OPM3® evaluation from PMI provides as a deliverable a customized roadmap for your organization's future performance improvement.

Details on all three company certification processes appear in Chapter 13; see Table 13-3.

TOP TEN QUALITY MANAGEMENT PITFALLS

1. Not defining quality standards or benchmarks early on in the project that the team can aim for. Often, team members are all sent off on their tasks with no metrics in mind for measuring their results.

2. Not auditing the quality process frequently enough, or failing to take sufficient action on the findings and recommendations after an audit.

3. Not checking in with your customer specifically to make sure you are on the same page regarding the quality goals and metrics of the project.

4. Not implementing the newest and best methods to do the job, but instead being ruled by the NIH (not invented here) mentality—wanting to continue doing things the same way you've always done them.

5. Rushing to meet a deadline at the expense of quality.

6. Failing to do thorough quality control—that is, conducting a proactive analysis of your team's quality procedures and testing, and making improvements where necessary.

7. Not creating realistic quality testing that would mirror the variables and stressors of the real world.

8. Not creating a sufficient testing environment, such as a fully redundant computer hardware and software system.

9. Failing to create proper contingency plans for maintaining quality in case problems occur.

10. Sacrificing quality for cost—for example, not hiring enough developers, depending on low-paid workers to ensure quality, testing too little, using low-cost materials, outsourcing without proper oversight… you name it.

ANSWERS TO THE SELF TEST AT THE END OF A50

As a challenge, take a look at Figure 6-6 and then answer the three questions below. This will reinforce the concept of control charts and will help you learn to determine which data points are considered out of control.

- **Based on our control chart scenario, are the three data points 4.6, 4.8, and 4.9 ppm out of control?** Yes. Even though all three are below the customer's upper limit of 5 ppm, they are *above* our chosen upper control limit (UCL) of 4.5.

- **What about points 3.3 and 3.2 ppm?** These also are considered out of control. In this case, they are above the customer's lowest allowable limit, but they are also *below* the LCL on which we based our testing.

- **What if in our control chart scenario, there were seven consecutive tests yielding the following data: 4.4, 4.3, 4.2, 4.3, 4.4, 4.2, and 4.3 ppm. Is this in control or out of control?** These data points are indicated in the figure as the cluster of points. The fact that there are seven data points might give you a hint on this one. These seven data points are all below our upper control limit, so at first glance, they might look safely in control. But they are also all above the mean. And in keeping with the rule of sevens that we defined earlier, the probability of seven consecutive data points randomly occurring above the mean is astonishingly low! Therefore, our process would be considered out of control here, by the rule of sevens. Cause needs to be assigned for those seven, and the process must be brought back into control.

Notes

1. Philip B. Crosby, *Quality Is Free: The Art of Making Quality Certain* (New York: McGraw-Hill, 1979).

2. Ibid.

3. Frank Langfitt, introduction by series host Ira Glass, "This American Life Tells the NUMMI Story," National Public Radio's *This American Life,* March 26, 2010.

4. James Womack, Daniel Jones, Daniel Roos, and Donna Sammons Carpenter, *The Machine That Changed The World* (New York: Macmillan, 1990).

5. Gina Kolata, "In Cancer Fight, Unclear Tests Confuse Therapy," *New York Times*, April 20, 2010.

CHAPTER 7

Controlling Risks on Your Projects

Risk is uncertainty that matters, and it matters because it can affect one or more objectives.

—Dr. David Hillson, "The Risk Doctor"

Before a key meeting with your stakeholders, do you make a backup copy of your presentation, then email yourself a second copy just in case? On top of that, do you take a trip to the meeting room in advance to test the file and make sure your slides display properly on the projector?

If so, the risk management discipline (RM) of project management is already right up your alley. But if not, that's all the more reason you will find RM a great opportunity to improve your project success.

Risk management means doing everything you can to expect the unexpected and to prepare in advance for it. One part is disaster recovery planning (also called business continuation), which some risk practitioners do as a full-time job. But RM applies to all projects and is probably the most important—yet most neglected—part of project management.

Risk management may seem mysterious to PMs who are not familiar with it. But the tools and techniques are straightforward and fairly easy to use once you learn what they are about, and they can make a huge difference in project success. PMs can get a great deal of bang for their buck by planning creatively and thoroughly. To those who ask, "Why worry about things that might not happen?" many seasoned risk managers would respond, "Pay now, or pay *more* later."

The Q&As in this chapter cover the key aspects of risk management, from the core concepts to the tools and best practices to the five RM planning steps, which are a tried and true recipe for success in the world of RM.

KEY DEFINITIONS AND TERMS

Q1. What are the definitions *risk* and *risk management* as part of project management?

A1. In one word, risk is defined as *uncertainty*. With so many variables and factors that can affect project success, a PM can never be sure in advance whether the project will be delivered on time, on budget, or correctly. Many unexpected events can crop up, jeopardizing a project's success. Yet projects must get done in spite of the constant uncertainty.

Therefore, the high-level purpose of risk management is to maximize project success by anticipating and managing those uncertainties. Specifically, this involves analyzing and predicting which risks would have the greatest impact if they occurred, while factoring in which ones have the highest probability of occurring. The PM then plans accordingly so that the project executes successfully and problems are avoided when possible and handled well when they do occur.

Q2. What skills do the best risk managers have?

A2. The best risk managers have several key skills and attributes:

- The ability to plan well, analytically, and in a well-organized manner. (The risk register templates and other tools provided in this chapter can help you with this.)

- The ability to think outside the box and creatively anticipate unexpected scenarios (which others might not see) and develop responses to those scenarios.

- The willingness and ability to come up with several alternative solutions to the same potential problem.

- Flexibility and willingness to quickly switch from one plan to another when the first solution isn't working. This is key; many PMs get too locked into their first idea, and by the time they recognize that it isn't working, it can be too late.

- The ability to foster a cooperative work environment and good relationships with the team. Solutions can't all come from the PM, but good PMs surround themselves with good people and encourage their cooperation and ideas. When team members are made to feel that they're all working toward a common goal and not just a paycheck, they're much more likely to suggest good risk solutions when needed.

- Mental toughness. In risk management, PMs must be able to work under pressure, weigh all the factors, and make the best decision. The best decision is not always the easiest or safest one. Often, it's the opposite—the hard and unpopular choice may be what's needed for the project. Being mentally tough by nature helps, for sure. But the more the PM plans for risks in advance, the faster and easier it will be to implement contingency plans when the risks do occur. There will be less need to improvise on the fly in high-pressure situations.

Q3. What are some of the most common risks on a project, and what does risk management mean for each?

A3. Two very common risk areas on every project are time management and cost management. There is a risk that the project will come in late or over budget (or both, since the two often go hand in hand). To manage both of these critical risks, PMs typically devote a lot of their attention to analyzing which issues are most likely to cause these risks to happen and planning how to avoid them.

PMs with an eye toward risk management will also take a look at the PM knowledge areas other than time and cost, think about what might go wrong in each, and then create a strategy to make sure the project succeeds in each area. Other kinds of risks that could occur include the risk that the quality of the final deliverables won't be to the customer's satisfaction (a quality management risk), and the risk that the contract will favor the other side, harming the project financially (contract risk).

Q4. What is a very specific example of managing a risk?

A4. Unless you are a company of one, there is always a risk that some of your best team members may quit the project. This is a critical risk, as many PMs know firsthand, because a good person quitting can kill a project. And yet many PMs ignore this common risk, hoping for the best (magical thinking!)

or because they believe they can't do anything about it. But a PM can do a lot to manage this risk. He or she might:

- *Cross-train team members.* Get team members up to speed on each other's job functions so the loss of a key player doesn't derail the project.

- *Hire an extra person if possible.* It might sound extravagant to hire one more team member than is absolutely necessary. But consider major-league baseball teams, which can only field nine players at a time but staff 25 (plus the farm teams). Of course, hiring another person is not always financially feasible, but if it can be done, it is better to err on the side of caution.

- *Require documentation.* As an alternative or supplement to cross-training, good PMs have their people document their roles, responsibilities, and test plans. This may sound time-consuming, but is nothing compared to the time you'll spend scrambling if a key player quits without leaving good documentation. It's also not a good excuse to use when telling a customer why a project is suddenly going to be very late.

- *Keep tabs on morale, and work to keep it high.* Savvy PMs are very aware of their team's morale and are not blindsided when people quit, citing morale issues. Moreover, they work proactively to improve and maintain their people's morale because they know projects suffer when teams lose good people.

Q5. Why is the definition of risk considered double-sided?

A5. Risk on a project has two sides: negative and positive. While we tend to focus on negative risks, it's considered a best practice for PMs to manage both sides of risk.

- *Negative risks (threats).* These include all of the unexpected events that can jeopardize a project. The PM should anticipate and plan for threats to prevent or avoid them whenever possible, as well as to best handle them when they do occur. Think of this kind of risk management as disaster planning for your project.

- *Positive risks (opportunities).* These are the unexpected things that could happen that might actually increase a project's chances of success. By anticipating and planning for positive risk, a PM positions the project to be ready to take advantage of those events if and when they do occur.

Q6. Why is risk management the most neglected area of project management?

A6. Some people think of risk management as red ink because the risks a team anticipates and plans for might or might not happen. In an effort to save money, sometimes PMs and companies think they can get away with neglecting risk—often at their peril.

Risk management is analogous to insurance. Why waste money on expensive comprehensive car insurance? You might never get into an accident or have your car stolen. But if you do have an accident, and your car and the other car are extensively damaged, the repairs may be so costly that the money saved by not paying for insurance is nothing in comparison.

That's why it's worthwhile to devote a little extra planning and resources to cover potential risks on a project. A neglected risk can cause an entire project to fail—or worse, it can lead to loss of future business and referrals or even a lawsuit. Remember, no one on a failed project ever got a medal for saving money by neglecting risk management.

Q7. With so many uncertainties in the world, how does a PM decide which risks to plan for?

A7. This is one of the key challenges for any PM. Identifying the right risks can often make the difference between success or trouble on a project. In truth, there is an infinite number of potential risks at all times. But proper risk management is about making the best decisions about which risks to prepare for and how much time and money to spend on each potential risk, best managing the limited resources at hand.

David Hillson is very well known in the project management world for his definition of risk as "uncertainty that matters," meaning that a PM needs to prioritize those risks that potentially matter most in terms of their impact (what would happen if the risk did occur), and their probability (the likelihood of the risk occurring).

Here are some examples of negative risks that could affect any given project:

- Your best technician might leave for a better position.
- A computer virus might clobber your system.

- The printer used by your department could break down and need to be replaced.

- The budget for your project might be reduced mid-project.

- A meteor could strike your building.

Of all five threats, the meteor would have the greatest impact (literally!). But the likelihood of it happening is so small that it's probably not worth worrying about or spending any resources on.

So it's practical, and good risk management, to eliminate the meteor from the list in order to better focus on the first four (the uncertainties that matter). For the first four threats, questions to consider with regard to RM include:

- Which are the most important of these threats to your specific project?

- Which are the most likely to occur?

- What can you do to prevent them, if possible?

- What would you be ready to do if any of these threats were to materialize?

Q8. What does it mean when risk managers talk about "known unknowns" versus "unknown unknowns," and how can a PM plan for both?

A8. The term *known unknowns* refers to events that have a degree of uncertainty, but the PM can very specifically identify, analyze, and plan for that uncertainty. The first four threats listed in the previous Q&A are all examples of known unknowns. The first threat, your best person quitting, is an especially good example of a known unknown because the PM:

- Knows who the best technician on the team is

- Understands the value of his or her role and can document what would happen if the team lost that person

- Can often make a reasonably good guess of the likelihood of that person leaving

- Can make plans in advance to minimize the damage to the project if that resource did leave.

Unknown unknowns, by contrast, are more general, and often can't be specifically planned for. The threat of a meteor hitting your building is an example. While it's true that a meteor *could* potentially strike any place, any time, if there are no known predictions of a meteor heading toward your building, the likelihood would be close to zero. So there is no advantage to dedicating any time or resources to manage such an unlikely threat, although it might be worthwhile to establish basic safety procedures to be followed in the event of more likely occurrences like fire or power outages. Also, creating a backup site for your project's data is something all large financial firms do nowadays, but this is a good idea for *any* company, in case of a physical threat to your facility. Many students have told me their company does not do this, and they realize the company would be in trouble if something happened to their data systems.

Allocating money and time to handle unknowns is called reserve analysis, the subject of the next three Q&As.

RESERVE ANALYSIS

Q9. What is reserve analysis?

A9. One of the core strategies of RM is figuring out how much extra money and time to allocate in your project budget and schedule for emergencies and other unforeseen problems. This is called reserve analysis, and it should be done carefully on every project. The idea is to estimate as accurately as possible how much extra money and time you might really need if certain risks were to occur. The trick to doing it right is to allocate enough, but not too much, to safeguard your project. It's clearly bad to underallocate because you won't have the reserves if you need them. But it also doesn't look good to overallocate, because the client may think that you are trying to pad your budget or schedule.

Q10. What are contingency reserves on a project?

A10. Essential to project success is setting aside additional funding in the budget, as well as additional time in the schedule, to allow the PM to handle unexpected costs or delays caused by anticipated risks—the known unknowns—coming to pass. This funding is called *contingency reserves,* which is the output of reserve analysis.

PMs can allocate extra funds by breaking them down as line items for each identified risk—for example, allocating $20,000 in case a replacement printer is needed. The line-item method is popular because clients like to see exactly what the risk is and where the money will go if it comes to pass. They also want to know that the money will *not* be spent if the risk doesn't occur.

PMs allocate extra time to the schedule in a similar fashion, and this extra time is also called contingency reserves. To manage the threat of your best technician leaving, you as the PM might allow three extra weeks to recruit, hire, and orient a new technician.

Reserves can also be added as a lump sum—for example, adding $50,000 to the project budget or five extra days to the schedule to manage any risks that arise. Alternatively, they be added as a percentage of the allocated amounts, e.g., 10 percent more money based on the overall budget or 5 percent more time added to the length of the schedule. Finally, reserves can be added, again as either a lump sum or percentage, to specific parts of the budget or schedule, such as the testing phase.

QII. How do management reserves compare to contingency reserves?

A11. Management reserves are large sums of money set aside by a company for large-scale (greater than on the project level) emergencies or changes, such as a damaging fire or a new government regulation that would necessitate major changes in the way the company does business. It would not be feasible for each PM to add huge reserve sums to their project budgets for such scenarios. But it does behoove the PM to know how such funding is allocated in the company and who controls it in an emergency, and to document high-level emergency funding procedures in the risk management plan.

RISK PLANNING

Q12. What are the key processes that a PM uses to plan for risks, and what are their outputs?

A12. As a best practice, the PM works with team members and SMEs to put together several risk-related documents over a five-step sequential planning process. The documents logically flow from one to the next.

In the following Q&As, we will cover them in the order they are created, beginning with the high-level risk management plan and culminating in the detail-driven risk response plan, which will become the key document for helping the PM and team manage risks throughout the project.

The five sequential risk planning processes and the key outputs of each are summarized in Figure 7-1.

1. Planning risk management →	Risk management plan
2. Identifying risks →	Risk breakdown structure (RBS) and risk register
3. Performing qualitative risk analysis →	Updated risk register (including probability and impact matrix and risks sorted into priority order)
4. Performing quantitative risk analysis →	Updated risk register (including expected monetary value for each risk)
5. Planning risk responses →	Risk response plan

Figure 7-1:   The Five Sequential Risk Planning Processes and Their Key Outputs

Note that an additional risk-controlling process, monitoring and controlling risks, is covered later in this chapter (Q&A 33).

Q13. How does a PM get started creating the risk management plan?

A13. The PM begins by compiling all risk-related points from the project charter, including all early risks documented at the inception of the project, as well as key constraints cited in the charter, such as deadlines, budget caps, and hiring issues, that are especially likely to pose risks to success.

The PM then begins outlining the approach and direction that the team will take to manage risks on the project. He or she documents:

- The risk tools, software, and documents that will be used on the project
- The names of the SMEs that the PM and team will consult regarding risks
- The historical information or lessons learned that will be used as references for handling risks
- How often risk will be addressed in team meetings
- Where the issue logs or other risk documents will be kept, such as in databases or on intranet sites, so the team can find and update them
- Risk strategies that will be employed on the project.

IDENTIFYING RISKS

Q14. How are the risks for a project identified, collected, and documented?

A14. Risks can be collected during status meetings, team meetings, by email, or through various communications between the PM and stakeholders.

A very popular way of capturing the key risks to a project is to hold a meeting strictly for this purpose. This is very similar to a requirements gathering meeting: The PM gathers people who can help generate a list of the key risks for their project. The meeting facilitator must skillfully create a safe environment in which stakeholders will not be afraid to say what they're really thinking. An atmosphere of openness is essential if the list of risks is to be comprehensive.

Some of the same tools and techniques used in requirements gathering are also used to elicit risks, especially:

- Brainstorming
- Flipcharts, whiteboards, and smart boards
- Mind maps/idea maps (and sometimes software products to facilitate these techniques).

Q15. Are there any suggestions for getting reluctant team members to talk about risks on their parts of the project?

A15. This is a significant and common problem. PMs must keep in mind that people are often unwilling to speak up about risks, especially in group meetings, sometimes because they worry that it may make them look bad in front of their coworkers. Figure 7-2 offers a few tips for getting team members to speak freely about risks.

Q16. How should the risk questions be framed to get more participation?

A16. Make your questions specific. Rather than asking, "Any risks anyone wants to share?" which may result in your team members looking down at their shoes, try saying: "Before we talk about risks, could everyone think about the triple constraint for a minute—scope, time, and cost—and then talk about parts of your project that might have risk issues in any of those areas."

- **Create an atmosphere in which sharing risks is encouraged or even rewarded.** At the beginning of the meeting, say that you'd like each attendee to mention at least one risk when they give their status. As an incentive, you might offer a free dinner voucher for whoever submits the best risk each month or for whoever takes on the role of project risk manager.

- **Distribute risk identification templates.** Before your meeting, give each attendee a document with fields for filling in new risks that have come up since the last meeting. Making an effort to do this underscores the value of risk-gathering as an ongoing process and encourages people to contribute their ideas.

- **Lead by example.** You can get the ball rolling at a risk meeting by talking about a risk you are grappling with. Make it clear that you do not expect everything to always go perfectly and effortlessly on the project, but the team can help make the project a success by anticipating problems in advance.

- **Don't go overboard.** For example, if you hold weekly status meetings, consider asking your team to hold lower-priority risks until the monthly meetings. A special segment of each monthly meeting should then be devoted to discussing risks.

- **Affirm risk success stories.** Provide occasional time in meetings for team members to share "risk successes," such as cases on the project where they anticipated a problem and nipped it in the bud, saving project time or money. This encourages others on the team to look for similar safeguards and solutions.

Figure 7-2: Tips for Getting Your People to Speak Up about Risks in Team Meetings

This often encourages team members to talk about risk issues they might not have brought up otherwise. For instance, team members may come back with responses such as:

- "For time—well, an issue did come up yesterday that might cause a delay..."

- "For cost... the new designer we hired is working out well, but just to let you know, we wound up having to hire her at a 30 percent higher rate than we had talked about in the kickoff meeting. And this may increase our part of the budget."

- "For scope, the client mentioned at yesterday's review meeting that he wants another new feature added. He said he knows it wasn't part of the original design, but he feels it's necessary anyway."

Q17. What does the risk breakdown structure look like, and how does it help the PM create an effective risk register?

A17. There are two outputs of the process of identifying risks. First, the risk breakdown structure (RBS) is created, followed by the detail-driven risk register. There are many ways to create an RBS, from drawing clouds or boxes on a whiteboard during a meeting to building a hierarchical graphic in Word, like the partial one shown in Figure 7-3. This RBS is similar in look and feel to a WBS.

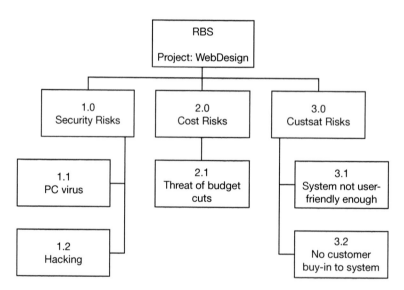

Figure 7-3: Risk Breakdown Structure (RBS) for
a Sample Web Design Project

The entire team contributes to the RBS-building process. To identify the project risks, PMs typically hold a brainstorming session with the team. The visual nature of the RBS and the interactive atmosphere of the session usually encourage team members to freely share risks that come to mind. The PM or appointed facilitator records the risks team members mention on a whiteboard, flip chart, or computer screen, sorts the risks into categories, and creates new groupings on the fly as needed.

In Figure 7-3, three broad categories of risk are shown: data security threats, cost risks, and customer satisfaction- (custsat-) related risks. This RBS is in the early stages—so far, only a few risks are listed. Once the RBS is more complete, the next step is to import the risks by category into the risk register, where they will be further analyzed, prioritized, and elaborated.

Q18. What is the risk register, and what are its key components?

A18. The risk register is the most important output of risk management. The PM takes all the risks identified in the RBS and puts them into list form, usually in a column in an Excel spreadsheet or Word table, and then adds columns for additional data as further research and planning are done.

A sample risk register template is shown below in three parts (Figures 7-4, 7-5, and 7-6).

In our sample template, there are 20 columns altogether. The fields are not all mandatory, and they do not need to be created in the order depicted from left to right. Feel free to omit some of these, add some of your own, and tailor them to your own industry and project.

Note that for the sake of clarity, the Risk ID column is carried down into all three parts of the sample template. In the real world, you would have one combined spreadsheet, and this field would only appear once.

The first four fields in part 1 of the template are basic: numbering, naming, categorizing, and describing each risk in detail. As you can see, if the PM used an RBS to build the list of risks, the first three columns will come from the RBS.

Note that it's a best practice to keep the RBS and risk register in sync (like the schedule, WBS, and WBS dictionary). Updating both outputs as new risks are added throughout the project helps team members see the big picture and also keeps any risks from slipping through the cracks.

The remaining fields in parts 1, 2, and 3 of our sample risk register are the subject of the following Q&As.

Risk ID	Risk Name	Risk Category	Detailed Description	Contingency Plan (Plan A)	Backup Plan (Plan B)	P (Probability from 1–10)	I (Impact from 1–10)	P * I (Probability times impact)
1.1	PC virus	Security				8	5	40
1.2	Hacking	Security				8	8	64
2.1	Budget cuts	Cost				1	10	10
3.1	System not user-friendly enough	Customer satisfaction				2	10	20
3.2	No customer buy-in on system	Customer satisfaction				4	10	40

Figure 7-4: Risk Register Template, Part I
Includes calculation for P * I (probability times impact)

Risk ID	P2 (Probability as a percentage)	I2 (Impact in dollars)	P2 * I2 (Expected monetary value, or EMV)	Cost of Contingency Plan	Cost of Backup Plan	Project or Company's Strength for Handling the Risk
1.1						
1.2						
2.1						
3.1						
3.2						

Figure 7-5:   Risk Register Template, Part 2

Risk ID	Assigned to	Current Status	Steps Being Taken to Avoid This Risk	Notes	Risk Trigger
1.1					
1.2					
2.1					
3.1					
3.2					

Figure 7-6:   Risk Register Template, Part 3

RESPONDING TO RISKS

Q19. What is a contingency plan?

A19. A contingency plan is a plan for what the team would do if a specific risk were to occur. Coming up in advance with a contingency plan for each identified risk is one of the biggest keys to project success. The contingency plan column is probably the most important one in the risk register (See Figure 7-4).

Q20. What is a backup plan, and how does it differ from a contingency plan?

A20. If the contingency plan is the most important part of the risk register, you could say the backup plan, also called the fallback plan, is the second most important. If the first planned response doesn't succeed, the PM should be ready in advance with a clearly documented alternative plan.

Let's say that a football team plans a strong passing game against an opponent. If they come out passing and immediately get intercepted on their first three passes, they must be ready with an alternative strategy, such as a well-practiced running game, as a contingency plan. And if their first few running plays don't provide the needed results, they won't win unless they have a backup plan behind the initial running attack, such as a different offensive line formation.

In RM, when the PM can pull out a second plan, implement it, and solve the predicted risk, it is a very good day.

Q21. What can a PM do if neither the contingency plan nor the backup plan work?

A21. There are two answers (and neither one involves going home and taking a nap!):

- *Workaround.* When you run out of risk response plans, the PM must come up with a new solution on the fly. This is called a *workaround.* As good as your risk planning may be, sometimes the response plans don't work. The ability to recognize (and admit) that the plans aren't working, come up with a creative new solution, and quickly and confidently implement a new solution are all valuable skills for PMs. Hopefully the workaround will succeed where the contingency plan and backup plan failed.

- *Have more than one backup plan.* There's no rule that says that you need to have *only* the one-two punch of a contingency plan and one backup plan. That is a recommended *minimum.* But having several good plans ready to go provides extra safeguards and makes it less likely that you will have to scramble around to establish a workaround on the fly. Depending on the industry, corporate culture, and the nature of your project, some PMs will design several contingency plans for key risks, making their projects that much more secure.

Q22. When is the process of planning risk responses performed, and what is the name of the output?

A22. Identifying and analyzing potential risks and coming up with the plans to handle them—both the contingency and backup plans—comprise the formal PMI process of planning risk responses. The PM often starts planning responses to risks as soon as they are identified, sometimes as early as during the creation of the project charter.

Some PMs begin documenting the contingency plans and backup plans as soon as they've created the risk register. That's why both of these columns are shown in part 1 of our sample template. Once the risk register is complete, some PMs call the spreadsheet the risk response plan; others continue to call this document the risk register.

The exact order in which the PM executes the risk planning processes is a matter of personal preference to some degree, and the processes can overlap. But many PMs prefer to do further analysis after identifying risks and before planning risk responses. Per version 4 of the *PMBOK® Guide* (and as shown in Figure 7-1), two more risk planning processes, performing qualitative risk analysis and performing quantitative risk analysis, should be completed before the process of planning risk responses. The next three columns in the risk register template—probability (P), impact (I), and the P * I formula—take us into the next sequential risk management process: performing qualitative risk analysis.

RISK ANALYSIS

Q23. What exactly is meant by *qualitative risk analysis*?

A23. Qualitative risk analysis sounds very mysterious and complicated, like something George Costanza might go on about on an episode of *Seinfeld*. But the concept is very straightforward. It means prioritizing risks so the team knows in advance how much analysis, effort, and resources to put into each one.

A popular method is to rank each risk, either with a number or with a designation such as *high, low,* or *medium.* Once all the risks have been ranked, the PM later sorts the risk register in order of the priority (or quality) of each risk.

Q24. How do probability and impact come into play in the qualitative risk management process?

A24. A best practice, as shown in Figure 7-4, is to rank each risk for both probability and impact on a scale of 1 to 10.

In our example, the probability of a PC virus (risk 1.1) is judged to be high (8, on a scale of 1 to 10). Also, its potential impact on the project is estimated to be 5 out of 10. Risk 3.1, where the impact of the deliverable being considered is insufficiently user-friendly, is a 10. This may seem to be a very serious risk because if it occurred, it could jeopardize the whole project, but the PM and team estimated the probability of this risk to be only 2 out of 10.

By assigning both a P and an I to each risk, the PM can compare all the risks on the project relative to each other.

Q25. How are these probability and impact numbers used in a formula?

A25. For risk 1.1 (a PC virus), by multiplying the P and I, we get 40, as follows:

$$P * I = 8 * 5 = 40.$$

For risk 3.1 (delivered system is not user-friendly), we get a much lower 20:

$$P * I = 2 * 10 = 20.$$

So even though risk 3.1 has a much higher potential impact (10 compared to 8), its lower probability makes it only half as great a risk, mathematically speaking. The purpose of using the formula is to reveal the threat each risk really poses by showing its combined probability and impact.

To complete our math for the remaining two risks with P and I assigned:

For risk 1.2 (hacking), by multiplying the P and I, we get 64, as follows:

$$P * I = 8 * 8 = 64.$$

For risk 3.2 (no customer buy-in), we get 40:

$$P * I = 4 * 10 = 40.$$

Q26. When and how does the risk register evolve into a probability and impact matrix?

A26. As soon as the P * I formula has been applied to all the risks being considered, the risk register can also be called by a new name—the probability and impact matrix.

Risk ID	Risk Name	P (Probability from 1–10)	I (Impact from 1-10)	P * I (Probability times impact)
1.2	Hacking	8	8	64
1.1	PC virus	8	5	40
3.2	No customer buy-in on system	4	10	40
3.1	System not user-friendly enough	2	10	20
2.1	Budget cuts	1	10	10

Figure 7-7: Probability and Impact Matrix

Figure 7-7 shows how the PM can take the process of qualitative risk analysis one step further by re-sorting the list based on the calculated probability and impact.

- Risk 1.2 (hacking) has the highest P * I (64), so it appears at the top.
- Risks 1.1 and 3.2 tie at 40, so they are shown in the middle of the matrix.
- Risk 3.1, at 20, moves below these three risks.
- Risk 2.1 (budget cuts) gets sorted to the bottom. At only a P * I of 10, it requires the least attention at this time.

Q27. How does quantitative risk analysis differ from qualitative risk analysis?

A27. Quantitative risk analysis is the next sequential risk planning process, per the *PMBOK® Guide*, and it is essentially a drilling down from its similarly named predecessor, qualitative risk analysis. Here the idea is to calculate the effects of each risk in monetary terms.

In Figure 7-5, the second part of the risk register, there are again two columns for probability and impact. We can assume for the sake of our example that the risk register is already sorted, with the greatest risks appearing at the top (as shown in Figure 7-7).

Next, we'll take the original probability numbers for the five risks discussed earlier, sharpen our pencils a little, and refine these numbers into percentages. To differentiate from *P* (used for our qualitative risk analysis), we'll call this probability value P2. A probability of 8 out of 10 might translate to 80 percent; 2 out of 10 would translate directly to 20 percent, but the PM might recalibrate it at 22 percent, possibly taking into account some new information discovered since qualitative analysis was done; and a probability factor of 4 might be reestimated now as 38 percent.

The harder part is to take the original impact for our risks, originally estimated on a scale of 1 to 10, and reestimate them as dollar amounts. We'll call this second impact value I2. In our example, risk 1.1, a PC virus, might shut down our online system for a few hours. The financial impact of that risk might be $50,000. But let's look at risk 3.1. Suppose this is a $1,000,000 project. If the customer doesn't think the system we built is sufficiently user-friendly and wants to cancel the project or cut off funds early, the impact could be significant: perhaps $500,000.

Q28. What is expected monetary value, and how is it used in quantitative risk analysis?

A28. Expected monetary value (EMV) is calculated by multiplying our new probability, P2, by our new impact, I2, for each risk. The formula, then, is P2 * I2.

If we apply the EMV formula to risks 1.1 and 3.1 in our example, we would get the results shown in Figure 7-8.

If we compare these two risks again in light of the new EMV information, risk 3.1 suddenly looks like it may deserve more attention than we originally thought. The PM and team might act accordingly by allocating more resources to researching and planning for this risk.

Risk ID	Risk name	P2 (Probability as a percentage)	I2 (Impact in dollars)	P2 * I2 (Expected monetary value, or EMV)	Original P * I numbers
1.1	PC virus	80%	$50,000	$40,000	40
3.1	System not user-friendly enough	22%	$500,000	$110,000	20

Figure 7-8: Expected Monetary Value for Two Sample Risks

PMs are free to make some style choices when it comes to risk analysis. For example, some PMs and risk managers perform quantitative risk analysis and apply the EMV formula for only the most significant risks selected in the earlier qualitative risk analysis process. This saves time and resources and maintains focus on the key risks. For instance, if the risk identification process produces a list of 75 risks, the PM might whittle the list down to a top ten list through qualitative risk analysis. He or she would then calculate the EMV for just those top 10 risks.

Some PMs and risk managers re-sort the risk register after performing quantitative risk analysis and running the EMV formula. In the probability and impact matrix based on our qualitative risk analysis (Figure 7-7), risk 1.1 (a PC virus) appears higher on the list than risk 1.3 (system not user-friendly). But after drilling deeper into quantitative risk analysis, the PM or RM might decide to move risk 3.1 above risk 1.1 because it has a much higher EMV and is therefore a greater threat to the project's success.

Q29. How does the PM complete the next fields in the risk register, cost of contingency plan and cost of backup plan?

A29. It's important for the PM to have a rough idea of what potential contingency and backup plans would cost the project as part of deciding on these plans. For instance, if a possible contingency plan would be so expensive to implement that it would destroy the project's profit margin (even if it worked), the PM should go back to the drawing board.

That said, these costs are not expected to be estimated in detail the way the other project costs are estimated because with luck, these costs won't be incurred anyway, and you don't want to go overboard detailing the estimates. But the estimates should be as realistic as possible without spending too much time on them. The estimating techniques discussed in Chapters 4 and 5 can all be applied toward estimating the costs of possible contingency and backup plans.

Q30. What is the purpose of the field in the risk register "Project or company's strength for handling the risk," and how is it used?

A30. This field is not as standard as most of the others, but I know of some companies that use it and find it very valuable. To use this method, the PM analyzes how strong the project team would be in handling each risk and records that assessment next to each risk in the risk register. The field is then used as part of the probability and impact calculation. In addition to the two variables, P and I, the PM also assigns a variable called *S* for *strength*. And instead of using a scale of 1 to 10 for P and I, the PM uses a scale of 1 to 5 for all three variables, P, I, and S. The calculation when using three variables looks like this:

$$P * I * S$$
(for **P**robability times **I**mpact times **S**trength).

So instead of a maximum risk score of 100 (10 * 10) as in the basic P * I model, a score can go as high as 125 (5 * 5 * 5) when the strength variable is brought into the mix.

Q31. The next four fields in the risk register all look pretty straightforward. Are there any special points to be aware of?

A31. Here are some key points.

- *Assigned to:* To make sure that risks don't get forgotten, it's good to attach people's names to the risks early on, and generally, it's a best practice to assign a single owner to each risk. This increases direct accountability and also keeps people from delaying each other's work or stepping on each other's toes. The stakeholder assigned to the risk is sometimes called the risk response owner.

- *Current status:* Once the risk register is created, it's important to maintain it as a living document and not think of it as "finished," which can lead to complacency. The PM might update it after each status meeting.

- *Steps being taken to avoid this risk:* A proactive approach is often best. Risk management is largely about planning how to handle risks after they occur, but it's even better to completely *avoid* them if possible. And looking for creative preventative measures helps keep your team focused on risk management as an ongoing part of the project.

- *Notes:* This column is a catchall place to note any additional information you feel is important, such as cross-dependencies a particular risk may have with other risks or with other planned changes, the name of the stakeholder who contributed the risk, and the date the risk was submitted.

Q32. What is a risk trigger, and how is documenting it helpful to the RM process?

A32. A risk trigger is a sign that a risk may be about to occur or is occurring. As soon as the PM notices a trigger, he or she should implement the contingency plan to counter that risk.

Let's return to the risk that the team's lead technician will quit, which, if it occurred, might strongly impact the project. Here are three triggers that could indicate this risk is going to happen:

- A rumor that the team member is looking for a new job starts going around.
- The PM notices that the technician appears to be going to interviews. This is a stronger trigger than a rumor.
- The technician submits her letter of resignation. In our example, this is obviously the definitive trigger. The PM would be ready in advance to respond to it with a contingency plan, such as quickly reassigning the team member's workload to mitigate the impact of the staff member leaving, while also initiating the process of recruiting a replacement.

A PM can take positive action any time a trigger emerges. If the PM in the scenario above thinks the technician may be looking for a new job, he could meet with her to talk about how her work is going and try to make conditions better for her in an effort to retain her, and hopefully he will be able to keep her. He could also take action to better position the team in case the lead technician does leave, by offering thorough cross-training and by documenting as many technical processes as possible.

THE LAST RISK PROCESS: MONITORING AND CONTROLLING RISKS

Q33. What is the process of monitoring and controlling risks, and when is it performed?

A33. Creating a solid risk register complete with risk responses is only half the job of risk management. The PM needs to constantly make sure that the risk plan is up to date, that the documented risks are being watched for, and that when risks do occur, they are being properly handled, as per the plan, and that status updates are recorded.

The team also should always be watching out for new risks and adding them to the risk register as they come up. A popular way to do this is to reserve part of each team meeting or, if feasible, every monthly meeting, for discussion of ongoing and new risks. Of course, team members and other stakeholders should also feel comfortable immediately bringing important risk issues to the PM's attention as they come up.

A FEW MORE IMPORTANT RISK CONCEPTS, TOOLS, AND STRATEGIES

Q34. What are the four strategies for dealing with negative risks (threats)?

A34. There are four widely recognized general strategies for dealing with negative risks: mitigate, avoid, transfer, and accept. Each is defined in Figure 7-9, and examples for all four are provided in the figure, all based on a particular risk: A PM has a fear of flying, but the client has asked him to attend a meeting in a far-off city to discuss the project. The PM is trying to determine how best to handle the request.

Q35. What are the four strategies for dealing with positive risks (opportunities)?

A35. As with negative risk, there are four accepted strategies for dealing with positive risks: exploit, enhance, share, and accept. Each is defined in Figure 7-10. Here, the examples are all based on the same positive risk: A PM is currently managing six projects and has just been told by senior management that one of the six (we'll call it Project A) will likely become key to the company's overall success in the upcoming year.

Q36. What are secondary risks, and how do they relate to risk strategies?

A36. Unfortunately, implementing one risk strategy often causes a new risk to occur. In other words, the solution brings a new problem. For instance, someone afraid of flying might drive to the meeting instead, get lost, and be delayed, or he might have an accident and miss the meeting. Or, if he video-conferences in, the client might be displeased that that the PM didn't attend the meeting in person. In both cases, the success of the project could be impacted, even though the primary risk (fear of air travel) was avoided.

Risk strategy	Definition	Example of each strategy (Based on fear-of-flying scenario)
Mitigate	To take action aimed at reducing: • The probability of the risk occurring • The impact of the risk if it does occur.	• Pick the airline with the best safety record. • Wear your seat belt, and choose a seat by the emergency door.
Avoid	To completely eliminate the risk by taking a different course of action.	Drive to the meeting instead of flying, or videoconference into the meeting.
Transfer	To give the risk to someone else.	Buy flight insurance, which puts the risk (the financial risk, anyway) on the insurance company.
Accept	• To take no action to avoid or mitigate the risk for the time being. • To hope for the best for now, but keep an eye on the risk and be prepared to gear up and take action if the threat increases over time or if other circumstances change—for instance, if technology that could help mitigate the risk becomes more affordable.	Bring a DVD player and a good movie, and do your best to enjoy the flight.

Figure 7-9:   The Four Strategies for Dealing with Negative Risks (Threats)

The fact is that every action can have unintended consequences. So it behooves PMs to be all the more careful about analyzing and selecting the best possible risk mitigation strategies they can, to increase the odds that the risks out there in the world won't negatively impact their projects.

Q37. What are residual risks?

A37. Even after actions are taken to mitigate a risk, the threat sometimes still remains (like the *residue* of a drink in a glass—hence the name *residual!*).

Risk strategy	Definition	Example (Based on the scenario of the PM managing six projects)
Exploit	Taking strong, proactive action to eliminate the uncertainty around an opportunity by doing everything possible to make it happen.	The PM takes some of the best team members from each of the other five projects and puts them on Project A.
Enhance	Analyzing the underlying drivers behind each risk and doing whatever is possible to positively influence each one.	The PM analyzes the various aspects that appear to be key to the success of Project A and carefully tweaks each one. For instance, the PM could facilitate advanced training to an engineer on the critical path.
Share	Instead of taking on an opportunity alone, partnering or merging with another team or company, pooling resources with another department, scheduling meetings with another PM to exchange ideas, among other collaborative actions.	The PM subcontracts some of the work of Project A to an industry-leading consulting firm to take advantage of the firm's superior expertise in areas key to the project.
Accept	Taking no action for now, but keeping an eye on possibly pursuing the opportunity in the future. Perhaps the opportunity will become more appealing later, easier to obtain, or more important to the project.	The PM continues to manage the six projects with no immediate changes, but is watchful and alert to the possibility that the focus on Project A may require a change in priorities. The PM is open to that change.

Figure 7-10: The Four Strategies for Dealing with Positive Risks (Opportunities)

Suppose that to avoid the general threat of computer viruses attacking your laptop, you install the world's best protection software. But even with this software in place, there is always the lurking threat of a new virus that could get past your defenses and infect your system. So the risk of potential harm to your project remains, even though you took appropriate action to mitigate it.

A best practice for residual risks is to create what is called a *watch list*. List all of the residual risks in a particular file that stakeholders can access and monitor to see if the risks' priority or likelihood changes over time. Alternatively, some PMs designate residual risks as such on the risk register, for instance in the "Notes" field.

Q38. How do SWOT analysis and the SWOT diagram help a PM make risk-related decisions?

A38. Before deciding how seriously to take a threat (negative risk) or how many resources to invest in an opportunity (positive risk), it's important to measure the risk in two ways: how large it is, and how strong or weak your team or company is at handling that kind of risk. A technique called SWOT (strength, weakness, opportunities, and threats) analysis can be a helpful tool for measuring risks, and it works equally well for both positive and negative risks.

SWOT analysis is often done using what's called a SWOT diagram, which can be drawn on a whiteboard, on paper, or using a software tool. The diagram is shaped like a square with four quadrants, as shown in Figure 7-11. The idea is to rate each risk in two ways—on its size and on the team's capability of handling it, plot the rating points on the SWOT diagram, and then see where the risk falls in the grid.

- *Opportunities* are rated on the size of the benefits they would bring, as well as on the project team's or company's relative ability (strength or weakness) to support that opportunity and make it succeed. The best opportunities would fall in the upper right-most corner of the upper-right quadrant, as shown, because:
  - o Their benefits would be large
  - o The team or company also has significant strengths to support that opportunity.
- *Threats* are rated on how much danger they pose, and again, on the company's or team's relative ability (again, strength or weakness) to handle that threat. The worst threats—those that are severe and that the company or team does not have a strong capacity to handle—would fall in the lower left-most corner of the lower left quadrant.

SWOT analysis can be done early on when risks are first identified and later, as ongoing analysis is done to determine the relative size of each risk through qualitative and quantitative risk analysis.

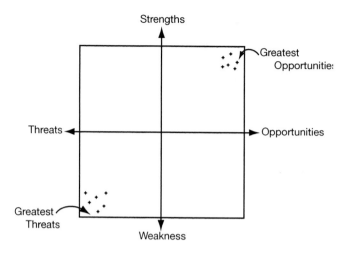

Figure 7-11: SWOT Diagram

Q39. How can Monte Carlo tools help the PM with risk management?

A39. Many software tools can help PMs and risk managers analyze and identify risks. The tools, which can crunch numbers very rapidly, are called Monte Carlo tools, named after the famed casino in Monaco. Monte Carlo tools are commonly used for analyzing complex project schedules. The tools can scan the paths and identify schedule risks that might not be apparent to the human eye.

Q40. What is the correlation between assumptions and risks?

A40. Assumptions and risks are closely related. Often, when an assumption is made on a project, a risk can hinge on whether the assumption will turn out to be true or not. An example is the assumption that a project will receive the full funding stated in the requirements. Suppose that $500,000 is the estimate for a project, and the funds are expected to be disbursed over a six-month period. But if there is some doubt that the full $500K will be disbursed, this project is under a cost risk. And if less than the full $500K is actually disbursed, the project could be put at risk in several ways. Among other possible risks, it could be at risk of coming in late (schedule risk) or of not meeting the agreed-upon quality level or scope.

A strong understanding that such assumptions can lead to risks can play a key role in the success of a project. For that reason, assumptions, along with risks, are often documented early on in the project charter. They are sometimes carried over and continually updated in the risk register, perhaps in the "Notes" field or in their own "Assumptions" field if preferred.

TOP TEN PROJECT RISK MANAGEMENT PITFALLS

1. Insufficient risk planning. This is the killer. Many projects develop severe problems or fail because the PM does not adequately plan for risk. Sometimes overconfidence in the project is to blame, but often, management asserts that there aren't enough resources to try to address risks that may not even happen. It is up to the PM to push for the degree of RM he or she believes is necessary to ensure the success of the project.

2. Insufficient funding. Even when the PM has the best intentions and wants to provide for risk management on a project, management may deny the request for resources or funding. The PM should not fail to push back. He or she can prevail by making a convincing case that risk management is in the best interest of the client and the project. It's hard to argue with that!

3. Overly bureaucratic risk planning. Some PMs get so carried away with risk planning that they truly go overboard. Risk management can be a waste of time and resources if done to the extreme. When risks occur, crisp, clean solutions are needed, not mountains of paperwork.

4. Planning for the sake of planning (for the auditors' benefit). Unfortunately, PMs sometimes create risk plans that are not really actionable but that exist largely for the purpose of showing them to an auditor or senior management. Also known as paper plans or plans in a drawer.

5. Analysis paralysis. A team may have created, or at least discussed, good contingency plans, but sometimes when problems arise, the stakeholders can't agree on how to respond. Solid planning is the key. A risk response plan (part of the baseline project plan) should be agreed on in advance and ready to go in case of emergency.

6. Insufficient testing. Backing up your data but failing to test whether it can be quickly and rapidly restored is one example. Contingency plans should always be tested in advance when possible. In the case of

Hurricane Katrina, there were documented evacuation procedures, but they were not sufficiently tested. Doing evacuation drills in advance might have exposed flaws in those plans, which may have saved lives later.[1]

7. Not assigning a single owner to each risk. Assigning a single owner to each risk is a best practice because it best ensures that the risks are handled. A risk owner column appears in the risk register template in this chapter.

8. Not looking in advance for lessons learned. When it comes to risk management, trying to reinvent the wheel can be more than a waste of resources—it can mean a failed project.

9. Not sufficiently challenging assumptions. Even if assumptions are identified as such, they often go unquestioned far into a project's life cycle. For example, you might assume that the bugs in a vendor's early version of a software product will be fixed in the production version by the time your project critically needs the software. This often turns out not to be the case, as vendors may have other customers and priorities, and a fix that is key to you may get lost in the shuffle. If the project requires that certain bugs be fixed, you can't rely on an assumption. You must be proactive about pushing for the fixes to get done.

10. Complacency. Complacency is the single biggest enemy of risk management. People tend to get all bent out of shape when a disaster happens, demanding explanations and clamoring for protection from future occurrences. But inevitably, other priorities come up and entropy sets in once more, and it becomes difficult to justify putting resources into risk management. But a good PM is willing to do what's right for the project and not just what's popular.

Note

1. For more information on insufficient testing of evacuation procedures, see Jeff Furman, "Advance Disaster Planning: A Q&A with Three Senior Risk Managers on How Preparedness Is Changing after the Hurricanes of 2005," *Technical Support Magazine* (March 2006).

CHAPTER 8

Procurement and Contracts

The decisions a PM makes about procurement and contracts can be the most important on any project. Deciding which customer deliverables will be procured from outside vendors versus which will be built by the team (called the buy-or-build decision) can be a highly significant factor in a project's success. Equally important are the choices the PM makes about which sellers will be selected from the vast world of vendors.

The right contract also can make or break a project. The specific terms of a contract can either put a project in a secure position or in one of high risk. And the type of contract you choose also can impact success, either by shielding the project from risk or by exposing the project to greater risk.

The procurement and contract processes tie heavily into all of the other PM knowledge areas. For instance, the vendor the PM chooses for procurement directly affects the quality of the final deliverables, while the terms of the contracts the PM arranges with sellers can be the single biggest factor in determining whether the project comes in on scope, on time, and ultimately, on budget.

Whether your PM work places you on the customer side or the seller's side, this chapter will answer many questions about procurement and contracts that can help you on your projects.

PROCUREMENT

Q1. What are the keys for a successful procurement on a project?

A1. There are several important factors:

- First, solid requirements gathering and scope definition are essential, so that the PM will know exactly what must be procured and contracted for.

- Second, it is essential for the PM to give very clear specifications to the procurement and legal people to make sure that the procurement documents explain exactly the goods and services that must be acquired. Care must be taken in putting together all of the descriptive documents that will be used in the procurement process, such as the request for proposal and statement of work (discussed later in this chapter).

- Deciding *how* you will choose your vendors—whether through a request for proposal process, a bidder's conference, or some other method—is key.

- Checking up on references is not a new idea, but it is a critical one. Just as you would put time and care into choosing a service provider such as a dentist to a baby-sitter in your personal life, put the necessary effort into checking the references of vendors for your (multimillion-dollar, important) project.

- Finally, choosing the best vendor to fit your project is a key decision. It is normal, especially in a tight economy, to want to put cost above quality. But choosing a vendor solely based on cost is almost always the wrong decision. If the project doesn't achieve its quality goals, the customer will not be happy in the end, and the project won't be seen as a success.

Q2. What are the keys for successfully managing the legal side of a project?

A2. Here are some important legal aspects.

- ***Selecting the right attorney.*** A PM often has more control in choosing the contract attorney for a project than he or she may realize. This is a key decision that can affect how effective the contract will be and thus the success of the project. Even in a large organization in which many lawyers and managers are involved, PMs often can request a specific lawyer based on the technical needs of the project. Lawyers vary a great deal in experience and background, and you as the PM should always try to ask for the most qualified attorney to handle the specific needs of your project. (If you don't ask, you don't get!)

- ***Strong involvement in the legal process.*** It's essential for the PM to be as involved as necessary with the legal processes on any project. The PM knows best what will make the project succeed for the client, and by working closely with the lawyers, the PM can ensure that the goals and best interests of the project are protected. Sometimes lawyers may have their own agenda, conflicting with the project's. In other cases, senior management wants to bring other issues or products into a negotiation with a vendor that can slow down or hinder your contract. The PM does not want to *oppose* legal or senior management but should maintain an active presence to make sure the project's priorities are best represented in the process.

Q3. What is a recommended approach for working with vendors on contracts?

A3. The expression "You can attract more flies with honey than with vinegar" strongly applies here. In my experience, I have achieved very good results consistently by treating vendors as business partners (not as the bad guy) and going for cooperation and shared goals, rather than trying to bully them as many customers do (because as the customer, they can).

- *On negotiations:* Treating vendors fairly is particularly important in contract negotiations. I can attest that in many cases, I gained more for our clients by being fair with the vendors than I believe we would have by playing hardball.

- *On day-to-day contract administration:* My team often worked closely with our vendors to help them identify and fix any bugs we encountered in new software. When the vendor supplied fixes for the bugs, we often would test the vendor's fixes in our environment, and when we confirmed that they worked, we would notify the vendor ASAP. This was mutually beneficial. It helped us because it sped up the process of getting a certified fix into production in our environment, and it also helped the vendor because our testing verified that the vendor's fix would also work for its other customers. By doing this, we were able to build goodwill with the vendor on that project as well as future efforts.

Q4. Why is it critical for a PM to push the legal department for a win-win negotiation?

A4. The PM should proactively work to foster a positive relationship between the legal people on both the customer and the vendor side. This is because in any procurement/contract situation, the best long-term results are attained when there is a win-win: both companies feel satisfied that the contract is fair.

One might say that some lawyers like to shoot for a win-lose with a contract that is good for their side and bad for the other. But this can be a Pyrrhic victory, or an instance of winning the battle and losing the war. Vendors who wind up on the wrong side of a bad contract often will try to find ways to get back at the other side—for example, by doing the bare minimum specified in the contract instead of sending their best people to do the best job for your customer. This is why the PM should push for a win-win—a situation in which both sides will be happy and productive. Going for a win-win can make a big difference in the likelihood of the project succeeding and can also pay long-term dividends for the vendor in the form of future business with the customer and referrals for more business.

Q5. From a procurement/contracts perspective, what are some of the most favored best practices today for saving money on projects?

A5. Two of the biggest ways to save money are by making the right buy-or-build decisions (covered later in this chapter) and creating a well-planned, well-crafted contract. There are many other ways to keep project costs down, but if you as the PM didn't make the right choices about what to procure with which sellers and didn't sign a good contract, all other cost-cutting efforts will feel like working with one hand tied behind your back.

Other common cost-saving measures include outsourcing and virtual teams.

- *Outsourcing* work to places with cheaper labor and materials costs, such as India and China, can save money, but outsourcing brings many management challenges and is not necessarily a silver bullet. (See more on outsourcing in Chapter 11.)

- *Virtual teams.* Often linked with outsourcing; a PM in one office manages people in different locations, often overseas. Virtual teams also pose many management challenges, discussed in detail in Chapter 11, but they can bring cost savings, as well as many other benefits, if managed well, so this method is worth considering.

CONTRACTS AND CONTRACT TYPES

Q6. What is the definition of a contract, and what makes for a good contract?

A6. A contract is a legally binding agreement between two parties, where one side (the seller) agrees to do some kind of specified work (creating goods or services—the deliverables), and the other side (the buyer, or customer) commits to reimbursing the seller for the work. The reimbursement is, of course, usually monetary, but occasionally contracts can spell out other terms, such as barter, in which goods or services are traded off for each other.

In the PM world, a contract is almost always a written document, signed by both buyer and seller, and often cosigned by the legal teams representing both sides (though verbal contracts can also be valid and binding). Once a contract is signed, both parties are legally obligated to follow their share of the terms or else be subject to possible legal action. The seller must complete the work per the stated time frame and other specifications, and the buyer must reimburse the seller per the agreed-upon amount and documented payment schedule.

A good contract is clear, precise, thorough, and also fair. It specifies exactly what both parties need to agree on in order to get the work done properly and to the customer's satisfaction. And its language protects both parties from being taken advantage of by the other. (A contract that is clearly one-sided, favoring one party over the other, is not only unfair but, also, will probably not yield the best results.)

Q7. What exactly is a concession on a contract?

A7. A concession is something one side (usually the customer) is asking to be added into the contract that would not otherwise be provided. As the word implies, concessions usually mean that one side must give in to accommodate a strong need on the other side.

Because the party being asked to grant the concession generally has some interest in not granting it, a couple of key principles generally apply:

- If you ask for too many concessions, you may not get the most important ones, so choose carefully which ones are really worthwhile. If a concession from the other side is really worth it to you, be prepared to give something up in return.

- Sometimes people unintentionally ask for a concession that is truly unfair to the other side, and this can derail a contract if the asking side is too rigid about the request. When possible, it's best to be willing to see the other side's point of view. If the concession you're asking for is really not feasible, or is counter to the other side's interests, be ready to accept a no for the greater good of the project.

Q8. What are maintenance and expenses on a contract?

A8. Many contracts, such as for those for software, whether it is purchased or custom-built, come with maintenance and expenses—commonly called M&E—clauses. They usually involve an annual fee for continued support of the system after the build project has been completed. For instance, if the customer is charged $300,000 for the build, there may be an M&E charge of 5 percent annually, or $15,000 per year.

The customer should watch out for hidden M&E charges that it might not realize are part of the contract. Some vendors also try to put in graduating M&E charges—for example, none the first year, 5 percent the second year, and 7 percent the third year. These can often be negotiated to a fixed rate or a capped charge, which can be a significant savings for the customer.

Q9. What is a boilerplate contract?

A9. It is the standard contract a seller/vendor offers to clients. Vendors will try to get an unsuspecting or naïve customer to sign their boilerplate contract, often saying things like, "All our customers sign this standard agreement," or "Don't worry, it covers everything. We've done a lot of these." Signing a boilerplate contract is almost always a very bad idea for the customer because it doesn't take the customer's specific needs into account. If you showed one to a lawyer on your side, he or she would probably not let you sign it.

Q10. Does the PM need to be concerned about the specific contract type, or is that best left to the lawyers?

A10. While this decision is usually made by the lawyers, the contract type can play an important role in the success of a project, so it's good for the PM to be very aware of the specific types and sometimes to play an active role in choosing one. Many PMs are not aware that some contract types inherently carry more risk for one side or the other (buyer versus seller). The contract type can place one side at a disadvantage, just as any clause within a contract can benefit one side over the other.

Q11. What are the two main categories of contract types usually used on projects, and which are lower risk for the buyer versus the seller?

A11.

- *Fixed price (FP):* Also called firm fixed-price (FFP) or lump sum contract. Here the buyer and seller agree in advance to a set fee for the project, which is then put down in writing in the contract. Generally, this is better for the buyer (less risk) because no matter how long the project takes, the buyer will only pay the agreed-upon amount. This means that if the work winds up taking a lot longer than planned, the seller is at a great risk; because time is money, the seller will lose even if it receives the full payment.

- *Cost plus (CP):* Here, payment is open-ended because the buyer is agreeing in advance to pay whatever *costs* the seller incurs on the project, *plus* an additional fee. This contract type heavily favors the seller because the longer it takes on the project, the more money it will receive. This clearly puts the buyer directly at risk because the costs are uncertain. But there are ways of mitigating the buyer's risk on CP contracts, including adding price caps, incentive clauses for getting the job done faster or meeting other metrics, penalty clauses that punish the seller for finishing late, or a point of total assumption clause (discussed in Q&A 42 in this chapter).

Q12. What are the most common contract types within the fixed-price and cost-plus categories?

A12. These are the most common.

Fixed Price

- *Fixed price or firm fixed price:* The general fixed price contract described in Q&A 11.
- *Fixed price incentive fee (FPIF):* A fixed price combined with an incentive fee: The seller will receive a bonus for finishing early or surpassing other metrics agreed upon in advance, such as quality. Incentives can be win-win for buyer and seller. They help motivate the seller to finish faster, which is good for the buyer, and also reduce the risk that the seller will work longer for less.
- *Fixed price economic price adjustment (FPEPA):* Here the buyer agrees in advance that it will adjust the pay rate to changes in economic conditions, such as:
  o Cost of labor or materials
  o Fluctuations in currency rate conversions
  o Inflation.

This contract type also mitigates some of the risk on the seller.

Cost Plus

- *Cost plus, cost reimbursable, or cost plus fixed price (CP, CRP, or CPFP):* This is the common cost-plus contract: The buyer reimburses the seller for costs and pays the seller a fixed fee. As noted in Q&A 11, the cost-plus category of contracts generally is more favorable to the seller because the costs are open-ended. This implicitly gives the seller an incentive to take longer, unless other language in the contract is added in to motivate the seller to work faster, mitigating the risk on the buyer.

- *Cost plus award fee (CPAF):* This is a unique contract type under which the customer will cover the seller's costs, plus it will award an amount of additional money based largely on the customer's assessment of how well the seller performed. The amount of the award can be up to the buyer or can be based on metrics that were agreed upon and specified in the contract.

- *Cost plus percentage of costs (CPP):* Here the vendor is reimbursed for all costs, plus a percentage of all costs. (This is loosely referred to as *double-dipping*.) The percentage is flat, so the fee owed rises in direct proportion to the costs. So if the costs are $1 million and the percentage is 10 percent, the percentage on those costs would be $100,000, for a total of $1,100,000. But if the costs balloon to $2 million, the percentage on those costs would become 10 percent of $2 million, or $200,000, for a total of $2,200,000—double the original costs, plus the percentage.

  A CPP is basically considered a bad contract type from the buyer's perspective because it puts the buyer at risk of being taken advantage of by the vendor, who has a double incentive to stretch out the schedule. If this type of contract is required for some business reason, putting in a cap to prevent costs from going over a strictly specified limit is the customer's best defense. If possible, buyers should avoid this contract type whenever possible. Note that some U.S. government agencies are strictly prohibited from getting into this contract situation as a customer.

Q13. Why is the time and materials contract in its own category?

A13. Conceptually, time and materials (T&M) contracts are similar to cost-plus contracts—here again, the buyer is paying the seller's costs at an agreed-upon rate for the seller's time, plus the seller's costs for materials. T&M is very useful for smaller projects and for contracts in certain industries, such as construction, in which projects may be fairly standard, so more complicated contract types are not necessary. T&M is also a popular choice whenever both parties prefer a quick contract to save resources.

Like cost-plus contracts, T&M contracts inherently hold more risk for the buyer because the units of time and materials are not strictly specified, and so they are open-ended, which is a disincentive for the seller to hurry. Buyers would generally try to avoid T&M contracts, but in many cases getting a contract finalized quickly and signed outweighs the risk of entering an open-ended agreement.

THE STATEMENT OF WORK

Q14. What is a statement of work (SOW)?

A14. The SOW is the document created by the customer that will specify for the vendor, or potential vendor, what the customer wants done on the project—what goods it wants created or what services it wants performed. The SOW can be fully detailed or more high level. It can be very similar to the scope statement created internally by the project team, but translated into what the customer wants the vendor to see. It often also includes timelines for getting the work done.

On projects where a request for proposal (RFP) or similar documents (a request for information or quotation) are sent out to potential sellers, the SOW is often included as a companion document, providing the technical detail of the customer's requirements. This helps the vendor determine what questions and areas to address in its proposal to show the customer that it is capable of properly delivering the project results.

Q15. What are the three common types of SOW?

A15. There are three typical SOW types, differentiated by the level of detail that goes into describing the customer's requirements. They are described below in ascending order of customer knowledge about the project. The best position for the customer to be in is #3 (design level) to prevent the vendor from having the upper hand in contract negotiations. The three types are:

- *Performance SOW, "the problem":* Here the customer has the least amount of knowledge. It has a rough idea of what it wants as a final deliverable but not much knowledge about how the work would be performed. This type of SOW is called "the problem" because the customer knows the problem it wants solved, but not much technically about the solution the vendor will need to come up with. This is the least desirable of the three positions for the customer to be in because the vendor can potentially take advantage of the customer on the contract and later on the project. If you as the customer find yourself in a situation like this, hiring a subject matter expert to at least help with the negotiations may be worthwhile. You'll spend a little to potentially save a lot.

- *Functional SOW, "the features":* The customer knows much more specifically what it wants—more so than with a performance SOW—and can list the features in good detail of the desired deliverable.

- *Design SOW, "the blueprint level":* Here the customer knows exactly what it wants and a lot about how to build it. The customer could probably do the work on its own but is choosing to outsource it.

Q16. How does an SOW differ from a contract?

A16. The SOW can be a companion document to a contract, or it can be considered a contract in itself.

- *As a companion artifact to a contract:* Often, an SOW is created to be sent out to potential sellers along with an RFP. Sellers analyze the SOW to see if they can adequately perform the work of the contract and send back a proposal to the customer. Once a seller wins the project, a formal contract is created and signed by both companies. The SOW often is retained as an artifact and becomes an attachment to the contract.

- *As a contract itself:* Sometimes an SOW is created, shared with the vendor, duly signed by the customer and the vendor, and used to guide the project. A formal contract is never created—the SOW is used in lieu of one. It is considered a legally binding agreement, and for all practical purposes, it becomes the contract for the project.

BIDDING AND EVALUATION

Q17. What does a PM need to know about the bidding process?

A17. Sometimes it is advantageous to open a procurement up to bidding. The customer side will offer some, or all, of a contract to be done by an outside vendor, and various sellers are given the opportunity to compete for the work. Usually, price is the key issue; vendors submit offers, and the lowest number wins, like at an auction. But in many cases criteria other than sheer price determines the outcome in a bid.

A formal written document, called an invitation to bid, is sent out to potential bidders. Bids are sometimes submitted by mail or email, but the bidding process itself often is done through a bidder's conference, where various potential vendors are gathered at a hotel or conference center, presentations are given by the customer, and bids are offered live at the site. There are strict rules governing the bidding process to maintain fairness. PMs have a strong obligation to maintain a level playing field for all invited bidders. It's especially important not to share any information with one bidder that could put them at an advantage over the others.

The key to a good bidding process is that before vendors are invited to submit their bids, the PM takes care to prequalify the bidders to make sure that their services will be considered acceptable if they win the bid. This is done through:

- Carefully researching and vetting potential bidders in advance
- Limiting the potential bidders to only those listed on an approved sellers list, in some cases (see Q&A 35 in this chapter)
- Constructing evaluation criteria (see Q&A 19).

Q18. What is a sealed bid, and when is it useful in the bidding process?

A18. A sealed bid is what it sounds like: The bid price a seller is offering for its services is literally sealed inside an envelope, and no one can see the contents until the customer is ready to open all of the bids at the same time, preserving confidentiality. Often, a witness must be present along with the contract officer opening up the bids to keep the process kosher and make sure the bids are handled properly.

An underlying reason for doing a sealed bidding process is that the buyer may not want to look at the bid price right away. It might want to look at various vendor proposals first to see which vendor appears to be the most qualified. After narrowing the bidders down, from, say, ten bidders to three, the buyer might open the sealed bids and just look at the price quotes from the final group of three. This way, the buyer lets the qualifications of the sellers be the primary consideration and the bid price the secondary factor, as opposed to bid situations in which the cost of the bids is the key consideration.

Q19. How do PMs create evaluation criteria, and what are weighted evaluation criteria?

A19. A best practice is to formally create a set of evaluation criteria in advance of a bidding process or an RFP/proposal process. This is another situation in which putting a little more effort into the planning can yield much better results for your customer. Instead of simply reading a number of vendor proposals, the PM should first create a solid set of evaluation criteria that the customer and other key stakeholders agree with.

This document might be a top ten list of features the customer cares most about, out of many more potential features. Or it might include two lists, a mandatory list and a wish list. The mandatory list would contain the features the vendor absolutely must provide; the wish list might include features that would be nice to have. Vendors' ability to provide features on the wish list may be a determining factor when the PM later tries to differentiate among the vendors and choose one.

A popular and convenient way to compile information on vendors' capabilities is to create a spreadsheet. The criteria are listed in one column, and each vendor is given its own column. Based on each vendor's proposal, the proposal evaluators rate the vendor by scoring it on how well it meets each criterion. Some companies find it very helpful to create a weighting system, where a multiplication factor is used to place more value on some features over others. For instance, if the customer is most focused on five features out of 20, whatever rating each vendor receives on those five features might be multiplied by 3, boosting the scores of the vendors who excel in those five categories.

THE BUY-OR-BUILD DECISION

Q20. What is *buy-or-build analysis*, and what are the most significant factors in a PM's decision to buy or build?

A20. Buy-or-build analysis, also known as make-or-buy analysis, is the research and decision-making process a PM goes through before deciding to contract with one or more vendors for a product or service or build the product or service internally, using the company's own people. If the customer decides to make its own product, that's called *build*, but if the customer decides to procure a product or service from a vendor (seller) instead, that's called *buy*, which results in procurement.

Q21. What are the benefits of building as opposed to buying?

A21. Building:

- May be cheaper
- Is more customizable
- Creates buy-in from within the company, avoiding the "not invented here" syndrome, which can block acceptance of a product within a company. (See Chapter 12, Q&A 47, for more about this pitfall.)

Q22. What are the benefits of buying as opposed to building?

A22. There can be many benefits to buying a product from a vendor, rather than making your own. These include:

- *A stronger guarantee of getting the work done.* Buying from a reliable, well-known vendor that is unlikely to go out of business and that you can investigate in advance by gathering customer references is often much less risky than building your own product. Unfortunately, PMs take a chance and venture into unknown territory when trying to build a solution for the first time. Key people can quit the project or be reassigned, internal priorities can and frequently do change, and the creation of a new system can prove much more complex than estimated.

- *A more solid estimate.* A quoted estimate from a substantial vendor is a number you can trust, especially if the vendor has delivered this product or service already to other customers—its cost and time estimates are based on already-proven numbers. If your own internal people are creating a product for the first time, their price estimate may be very inaccurate, and therefore may put the project at schedule risk, budget risk, or both.

Q23. Why is there lower risk in many ways when buying from a vendor, rather than building your own product?

A23. Focusing on the level of risk is often a way of justifying a buy over a build. Generally, risks *can* be lower on a buy for two reasons:

- *Been there, done that.* Buying from a reliable, well-known vendor who has already done the kind of work you are looking for is obviously safer than having your team plunge into the unknown, experimenting in a new area for the first time. The longer the vendor has been in business, and the more you trust it to stay in business, the lower the risk.

- *More solid estimates,* as detailed in the previous Q&A.

Q24. How does corporate culture figure into buy-or-build decisions?

A24. Corporate culture (a subset of what the *PMBOK® Guide* calls "enterprise environmental factors") can factor heavily into this kind of PM decision. If you, as the PM, work for a company or client where there is a strong preference toward either buying or building, make sure that you are aware of this preference, regardless of which option you will ultimately choose. For example, if your company tends to outsource software builds, but you want to build your own system as part of your project, you might choose to do what the company prefers, if you determine that building is not worth fighting the battle. If you do decide to swim against the corporate tide and build the system, you should be prepared to make a very strong case for why it is worth building for this project.

Q25. Why are historical information and lessons learned especially useful when making a buy-or-build decision?

A25. Doing a little quick research into what other PMs have done when faced with similar situations is often a great starting point and a great way to save money on your project. It's usually pretty easy to obtain this kind of information by simply asking the vendors for references about their recent similar work on other projects. When trying to make the buy-or-build decision, PMs should ask:

- Were other companies successful at building similar products?
- Are successful vendor solutions out on the market?
- How satisfied are customers who bought the vendor solutions?
- How much money, if any, did the outsourced product or service actually save those companies, compared to the probable cost of in-house solutions?

Q26. How can the expected monetary value (EMV) formula help a PM make and justify a buy-or-build decision?

A26. One way to grapple with the unknowns of a buy-or-build decision is to try to quantify the decision using the EMV formula (see Chapter 7,

Q&A 28). In procurement management, the biggest decision you must make is often whether to create your own product internally or to outsource it. This decision can have a huge impact on the entire project's success. The EMV formula can help by showing you which choice will yield the higher positive dollar value.

For example, contrast the following buy-or-build scenarios. You are a PM in a factory, and you are planning either to buy a new system for producing your company's product line or to build your own new system as an upgrade to your existing equipment, using your company's engineers and technicians.

- *Buy:* Your up-front analysis leads you to an estimate that the vendor solution would have a very high chance of success: 80 percent. This also means it would have a chance of failure of 20 percent.

- *Build:* You determine that if your own people build the new system as an upgrade to the existing setup, the work would be less likely to get done on time, and it also might not contain as many high-quality features. The vendor product is robust and has already been out on the market for more than a year. So you estimate a higher risk of failure, 35 percent, equating to a 65 percent chance of success.

Your senior management estimates that with either solution, if the project fails, your company will lose some $2,000,000 in revenue after the first year because the new system won't be up and running. These numbers can be fed into the EMV formula, per Figure 8-1.

From the point of view of potential cost of failure, the buy looks like the much safer decision because it has a significantly lower risk cost: −$400,000 EMV compared with −$700,000 EMV on the build/upgrade in this example.

The Cost of Failure If the Buy Fails	The Cost of Failure If the Build/ Upgrade Fails
Buy EMV = probability of failure * impact	Build EMV = probability of failure * impact
Buy EMV = 20% * −$2,000,000	Build EMV = 35% * −$2,000,000
Buy EMV = −$400,000	Build EMV = −$700,000

Figure 8-1: Using Expected Monetary Value (EMV) to Help Make a Buy-or-Build Decision

Q27. How can a decision tree help a PM make decisions, and how can EMV be used to build a decision tree?

A27. A good buy-or-build decision must factor in the purchase price of the buy versus the internal costs of the build. This is where a decision tree comes in. It works hand-in-hand with EMV.

- **Buy:** You've been given a quote from the vendor for $800,000.
- **Build:** Your team's estimate for the internal build is $550,000.

Figure 8-2 is a decision tree showing which path looks like it will be more cost-effective based on your best estimates.

The buy path (top) shows the up-front purchase price of $800,000, and the EMV of the cost of failure, as determined in the previous Q&A, is −$400,000. Adding these two costs, the diagram depicts the total cost of this path as:

$$\text{Purchase price} + \text{EMV of cost of failure} = -\$800,000 + -\$400,000 = \\ -\$1,200,000.$$

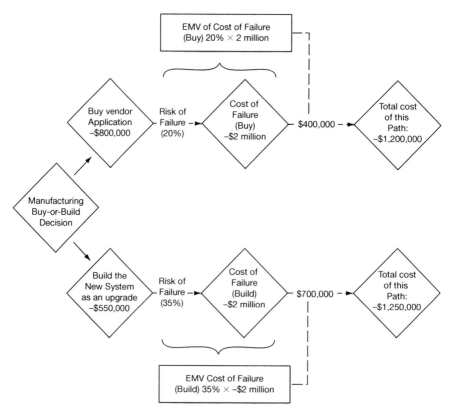

Figure 8-2:   Buy or Build Decision Tree

The build path (bottom) shows the lower internal cost of –$550,000, but combined with a higher EMV cost of failure of –$700,000, the calculation is:

$$\text{Build price (estimate)} + \text{EMV of cost of failure} = -\$550,000 + \\ -\$700,000 = -\$1,250,000.$$

The buy still looks like the better decision, but the numbers are now much closer.

It's important to keep the following recommendations in mind when doing EMV and decision-tree analysis:

- **Don't be ruled by the numbers.** Remember that the numbers are derived from estimates, which are always based on variables and assumptions. This means that your EMV numbers are estimates in a sense as well. So you always want to question the numbers behind the numbers. Don't be afraid to let your experience and intuition play a part in your decisions.

- **Don't forget the intangibles.** If building your own system lets you tailor the deliverable better to the client, which might lead to increased customer satisfaction, that in itself could be a reason to do the build, even if the numbers lean slightly the other way. Another intangible is morale—teams often work better when they are building the system themselves, because they take more pride in doing original, unique work. Try to consider which intangibles might be most impactful when making buy-or-build decisions.

- **Look for side benefits.** Doing EMV/decision-tree analysis often forces all the team members to make more thoughtful, accurate estimates. Focusing, for instance, on the relative risks of the buy can sometimes force all the team members to drill deeper to consider the relative functionality benefits that the vendor solution might bring. As the different sides defend their respective positions, a deeper and more thorough analysis often emerges as a side benefit.

- **Don't just look at the threats.** You can use EMV/decision-tree analysis to factor in potential opportunities as well. In the example depicted in Figure 8-2, the PM could add branches coming off the buy and build paths that represent the varying profits expected from each. For example, if the vendor solution has the potential to bring in $5 million in profit, but the build/upgrade solution has the potential to bring in only $3 million, that would tilt the scales heavily toward the vendor solution. Here the decision tree can make a difference, because people often overly focus on the costs of each choice without considering potential gains.

SOLE SOURCE VERSUS SINGLE SOURCE PROCUREMENT

Q28. What is *sole source procurement*, and how should it factor into a PM's procurement decision-making process?

A28. In a sole source procurement, there is only one company in the world that makes the needed product or offers the needed service. If a PM is considering procuring from a sole source seller, he or she must carefully weigh the unique risk factors this entails, including:

- What will happen (on the project or after) if the vendor goes out of business, and there's no other vendor with a comparable product or service?

- If the vendor unfairly raises its prices, how would this affect the project or customer? How likely is it that the vendor will do this?

- What if the vendor decides to discontinue the needed service or does not put the high priority on the service that the customer expects?

Q29. What is *single source procurement*?

A29. In single source procurement, there *are* multiple vendors who can provide similar products or services, but the customer chooses to buy from only one. For example, out of all the many companies who make printers (Xerox, Canon, and HP, among others), a company chooses to buy Canon copiers exclusively. Figure 8-3 shows the primary pros and cons of single source procurement.

PROPOSALS AND RELATED DOCUMENTS

Q30. What is a *proposal* in the PM world?

A30. A proposal is a written response from a vendor to a request for proposal (RFP) from the buyer. The vendor tries to answer all the questions in the RFP as best it can to demonstrate why the buyer should feel confident in choosing the vendor as its solution provider.

Vendors usually include price in their proposals, although sometimes pricing information is withheld until later in the process. Also included are

PROS	CONS
Strong discounts on large bulk deals	Lose the benefits of diversity/competition among sellers
Easy maintenance (same for all units)	Vendor can overcharge or underperform, especially if complacency sets in over time, because the vendor doesn't have to work hard to retain the business
Centralized support and single point of contact with which the project team communicates	

Figure 8-3: Single Source Procurement: Pros and Cons for the Customer

technical details, which are often high level but sometimes very specific, about how the vendor would perform the work of the project. In a competitive situation, such as a bid, vendors consciously attempt to win the contract by making sure that the substance and form of the proposal are high quality.

Q31. What exactly is a *request for proposal*, and when and how does a PM use it?

A31. A request for proposal is a request that one or more potential sellers submit a proposal to provide a product or service. Let's say that a PM is leading a project to build a software system. He wants to choose between three vendors. So he writes an RFP, perhaps with the help of a technical expert, and sends it out to the vendors. If all three of the vendors respond with proposals, the PM will analyze all three proposals to determine which vendor is best. The price quoted in each proposal will be one of the criteria.

Q32. When would a PM use a *request for information* (RFI) instead of an RFP?

A32. A PM might send out an RFI if he or she is in the exploratory stage, just starting to look for a potential vendor, and is only looking for information for the time being. The PM is not ready to commit to one vendor, or even to take a serious look, and so he or she does not want to spend the time and resources preparing a detailed RFP. Also, if the PM is not yet in a position to make a contract award, it is too early and unfair to ask vendors to put in the effort needed to create a proposal.

Q33. Under what circumstances would a *request for quotation* (RFQ) be best?

A33. When a PM already knows what is needed, mainly cares about price, and does not need to know the details of how each vendor will create the solution, sending an RFQ can be the most efficient and best way to go.

Suppose that a PM needs to buy ten large printers for a project and is trying to choose between some of the big manufacturers, such as Canon and Xerox. In a case like this, price is the main object. The PM can make the fairly safe assumption that all of the big printer companies make a pretty comparable product, so he or she would not need to spend time and resources asking for a full proposal, then analyzing the proposals to determine which vendor is best. Vendors' responses to the RFQ will quickly give the PM the needed price information; he or she can then choose the vendor that offered the lowest price.

Q34. When does RFQ mean *request for qualifications*, and which industries use it that way?

A34. Several branches of the New York City government use this document when the need arises to add a vendor that the agency can consider for an upcoming bid to the agency's select sellers list. The agency sends the vendor an RFQ, and the vendor responds with a document describing its qualifications. If those qualifications are deemed satisfactory, the agency adds the vendor to its list, and the company becomes eligible for the agency to include it in RFPs or to invite it to bid.

A FEW MORE KEY TERMS AND CONCEPTS

Q35. What kind of companies use a preferred or select sellers list, and how does a vendor get onto the list?

A35. Many organizations, especially government agencies, have rules prohibiting contracting with vendors who are not on their preferred sellers list. For example, the U.S. federal government requires procurement people to select only from vendors on the approved list, which is called the General Services Administration (GSA) Schedule. In private industry, selecting vendors is generally up to the discretion of the company's management and bylaws.

How does a company get onto a preferred sellers list if it can't get experience because it's not on the list? This sounds like a catch-22, but companies are added to these lists all the time. In some cases, they can be added via recommendations; in others, particularly in government, they simply need to go through the formal application process required by that agency, and as long as they meet the qualifying criteria, they will usually be added to the list.

Q36. What is exactly is meant by *performing due diligence?*

A36. A PM performs due diligence by doing everything in his or her power to analyze potential vendors' qualifications and choose the best vendor possible for the client. Due diligence includes not only research but being fully aboveboard and ethical at all times. Actions include:

- Thoroughly researching the marketplace
- Giving all potential sellers a fair chance (within reason)
- Avoiding favoritism and keeping vendors on a level playing field
- Honoring all nondisclosure agreements (discussed in Q&A 40 in this chapter)
- Following rules and regulations regarding bidding protocol
- Conferring with the legal team on the proposal and contract documents
- Considering all pertinent requirements (e.g., taking quality and risk into account, not just price)
- Asking for references and contacting the references
- Establishing proper evaluation criteria (discussed in Q&A 19 in this chapter).

Q37. What is a *dispute resolution system* (DRS) clause, and how can it help a PM avoid lawsuits?

A37. A dispute resolution system (DRS) clause is a contract clause specifying that in the event of a major issue or disagreement between customer and seller, both sides pledge that they will not initially file a lawsuit, which is very costly and resource intensive for both sides (even for the one that wins). You as the PM can ask your legal team to include a DRS clause in your contracts if doing so is not standard at your company.

Under a DRS clause, the first step for both parties is usually to submit to arbitration—both parties agree to let the issue be resolved by an impartial mediator. In some contracts, the DRS specifies what is called an order of operations, meaning a sequence of steps for resolving a conflict in the event that the first step specified, such as arbitration, does not work.

There are a few cautions regarding the DRS clause. It is worth reading the fine print on any DRS clause to make sure it specifies that arbitration would be the first response but not the only response. This is known as forced arbitration and should be avoided. Whether the PM is on the customer's or the seller's side, he or she does not want to give up the right to take further legal action if the arbitration does not yield satisfactory results.

Also, be aware that in some industries (such as brokerage), professional arbitrators may be known to lean toward one side; this is the nature of the industry. Arbitrators' leanings are worth researching in advance and should be a consideration when deciding whether you want a DRS clause in a particular contract or not. One way to handle this situation is to put language into the DRS clause specifying that both parties will have approval rights over which arbitrator is chosen.

LEGAL DOCUMENTS AND TERMS PMS SHOULD KNOW ABOUT

Q38. What is a *service level agreement* (SLA)?

A38. An SLA is a legally binding contractual agreement between the customer and the seller that is specifically tied to service. The seller commits in writing to provide specific levels of service for the buyer, in agreement with the levels that the customer expects to receive and is willing to accept.

Beyond detailing service levels, SLAs may also include quality metrics the customer will expect, guarantees and warrantees it is entitled to by the SLA, and rules regarding overtime for the vendor's support.

An SLA should be as specific and clear as possible, with measurable and verifiable parameters. Figure 8-4 suggests some sample language.

Q39. What is an *enterprise-wide license agreement* (ELA)?

A39. An enterprise-wide license agreement is a firm-wide (enterprise-wide) contract that can offer significant volume-based cost savings for PMs working in very large companies. Instead of simply buying a product or service just for the current project or just for one department, large discounts are often available for companies willing and financially able to make large-scale licensing deals.

- The seller will provide 24/7 Level 2 hotline support.
- The seller will only provide Level 1 support Mondays through Fridays, from 9:00 a.m. to 5:00 p.m.
- The software system created by the seller for the customer is guaranteed to be fully operational and available to the customer from 8:00 a.m. to 11:00 p.m., seven days per week.
- This software system will be down for maintenance from 11:01 p.m. to 6:59 a.m., seven days per week.

Figure 8-4: Sample Service Level Agreement Language

SLAs are common nowadays in many different industries, but ELAs are usually for the purchase and licensing of hardware and software. For example, a large company, such as a Fortune 500 financial firm, might license numerous hardware and software products from one of the giant providers, such as IBM or Microsoft.

ELAs can be very mutually beneficial. The buyer gets greatly discounted pricing; the seller gets a guaranteed large sale. And both sides gain efficiencies in the procurement and legal processes, with one contract, one set of signatures, and one group of procurement rules that cover all of the many small business units making up the buyer's company.

Q40. What is a *nondisclosure agreement* (NDA)?

A40. A nondisclosure agreement is a legally binding commitment to protect the intellectual property of a company, including inventions, pending patents, and original artwork, as well as software code, computer files, databases, and information contained on intranet sites and in reports and other internal documents that the company considers confidential and proprietary. Some companies have employees sign NDAs as a matter of course.

The ease of scanning and saving information on CDs and flash drives and carrying it with you off-site, or transmitting it electronically, is ever increasing. But divulging information covered under an NDA is a serious violation because it can hurt your employer and help its competitors. You, as the PM, must remember that it is unethical, as well as illegal, to violate an NDA that you promise to abide by when you sign it.

Q41. When is a *letter of intent* (LOI) needed?

A41. Sometimes a customer is not ready to make a deal with a seller but wants to express a certain level of commitment to working with that seller. The customer can send the seller a letter of intent, a document that allows the PM to clarify his or her client's needs in writing, to demonstrate sincere interest in working with the seller, and to indicate that his or her company intends to negotiate with the seller in good faith. An LOI does not obligate the customer to complete a deal with the seller.

An LOI can be optional, but there are business situations in the PM world in which writing an LOI is a necessary requirement for moving forward. In some cases, a vendor may not be willing to allocate any of its resources without the commitment of an LOI. Some vendors may require that a customer pledge in a written LOI that it will be exploring a contract exclusively with their company. And some branches of government have regulations stipulating LOIs as a mandatory part of their process.

PMs should note that while an LOI may not be binding toward completing a deal, it may contain wording that *is* legally binding, or it may attach to an NDA. As with any document for signature, a PM should be careful about signing any LOI and should only do so with the approval of his or her client's legal department.

Q42. What is the *point of total assumption* (PTA), how can it help the buyer, and what is the formula for calculating PTA?

A42. PTA is an optional contract clause designed to protect the customer from being charged for costs going beyond a certain threshold. It is often included in fixed price incentive fee contracts to specify that once a specified spending limit has been reached, the seller will assume total responsibility for all costs exceeding that limit.

To understand the PTA, it helps to know that there are actually two limits. First, the seller wants to avoid spending beyond the point at which the customer will stop reimbursing in full for expenses incurred and will begin only partial reimbursement. This first limit is the target price, as specified in the contract. The second limit is the actual PTA, the point at which the seller takes over full responsibility for expenses. The example in Figure 8-5 shows the four variables used in the formula to calculate PTA.

- **Target price:** The *planned* amount the buyer is expecting to pay, e.g., $900,000.
- **Ceiling price:** The *maximum* amount the buyer is agreeing to pay, e.g., $1,000,000.
- **Customer's share of cost overruns:** The percentage of costs the customer will reimburse the seller for, on costs that fall between the ceiling price and the target price, e.g., 75 percent.
- **Target cost:** The planned expenses the seller expects to spend, e.g. $800,000.

PTA = ((Ceiling price – target price) / customer's share of cost overruns) + target cost

PTA = ((1,000,000 – 900,000) / 75%) + $800,000

PTA = ($100,000 / 75%) + $800,000

PTA = $133,333 + $800,000

PTA = $933,333 ← The point at which the seller will assume all subsequent costs.

Figure 8-5: Sample Calculation Using the Point of Total Assumption (PTA) Formula

So in the above example:

- The customer will reimburse the seller for all expenses *below* the $900,000 mark.
- The customer will reimburse 75% of expenses in the range *between* $900,000 and $933,333.
- The seller will be fully responsible for all expenses incurred *beyond* the $933,333 mark.

Q43. What is a *source escrow clause*, and when is it worth fighting to get one into your contract?

A43. Putting a source escrow clause in a contract is a little like putting money on ice, but the "money" is software source code. The legal department representing the customer side on the contract gets the seller to agree that if it ever goes out of business, the customer would have the rights not only to continue to use the purchased computer application but to modify, run, and maintain the source code behind the vendor's application. This is a great idea that can save the day for the customer. Without the clause, the customer definitely does not have the right to use the vendor's source code; in fact, it would be illegal.

When is a source escrow clause worthwhile, and when is it not?

Worth it when:

- A vendor has built a customized, unique app just for your company; you need the source code to maintain the app.
- It's an off-the-shelf product, but the vendor is a sole source, and there is no comparable product on the market.

Not worth it when:

- There are similar products on the market with which you could quickly replace the app in the event the vendor does go out of business.
- You wouldn't have the resources to take the source code and modify it, and a viable alternative could be implemented. If it would be faster, easier, and less resource intensive to switch to another vendor if your vendor were to go out of business, it might not be worth fighting to get a source escrow clause into your contract. The PM might do better asking for other concessions instead.

Q44. What is the legal concept of *privity*, and how can PMs apply it to projects?

A44. Privity is a legal principle defining who the PM is allowed to go to when there are more than two companies involved in a procurement, and going to the wrong company can cause trouble. For example:

A PM for company A (the customer) has a contract with company B (the seller), and the seller outsources some of the project work to subcontractor company C. If the PM for company A is not happy with the work of subcontractor C, can the PM go directly to C because C is ultimately under A? Or must the PM for A go directly to B? The answer is that the PM for A *does* need to go to B because A's contract is with B. This is simply a matter of following the contractual agreements. Jumping from A to C would be a contract violation that could have ramifications. It could lead to friction between the manager who was left out of the loop, and on a larger scale, it could also lead to bad blood between all the companies involved, possibly resulting in a loss of future business.

> ### Avoiding Privity Issues
>
> To avoid this situation altogether, company A could have specified in the contract that vendor company B cannot outsource work to any subcontractors. Or if that's not feasible for the project, company A could have put language into its contract with B that granted A certain rights over any other subcontractor B might hire on the project.

PROJECT CLOSEOUT

Q45. What are keys for successfully closing out a project on the legal end?

A45. It is critical to make sure that all required final signatures are obtained. Often the project's contract includes a specific list of needed signatures, such as the project sponsor's and sometimes the company's attorneys', officially confirming that the project has been satisfactorily completed from the client side.

In the rush to jump into the next project, final signoffs are sometimes neglected. When a project ends, it may seem obvious that it's over, and everything that had to be done has been done. Not getting final signoffs may seem like a minor omission, but it can lead to repercussions, ranging from late fees to additional maintenance fees and even to potential lawsuits, that can potentially more than undo the positive results of a project. To protect the project and company, it is the PM's responsibility to make sure that all required signatures are obtained and that copies of the signed documents are distributed to the appropriate parties and saved on file.

Q46. What are requirements for closing out procurements on the customer side?

A46. On the customer side, the PM needs to:

- Make sure that *all final deliverables* have been given to the customer. It is not uncommon for some of the more minor deliverables to be neglected, and this can undercut the success of a project. For example, the main product may have been delivered, but the PM or customer might not realize that the providing organization is also contractually obligated to provide on-site training or a certain number of free service calls to the customer.

- Make sure all ***internal signoffs*** have been obtained; sometimes signatures within the customer company are required (in addition to legal signatures between the customer company and the seller's organization). In addition to the signatures, this should also include updating project checklists, spreadsheets, and other such project documentation to indicate that all procurements for the project have been fully delivered and signed off on, and that the project is complete.

- Make sure that ***all final payments*** have been made to the seller. Even after the main payments have been made, the PM is responsible for making sure that the customer does not owe any kind of payments to the vendor, including travel and expense payments, performance awards promised in the contract, or any other kind of payment or financial documentation, such as that for tax purposes.

- Conduct a ***procurement audit,*** the subject of Q&A 50.

Q47. What are the requirements for closing out procurements on the seller's side?

A47. The seller's responsibilities at closeout time are a little more obvious.

- ***Make sure the customer receives all final deliverables*** and signs off on them, so it can't come back and say it didn't receive everything. Make sure that all incidental deliverables also have been taken care of. Incidental deliverables are items thrown into a contract by the legal team or senior management that the PM may not be aware of. They can include concessions such as free training or a certain number of free on-site support calls. The seller is obligated to honor any and all commitments in the contract, big and small. And it also is good business to do so—the customer will especially appreciate it if you remind them that you are seeing to it that they receive something they are entitled to by the contract but may have missed.

- ***Provide upgraded products, bug fixes, and more:*** Some vendors are very attentive while the contract negotiations are going on but become neglectful once they have clinched the deal, while some continue to be helpful even after the project is officially over. A vendor's behavior after it has received the last payment for a project often differentiates superior vendors from the competition. It's always good for the vendor to keep future business in mind.

- *Complete any and all documents the customer needs* as specified in the contract, such as required information for a procurement audit.

Q48. What is a *buyer-conducted performance review*, and how does it help the customer?

A48. In a buyer-conducted performance review, the customer initiates a visit to the seller's site to review the project progress to date and to discover, document, and promptly address any issues. Usually, this review entails bringing together technical experts as well as PMs from both companies and taking a close look at the deliverables created so far and, in some cases, the processes of the project. The goal is to confirm that the project is on track. If it is not, the customer and seller must come to an agreement on implementing corrective actions that will get the project to where it should be in a mutually agreed-upon manner and time frame.

A key point about this kind of performance review is that if the customer PM wants these reviews to be part of the project's life cycle, the customer's legal team must include language in the contract providing for them. This language should specify how often the review process will take place, what the inspection process will cover, and the expected fix time for issues discovered in the reviews. If such reviews are not mandated in the contract, the vendor is under no obligation to comply with ad hoc requests for such meetings—and it would not be fair to ask for them.

Q49. Is offering to be a reference for a vendor considered a best practice?

A49. In some circumstances, yes, but three considerations should rule a PM's decision to do so:

- *Company rules:* First of all, you as the PM may only do this if your company's policy supports it. Many government agencies prohibit giving references outright, and not all private companies allow it, either.

- *Permission/disclosure:* Even if your company's guidelines allow you be a reference for a seller, it's important to obtain specific permission. Your reference must be in the best interests of your company, and you must be sure to avoid any conflict of interest. Just because you'd like to recommend a vendor (and possibly get a free lunch or gift out of the deal) doesn't mean your organization will agree that doing so is a good idea. Asking for permission takes any guesswork out of this decision. If it's not possible to obtain advance permission, be sure to disclose to your company that you've given a reference after the fact, for the same reasons.

- *Only if warranted:* If a vendor provides the best product on the market or has given you exceptionally good service, offering to provide a reference to other customers is legitimate, can help your vendor, and can generate a great deal of goodwill.

Q50. What is a *procurement audit*, and how can it help a PM's company?

A50. Knowledge often goes undocumented and walks out the door when a PM leaves a company. A little-known best practice, the procurement audit, can help a company retain knowledge about the procurement and legal processes on a project.

The PM takes a little time at the end of a project to collect and document how the project went with regard to the procurement and legal processes. Think of this is capturing lessons learned about the procurement and legal processes (or if you like mnemonics, here's one: LLL = legal lessons learned!).

The PM might try to answer questions such as the following as he or she conducts the procurement audit:

- How was the outsourcing company to work with? Were the seller's technical support people responsive to the company's needs?
- Were the vendor's procurement and legal people lawyers cooperative about getting the contracts completed and signed in a timely manner?
- Were the corporate attorneys from the other company fair about the contract, or did they try to rush you, bully you, or hide the facts?

This documentation can be extremely helpful for the company the next time it is making decisions about possible vendors to work with.

TOP TEN PITFALLS IN PROCUREMENTS AND CONTRACTS ON THE CUSTOMER SIDE

1. Starting a project without a contract or before the contract is finalized. (This may sound funny, but it happens!)
2. Not thoroughly checking a seller's references. (People sometimes read the written references, but they don't follow up with a phone call.)

3. Going with the lowest-cost seller, but not the *best* seller to meet your customer's needs.

4. Deciding to outsource for financial reasons, but failing to make up for the loss of control outsourcing brings by adding additional oversight.

5. Signing any legal document, such as an addendum to an already-signed contract, without consulting a lawyer.

6. Signing the vendor's boilerplate contract.

7. Using the wrong contract type for the needs of your project.

8. Leaving something you discussed with the seller out of the contract because you assumed it would be honored based on the conversation.

9. Making assumptions that certain features or services would be included with the project (e.g., free support for a certain period of time), even though they were not specified in the contract.

10. Missing opportunities by thinking small—for instance, by signing a quick individual contract with a vendor for a minor, specific project, without first considering whether a larger, company-wide contract might be more cost-effective for your firm.

TOP FIVE PITFALLS TO AVOID ON THE SELLER'S SIDE

1. Taking advantage of the customer's lack of knowledge and pushing through a one-sided contract that is unfair to the customer. This might seem like a good idea initially, but over the long term, the customer might wind up feeling cheated and no longer trust your firm.

2. Exploiting a customer's deadline and overcharging them when you know the customer is under internal pressure to close a deal.

3. Rushing the customer by imposing your company's deadline.

4. Overcharging for short-term gain, risking potential future business for your company.

5. Taking on a contract that you know is not the best fit for your company just to get the short-term money or to try to get a foot in the door toward future business with the customer.

TOP FIVE PITFALLS TO AVOID ON BOTH THE BUYER'S AND SELLER'S SIDES

1. Letting your legal people spend too much time haggling over issues not critical to your agenda.

2. Staying out of the legal negotiations and relying too much on your legal people to handle it all for you.

3. Letting your attorneys go for a win-lose result, instead of pushing them to come up with a win-win that might create a more positive and long-lasting relationship with the other company.

4. Exploiting a mistake in the language of the contract after it is signed to gain something that was not intended by the spirit of the contract.

5. Trying to put language into the contract for the wrong reasons—for example, a clause that your own company favors but that you know is not best for the contract at hand.

CHAPTER 9

Ethical Considerations PMs Face on the Job

Don't be evil.

—From the Google Corporation's Code of Ethics

One of the toughest parts of any PM's job is making decisions that are the best under the circumstances as well as the most ethical. And while the cynical might question whether it is possible for good business decisions to also be ethical decisions, any company that values long-term profitability knows that the most ethical choice is also the best business decision. The wrong ethical choice can cause long-term problems for your business, greatly outweighing any short-term gain. Unintended consequences can range from loss of business to negative word of mouth to a dramatic collapse like Enron's.

We all tend to think of ourselves as ethical people who make ethical decisions. But ethical compromises in the business world are all too common. One look at the daily newspaper and you can almost always find coverage of the latest business fiasco, often directly traceable to a breach of ethics. These are not always as obvious, or as clearly intentional, as a Bernie Madoff–style Ponzi scheme. Sometimes ethical lapses are fairly subtle; a PM takes shortcuts to cut costs or makes a compromise to gain favor with a customer. And sometimes the PM may not even be aware he or she is doing something wrong if he or she is in an environment in which his or her associates take similar actions.

In a current trend toward taking the high road in business, approximately 20 percent of the graduates of both the Harvard Business School and the Columbia Business School now voluntarily sign an ethical pledge before they go out into the business world (Wayne 2009). Also worth noting is that PMI has long required all of its certification candidates to sign PMI's *Code of Ethics and Professional Conduct* as part of the credentialing process. A quick summary of this code appears later in this chapter.

This chapter covers ethics for PMs, from individual responsibilities and challenges to ethical decision-making as part of an overall strategy for short- and long-term success. And with permission from PMI, this chapter also includes a summary and key citations from the *PMI Code of Ethics and Professional Conduct*, to help PMs see real-world applications of PMI's standard.

ETHICS IN PROJECT MANAGEMENT

Q1. How is the term *ethics* defined in the project management world?

A1. The fundamentals of ethics in project management are not so different from those emphasized in Boy Scouts, Girl Scouts, or Sunday school: being honest and forthright, and following the golden rule of doing unto others.

In the project management world, however, key decisions are expected to lead to project success and profitability. This makes things complicated for PMs, who are often caught in the middle between competing requests from the customer and their own company. But one of the indicators of a good project manager is a reliable commitment to making the best and most ethical decisions.

Q2. What are examples of real-world ethical challenges PMs face?

A2. PMs face ethical issues every day. Here are a few typical examples, all of which involve making difficult choices:

- *When hiring new team members:* Will you choose the best and most qualified candidate for the position? What if someone at your company is asking you to hire his friend?

- *When selecting a vendor:* Will you establish a fair selection process and choose the seller best qualified to fulfill your client's needs? What if your performing organization is pressuring you to go with a cheaper vendor to increase its profit margin?

- *When managing your team:* Will you be equally fair to all personnel? What if some staff are permanent and you're worked with them for years, and some are consultants, employed by a faraway outsourcer, who have their own direct manager and who frequently come and go?

Q3. Where do ethics fit in within the PM knowledge areas and processes?

A3. Coverage of ethics within the *PMBOK® Guide* is a little like a 13th-floor elevator stop—you can't see it, but it really is there! The *PMBOK® Guide* does not include a chapter on ethics, but it *does* make explicit reference to the *PMI Code of Ethics and Professional Conduct*, which strongly encourages PMs to behave ethically in all of their dealings as a core component of professionalism. The PMI exams for more experienced managers (e.g., PMPs and PgMPs) also emphasize ethics in many of their questions. Ethics, then, underlies *all* of the project management knowledge areas. (For this reason, some PMs find it helpful to think of ethics as the sixth process group.)

Q4. Does PMI attempt to *enforce* its code of ethics, or does it just *encourage* ethical behavior?

A4. The answer is yes to both. PMI *encourages* ethical behavior by stressing it in its published literature, including the *PMBOK Guide*, monthly and quarterly magazines for members, and its code of ethics and professional conduct (available to all as a free downloadable PDF at http://www.pmi.org/About-us/Ethics/Code-of-Ethics.aspx). Ethics in project management is a popular topic at local chapter meetings, conferences, and global congresses as well. Per PMI, 9 percent of the questions on the PMP® exam address ethics and social responsibility, motivating candidates to study ethics as part of their test preparation (and ideally apply what they learn back in the workplace).

PMI *enforces* awareness and practice of ethics in two key ways. All candidates applying for all of PMI's exams are required to sign off on PMI's *Code of Ethics and Professional Conduct*, meaning that they have read it, understand it, and pledge to follow its principles in their PM work. PMI also has a formal mechanism for reporting ethical misconduct by PMI members, PMI-certified PMs, or volunteers taking part in PMI activities or events. Anyone wishing to submit a complaint in writing can download and complete PMI's *ethics complaint form*, available at http://www.pmi.org/About-us/Ethics/N/media/PDF/ Ethics/ap-complainttemp-edited.ashx.

Q5. What exactly is covered in PMI's *Code of Ethics and Professional Conduct*?

A5. The PMI code of ethics covers four individual values: *responsibility, respect, fairness,* and *honesty.* For each of the four values, two levels of ethical standards are described—aspirational and mandatory. Aspirational standards are considered goals that PMs need to *strive for;* mandatory standards are considered *musts* that PMs are *required to follow.*

The complete code is several pages long, and we recommend reading it in full. Figure 9-1 offers a quick summary that cites the four values and lists key standards, both aspirational and mandatory, for each.

Q6. When can behavior be legal but unethical?

A6. Many behaviors are both unethical and illegal. Consider a mugger stealing someone's money: It is morally wrong to hurt anyone or take their belongings, and stealing money is a violation of the law.

But in the business world, many behaviors are unethical but not illegal. PMs and project team members nevertheless should scrupulously avoid engaging in them. Imagine that a PM leads his customer to believe that he and his direct team will do all the work of the project. The PM then outsources some of the work to a less expensive seller to reduce his costs. If the contract does not prohibit outsourcing, the customer has no legal recourse. But this behavior is highly unethical for two reasons: The PM deceived the customer, and he is trying to boost profit at the expense of delivering quality for his customer. This breaches two specific clauses in the PMI code of ethics:

Clause 3.3.1: "We negotiate in good faith." (Mandatory standard, Chapter 3, Respect).

Clause 5.3.1: "We do not engage in or condone behavior that is designed to deceive others..." (Mandatory standard, Chapter 5, Honesty).

Our second example is not as clear cut. Let's say that a small-business owner hires a personal friend over a more qualified job applicant. Government agencies and larger companies with established HR departments and well-documented interview processes closely follow the laws prohibiting unfair hiring practices. But even if you are the owner of a very small company, your conscience should direct you to hire the best candidate for the job, out of fairness to the candidates and to your customer, who could be affected by your choice.

Ethical Value	Summary
1. Responsibility	*Aspirational:* Always striving to take full ownership for our behavior; only accepting work we are fully qualified to do; fulfilling all commitments; caring about society and the environment as well as the company; protecting proprietary and confidential information. *Mandatory:* It is required to follow all work-related policies, rules, regulations, and laws and to report violations of the PMI code to the appropriate parties. Anyone reporting a violation will be asked to furnish proof in order for action to be pursued. Additionally, disciplinary action will be taken against any reported individual who retaliates against the reporter.
2. Respect	*Aspirational:* People's customs and differing points of view should all be treated with respect. And we should strive to always deal with people directly in the workplace, instead of discussing our problems with colleagues or supervisors. *Mandatory:* We must negotiate in good faith and must not abuse others, bully them, or in any way take advantage of them based on having superior power over them (including relationships between boss and subordinate as well as customer and seller).
3. Fairness	*Aspirational:* We should be impartial, transparent, and fair in all business dealings and job hirings. *Mandatory:* We must disclose conflicts of interest in business dealings and obtain approval from management to proceed after disclosure. We must not discriminate, punish/reward, hire/ fire, or violate the rules of the organization based on favoritism or prejudice of any kind.
4. Honesty	*Aspirational:* We should seek to understand the truth; to be truthful in communications and in anything promised; and to foster an environment where people feel safe to speak the truth. *Mandatory:* We must avoid any kind of behavior that is deceitful or attempts to hide the truth, and we must refrain from communicating any untruths for personal gain or to injure another person.

Figure 9-1: Quick Summary of PMI's *Code of Ethics and Professional Conduct**

*Project Management Institute, *PMI Code of Ethics and Professional Conduct*, Project Management Institute, Inc. (2006). Copyright and all rights reserved. Material from this publication has been reproduced with the permission of PMI.

Again, there is a specific clause in the PMI code of ethics that applies very well here:

> *Clause 4.4.3:* "We do not hire or fire, reward or punish, or award or deny contracts based on personal considerations, including, but not limited to, favoritism, nepotism, or bribery." (Mandatory standard, Chapter 4, Fairness).

Q7. How should ethics affect the core decisions a PM needs to make on the job?

A7. When considering a change or making decisions on a project, a PM should ask two key questions whose answers, taken together, will often help lead to the best decision:

1. How will this change affect all of the competing elements of the triple constraint?

2. How do I weigh all the competing factors and make the best, and most ethical, decision?

It may sound complicated to factor so much into a decision, but that's why skilled, experienced PMs are necessary. For example, whenever vendors are being evaluated, the least expensive one would be always be the best choice if all the other factors on the triple constraint could be ignored. But it takes skill, sound judgment, and sometimes courage to also factor scope, quality, risk, and customer satisfaction into a procurement decision and to be willing to stand up to your company to recommend a more expensive solution.

Ethically speaking, it would not be fair to your customer to choose a cheaper vendor to boost your profit margin but then underdeliver on the scope and quality you promised. Qualified vendors also would consider it unethical for you to choose a cheaper seller over a more qualified provider, unless your agreement with your customer very explicitly stated that cost was the chief criterion.

There are two specific clauses in the PMI code of ethics that are applicable to contracts and vendor selection:

> *Clause 5.2.4:* "We make commitments and promises, implied or explicit, in good faith." (Aspirational standard, Chapter 5, Honesty).

> *Clause 5.3.1:* "We do not engage in or condone behavior... that if known, would render our statements as misleading or incomplete." (Mandatory standard, Chapter 5, Honesty).

Q8. Should a PM's loyalty be to the customer or to his or her own company?

A8. This is probably the single biggest ethical issue most PMs face. It comes up all the time on projects. In short, the better the PM, the better he or she will handle this kind of conflict.

It is crucial to remember that the old cliché, "The customer is always right," may be a great customer service motto, but it is definitely *not* a fact. The customer may ask for more features, a broader scope, or more support, and a good PM strives to put the customer first wherever possible. But customer requests can be very self-serving: good for the customer but bad for the performing organization and even, at times, for the project itself. Saying yes to every customer request at the expense of other stakeholders and considerations is a recipe for disaster and is not recommended.

A good rule of thumb for PMs to keep in mind: Think of yourself as having three clients—the customer, the project, and your company.

- *The customer:* PMs should put the customer first when possible.

- *The project:* At the same time, the PM must always keep in mind the big picture—the project as a whole—and view all customer requests in this light.

- *The company:* It's also critical to stay focused on what's best for the PM's organization, both on the current project as well as long term.

Q9. Could the customer, the project, and the company be thought of as an "ethical triple constraint"?

A9. Yes. Imagine three forces tugging at you at once as you're trying to make ethical decisions: the customer, the project, and the company. Figure 9-2 illustrates these forces as a triangle much like the classic triple constraint triangle. The project is the base of the triangle, representing the work, while the left and right sides of the triangle are the customer and the performing organization, which ideally should work together in concert to help deliver the project. Often, however, the customer and the company have conflicting agendas that need to be balanced skillfully by the PM.

You can think of this as a corollary to the classic PM triple constraint, as follows:

- Here, all three components—customer, project, and company—need to be constantly taken into account to produce the best results.

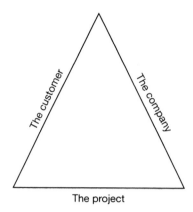

Figure 9-2: The Ethical Triple Constraint

- Like the classic triple constraint, each of these three components is sensitive to change or pressures from the other two, and changes to any one component can affect either of the other two.

Q10. What are some examples of how one element of the ethical triple constraint can affect the others?

A10. Here are three of many examples that come up frequently:

- If the customer demands too many changes, the project as a whole can suffer, coming in late or over budget.
- If the performing organization puts its own needs first—for instance, outsourcing some of the work to decrease costs—the quality of the project may suffer, leading to customer dissatisfaction.
- If too much focus is placed on the project as an entity, there may be too much emphasis on meeting the target dates and keeping on budget and not enough on providing quality deliverables to the customer or fulfilling change requests. This damages the relationship with the customer and ultimately hurts the performing organization, too.

Q11. What is *careerism*?

A11. Careerism is the opposite of putting the customer, project, and company first. When someone makes a choice that is good for his or her own career at the expense of the greater good of the project, company, and customer, his or her behavior is called careerism. For example, a careerist PM might throw a contract to a friend's company even though that company is not the most qualified seller, hoping that the friend will someday repay the PM in kind, possibly with a position at the other company.

PMs who are overly willing to comply with directives from management demonstrate more subtle careerism. These PMs *seem* to be doing the right thing but are really doing the *wrong* thing for the firm. For instance, a company may be trying to reduce costs across the board. Careerist managers may make decisions they don't really believe in under the banner of the cost-cutting directive: They might agree to a voluntary staffing cut, claiming that it will not impact their results (even though they know it will) because they are hoping they will eventually be rewarded for their austerity by the company.

Q12. What if a person's personal ethics conflict with a company's mission or values?

A12. People's personal ethics are deeply rooted in their family values, political leanings, and religious beliefs, and no one wants to take actions on the job that contradict their strongly held core values. But personal values must be kept subordinate to the greater good of the customer, project, and company. Suppose someone is a strict vegetarian and has very valid moral or religious reasons for her vegetarianism. But if she works for a food company that produces meat products, she isn't entitled to become a saboteur and hurt the firm. If a person's beliefs are so strong that he or she can't do his or her job professionally and well, the answer is that he or she should not work for that company.

MANAGING OTHERS' EXPECTATIONS ETHICALLY

Q13. What's wrong with putting the customer first?

A13. There are two main reasons why this can sometimes be the wrong thing to do.

- *There can be unintended consequences.* A customer may want something, not realizing that their request could harm the project. If the project's PM goes along with the idea, knowing full well that it's not best for the project, this is unethical: It jeopardizes the project and the performing organization, per the ethical triple constraint above.

  For example, suppose a customer asks the PM to cut corners and hire his friend, who's an unlicensed electrician. The friend doesn't perform the work up to code. There may be many negative consequences, including poor quality, a fine from an inspector, or the worst-case scenario: personal injury and lawsuits. The PM would likely be considered legally liable for knowingly doing the wrong thing (even though the customer asked the PM to do it).

- ***There might be an expectation of quid pro quo.*** The PM may expect something in return for going along with such a request. For instance, suppose a customer asks a PM to hire her personal friend onto the project team, even if he is not very well qualified. The PM may do so and tell his own management that he is doing it to please the client. On the surface, this sounds as if it might also be good for the performing organization. But the PM might have an agenda: He may think that the client owes him a favor (quid pro quo). Perhaps the PM hopes that the client will someday offer him a job. The PM's ulterior motive makes hiring the customer's friend an unethical choice.

  Further, keep in mind that if the client's friend doesn't do a good job, the project may be harmed in the short run and in the long run, as can the performing organization and the reputations of all the members of the project team.

Q14. How can I say no to the customer when necessary?

A14. PMs need to be able to say no with finesse. You must be willing to stand up for what's best for *most* stakeholders, even when a decision might not satisfy *all* stakeholders. I have personally found that explaining that you're not trying to say no, but rather, you're advocating for what's ultimately best for the client and the project, is an effective way of handling client requests that you are not willing to fulfill. Sometimes the customer doesn't know the full facts, and it's up to you to show him or her. You may have to do some research and analysis until you are able to translate your reasons into terms the client can understand. Always try to present your case as fact-based and objective, avoiding opinion, conjecture, emotion, or a "this is how *we* like to do things" attitude. Chapter 10 details the soft skills and diplomacy that are essential in these situations.

Q15. What can I do if the customer refuses to take no for an answer?

A15. If you can't persuade the customer to do what you think is best for the project, you must escalate the conflict, either to the sponsor, your boss, or your customer's boss—whichever way the politics would work best in your environment. Many PMs make the mistake of caving to the customer, but going along with a poor choice is not sustainable for the project. Also, keep in mind that the customer whose loyalty you may think you've won by agreeing to the extra features he requested will be the same guy who blames you later if the project comes in late or over budget (even if it was his request that caused the slippage).

Q16. What if I work for the client, and my firm is trying to get me to take unfair advantage of the performing organization?

A16. It's always best to strive for fairness and to treat the performing organization as a business partner rather than an adversary. Some customers try to get a lot of extras from their vendor simply because they can. This not-very-nice behavior is known as *getting over*, and if it hurts the other party's business, it may be unethical. Note that the PMI code of ethics prohibits exercising position power:

> ***Clause 3.3.2:*** "We do not exercise the power of our... position to influence the decisions or actions of others..." (Mandatory standard, Chapter 3, Respect).

Empathy for your PM counterpart on the vendor side should be your ethical guide.

Keep in mind that getting over doesn't always yield the best results for the customer. If you manage, for instance, to get extra features added for free to your deliverable, your request may come back to bite you if, in the team's rush to get everything done for you, it winds up delaying your project or lowering the overall quality. (This is a very common pitfall!)

ESCALATION, WHISTLE-BLOWING, AND ETHICS BOARDS

Q17. What if my own management refuses to accept a no from me, the PM?

A17. PMs must be open to the idea that their senior managers may know something they don't. They may have confidential information they are not able to share with PMs. For instance, there could be an upcoming corporate merger, and the project you are leading may be a linchpin to the success of the merger or even a precondition for the agreement. So you may be saying no to your manager about a project detail, but he or she may know something about the big picture that he or she is not allowed to share with you. Good PMs don't fall into the trap of believing, "It's my project, so I always know best." They are open to their managers' points of view, as well as those of other stakeholders.

If you have made the best, most sincere case you can, and your manager still doesn't agree, you either need to defer to his or her better judgment or escalate the situation. There are several ways to kick things upstairs, but all of them can endanger your position and your career and are to be avoided whenever possible. You should employ them only after you have worked hard to come to an agreement with your manager, and failing that, only if you believe it's really worth the possible downside.

Q18. Is there a right way to escalate when necessary?

A18. When you have exhausted all attempts to come to an agreement, and you feel that your manager is trying to push you to do something that is unethical or that could damage the project in a significant way, escalation is sometimes necessary. But this does not mean you have to go behind your manager's back. It is recommended that even when you are escalating a problem, you try to be as open, up front, and honest as possible. Bypassing your manager would likely be seen in itself as unethical (even if you have a good reason) because it's a betrayal of trust.

The best way to escalate an issue is to be upfront and professional. Say to your manager, "I believe that this situation is important enough that we need input from senior management, and I'd like to schedule a meeting where you and I both can be present." This approach is the "high road," and it allows for four possible outcomes:

- *The best-case scenario:* Your manager realizes that you are serious, reconsiders, and lets you have your way. Even if this doesn't happen, at least you haven't burned your manager by sneaking around behind his or her back.

- *The second-best outcome:* Your manager agrees to meet with senior management. You each get to make your case, and the situation is resolved at the meeting (perhaps to your liking, perhaps not).

- *Your manager stands firm,* saying, "If you want to try to escalate this, you'll have to go ahead without me, because I'm firm on my decision." You can either accept the manager's decision or escalate the conflict.

If you do escalate, at least it's not a surprise to your manager. In fact, he or she has given *tacit approval*, meaning unspoken but understood approval, for escalation.

- *The least desirable outcome:* Your manager tells you to just do what you're told and forbids you from escalating. If this happens, you either have to do as ordered or consider the options discussed in the next few Q&As: whistle-blowing, snitching, or going before your company's ethics board.

Q19. What exactly is *whistle-blowing*, and is it ever a good idea?

A19. Whistle-blowing is exposing corporate behavior you believe is unethical, usually by jumping over your direct manager's head and going high up in the company or even outside the firm. It is often done to expose a major grievance, such as corporate crime (also known as white collar crime or corporate malfeasance). Whistle-blowing is sometimes covered in the media, usually when the company is large and the violation is severe.

Whistle-blowing can get results, but it should only be used as a last resort because there are two big problems associated with it:

1. *It's very risky.* Many people have been fired from their jobs for this, and further, have been blackballed in their industry, preventing them from getting other jobs. This is such a high risk that there have been laws passed in the United States. and other countries to protect whistle-blowers. But even with that protection, people sometimes get fired for it anyway. They can try to sue their companies under these laws, but there is no guarantee that they'll win the lawsuit, get their job back, find a new job, or regain their reputation, which is often permanently tarnished with the label of whistle-blower.

2. *Even when you win, you lose.* Even if your case is factually correct *and* your company resolves the problem you've exposed (two big ifs), your reputation may still be ruined. You will probably be seen as disloyal to the company for blowing the whistle, even if you tried going through proper channels first.

Q20. What about *snitching*?

A20. Snitching is akin to whistle-blowing, but the term usually refers to smaller-scale behavior, such as garden-variety complaining about a coworker to a higher-up. It is not easy to report on another person's bad behavior, but if you become aware of a violation at work and don't report it, you could be considered an accessory. In cases like this, most ethics experts would side with you, as the reporter. Reporting bad behavior is necessary for things to run properly in companies, as well as in society. But your motivation is important. Anyone who snitches should be doing it to stop the bad behavior, to help the victim, and to improve the working environment and help the firm as a whole. Snitching becomes unethical when it's done for personal gain—in other words, reporting to make oneself look good.

Q21. What is an *ethics board*, who sits on such a board, and when should a PM or other employee approach an ethics board?

A21. Many companies have some kind of ethics board, which provides a forum for airing grievances about ethical violations. Usually, they are made up of senior managers from HR and other areas of senior leadership.

Ethics boards are necessary in cases in which directly confronting the offender is not feasible—for instance, if an employee is being sexually harassed by his or her own supervisor.

But be aware that raising an issue to an ethics board is not always a walk in the park. It is a kind of whistle-blowing because it is a backdoor approach to resolving a problem, unlike confronting the offender or going through normal reporting channels.

Going before an ethics board should be a very carefully considered decision for two reasons:

- *Being direct can bring faster, better results in some cases.* Ethics boards tend to be extremely thorough, so investigations can be very time consuming.

- *The complainant or other witnesses may face consequences.* Ethics boards usually offer confidentiality and safety, but full anonymity is not always possible. A good ethics board has to be fair; it must protect anyone accused of wrongdoing as well as any victim. Sometimes the complainant (and other witnesses) may be asked to testify to the board. They may have to name names and reveal secrets, and things can be said that wind up being held against employees. This sometimes happens even if there is a confidentiality policy and despite the best intentions of the board.

Q22. What could be wrong with an open-door policy?

A22. Senior management in some companies encourages an open-door policy. Employees are told by some higher-up, "My door is always open—you can always come to me with any issue." This approach can serve some useful purposes. For example, it can enhance morale: Employees like to feel as if their opinions matter and that others are listening. But the danger of an open-door policy is that it can make it too easy for people to become snitchers or whistle-blowers. (I have seen this happen on a large scale!) Again, these actions should be a carefully considered last resort. For an open-door policy to be effective and ethical, ground rules about which topics are appropriate for discussion can be very helpful, along with clearly stated policies about how confidentiality will be maintained.

UNETHICAL BEHAVIOR

Q23. What is *lying by omission*, and is it really lying?

A23. In one of the classic *Pink Panther* movies, Inspector Clouseau asks an innkeeper, "Does your dog bite?" The innkeeper says no, the dog bites Clouseau, and when confronted, the innkeeper explains: "That is *not* my dog." Many PMs and other businesspeople use this tactic, rationalizing that it isn't really lying. But withholding information in this way can cause damage and is known *as lying by omission.* Here are two common examples in the PM world:

- A client asks a PM if a milestone will be met, and the PM (knowing that the milestone will be late) answers: "I have not been told by anyone on my team that we won't meet our deadline."
- A PM asks a vendor whether a bug fix will be part of the next version of its code. Knowing it that will not be included, the vendor answers: "I have been given no information about whether the fix will be included."

While some might say these answers are not technically lies, the PMI code of ethics makes crystal clear that lying by omission is unscrupulous behavior and is prohibited for PMs. Chapter 5 of the code, on honesty, states: "We do not engage in... making misleading or false statements, stating half-truths, providing information out of context, or withholding information that, if known, would render our statements as misleading or incomplete."

Remember, any kind of lie (whether by omission or commission) can be destructive because it erodes trust and respect. For more on the problems caused by dishonesty in communications, see the Q&As on *smoothing, spin,* and *white lies* in Chapter 10.

Q24. What is a *non-apology apology*, and why is it unethical?

A24. No one likes to admit that he or she is wrong, but it's necessary sometimes (and people admire you for it) to take responsibility for one's mistakes and to apologize sincerely and in a straightforward manner. The non-apology apology is *not* an admission of responsibility and is neither sincere nor straightforward.

Suppose a PM subcontracts out part of a project, and the subcontractor doesn't do a good job. The customer is understandably unhappy with the results, and the PM knows an apology is warranted, but he doesn't want to look bad. So the PM says to the client: "If you feel that the results were not what you expected, I sympathize, but just so you know, the part you are objecting to was not done by my people."

What's wrong with this picture? First, the PM is not quite admitting that the results were different than promised. He is placing some responsibility on the customer, couching his remarks with: "If *you* feel that the results...," as if to suggest that the customer is perhaps being unreasonable. Then, instead of saying, "I apologize," the PM says, "I sympathize," which may make it sound as if he is empathetic, but this is not a real apology.

What should the PM have said? He should have taken ownership of the unsatisfactory work and offered a real apology, e.g., "I understand that our team did not deliver the results you expected. I would like to apologize to you personally and offer to do whatever I can to make it up to you."

The non-apology apology in this example not only fails to give the customer emotional satisfaction or closure, but it also has an element of dishonesty. The PM is twisting the facts to make it sound as if the customer's dissatisfaction is not really his fault, when he knows it is.

Q25. What exactly is *doubletalk*, why is it used, and why is it considered unethical?

A25. Suppose the PM in the previous Q&A had said to the customer: "I understand you feel you didn't get what you want, although my people did deliver what they thought you wanted. There were some issues with the specs between my technicians and your assistant... that may be something you want to look into on your end down the road, word to the wise. Nevertheless, let's see if it's something we need to fix for you."

You might say that this PM is multitasking with his mouth (triple-talk?!). First, he is insinuating that the customer's communication skills are poor. This is unfair (as well as tacky and rude) because the PM is making accusations about the specs being unclear without giving evidence, at a time when the customer can't really refute them. Second, he is blaming the customer at the same time he is apologizing. He is even casting doubt on whether any fix is warranted or will be forthcoming.

People sometimes use doubletalk as a deliberate tactic because they believe that "the best defense is a strong offense." This strategy may sometimes work in sports, but it is definitely not considered ethical behavior for a PM and is also often counterproductive.

Q26. What is *greenwashing*?

A26. Greenwashing is a modern form of doubletalk that frequently appears on corporate websites, social media pages, or TV advertising. The name is derived from the term *whitewashing*, which means covering up (painting over) the truth. Greenwashing goes a step further by putting an environmentally friendly ("green") spin on top of the cover-up.

For example, suppose a particular company suffered a major accident that led to significant environmental damage. Yet the company is also currently spending some of its research and development money to develop methods that would allow it to leave a smaller carbon footprint. The company is not ethically required to remind everyone about the accident on its corporate website. This would be going overboard. But if the site plays up the company's concern about the environment while the overall facts contradict that claim, the company is telling a lie of omission and painting over that lie by greenwashing. Furthermore, it is dishonest to present the information in a way that is an intentional attempt to take advantage of people who aren't aware of the accident.

AVOIDING UNETHICAL BEHAVIOR

Q27. What is *disclosure* in the PM world?

A27. Disclosure means sharing your knowledge in an open, honest fashion, as opposed to covering up information or being secretive about it. It is a core principle for PMs.

For example, let's say that you work for the government and are tasked with finding the best outsourcer for your customer's project. Suppose your research and best judgment lead you to choose the outsourcing company where your best friend happens to work. If you disclose the fact that it's your best friend's company, your customer and your management can factor that information into the decision to use that company or not, based on the true merits of your friend's company. But if you don't disclose the relationship, you are putting your agency at risk of getting in trouble for unfairly favoring your friend. You are even risking harm to your friend's reputation in the process because it could come out that they won a bid unfairly, when maybe they would have won the bid anyway, even if you had disclosed the relationship. The best thing to do is disclose your relationship with your friend, make the case for why you think her company is best for the project, and then let your management make an informed decision.

Q28. What does it mean to *recuse* oneself from a project, and why and when is it done?

A28. Sometimes it's best for a PM to resign from serving on a particular project. The situation above, in which the PM's best friend works for the company she is recommending for a government project, is a classic example. If the PM stays on the project that her friend's company was awarded, the government agency may be vulnerable to accusations of favoritism in the selection. But if the PM was upfront in disclosing the relationship and recused herself from the project, her department can safely use the outsourcer.

Q29. What is meant by the term *appearance of impropriety?*

A29. Even when a company is not doing anything unethical, if it *looks as if* it may have committed some wrongdoing—in other words, if there is an appearance of impropriety—the company can be hurt. Per the example in the previous two Q&As, even if the PM discloses the relationship and recuses herself from the project, and even if the government agency chose the outsourcer because it truly was the best-qualified seller, someone could still *say* that the outsourcer was chosen because of the friendship between the government PM and the outsourcer's employee. Unfortunately, this means that sometimes you cannot choose the best seller for your project because of the potential trouble that the appearance of impropriety could cause.

Q30. What is a *conflict of interest* in the business world, and how can they be avoided?

A30. The reason for the appearance of impropriety in the example above is the conflict of interest at the root of the situation. The PM who is recommending her friend's company may have two interests: She cares about helping her agency's project, and she also may care about sending business to her best friend, who stands to make a lot of money from the contract if the work gets awarded to her.

The PM's first loyalty should be to her government agency and customer, so her first priority should be to choose the best outsourcer. But what if she is in conflict between her loyalty to her job and her loyalty to her friend? She might think, "Well, there are a few good outsourcers. They are not too different, and my friend needs to put three kids through college, so let's say her company is the best!" It's human nature to want to help friends, but there is a clear conflict of interest here—and the PM and his management could get into trouble. This is why disclosure is so important and why recusal is also sometimes a recommended option.

OTHER ETHICAL CONSIDERATIONS

Q31. What is the difference between a *bribe* and a *kickback*?

A31. Bribes and kickbacks are related. They are both unethical, and in many circumstances are also both illegal. On projects, bribes and kickbacks typically involve a buyer/seller relationship. The seller offers the buyer money in exchange for selecting his company for the contract award. The main difference between a bribe and a kickback is the timing.

- *Bribe:* Suppose a PM's friend gives him an unusually large cash gift for his birthday. The friend knows that the PM is considering awarding his company with a contract. And to make the situation less subtle, suppose he talks a little like Tony Soprano. He says to the PM, "Happy birthday, and by the way, not for nuttin', but I hope my company gets that contract I know you was considerin' us for!" This would clearly be a bribe: He is giving the money with the expectation that the gift will influence the PM's decision.

- *Kickback:* Suppose no money was exchanged in advance, but *after* the PM's friend's company was awarded the large government contract, suddenly a new car appeared in the PM's driveway. The Soprano-kinda-guy drops by and says, "It's no biggie. It's for your son. In college."

- It is easy to see why accepting either kind of gift could ethically compromise a PM. This is the kind of offer you have to refuse.

Q32. Is it all right to use bootleg copies of software on a project?

A32. Even though money does not change hands in this situation, and software piracy is common, using bootleg software is unethical and illegal. Yes, modern technology has made it much easier to copy software. But that does not mean that stealing is suddenly OK!

Many kinds of documents, including internal research and development papers and presentation materials, as well as a lot of software products, fall under the umbrella of *intellectual property*, which is protected under copyright infringement laws. This guards the rights of the people who put in a lot of time and effort to create these materials. They are entitled to be asked permission for copies and usage and to be compensated for them, per the terms of the legal and corporate agreements.

Q33. Can I use materials I created at my old company at my new company?

A33. Surprisingly, the answer is often no, unless you were working under a contract that granted you the rights to those materials. In most cases, even though you created the materials, you did so under the employ of your former company, so usually, the material legally belongs to that company. Furthermore, it's highly likely nowadays that the company required you to sign a nondisclosure agreement (NDA) specifying that any intellectual property you developed while working at the company became and remains the excusive property of that company. (For more about NDAs, see Chapter 8, Q&A 40.)

If your former employer holds the rights to the materials, you would need to get their *express* written permission to reuse them. This means the company would grant you the right to reuse the material only for a specific purpose and only during your tenure at your current company. Express permission sometimes includes other restrictions as well; it may only allow usage within a certain time frame or may permit the use but not the *sale* of the materials.

Q34. Are there special ethical considerations in bidding situations?

A34. The PM always must be ethical and fair in any buyer/seller relationship but especially so in a bidding situation. For instance, you may be used to letting your vendors take you out to lunch to discuss business. But they were not bidding on contracts at the time—you routinely bought their goods and services as you saw fit. When you allow competing companies to bid on contracts, new rules apply: You are no longer allowed to favor one prospective seller in any way, whether by having lunch with its employees, accepting minor gifts, or exchanging any information that could give that company a competitive advantage over another seller.

Showing favoritism to prospective contractors is a very real problem. And more than a few people have even gone to jail over kickbacks, bribes, or other favoritism in the bidding process. So it is absolutely necessary that you maintain a level playing field for all vendors in a bid situation. You can't go wrong taking a 100-percent-professional approach in *all* of your dealings with vendor candidates, whether you're in a true bidding situation or in some less formal process of selecting your sellers.

Q35. What is *xenophobia*, and how is it expressed in communications on projects?

A35. Xenophobia is fear, distrust, or dislike of foreigners, and it can cause problems for PMs. Even if the PMs themselves are fair and equitable, they can get caught among stakeholders who harbor such feelings about other stakeholders. For instance, let's say that most of a team is located in one country, but some of the work is outsourced to workers in another country. This often causes resentment among employees who feel the outsourced workers are trying to take away their jobs and the jobs of their coworkers.

The best way to handle a situation like this is to aim for 100 percent fairness at all times and to have a policy of zero tolerance for xenophobic behavior. Note that it is entirely unacceptable for a PM to side with whichever group he or she is talking with at the time, as sometimes happens in these situations. This is a kind of double-talk that doesn't really help anything.

Q36. What are *microinequities*, and how do they relate to xenophobia?

A36. Microinequities are minor examples of xenophobic behavior. Many people in the business world may, in general, treat people of all backgrounds fairly, yet they might be guilty of furthering microinequities, possibly without even realizing it.

The current trend toward virtual teams and offshore outsourcing has fostered microinequities. Many American-based companies employ workers in foreign countries, primarily because labor is cheaper overseas. This can exacerbate sentiment against foreigners. The foreign workers may be well-treated in general, but there may be small, subtle cases of insensitive or rude behavior on projects. On top of being unethical, this of course can hurt the project, which requires the full cooperation of everyone on the team.

For example, the native English-speaking team members in the United States may not be tolerant of the less fluent language skills of team members on the other side of the ocean. This is sometimes expressed as impatience, or in jokes, or in a variety of other ways that show a lack of respect for the people on the other end of the call. Though these behaviors may be subtle, they can still be hurtful. (On top of that, it's unfair to treat the people to whom *we* outsourced the work with disdain as if it were *their* decision!)

Q37. Just to review the ethical issues we've discussed, how many ethical violations were apparent in the subprime mortgage crisis?

A37. A creative way to review ethics is to try to determine the underlying ethical problems that led to a real-world problem. Since everyone reading this book has probably heard about the subprime mortgage crisis and its link to the global financial meltdown of 2008–2009, how many ethical issues can you think of that may have played a role? Here are a bunch—can you add more?

- Many banks gave loans to people without verifying the borrower's income, probably in many cases to get the commission on the transactions, even though they knew that some of those loans could not be repaid. This is called predatory lending.

- The agents making the loans did not disclose to the borrowers how rising and sliding interest rates would make the borrowers' payments go up over the years—so much so that they could no longer afford them.

- On paper, the banks exaggerated the health of the loans for their balance sheets, while secretly referring to them internally as "toxic assets."

- Banks went ahead with these loans on the assumption that real estate values would, on a system-wide basis, *only* go up, when they knew, based on history and some contemporary regional examples (and common sense!) that this could not always be true.

- Taking these subprime loans and splitting them up into a sausage known as *mortgage-backed securities* (referred to as *slicing and dicing*) was something of a Ponzi scheme because, by definition, subprime loans are very high risk.

- The agencies rating both the loans and the securities based on these loans deliberately overrated them.

- Many borrowers knowingly misrepresented their income and assets to help them get loans they felt they needed but knew they were not qualified for.

CREATING AN ETHICAL WORKPLACE

Q38. What can I do to improve my company's ethics?

A38. If you notice an ethical problem at your company, there is probably something proactive you can do to help try to fix it. What if there are, for instance, microinequities in the way the team works with its outsourced staff? Maybe you can come up with team-building activities that could improve the work environment and even enhance team members' relationships. Sometimes just raising awareness of such situations in a discreet, professional way can make a difference, leading to more positive results for the team and the project.

Ethics is a factor to take into consideration the next time you are looking for a new job. In the days of corporate websites, online discussion groups, and YouTube videos, a wealth of information is available about many companies' corporate culture. If corporate ethics is important to you, why not spend a little time specifically researching that part of a prospective employer's makeup?

Q39. Should project team members ever work for free?

A39. If you think *of course* no one should ever be asked to work for free, then you probably have never been personally exploited in this way. It is one thing when an employee voluntarily does extra work for free, for the sake of helping the company or in the hopes of getting ahead. But an ethical line is crossed when the employee feels he or she can't say no to a request from a manager out of fear of retaliation. Two common examples follow:

- *Work now, maybe get paid later.* Consultants are sometimes told they will be paid down the road, once the project starts making a profit. That time may never come.

- *Work to get the work.* Workers are sometimes asked to put in unpaid hours to create proposals, build sample deliverables, or complete some other task that will hopefully, but not necessarily, help close a deal for the sponsor pitching the proposal. Workers should be paid for all such activities.

As a PM, you want to do everything you can to avoid situations like these for yourself, as well as for your team members.

Q40. What can a PM do to foster good ethics on his or her projects?

A40. For PMs, denying responsibility definitely will not cut it! For a project to be fully successful and avoid ethical problems that can lead to unhappy clients and lost business, it should be able to pass an ethical litmus test. And the best way to accomplish that is for the PM to:

- *Be fully accountable* for problems and mistakes on the project.
- *Lead by example.* If you want people to behave ethically while working on your project, you need to set the bar high by modeling good behavior in your treatment of stakeholders and in all the decisions you make as a PM.

- *Include ethics in your hiring criteria.* Don't be afraid to ask for references and to check them thoroughly. Also, consider including a question or two about ethics in the interview, such as, "What's an ethical challenge you have faced on a project, and how did you resolve it?" or "Does your current company have an ethics board, and if so, could you tell me about any involvement you may have had with the board?" or "*Business ethics* is a hard term to define—what's your take?" If an applicant finds it irresistible to try to be funny with an answer like, "It's what you say you'll do, but not what you'll really do," you'll be very glad you asked and think to yourself, "Next applicant, please!"

TOP TEN ETHICAL PITFALLS

1. Sacrificing quality to cut costs. This is a *very* common mistake: The customer or the performing organization tries to cut costs, but then the deliverables lack their intended quality.

2. Going along with a customer's request when you know it's not best for the project.

3. Not standing up for what you believe is the right decision.

4. Going along with groupthink to avoid making waves.

5. Contracting to a seller that is not the most qualified because you have an ulterior motive.

6. Looking the other way and not speaking up when you see wrongdoing because a higher-up is the one behaving unethically, and you think you need to go along to keep your job.

7. Asking staff to do extra free work.

8. Pressuring team members to sign petitions, support causes, or donate money to your favorite charities—and making them feel as if they have no choice.

9. Showing favoritism toward certain team members based on personal friendships or other non-merit-based reasons.

10. Lying by omission and dealing in bad faith.

CHAPTER 10

Communication Skills for PMs

Never say, "You're wrong!"

—Dale Carnegie

Ask a PM which is the most important project management skill set, and he or she will likely tell you it's the soft skills. Besides speaking and writing, soft skills also include listening skills, interpersonal skills, and emotional intelligence (EI).

Everyone who works in project management knows some highly technical PMs who are less effective than they could be because their soft skills are weak. Without strong people skills, PMs are limited in their abilities to gather requirements effectively, write team communications that get results, manage staff well, or interact successfully with their customers.

Missing a small cue by failing to read between the lines when conducting an interview can result in hiring the wrong team member, which can hurt a project. And misunderstanding just one aspect of a requirement, or failing to document it clearly, very often leads to rework and wasted resources.

This chapter explores many communication best practices, including tips on active listening, a discussion of how the five PMI communication processes and their outputs can help you, and valuable concepts from several of the most influential theorists. And because much of this skill set lies in avoiding common bad behaviors, this chapter includes a section on communication *worst* practices as well.

LISTENING SKILLS AND EMOTIONAL INTELLIGENCE

Q1. What is *effective listening*?

A1. Effective listening is a general term for doing everything you can to really hear the other person in an effort to create the most positive communication outcome. Communication glitches are the root cause of many errors that occur on projects, so putting extra effort into listening as well as you can is well worth it.

Q2. What is *active listening*, and how does it improve the communication process?

A2. Active listening is proactively showing the person you are communicating with that you hear and understand what they are saying. An important part of active listening is nonverbal communication—conscious and unconscious behaviors such as nodding, making eye contact, smiling, and facial expressions, all of which indicate that you are paying attention to and understand what the other person is saying. Active listening greatly reduces the risk of miscommunication errors because the listener's responses *prove* that he or she hears the speaker.

Active listening also provides an additional psychological benefit that further helps the communication process. People like to know that the other person is listening because it makes them feel acknowledged and valued. They are more eager to work with and cooperate with active listeners.

Q3. What are some examples of active listening through verbal methods?

A3.

- *Paraphrasing,* or repeating back what the other person has said, is a reliable way to make sure that you are on the same page. It proves that the listener understands—or doesn't understand—what the speaker has said. If there is a misunderstanding, the speaker can immediately clear it up.

- *Asking questions:* When you ask a question, you can show not only that you're listening, but that you really understand the other person. This can focus and strengthen the discussion, move the communication along, take it further than it might otherwise go, or even take it in a new direction.

- *Clarify and confirm:* At the end of a meeting (or at any point during a discussion), the participants take a minute or two to quickly summarize key points and make sure that everyone knows what they need to do to follow up on the conversation. In my experience, this technique is highly effective, and it is recognized as a best practice.

- *Sending a follow-up memo:* Summarize key points discussed and expected follow-up actions. This is like a written version of clarify and confirm. The memo does not have to be long; in fact, shorter is usually better. By covering the key points from the meeting, miscommunication, and, more important, performing the wrong work as a result of miscommunication are avoided.

Q4. What is *commit-to listening*, and how is it applied in practice?

A4. TV newspeople demonstrate commit-to listening when they lean all the way in toward an interview subject and stick their microphone right in the subject's face as they ask questions. Talk show host Phil Donahue did this so dramatically that it was parodied by the late Phil Hartman on *Saturday Night Live*.

In the PM world, it isn't necessary to go overboard like this; it would make the person you're listening to uncomfortable. But you should always show that you are totally focusing on him or her, through your body language, posture, facial expressions, and by making eye contact. A commitment to listening works because it demonstrates very strongly to the other person that you are listening to him or her. This reassures them, and makes them want to continue.

To fully focus on the other person, it is essential that you avoid distractions. For example, even if you are under pressure to get your work done, don't glance at your smartphone or laptop to scan your email or send off a quick instant message. There is a term for these distractions: noise.

Q5. Why is noise considered a barrier to communications?

A5. Anything that interferes with listening, such as looking at a cell-phone screen or laptop or wearing earphones, is considered noise. Even if the listener has a very important reason for needing to stay connected to his or her messages at the time, the other person doesn't know this. To him or her, it looks as if you are distracted or, worse, rude and disrespectful.

If you find yourself in a situation in which you must keep your eye on your incoming email or phone calls, apologize to the other person up front and let him or her know that you may need to take a call from your wife at the hospital, for example. The other party will almost certainly understand, and he or she will appreciate your respect for his or her time and feelings.

Q6. What is *empathic listening*, and how can it help in communications?

A6. Empathic listening is a term coined by David R. Covey and used in his book *The 7 Habits of Highly Effective People*. It is based on the idea that the more empathy you have for the person you are communicating with—in other words, the more easily you can put yourself in his or her shoes—the better you can really *hear* the other person, which helps you understand and work successfully with him or her.

Like active listening, it's a proactive approach. Let's say that you are a PM negotiating with a stakeholder. Empathic listening would include elements of the following:

- *Letting the other person talk first* about his or her needs, before you talk about what you want. As a PM, for example, it might be to your advantage to let the resource management speak first when negotiating resources.

- *Going for a true win-win result* by asking questions like: "I hate to take your best designer, but you know I need her for next week's brainstorming session. Which twenty-hour period would work best for you next week?"

- *Making sure the other party feels listened to, understood, and appreciated.* "I know how rough it's been for your team working all that overtime for the client. We especially want to thank you for lending us their expertise last night on that after-hours bug."

Q7. How can an awareness of paralingual vocal qualities help PMs hear between the words and foster better listening?

A7. Some PMP® prep books use the word *paralingual* to describe the messages a skilled listener can hear in someone's voice, beyond the words themselves. Misunderstandings often arise because a person's words don't fully express what he or she is trying to say. This happens in electronic communications all the time, but it also happens quite often in spoken language, even when people are communicating face to face.

Paralingual Quality	What Can It Indicate?
Volume	An overly loud voice can indicate anger, impatience, or nervousness.
Tone	Tone may suggest feelings, such as anger, suspicion, or apprehension, that are not expressed in the speaker's words.
Rhythm/ cadence	How fast someone is talking, and how long he or she pauses between words or phrases, can also indicate how he or she is really feeling.
Inflection	Did the speaker's voice rise in pitch at the end of a sentence, indicating that he or she was asking a question or that he or she feels uncertain or indecisive? Or did his or her voice drop in pitch at the end of the sentence, suggesting that the speaker has confidence in what he or she is saying?

Figure 10-1: Paralingual Vocal Qualities

Figure 10-1 lists of a few of the most important qualities to listen for in someone's voice and what each may indicate to a listener who is trying to hear between the words.

Test Your Listening Skills

- If your interpersonal skills are already strong, you can probably name several paralingual qualities in addition to the ones listed in Figure 10-1. Take another look at the list and then spend a few minutes to think of others you would add.
- If you think that a team member should improve her listening skills, show her the list in Figure 10-1, and challenge her to try to add five more of her own.

For example, paralingual qualities can tell us about a speaker's:

- ***Mood and confidence:*** Even if a team member claims that his work is going well, his voice may reveal his true feelings. A shaky voice or speaking in a lower or higher pitch than normal could all betray a lack of confidence in the estimate he is giving you or suggest that he has a problem he's not telling you about.
- ***Truthfulness:*** A reliable ability to tell when someone is lying is priceless for PMs. For example, it's helpful to be able to determine if a vendor is

not telling you the truth about whether a bug fix has been fully tested. Some questions you might ask to determine this: When a vendor tells you a bug has been fixed, do they say it like they want to sit down and talk about it further? Do they bring up how they verified the fix? Or do they speak briefly about it, as if they want to quickly move on to the next agenda item?

Another situation might involve vendor references. When you ask a vendor for a reference, do they say, "Yes, we have references we *could* furnish?" Or do they say, "Yes, we have five customers that we would *love* to connect you with so you can hear how much they like our app!" In the first case you can hear hesitation; in the second case the vendor seems to be exuding confidence and an eagerness to discuss references.

Q8. What is *emotional intelligence*, and how is it related to listening skills?

A8. A lot of what is called emotional intelligence, or EI, is the ability to read other people. Part of it is listening skills: hearing what people are *really* saying, which often is very different from what they are actually saying in words. EI is also about picking up cues from others' body language and facial expressions, which specifically is sometimes called *emotional awareness*. This is a person's ability to *interpret* others' attitude, emotions, and all of the other information they communicate, intentionally and unintentionally. The way a person treats others, and his or her instincts about other people, are also components of EI.

Related to the ability to interpret nonverbal cues is the ability to read silences. When you say something to your team and no one answers, do you assume they are agreeing with you? Silence always sounds like silence! The key to being emotionally astute in situations like this is to read faces very carefully and ask follow-up questions, to make sure you're not missing something that no one felt comfortable mentioning. PMs often don't follow up this way because they are assuming that if anyone disagreed, they would speak up, which isn't always the case.

Many people feel that EI is largely innate. But much of it is a matter of using effective listening and interpreting skills and picking up nuances in what people say. EI is critically important for PMs because managers with very strong EI tend to hire the right people, choose the best projects, and, in general, show good instincts in making decisions about people. Think about how valuable these business decisions can be and what a difference they can make in a PM's career.

THE PMI COMMUNICATIONS MANAGEMENT PROCESSES

Q9. What are the five communications management processes discussed in the *PMBOK*® *Guide*?

A9. The PMBOK® Guide discusses these five processes:

1. Identifying stakeholders
2. Planning communications
3. Distributing information
4. Managing stakeholder expectations
5. Reporting performance.

Each of these communication processes is discussed individually in the following five Q&As, which emphasize how the processes and their outputs can help you on your projects.

Q10. What is the purpose of the stakeholder register, and when is the stakeholder identification process executed?

A10. The stakeholder register (covered in detail in Chapter 3) is created during the process of identifying stakeholders, which is done very early in a project. The register is a PM best-practice document designed specifically to improve communications on your project.

If you are a PM who has great people skills and a high EI, you may be able to remember the name and role of every stakeholder on your project. But not everyone can do this, especially on large, dynamic projects, and not all team members interact with all the stakeholders the way the PM does, so they would have no way of knowing the same details. A stakeholder register gives you a place to document key information about project stakeholders. It's a quick, easy way to share information that you want your team to know, and it's very easy to create. A simple spreadsheet in Excel or Word is all you need. Create one column for the stakeholders' names and another for their roles and responsibilities. Other columns for additional data, such as the name of each stakeholder's manager, the department he or she works for, and his or her agenda, goals, and issues, might also be useful (see Figure 3-2).

Note that this document also becomes an important input to the process of collecting requirements and can be a precursor for one of the key documents created in that process: the requirements traceability matrix (also described and illustrated in Chapter 3; see Figure 3-3).

Q11. What is a *communications management plan,* and what should it include?

A11. The communications management plan is also created early, during the communications planning process. Many PMs I meet tell me they have been badly burned at one time or another by a communication snafu. And yet most also confess they have never created a communications management plan, the purpose of which is to avoid such snafus by putting communication *ground rules* in place and laying out in writing how information will be distributed on your project.

PMs should speak with their customers early on to determine the kind of information they want, as well as the desired format and the frequency of updates. Put these agreements in writing. This will serve as the communications part of your project plan.

When you are building a communications management plan, think about situations in which a miscommunication caused trouble for you or your team. Could a written ground rule have prevented it?

- Did one of your team members send information he or she shouldn't have to a client?

- Have two of your stakeholders ever come to a meeting with different versions of the schedule or project plan?

- Did you ever find out too late that a client felt that it was receiving updates on the project too infrequently (or too frequently)?

Figure 10-2 lists sample ground rules PMs commonly include in communications management plans as well as examples of the kind of problems each ground rule can help prevent.

Ground Rule	What this Rule Is Intended to Prevent
On this project, only the following three managers may send notes directly to the client: Jane A. (project manager), Bob S. (project scheduler), and Susan J. (quality manager).	The release of information that shouldn't be sent to the client. (Note that this may work best if, as in this example, more than one person is listed, so that the PM does not appear to be overly controlling.)
Updated versions of the project plan will be distributed weekly to all stakeholders on Tuesdays at 3:00 p.m. • The new baseline will be uploaded to the intranet site at the following URL.... • These updates will also announced by email, and a hotlink to each new version will be included. (Note to team: Please test hotlinks before sending out the email!)	Lack of awareness of when updates will be distributed and confusion about how to access new versions of the plan.
Please be sure that all project-related communications take place using *company-issued* cell phones, laptops, and email accounts.	Delays, snarls, and frustrations when email attachments cannot be opened because stakeholders are using personal equipment and protocols.

Figure 10-2: Ground Rules in the Communications Management Plan

Q12. What does the process of distributing information cover?

A12. This is the catch-all process for doing everything you promised to do in the communications management plan. It encompasses all of the primary written and spoken communications for your project. The process includes conducting meetings with your team and customer, sending out notes to your stakeholders, updating documentation databases—in other words, interacting with people on your project.

Note that PMI considers the process of distributing information to be part of the executing process group. This process is all about conducting the everyday communications necessary to get the main work of the project completed. It does *not* include the preparation or distribution of performance reports, which are the output of the next process discussed in Q&A 13.

Q13. What are performance reports and the process of reporting performance, and how does that process differ from distributing information?

A13. Performance reports, created in the process of reporting performance, are communications that deal specifically with variances, meaning any situation in which a project is not performing according to plan—whether it is late, over budget, underperforming, ahead of schedule, or overperforming. When PMs calculate earned value (covered in detail in Chapter 6), they compile the results into a single report, referred to as a performance report, and send it to their key stakeholders.

To emphasize the distinction between performance reports and more common memos, PMI designates the creation of these reports as the process of reporting performance, separate from the process of distributing information. Reporting performance is part of the monitoring and controlling process group because its purpose is to keep a constant eye on the project to make sure that it is staying on plan and to home in as soon as possible on any deviation from the plan and nip it in the bud. When a project deviates from the plan, the PM must determine whether the variance is a problem, analyze it to see if it might indicate a trend, report it in a performance report, and, most important, try to correct it wherever possible.

Q14. What is the PMI process of managing stakeholder expectations?

A14. Technical success on a project is not worth very much at the end of the day if you don't have satisfied customers, and one of the keys to customer satisfaction is effectively communicating with them to keep them in the loop and prevent unpleasant surprises. This is the process of managing stakeholder expectations. An important part of managing expectations is *level-setting* customers—meaning fully sharing plans, updates, and changes with them, so they know what to expect and can plan accordingly.

Many PMs make the cardinal mistake of doing the work correctly but not communicating fully with their clients. Suppose a client asks for a bug fix. The PM asks her developer to create this fix, and the developer plunges feverishly into the work and completes the fix, maybe a little late, all without saying a word to the customer. The result? The customer doesn't know if the fix was even begun, much less completed, when the deadline comes and may assume the worst. When the deadline comes, the customer may call the PM and ask if the work is done. The PM asks her technician if the work is done and is told no. The PM then has to tell her customer, no, the work isn't done. If the customer had been kept in the loop, he might have been satisfied that things were moving along well enough and appreciate the team's hard work and progress on fixing the bug.

The result of inadequate communication, all too often, is stakeholder unhappiness, which spills over into the rest of the project. But by proactively taking the time to manage the expectations of customers, the sponsor, and other stakeholders, a PM can often boost the overall success of a project. One example of managing expectations—sending a note to say that you'll send expected information later—is so effective that it warrants its own Q&A.

Q15. Why should I bother sending a note to say I'll be sending a note?

A15. Sending a note letting a customer know that you are not ready yet to send her what she wants, but that you will be sending it soon, on such and such a date and time, is a great way to manage her expectations. But it's often not done, because many PMs think that it's not as good as sending the expected information, so why bother? They may think that sending a note calls attention to the fact that the information is late. Or they may assume that the customer *knows* they are working hard, so it's not necessary.

But this is exactly the point of managing stakeholder expectations: Let them know when to expect deliverables, especially when you're running a little late. If you don't, you are making two mistakes: First, you are late, and second, you didn't inform the client in advance. But if you do inform the client, you will have made lemonade out of lemons. It is almost guaranteed

Managing Stakeholder Expectations Is Like Caring for Pets

We wouldn't want to compare your stakeholders to pets (we know how much you love your pets!), but many pet owners will like this analogy.

If you are trying to prepare your dog or cat's dinner, but she is impatiently barking or meowing for you to hurry up, you may be surprised to learn that, instead of trying to shush her into submission, you can show your pet the can of food and tell her you will feed her in a minute. This will quiet her down—now she will understand that her meal is coming right up.

You may already have realized that this is similar to the idea of sending a note to an impatient customer, assuring him that his report is midway to completion and will be in his inbox in two hours.

that she will appreciate the heads-up; and as a bonus, it will help build the client's trust in you.

COMMUNICATING WITH STAKEHOLDERS

Q16. What did communications expert Marshall McLuhan mean when he wrote, "The medium is the message," and how can PMs benefit from this idea?

A16. One of the secrets of success in communications is choosing the best delivery medium for your message. I once had a student who told me she won an award at work, but her company delivered it to her house on a Saturday. When the deliveryman came to the door, her first thought was that it was a pink slip, and she is still displeased with her company about this incident to this day!

While the message and the medium are clearly two separate things, McLuhan meant that they are linked, and the delivery method can alter the way the message is received and even how the content is understood. When crafting any message, it is always worth putting some thought into determining the best possible way to transmit it. If a face-to-face meeting is going to have the best long-term result (if, for example, you're presenting an award), you shouldn't take a shortcut by sending it to the recipient's house. This could diminish its value. With regard to project communications, think about the available communication channels—email, instant messages, phone calls, private meetings, or group meetings—and decide which one is most likely to ensure that your message will be understood the way you want it to be.

Q17. How can I decide whether formal or informal communication channels are most appropriate for my message?

A17. Related to "the medium is the message," it is important not only to choose the correct medium for each message, but to decide how formal or informal the communication should be within that medium. PMI addresses this issue because the relative formality of the medium can significantly affect how your message will be received and even how it will be interpreted.

For instance, suppose you have a serious announcement to deliver to your stakeholders, such as an upcoming merger. A typical email note might not be appropriate for this message because the impact would be lost in the shuffle of numerous emails. So you decide that you'd like to send a formal note to stakeholders, but you also need the speed and convenience of email.

A modern compromise might be to write your note in Word, in traditional memorandum format, but then cut and paste the memo into an email, keeping the original fonts and formatting from Word and maybe changing the usual background color. This would make the notice look more formal, and recipients would spend a little more time reading it.

Or, taking it up a notch, send the Word document itself as an attachment to your email. In the subject line you might write, "Important news we've been hoping for—please read the attachment carefully." This will notify the recipients that the message is somewhat formal and that they should give it more attention than they would a typical email.

Q18. What does the term *proxemics* mean, and what is its role in communications?

A18. Proxemics is the study of spatial closeness between people in interpersonal situations, particularly the decisions we make about our physical proximity to other people. For example, when you are interacting with someone you're just getting to know, do you want to move closer to establish friendship or intimacy? Or do you want to keep a distance to maintain a more business-like manner (and to avoid comparisons to the "close talker" character played by Judge Reinhold on the classic *Seinfeld* episode)? Do you want to shake hands when you meet someone new? Should you put your hand on a coworker's shoulder as you're waiting for the elevator?

Some of these choices come naturally as you meet and get to know people. The stronger your interpersonal skills and EI, the easier these decisions will be and the more likely you will be to make the correct ones. You can even plan situations in advance to ensure that people will be comfortable, which can make a difference in the quality of communications. For instance, for meetings, you can pick the best room, in terms of size and location, for the group and arrange the chairs and table such that people will wind up ideally situated near each other.

Q19. What is the communication channels formula, and why do PMs use it to plan communications on a project?

A19. Have you ever wondered how many possible one-to-one conversations are possible in a group? PMs use the communication channels formula to make this calculation. The formula is N (N − 1) / 2, where N is the number of group members.

For example, in a team of four people, Bob, Carol, Ted, and Alice, there are six possible one-to-one combinations:

$$N (N − 1) / 2$$
$$4 (4 − 1) / 2 = (4 * 3) / 2 = 12 / 2 = 6$$

Bob & Carol	Bob & Alice	Bob & Ted
Ted & Alice	Ted & Carol	Carol & Alice

While the formula has some specific applications for planning, most of the PMs I know tell me they use the formula in a more general way to remind their management that when they increase their group size by a certain amount, that it opens up x-number of new communication channels. This is important to know when considering how many people you might want to share confidential information with, for instance, because it sheds light on the number of exposures—people who might leak the information.

Note that the formula only counts the one-to-one combinations, or channels. Sometimes you may want to consider *all* possible channels, not just one-to-one combinations. For instance, if you are splitting your team into subgroups, it can be helpful to map out the list of all possible combinations when you're thinking about the best ways for the groups to communicate—via in-person meeting, teleconference, videoconference, online chat, screen sharing, or a blend of the above. Within our group of four people, we've seen that there are six one-to-one channels, but there would be 11 combinations altogether when you factor in the additional combinations of four sets of three, e.g., Bob & Carol & Alice, plus the group of four itself.

Keep in mind that PMP® and CAPM candidates are expected to know and be able to use this formula on the certification exams. (See Appendix B for all the PMP®/CAPM formulas.)

Q20. What communication secrets can we learn from alpha project managers—the top PMs?

A20. Andy Crowe, PMP® guru and author, led a study on what separates the very best PMs from all others. In case studies of more than 800 PMs, the top 2 percent were ranked as "alphas," and their stakeholders cited these PMs' communication skills as the number-one key to their effectiveness.[1] Here is a quick summary of his findings related to communications:

- Communication skills were the number-one differentiator between alpha PMs and non-alphas.
- The PMs rated as alphas outperformed the non-alphas by 31 percent in the area of communications.
- Many of the PMs who were rated highest as communicators were also rated highest overall (partly because of their high scores on communications).
- A much greater percentage of alphas cited communications as a tool that positively helped their projects.
- The alphas viewed communications as an ongoing *deliverable* of the project, not just as a tool in service of the project's deliverables. This means they put the same kind of care and thought into their communications that they did into their external deliverables.

USING COMMUNICATION TECHNOLOGIES

Q21. How can electronic communications cause management problems?

A21. Email and instant messages can be cold and impersonal, and they some-times lead to misunderstandings because they are *one-way* communications. When two people are talking together, they can hear nuances in each other's speech and can also quickly clarify any perceived misunderstandings. It's more difficult and takes longer to clear up misunderstandings that arise from an email or IM conversation.

Also, people may resent receiving work-related emails, instant messages, and text messages during their off hours—especially if the sender expects or demands an immediate response. Many people still prefer boundaries around their work time and don't want to be tethered to their phone or computer. Effective PMs respect these boundaries as part of professionalism and, also, as a measure against needlessly burning out their team members.

Q22. When is multitasking counterproductive to effective communication?

A22. Many studies have shown that true multitasking is largely a myth: People don't multitask as well as they think they do. Even *computers* don't really multitask—they just do things so fast that they appear to be doing them simultaneously. There is significant evidence that people trying to do two things at once are usually less effective at both and that it actually takes them *longer* to accomplish the tasks than if they did each one separately. So, when you try to scan your emails while you're talking to someone in the same room with you, you not only risk seeming rude, but you would process your messages more effectively and efficiently if you waited until after the meeting and devoted yourself completely to your email.

Q23. Is marking emails "urgent" or "confidential" worthwhile?

A23. As long as you don't overdo it, it is well worth taking advantage of some of your email application's mood-stamp features. For instance, to make a note more formal or to capture recipients' attention, some email protocols let you stamp a message "urgent" or "confidential" or "question" or "thank you" or "reply requested." And some also add on a visual icon appropriate to each stamp, such as a question mark when you mark it as a question.

If you have never used these features, they are very quick and easy to access and can help your messages make a strong instant impression. A word of caution, however: Don't overdo it. People who stamp "urgent" on everything become the boy who cried wolf, and overuse dilutes the impact of all these mood stamps.

Q24. Why are communication technologies such as teleconferencing and videoconferencing sometimes counterproductive?

A24. Many PMs love to embrace the latest technologies, but even truly great innovations in technology may have potential downsides. PMs who want to communicate as effectively as possible are careful to learn new technologies well in advance of using them and only use them when they truly will enhance communications.

Imagine that you're about to run a virtual meeting. Here are a few technology pointers to keep in mind:

- Don't assume that, from your client's point of view, your virtual presence is just as good as being there in person. Before you decide to conference in, ask your client if videoconferencing is really sufficient.

- Make sure materials are distributed in advance to all participants, instead of assuming everyone will get them. Often, people don't wind up pulling all the slides from the shared drive in advance or something else comes up if you're not careful to confirm such details. Even if you emailed everyone the materials in advance, call a participant or two well before the meeting to walk them through the download and any setup. They can then show the rest of their team in the remote location how to access the materials.

- Remember, no matter how amazing the latest and greatest videoconferencing tool might seem, don't assume everything will go perfectly. Be sure to set up and practice using any new software and hardware in advance, and allow a little extra time the first time you use it. Also, it's always good to have a backup plan. For instance, just in case a videoconference has glitches, think in advance about how you might deliver the same meeting without the video working. For instance, send everyone all the slides and other visual aids in advance so they could walk through the materials at their desks on a regular conference call if needed.

AGREEMENT AND DIPLOMACY

Q25. Why did interpersonal relations pioneer Dale Carnegie write, "Never say, 'You're wrong!'"?

A25. This is one of several core principles in Dale Carnegie's classic work *How to Win Friends and Influence People*. Most people have a strong aversion to being told they're wrong. Refraining from pointing out others' mistakes is one step toward getting along well with others.

- **If it's not an important mistake, don't correct the other person at all.** It's better to just let it go. For instance, if you're talking about holding a team meeting at a restaurant at the corner of Broadway and 46th Street, and someone says that it's called Macintosh's, but the name is really McTavish's, why point his error out to him, possibly embarrassing him? If everyone on the team knows where the restaurant is, it's better to be diplomatic and let it go. Your lunch will go a lot better this way—most people like being agreed with a lot more than they like being corrected.

- **If you do have to correct someone, make it sound as little like a correction as possible.** When it *is* necessary to correct another person, it's important not to hurt his or her feelings or, worse, shame him or her by calling attention to the mistake. This is also good for your sake, too, because you'll do better if you don't alienate any of your stakeholders. There are many subtle ways of saying someone is wrong without saying, "You're wrong." They just take a little extra thought, and they work like a magic trick. Try saying:
    - "I basically agree with you, but let me add this small point..."
    - "I think we're on the same page. But what we agree we want to do is this..."
    - "I'm not saying you're wrong, I'm just saying that..." (There's an obvious contradiction here, and yet, funnily enough, this approach works.)

Q26. Why should I pretend to agree if I really don't agree?

A26. There are two ways to answer the question, "Isn't the weather nice and warm today?" Most people instinctively go for agreement and say something like "Yes, very good for this time of year." But some people—maybe they're feeling crabby or contrary—might respond with conversation killers like: "Actually, it's five degrees colder than it should be for this month." Or "It won't last long—rain is predicted for the weekend."

In project management, you'll find that being agreeable will generally help you in your communications (note the root word of *agreeable* is *agree*!). People tend to avoid those who like to disagree for the sake of disagreeing and who seem to look for reasons to constantly tell people that that they're wrong. (For a hilarious example of how being disagreeable does *not* make for good customer service, watch a "Nick Burns: Your Company's Computer Guy" sketch from *Saturday Night Live.*)

For more about diplomacy—and why Nick Burns' shaming approach is not the recommended way to go—see the following two Q&As.

Q27. Can people learn to be more diplomatic?

A27. Some extraordinary people are so smooth in social situations that they seem to be born diplomats. But there are some tricks of the trade that I believe any PM can add to his or her repertoire. The next time you observe someone you consider very diplomatic, you will probably notice some common behaviors. Politeness and good manners are usually part of the foundation, and those are easily learned. But in addition to these, some people use language very diplomatically, with excellent results. (As an American, I have noticed that Europeans in particular seem to be able to use diplomatic language with finesse.)

Try:

- *Phrasing a request as a question, rather than like an order.* Instead of saying, "I need you to do this by tomorrow," consider saying, "Do you think you could work on this and get it done by tomorrow?" This approach:
  o Suggests that you are giving the other person a choice—though it's still very clear that you need him or her to do the work. Most people will be more willing to fulfill a request than follow an order.
  o Seems to imply that you are giving the other person a chance to determine whether the timeline is fair relative to the size of the task.
  If you soften the wording in this way, make sure to use a tone of voice that indicates you are serious. The words can form a question, but the tone should make it sound like a gentle yet firm request.

- *Giving the other person an out.* When making a request, make it sound like you are giving them the option to say no (even though you really aren't!). For instance, you might say, "Unless you're not able, I really need this by tomorrow." Be careful not to do this in a way that might make them feel they can push you around. The point is to get them to do the work by asking gracefully. But you do need to preserve the dynamic that you're the manager directing the assignment.

Q28. What is the concept of *no blame, no shame?*

A28. Children don't like being shamed, and adults don't like being made to feel like shamed children. Yet there is a lot of blaming and shaming in the business world. A best practice when talking with someone about a mistake he or she made is to stick to the facts and focus on lessons learned, with a future-oriented point of view. Talk as objectively as possible about how things will go correctly in the future by implementing a solution to the problem the team just experienced, rather than focusing on how this whole "mess" could have been avoided. Sometimes you may have to bite your tongue not to point out the faults, but blaming and shaming yield negative results, and if you get a reputation for being a blamer and a shamer, people won't want to work with you.

Q29. What is the best way to handle my own personal mistakes?

A29. No one likes to admit being at fault, so when a PM takes responsibility for his or her own personal mistakes, stakeholders and team members almost always respect the PM all the more for it. (This is especially true if the PM claims accountability for a team member's mistake.) Being able to admit responsibility for mistakes is one quality that separates true leaders from mere managers. So even though it's uncomfortable and a little scary to admit to a mistake in the corporate world, try taking ownership. You may get positive feedback and increased cooperation as a result.

Q30. What is going for a *win-win?*

A30. Working to ensure that both parties in a negotiation or conflict "win" is a project management best practice. Your communications should make clear that you want your side and the other side both to walk away satisfied. This sounds simple enough, and many PMs successfully negotiate win-wins all the time. But some PMs believe that to win, they have to make sure the other side loses. The problem is that a win-lose in project management doesn't get you a gold belt like in the boxing ring, and it isn't really a sustainable, long-term victory in the PM world. You still have to work with the other party, who may resent you for winning at their expense. If you have a choice between a win-lose and a win-win, a win-win will likely yield better results. The other party also will feel good about the project, instead of wanting revenge. And the happier the other side is, the better things will turn out for you, too—you will reap goodwill, referrals, and recommendations.

COMMUNICATION PRACTICES TO AVOID

Q31. What is *spin* in the PM world?

A31. Spin is not exactly lying. It is coloring facts with emotion or attitude. Imagine that a rumor that no one will receive a raise this year has been going around your company. When an employee asks about the rumor, a top manager says, "Well, let me address that. I believe I'm seeing signs that the company *is* starting to turn around! Let me tell you about some of the great things that are happening!"

The manager is putting a positive spin on the company's financial situation and skating by the employee's question about raises. Notice he has carefully chosen words such as: "I believe," and "signs" as opposed to "numbers" (so nothing he said is factually incorrect). But his response is a little *like* lying, because the company may or may not be doing well financially, but he is strongly implying that it is. He's putting a very positive spin on the situation. Meanwhile this makes the employee doubly frustrated because her question was not directly answered, and she probably is also very aware her manager was not being up front. (See also the definition of *smoothing* in Q&A47, Chapter 11.)

Q32. Is it all right to tell a white lie to spare a team member's feelings?

A32. People working on projects sometimes tell white lies in an attempt to avoid an unpleasant discussion or conflict. They rationalize doing so by claiming that the lies are intended to spare someone's feelings. While trying to avoid hurting people is great, white lies are almost never as good as direct, honest, open communication.

White lies often sweep problems under the rug and can create ripple effects. Suppose that a manager tells different versions of the truth to whichever employee he's speaking to. For example, he tells two employees that they each will be the only developer of an exciting new app. The manager's approach might prevent conflict in the short run. But when the two developers find out they will *not* be the sole developer—and of course they will eventually find out—animosity might develop between them, and they also will resent and lose respect for the manager for lying to them. If the manager had been up front in the first place, the developers could have remained friendly, and they would have respected the manager for having the courage to deliver the news, even if it wasn't exactly what either wanted to hear.

Q33. What exactly is triangulation, and why is it a poor strategy for resolving conflict?

A33. The best way to resolve an interpersonal conflict is one-to-one, directly and openly. This is a core PM principle. But it's a lot easier to simply complain to a third party and avoid the conflict. People find satisfaction in venting and also may hope that the third person will magically fix the problem. Involving a third person in a conflict is called triangulation, and it can lead to big problems. For example, if the person the injured party is complaining about finds out (and he or she probably will), he or she may feel betrayed and angry at the other two.

Unfortunately, unless the third party is Dr. Phil, triangulation usually accomplishes nothing, except to make the injured party feel better in the moment. The simple solution: When you have an issue with another stakeholder, always try to be direct with him or her, and cut out the middleman. Both the *PMBOK® Guide* and Dr. Phil would agree on this one!

Q34. How does passive-aggressive behavior affect projects?

A34. Passive-aggressive behavior is a way of expressing anger by taking *indirect* and usually counter-productive action. Often, an underlying issue or resentment causes this behavior, but that doesn't excuse it or make it an effective way to deal with a situation.

Here are two examples of how passive aggression might be manifested in project management:

- A project team member is angry at the PM, so he says something sarcastic to a team member in the morning meeting, under the guise of just being funny.
- A PM asks a competitive resource manager for a little training to help her team learn how to use the company's new content management system. The resource manager offers "help" in an uncooperative way by responding: "You don't need me to show you how to use the system. I believe there's a good document, in fact, that one of your own team members wrote. It's probably online, on a shared drive somewhere."

In the second bullet, the resource manager's response is passive aggressive in several ways:

- The help the resource manager offers—the document—is not the kind of help that the PM requested. She would prefer hands-on training.

- Whether or not the document truly is useful (or even exists), the resource manager doesn't go to the trouble of explaining exactly where it could be found.

- Throwing in that one of the PM's team members wrote the document is subtly insulting because it implies the PM should have known about it.

Q35. Is it ever OK to share confidential information in an effort to bond with a client or coworkers?

A35. Sharing secrets is a recipe for disaster. They tend to be revealed at inconvenient times, causing damage that cannot easily be undone. Moreover, it is unethical. For example, telling a client something that a colleague told you in confidence is a clear betrayal of confidence and a form of deception. Finally, many people will deem you unprofessional if you reveal confidential information to them. They will listen to your secret, but they may also make a mental note that you are untrustworthy for bringing it to them.

Q36. What is meant by *false balance*, and how can it harm a project?

A36. *False balance* is the presentation of information suggesting that an issue is more balanced between opposing sides than the evidence supports. Okrent's Law expresses this concept: "The pursuit of balance can create imbalance because sometimes something is true."

For example, we all know that Columbus landed in the Americas in 1492. This is a fact that can be backed up. But let's say that someone insisted that Columbus' journey actually took place in 1494. Obviously, it would not be reasonable to say, "Let's split the difference and go with 1493." Suggesting 1493 as an acceptable compromise is an attempt to achieve false balance. But you can see from this example how silly it is to compromise when that would be going against the facts.

False balance is unfortunately a common rhetorical tactic. False balance arguments are often used when one party *knows* they are not correct, but just wants to get their way. It can cause delays on a project because it puts the other party on the defensive, having to try to come up with arguments for why his or her facts are true (even though they are facts, not opinions). This is an impediment to getting at the truth of a situation and should be scrupulously avoided. (It's hard enough trying to solve problems *without* people playing rhetorical games!)

Q37. How can drawing false parallels get in the way of a positive discussion?

A37. A false parallel is an inaccurate comparison that is made with the intention of pushing an agenda. For example, when an idea is proposed during a meeting, a stakeholder who is against the idea will compare it to a scenario from another project—one that failed. The idea from the other project may not be similar enough to make it a worthwhile analogy. But in a quick meeting, there isn't always time to analyze all the similarities and differences. And once the comparison is made, it can stick in the other stakeholders' minds, unfairly linking the new idea with the failure of the old idea. It's best for the PM to nip this kind of tactic in the bud because it can prevent the best decisions from prevailing on a project.

Similar in nature to a false parallel is a specious argument, which is an argument that is intentionally designed to win a debate—but the person who is arguing the point doesn't believe it him- or herself.

Q38. What is arguing in bad faith, and why is it dangerous?

A38. In a well-ordered PM environment, everyone strives to be honest and up front and to stick to the facts. When there is conflict, they argue in good faith, saying what they mean and meaning what they say. The opposite of this is called arguing in bad faith: arguing based on an agenda and refusing to let those pesky facts get in the way.

For example, suppose on a buy-or-build decision, some key stakeholders want to stick with their old system and upgrade it, but the PM feels that the best solution is a brand new powerful app out on the marketplace. Maybe the stakeholders secretly realize that buying a new app is the best solution, but have an alternative agenda for sticking with the old system. So they come to a meeting with a list exaggerating the risks of the new product, and they claim that early adopters of that new app experienced *major* problems when maybe there were minor problems that were easily resolved by the vendor. False balance, false parallel, and spin are also specific tactics used when arguing in bad faith.

TOP TEN WRITTEN COMMUNICATION PITFALLS

1. Sending an email with no subject line (or an old subject line from an earlier message, or an unclear or off-target subject line). It only takes a few seconds to write a good subject line, and it can save your reader time and eliminate confusion.

2. Not writing a clean, concise first sentence and opening paragraph.

3. Sending a "reply all" when it isn't necessary for everyone to see the follow-up note. Unnecessary messages take up email storage space (and cause BlackBerrys to buzz when people are in the bathtub). Worse, carelessly hitting "reply all" can result in the wrong people receiving the email. (Imagine the client getting a confidential note about the client!)

4. Mass-mailing messages that would be more effective if you sent them individually and tailored them to each recipient. It's not always time effective to do this, but sometimes targeting the message to each recipient can make a big difference in the way they respond. Many people prefer the personal touch and pay more attention to messages that appear to be just for them.

5. Not clearly stating the follow-up action you want the recipient to take. Your request should be in a prominent part of your note, such as the first sentence of the first paragraph or the last sentence of the last paragraph—not buried somewhere in the middle.

6. Not checking your note for accuracy, grammar, and spelling before sending it out. Errors make you look unprofessional and distract the reader from your message. (And spell check only gets you so far. When in doubt, run the note by a team member or colleague first).

7. Not testing the attachments and links in your message in advance. Missing attachments and broken links frustrate the recipient and make you look careless.

8. Writing a note in all caps. Not only is all-caps text difficult to read, recipients may feel as if you are yelling at them. If you give recipients the impression that you can't be bothered to hit the shift bar, readers may think that you are implicitly saying that your time is more important than theirs.

9. Forwarding a note without explanation. Take a minute to write a new subject line and add one or two sentences at the top explaining why you are sending on someone else's note and what you expect the new recipient to do with it.

10. Emailing and sending IMs instead of communicating face-to-face with people who are nearby. This wastes more time than it saves, in many cases.

TOP TEN FACE-TO-FACE COMMUNICATION PITFALLS ON PROJECTS

1. Pushing blindly for your own ideas and not being open to what other stakeholders are saying.

2. Not practicing active listening.

3. Failing to clarify and confirm to make sure that you and the person you're communicating with understand each other.

4. Misreading the body language and nonverbal facial cues of the other party.

5. Not following the PM communication processes and failing to create their outputs, such as the communications management plan and stakeholder register.

6. Assuming that one type of meeting is equivalent to others (e.g., a teleconference versus an in-person meeting), and not planning accordingly to make the most effective use of the meeting format you choose.

7. Avoiding confrontation by telling white lies and being overly willing to compromise.

8. Deliberately misrepresenting the facts to push your own agenda by arguing in bad faith, promoting false balance, drawing false parallels, and spinning.

9. Failing to fully prepare for a meeting on the communications end (such as by sending out invitations early, getting the materials out to the participants in advance, confirming that materials were delivered and accessible, and choosing a good room for the meeting and arranging it to best effect).

10. Not giving your full attention to the person you're speaking with (especially if you're allowing yourself to be distracted by your newest electronic device).

Note

1. Andy Crowe, *Alpha Project Managers: What the Top 2% Know That Everyone Else Does Not* (Kennesaw, GA: Velociteach Press, 2008).

CHAPTER 11

Managing Your Human Resources

The challenges of managing and motivating your staff are the make-or-break elements on many projects. And the modern PM world presents much greater challenges in human resources (HR) management than ever before.

Technology has created an expectation of 24/7 availability and support, bringing many new stressors to manager/staff relations. And today's PMs find themselves overseeing many more projects at once than in the past, yet often with reduced authority and with team members reporting to multiple managers.

Outsourcing and virtual teams, more widely used every day, also bring unique added challenges, with PMs often leading groups in multiple locations and time zones. Supervising one team in person, while at the same time managing what feels like a shadow group continents away, makes things that much more difficult for any PM.

The good news is that the PMI standard offers a great deal of help with HR management. It includes four very straightforward processes, and each, along with its key inputs, outputs, and best practices, is presented in detail in this chapter.

PROJECT MANAGEMENT ENVIRONMENTS

Q1. How do project management work environments differ?

A1. PM work environments can vary greatly depending on industry, whether the organization is in the private or public sector, and on the size of the company. There are also major differences in the way project management itself is viewed in individual shops, which also can make a huge difference in the life of the PMs who work there. PMs taking on a new position should be very aware of how much difference these factors can make.

- *By industry:* Some industries are characterized by style, atmosphere, and even personality type. For instance, insurance companies tend to be cautious and preserve the status quo, whereas dot-com startups in the high-tech field tend to be much more risk friendly. An organization's culture affects many positions, but its effect is multiplied for PMs because they manage so many activities and roles. PMs, then, should carefully consider such enterprise environmental factors before taking on a position.

- *Private versus government:* Private and public organizations may handle HR management very differently. For example, in many government bureaus, there are rigid rules about hiring and firing, whereas in private companies, these decisions may be made at the discretion of PMs and HR managers.

- *By company size:* Smaller companies often give PMs more autonomy and decision-making authority and let them run more of the show, which also helps them learn a great deal. But many PMs prefer big companies because they have PM standards in place and shared templates to work from. The company knows how it likes projects run, the PM's roles and expectations are often very clearly defined, and many have PMOs to offer some guidance. Note, however, that at extremely large companies, there can be a lot of duplicated effort and confusion about which standard methods to choose from.

Q2. What are the three standard PM environments?

A2. Three types of PM environment—functional, matrix, and projectized—are recognized around the world as standard not only by PMI but by all project management bodies. Any organization that practices project management, whether it's public or private, big or small, probably will map pretty closely to one of these environments.

Figure 11-1 shows the three broad types of environment as a continuum, in order from left to right, of the PM's relative decision-making authority:

1. The PM has the least authority in the functional environment (far left).
2. The PM's authority falls somewhere in the middle in a matrix environment (center).
3. The PM has the greatest power in the projectized environment (far right).

Functional environment →	Matrix environment → Weak → Balanced → Strong →	Projectized environment

Figure 11-1: PM Decision-Making Authority in the Three General Types of Project Management Environment

Note that there are three subcategories within the matrix environment. The PM's power is weakest in the weak matrix, medium in the balanced matrix, and, you guessed it, strongest in the strong matrix.

Q3. What are the key characteristics of a functional environment?

A3. Imagine a large, old-fashioned company, like a big bank or manufacturing firm, that did not used to have any PMs at all. It is now starting to bring in PMs to run some of its projects, but it is still primarily organized into departments, each clearly run by what are called functional managers, or FMs (also called resource managers, or RMs).

- The main ***advantages*** of a functional environment for a PM are stability, job security, and significant accumulated employee knowledge that the PM can tap into for a project.

- The main ***drawback***—and it's a major one—of a functional environment is that PMs in this environment often have to battle to get resources because the resources are owned and controlled by the functional or resource managers. Given the importance of resources on a project, this makes it that much harder for PMs to succeed. The resources first and foremost report to the FM/RM, who also gives them their reviews, raises, and bonuses. The PM in a functional environment often has trouble getting resources assigned at all; when they are assigned, they are often assigned only part time to the project; and the resources often maintain primary loyalty to the FM/RM, causing problems for the PM and the project.

Q4. At the other end of the spectrum, what are the characteristics of a projectized environment?

A4. A projectized, or project-driven, environment is the most modern of the three, and in many ways it is the best for the PM to manage under. Here the company's projects are often clearly delineated in a project portfolio and have the support of a strong PMO.

- The many **advantages** for PMs include a high level of decision-making authority, and PMs receive full backing to get the resources they need. Projects in this environment often tend to use the latest and greatest PM methods, such as PMI processes, PMO support, and agile management, as well as state-of-the-art project management software.

- The single biggest **drawback** is that the jobs are temporary for the PM and the rest of the project team. Once the project ends, and the project budget along with it, there often is no more work or funding for the team, and its members are euphemistically said to be "on the bench" unless or until their company comes up with another project for them. While a projectized environment sounds like the best one for PMs in some important ways, it is not for everyone. The lack of job security is accompanied by a lack of associated benefits, raises, training, continuity, order, structure, and routine that are mainstays of the more traditional work environment—in other words, in functional environments.

Q5. What are the characteristics of a matrix environment?

A5. A matrix environment can be said to be halfway between a functional and a projectized environment. Many companies are in the process of transitioning from a traditional functional environment to a more modern projectized structure. In some ways, a matrix environment combines the best of both worlds, with some of the benefits of each as well as some of the drawbacks.

Remember that there are three subtypes of matrix environment—weak, balanced, and strong. A weak matrix has more in common with a functional environment; a strong matrix is close to a projectized environment.

- The primary **advantages** of matrix include a fairly high level of decision-making power and resource-acquisition authority for the PM, and a fair amount of the security, stability, knowledge base, and structure characteristic of a functional environment.

- There are two main **drawbacks:** A matrix environment is less permanent and structured than a functional environment, and PMs enjoy less authority than in a projectized environment.

HUMAN RESOURCES MANAGEMENT PROCESSES

Q6. What are the four HR management processes?

A6. Per the *PMBOK® Guide, Fourth Edition,* standard, there are four HR processes, defined here as follows, then covered in detail in their own Q&As.

1. ***Developing the human resources plan:*** Part of the planning processing group, in which you plan how you will staff and manage your project.

2. ***Acquiring the project team:*** Part of the executing process group, in which you actually hire your team.

3. ***Developing the project team:*** Part of the executing process group, covering how the PM develops his or her individual people and the team itself.

4. ***Managing the project team:*** This is a large part of what being a PM is all about. Note that this process is now part of the executing process group, but in the third edition of the *PMBOK® Guide* it was part of the monitoring and controlling group. This in itself shows how managing a team combines elements of both directing the work (executing) and making sure things are going according to plan (monitoring and controlling).

DEVELOPING THE HUMAN RESOURCES PLAN

Q7. What are the key inputs to the process of developing the human resources plan?

A7. As you start to plan the kind of team you will be putting together, the project schedule is your most important input. You will want to line up the personnel that can best accomplish all of the project activities detailed in the schedule.

When you are working with the schedule, you will probably find it handy to have on your desk all the supporting documents that went into creating it, such as the charter, requirements, scope statement, and WBS. Sometimes one of these predecessor inputs will contain important information that might not be apparent in the schedule but that may be key to staffing the project. You should also have the project budget on hand, as it will drive how you manage the hiring process.

Q8. What are the key outputs of the process of developing the human resources plan?

A8. There are five outputs that together make up what is called the human resources plan:

- Organization chart
- Responsibility assignment matrix (RAM), such as a RACI chart
- Staffing management plan
- Resource histogram
- Release plan.

Q9. How are organization charts used on projects?

A9. Organization (org) charts are the most commonly used artifact for planning the human resources for a project. This diagram provides an instant bird's eye view of the reporting structure of the entire team, illustrated as a pyramid-shaped hierarchy. (Org charts are very similar in appearance to a WBS; see Figure 3-4 for a sample WBS.)

An org chart shows all job functions, the personnel filling each title, and each staff member's immediate supervisor and, therefore, all of the chains of command on the project. The highest-level manager—either the PM or perhaps the program manager or sponsor—is shown at the top of the chart. Below the highest level are the direct reports who report up to that manager. On the next level down would be *their* direct reports, and so on down the chart.

Note that while org charts are very widely used for depicting departmental structure, they are not always used for representing project teams. This is a best practice for PMs.

Q10. What is a *RAM matrix*, and when is it more useful than an org chart?

A10. A responsibility assignment matrix is a lesser-known type of organizational chart. PMs who use them find them to be an extremely handy supplement to the traditional org chart because they are more specific and give a much truer picture of the roles and responsibilities of each team member. There are several variations; probably the most popular of these is the RACI chart (the acronym stands for *responsible, accountable, consulted,* and *informed*).

The classic RACI is a three-dimensional grid. All of the activities on a project are shown on the vertical axis, and the team members are listed horizontally across the top. For each activity, each team member is assigned a role that is designated by one of four letters—R, A, C, or I, depending on whether he or she is responsible or accountable for the task or should just be consulted or informed.

For instance, the PM might be the ultimately accountable party on one activity, so he or she would place an *A* in the PM column for that task. But the same PM might only need to be kept in the loop on another activity, so his or her role would be represented by an *I*, for informed. A stakeholder (who might not be on a traditional org chart at all if he or she is not part of the project team) might be designated with an *A* as the accountable party for that task.

The R, A, C, I designations are often much clearer and more useful than the generic job titles shown on an org chart because they specifically indicate what each person is supposed to do on each activity. Figure 11-2 shows that team members can be assigned to more than one activity and can play varying roles on different activities.

	Project Coordinator	*Web Architect*	*Web Designer*	*Web Writer*
1. Gather requirements	A	I	C	C
2. Create schedule	A	C	I	I
3. Build web pages	A	C	C	R

Figure 11-2:   Classic RACI Chart

Q11. How can a RACI chart be customized?

A11. The RACI lends itself well to customization. Figure 11-3 shows a few options:

- Substitute your team members' names for the job titles across the top column.
- Create your own abbreviated designations for roles, such as TE = tester and LT = lead tester, and document these abbreviations in a legend.
- Combine your role designations with the traditional R, A, C, and I designations to further specify team members' roles and responsibilities. For example, Bryanna is represented here as the business analyst (BA) on Task 3, and she needs to be consulted on this activity (designated by the letter *C*).

Task	Heidi	Bryanna	Daniel	Al
1. Analyze old test cases	PM, A	BA, I	LT, C	TE, I
2. Create new test cases	PM, A	BA, I	LT, C	TE, I
3. Conduct tests	PM, A	BA, C	LT, R	TE, R
4. Create reports on tests	PM, R	BA, R	LT, C	TE, C
5. Analyze results	PM, R	BA, R	LT, C	TE, C
Legend: PM = project manager; TE = tester; LT = lead tester; BA = business analyst				

Figure 11-3:   Modified RACI Chart for sample QA Testing Project

Q12. What is a *staffing management plan*, and how does it fit in as a part of the human resource plan?

A12. In a staffing management plan, PMs document how they are going to staff the project and manage those resources. The plan might cover:

- How many resources the PM thinks the project will need, and the level of those resources.

- How the PM intends to recruit for those positions. For instance, the plan might name the internal HR recruiter the PM intends to work with on the open requisitions.

- Training needs.

- Specific strategies for how the PM will manage the human resources on this particular project. For example, if the team is virtual, the PM might designate someone to act as second in command to supervise the overseas group.

Q13. What is a *resource histogram*, and how can it help the PM plan how to staff a project?

A13. Often, resource usage on a project is not constant. It may change considerably over a project's life cycle. This makes hiring and maintaining staff a challenge, both for the PM as well as recruiters he or she works with. A tool for keeping resource needs organized is a resource histogram, which can be a simple bar chart created in a product like MS Word or Excel. It shows periods of heavy staffing versus lighter resource activity.

It is also very useful for helping the PM budget carefully when the funding will vary over the course of the project. This can happen when the project goes through different phases during which the type of work will vary greatly. For example, on a typical IT project that involves designing, coding, testing, rollout, and follow-up support, more resources are often needed for the coding phase than for the other phases.

Q14. What is a *release plan,* and how can it help the PM wrap up a project?

A14. A release plan is a subcomponent of the HR plan that outlines specific plans for your human resources at the close of the project (e.g., terminations, reassignments). It can make wrapping up a project go much more smoothly and can help keep important procedures from getting lost in the shuffle. It answers questions such as:

- How will final payment be coordinated for all exiting team members?
- Will nondisclosure agreements need to be prepared, then signed by exiting staff?
- Who will schedule and conduct exit interviews and handle turnover documentation?

Q15. What additional planning needs to be done for virtual teams?

A15. If you're managing a virtual team, you'll need to plan for e-meetings, tend to contract issues, and make sure to meet everyone on the team at least once in person if possible.

- *Software considerations for e-meetings:* If you go virtual, you'll probably be holding many more e-meetings. Putting extra time into planning the meetings and making sure that the special software you will use to enable them is tested and ready to go will be critical. It's important to take into consideration that when you are holding a virtual meeting, you don't have the same flexibility to deal with technology glitches that you sometimes have with local meetings, such as jumping to another room or switching to a whiteboard or handing out paper copies. Having a backup plan is even more important for e-meetings.

- *Contract issues:* I remember a project on which everyone *except* the virtual team was required to be on 24/7 pager support because of an omission in the contract—and the main point of the contract was for the virtual team to provide the support! This caused a huge mess, and time and money were lost because the deal had to be restructured under new terms. As part of HR planning for virtual teams, PMs need to be especially careful when specifying requirements in the contract.

- *Meeting virtual team members:* Even if you and your local team meet the virtual team only once, this can make a big difference in managing and working with them. Of course, it may not be practical to fly your whole team across oceans. But if one group is in Washington, D.C., and the other group is in Chicago, why not plan for an occasional day of meetings and lunch? Even when long distances are involved, it may be well worth it in ROI to schedule at least one trip where virtual coworkers can meet face to face.

One cost-effective way for PMs to improve long-distance relationships is to send one team member at a time to spend a day with the other group. This gives the groups a chance to get to know each other and establish a strong working relationship. It also helps eliminate the risk, toxic to team development, of team members treating the other group as "the other"—the bad guy, who is never seen, who gets demonized for making all the mistakes (for more on this, see Q&A41 in Chapter 12).

ACQUIRING THE TEAM

Q16. What are the two biggest barriers to acquiring the right team?

A16. Hiring the right people is among the most important tasks a PM does on a project, and special care needs to be taken to do it properly. The biggest areas of difficulty are usually cost and time factors.

- *Cost:* PMs are often pressured by senior management to keep costs down in the hiring process (which is understandably part of the job of senior management). But it's the PM's job to push back and make sure the project gets staffed adequately.

- *Time:* Unfortunately, PMs often rush the hiring process. Either they don't put the time into interviewing enough candidates, or they skip key steps, like asking for references or checking the references they do get. (You may say, "Duh!" but in the haste to hire, managers often take a surprisingly skimpy look at references and call it a day.) Projects can suffer enormous losses of time and money when hiring is rushed and a team member doesn't work out.

Note that the PM's soft skills, especially negotiation skills, persuasion skills, and influencing skills, can be the deciding factor in whether he or she prevails in these situations. You have to persuade the powers that be that hiring the right people is good for *them*. Remember, in the end, your customer and senior management will only be happy if you bring in a successful project—not if you saved money on a losing effort.

Q17. What are some best practices for interviewing?

A17. Interviewing is key on staffing projects, but many PMs are not very skilled interviewers. It is highly recommended that they enlist the readily available aid of others who are, such as senior members on their team, as well as the company's HR recruiters. There also are many courses and books on the subject. Here are a few interviewing best practices:

- *Go the extra mile on prep.* Taking the time to analyze the truly critical needs of each open position and coming up with questions that will probe for those needs is well worth it and will pay off in dividends on the project.

- *Drill down.* A common mistake is getting locked into asking your set of prepared questions and not diverging from those questions. It's good to be flexible and prepared to probe deeper into the candidates' answers, especially if any answers don't satisfy you.

- *Don't ignore red flags!* How many times have you heard someone who regrets a hiring mistake saying, "I should have paid attention when they said such and such during the interview"? If you have doubts about any of a candidate's answers, it's crucial that you to take the time to probe further.

- *Listen to your gut.* No one's intuitive reactions are totally reliable, so you don't want to go overboard relying on gut feeling above all other criteria. But what you pick up from first impressions and nonverbal cues is going to be a good indicator of how other stakeholders on the project would likely respond to this candidate on the job if you hired him or her.

- *Allow enough time.* A common interviewing mistake is not to schedule sufficient time to give candidates the opportunity to demonstrate what they know (or don't know).

- *Meet candidates in person.* As much as it's tempting to save time by interviewing by phone only, it's always a good idea to meet any candidate in person before making the offer.
- *Don't use the same set of questions for everyone.* The benefit of asking all candidates the same questions is that it lets you compare their answers, apples to apples. But candidates may discuss the questions you asked them with other applicants. If you don't safeguard against this, the later interviewees will have an unfair advantage, undercutting your process.

Q18. What are some best practices for working with recruiters to help staff a project?

A18. PMs and other hiring managers often make the mistake of seeing the HR recruiter as an obstacle who they want to work *around*. Two heads are better than one, and you will get much better results if you view your HR recruiter as a respected business partner and join forces with him or her.

Think of yourself, the PM, as the customer on the project of staffing your team, where the deliverable is the hiring of good personnel. For best results, take the time to come up with the right requirements, treat the staffing process as critical, and enlist the aid of your HR recruiters, who can help you get the right staff for your project. In companies that don't have an HR recruiter, it is a best practice for PMs to work with a *retained recruiter* (retained by the hiring company) because this type of recruiter is primarily loyal to doing his or her best for the hiring company. This is considered by many to be a better way to go than working with *contingency recruiters* (a.k.a. *headhunters*) whose priority is placing their candidates.

Q19. Are there best practices for creating job specifications?

A19. Many PMs don't realize that including specific PMI keywords that best describe the environment and role in the job description can help narrow the field and speed up the interviewing process. Job listings should specify:

- *The type of environment*—for example, projectized or balanced matrix.
- *The PMI designation for the role.* Help your candidates differentiate among positions by stating who you're looking for: a coordinator, an expeditor, a project manager, a program manager, or a portfolio manager.

Describing your PM environment and the person you're looking for makes it much easier for candidates to know if they're a fit, and it saves you many hours of interviewing the wrong people.

Q20. Are there best practices for advertising PM positions?

A20. As social media evolve in functionality, employers have been using them more and more to advertise positions. Job postings that would have appeared only on corporate websites a year ago are now popping up on sites such as LinkedIn, and recruiters are also posting them on companies' pages on Facebook and under discussion links in relevant LinkedIn subgroups. (See Appendix A for a list of PM-oriented LinkedIn groups.)

Some job seekers prefer finding listings this way. Listings on their favorite social media sites may seem more targeted, relevant, and current. Many candidates think corporate recruiting sites are cumbersome and intimidating. There are a lot of screens to wade through, and candidates know that positions they are viewing on the site may no longer be open, as opposed to a fresh note popping up in their inbox from a member of one of their favorite virtual groups.

Q21. How do negotiation and influencing skills come into play when acquiring a team?

A21. Every company has limited resources, and if two projects are competing for the same resources, one project will always be seen as the one that is on the critical path to the department's success. That one will, predictably, get the more talented and more experienced people.

You, as the PM, are challenged to make the best case you can to justify why you need the best resources to succeed and to explain how the success of your project will help drive the company's success. Your negotiating and influencing skills are essential here. You really can't *make* your management give you the people you need, but you can make them *want to* give you good staff.

Q22. Do you know your company's protocol for working with recruiters?

A22. A common mistake PMs make is to unwittingly (or sometimes intentionally) break their company's recruiting rules. Does your company have an HR recruiter you are expected to work with, and does the recruiter have a list of approved headhunters you are obligated to work with? It's always best to follow protocols like these or, when necessary, to request formal permission to deviate from those rules. A good HR recruiter will even offer to give you some guidance in cases like this, when you choose to conduct your own interviews.

In many cases, if you want to use a headhunter who is not currently on your company's preferred resource list, you just need to go through a process to get him or her added to the list. That way, you get what you want while still following company rules. For those of you who are rebels—and rebels make some of the best project managers—it's still always better to respect the HR department and show that you are playing ball with them by working within their procedures. This may come in handy down the road when you need HR's help.

Q23. What is resource preassignment?

A23. Sometimes a project hinges on having certain key human resources in place, who are assigned in advance, before resource requirements are formally allocated. Other times, the opposite happens: PMs are told in advance that certain people will be assigned to their teams, even if they are not necessarily a perfect fit or someone who the PM would have chosen. Both of these situations fit into the category of preassignment because they precede the formal role-assignment stage of the project.

It's recommended that PMs approach any preassigned asset with a highly positive mindset. Think, "How can I maximize the value this person can bring to my team?" Even if you are preassigned a resource who would not be your first choice, you must still maintain an open mind and do your best to help that resource succeed.

Q24. What outputs, other than hiring the team members, are created from the process of acquiring the project team?

A24. There are two primary outputs:

- *Resource list:* Most PMs use electronic software such as MS Project not only to schedule the activities of the project but also to keep track of resources. As each team member is hired, the PM adds him or her as a resource to the resource list within the program, along with the resource's hourly rate.

- **Resource calendar:** If some members of the team observe different holidays, which is especially common if the team is virtual, the PM also often creates a separate resource calendar for those staff members. For instance, if half of the team is in the United States and the other half is in London, the PM will work with two resource calendars, each showing the eligible working days and holidays for that group. For example, Christmas Day, December 25, would be listed as a holiday on *both* calendars, but Boxing Day, December 26, would only be designated on the London resource calendar. The software will then automatically count Boxing day as a day off for just the London staff.

Q25. Which parts of the project plan should be updated as staff are hired?

A25. The WBS, project schedule, and budget (all key *inputs* to acquiring a team) should be updated as necessary as staff come on board. Adding staff of course directly affects the budget, sometimes in ways that were not exactly expected—for instance, if new hires wind up costing more than the PM originally budgeted for them. When hiring goes either faster or slower than planned, schedule and network diagrams may have to be updated. Having fewer or less experienced staff members, for instance, may mean that the PM will need to push back deadlines and update all pertinent planning docs.

DEVELOPING THE PROJECT TEAM

Q26. What are the expected stages of team development?

A26. Sometimes PMs come roaring in to get their team started on a project, but they encounter stiff resistance. Instead of accepting the PM's authority and quickly gelling into a productive team, team members question who is in control, who knows more, and who should lead and perform which tasks.

Has this happened on one of your teams? It's not your fault! This behavior is characteristic of the storming stage, the second of the five sequential stages of team development that comprise the Tuckman model, named after Bruce Tuckman, the psychologist who identified them.

1. **Forming:** In this stage, the PM puts the team together and assigns the various roles and responsibilities. In accordance with the PMI model, the PM has already performed two processes to get to this point: developing

the HR plan and acquiring the project team. But before the team begins performing productively, there often is a storming stage.

2. *Storming:* Before teams gel and become productive, they often go through some birth pains and growing pains. Although this is typical, a good PM can minimize the length of the storming stage and can quickly move the team on to the desired next stages.

3. *Norming:* Group members settle in, putting any issues about accepting the PM or their teammates or their role aside. Everyone falls into line and starts thinking about how they can start contributing toward the goals of the project. In this stage, the team is like a carpenter's level set on a table—after the bubble bounces around from side to side (in the storming stage), it settles (hopefully in the middle).

4. *Performing:* Now the project is under way, and the team is working together to execute its goals, like a baseball team that has gotten through spring training and has entered the regular season.

5. *Adjourning:* Before the project ends, the PM does everything necessary to smoothly close out the project so that each team member will be free and clear and ready to move on to his or her next assignment (e.g., paperwork, terminations, exit interviews, resource reassignments).

Note that various management theorists have offered several variations on this model over the years, adding additional steps such as renorming, reforming, and high performing.

MOTIVATIONAL THEORIES IN PROJECT MANAGEMENT

Q27. What are considered best practices for motivating staff today?

A27. PMI has recognized six leading theories for motivating staff as best practice methods. They come from a variety of psychologists, scientists, and engineers.

- Maslow's hierarchy of needs
- Herzberg's theory of hygiene factors and motivational factors
- McGregor's Theory X and Theory Y
- Fiedler's contingency theory

- Vroom's expectancy theory
- McClelland's achievement theory (or the three-need theory).

To effectively motivate employees, it is important for PMs to understand that each team member has different needs and that the key to motivating one person might not work for someone else. Each of the above theories can help you in some situations, with some employees. Sometimes, combining elements of the above theories will work best, tailored to the employee and the situation.

Q28. How does Maslow's hierarchy of needs apply to managing project teams?

A28. Abraham Maslow, known as the "father of the humanistic psychology movement," developed the influential theory that people have a hierarchy of needs, which he represented as a pyramid (see Figure 11-4). A person's lowest-level needs (starting with basic needs, at the bottom) must be satisfied first. Only then can his or her higher-level needs be addressed and so on up the ladder.

Maslow also made an important distinction between the four lower-level needs and the highest level, self-actualization. He characterized the lower-level needs as *deficiency needs*, meaning motivation to fill gaps that people feel. Maslow contrasted these with what he called the *growth needs* related to self-actualization, which is discussed in the next Q&A.[1]

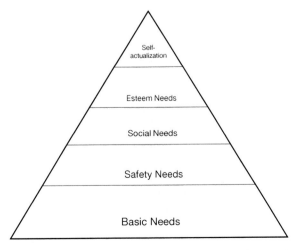

Figure 11-4: Maslow's Hierarchy of Needs

Q29. What did Maslow mean by the need for self-actualization, and how can managers help their people rise to that level?

A29. In a separate category at the top of the pyramid, Maslow identified the need for self-actualization (growth needs). Once the basic needs are satisfied (levels one through four), individuals are no longer deficient, and their *impulses,* as Maslow called them, for personal growth are free to come into play. He described self-actualization as the need for character growth, character expression, maturation, and development. Self-actualization also includes looking out beyond one's self toward others, a view he summarized as problem-centered rather than ego-centered. Per Maslow's model, being self-actualized means doing what you are best at or what you are born to do.[2]

Maslow's approach has been applied for many years toward motivating employees. Managers analyze what it would take to best motivate each employee to rise through his or her own individual pyramid. This requires determining each team member's current level of needs, thinking about what their next level would be, and then strategizing how to help him or her get there.

For a larger-than-life modern example, Oprah Winfrey epitomizes a dramatically self-actualized person in two key ways. First, she ascended to a point in her career where she is fully using all her talents and skills (her creativity, her communication and interpersonal skills, her emotional intelligence, and her performer's abilities). Second, as she moved toward the top of the pyramid, Oprah was able to look beyond herself and turn her talents toward helping others: She changed the focus of her TV show, started a world-famous book club to encourage reading, and became heavily involved in large-scale charitable projects.

For PMs, the goal is not to try to make everyone on your team an Oprah but to motivate each team member to do their best work for your project and company. This includes focusing on priorities outside the self, such as putting the customer first, thinking about the greater good of the project, and helping out your teammates. This can also include taking part in programs such as corporate volunteer days, where employees perform charitable work in the local community.

Q30. How does Herzberg's theory of hygiene and motivational factors depart from Maslow's theory?

A30. Frederick Herzberg is known as the father of job enrichment. His *motivation-hygiene theory* is based on his extensive research and satisfaction surveys that focused specifically on employees' needs in the workplace. Unlike Maslow's linear hierarchy, Herzberg theorized that there are two types of factors that both must to be present for employees to be motivated, hygiene factors and the motivating factors. People are dissatisfied by a bad environment or the extrinsics of the job, but they are not necessarily satisfied by good environment. Rather, they are satisfied by the intrinsics of what they do or the *motivators*. Hygiene and motivating factors are defined further:

- *Hygiene factors:* Certain factors are a *prerequisite* for getting good work out of employees, though they are not sufficient in themselves to motivate employees to work harder and go beyond the minimum level of expectations. Rather, certain factors must be present as a foundation, including:
  o Providing a good work environment
  o Offering fair pay
  o Creating good relationships between manager and worker.
- *Motivating factors:* In a separate category, Herzberg placed those things he felt would incentivize staff to do more and better work, especially:
  o Offering feedback and recognition for achievement
  o Completing a job for a client, which is satisfying
  o Providing greater responsibility
  o Providing opportunities for advancement and growth.[3]

In short, to motivate their teams, PMs need to make sure the hygiene factors are in place while also acknowledging that those factors alone won't satisfy their team completely (e.g., "I gave them all bonuses, I don't know why half my team left!"). PMs must also offer motivating factors, which offer challenging and satisfying work.

Q31. How can an awareness of McGregor's motivational theory help PMs better manage and motivate their people?

A31. Douglas McGregor categorized managers into two groups, which he called Theory X managers and Theory Y managers, based on their style of motivating others.

- *Theory X managers* believe that workers must be carefully watched and managed because they would not work hard if left to their own devices.

They are similar to what we call micromanagers, but not only do they want to manage the minutia, they also act like taskmasters.

- *Theory Y managers* believe in people's intrinsic need and desire to work hard. Their management style is more hands-off. They operate as guides and mentors, giving their people as much autonomy as they can handle and making themselves available only as requested or when they see specific needs.

McGregor's related his X and Y theories back to Maslow. He wrote that Theory X management cannot work in a lot of cases, because Theory X works only with deficiency needs—needs on the lower-end of Maslow's hierarchy. Many people have growth needs, however, and Theory Y management motivates people by cultivating self-actualization.[4]

McGregor himself was aware that his theory was often somewhat misunderstood. He emphasized that he did *not* advocate that all managers be Y managers all the time. While he clearly did stress that Theory Y was the better way, and not just one of two equal choices, he recognized that not all employees are necessarily ready to respond productively to Theory Y management.

From my own experience managing and observing many other managers, I have found that it's best to be able to operate as both a Theory X and Theory Y manager—whichever style is needed in the situation. The best managers are flexible and responsive to the differing needs and personalities of each team member. Employees who will thrive under more autonomy will respond better to Theory Y management, while employees who need close supervision will be more productive under Theory X management. Also, if a manager has a primarily Theory X dynamic with a team member, gradually adjusting the relationship to more of a Theory Y dynamic might help the team member become more independent and productive over the long term.

Q32. What is *Fiedler's contingency theory*, and how does an awareness of contingencies help a PM better motivate his or her people?

A32. One PM may be very effective in many situations and thus considered the better manager. But when the environment changes, another PM might suddenly be viewed as a better fit. For example, Susan might perform better under pressure, but Steve might thrive when economic times are good and he has a lot of resources that allow him to be experimental and creative.

Fred E. Fiedler explored this dichotomy in detail in his contingency theory, which states that some managers are more effective at motivating and leading, *contingent* upon certain circumstances. The employees making up the manager's team are just as important or more so to a manager's success or failure as his or her own intrinsic skills.[5]

In the movie *The Godfather*, Robert Duvall plays Tom Hayden, the highly trusted and effective advisor and attorney (consigliere) to Don Corleone (Marlon Brando). But when events change drastically (Don Corleone dies, and the mob families go to war), he is told by the new boss, Michael Corleone (Al Pacino), "Tom, you're not a wartime consigliere... you're out!"—meaning that in the new world order, he is no longer the critically important figure he had been to his management and team (such as they are!).

Fiedler took this further to suggest that group or organizational performance could be improved "either by changing the leader to fit the situation or by changing the situation to fit the leader." He suggested that leadership training should recognize this and should emphasize the need for managers to learn how to recognize the conditions under which they can best perform and to modify the situation to suit their leadership style.[6]

PMs must realize that outside factors can change significantly, and they need to be flexible enough to adjust their style accordingly. For example, the sponsor or key client can appoint a successor, and suddenly the game changes. The PM who can best recognize change and react accordingly—for instance, by adjusting priorities and personal style—will be the most successful.

Q33. What is the *expectancy theory*, and what do PMs need to know about employees' expectations?

A33. Employee motivation can often be directly linked to *expectations* on the job: The more a worker knows what is expected of him and knows what the rewards will be if he meets those expectations, the more motivated he will be. Victor Vroom wrote about some intriguing motivating factors that PMs might not typically be thinking of when assigning work[7]:

- *Valued abilities*. The more an employee uses abilities that she herself values, the better the work results will be. For instance, employees who consider good communication skills important will perform better on tasks that require those skills.

- *Knowledge of results.* Employees will do better when they receive feedback confirming they are meeting job expectations.

- *The cue function.* It can help motivate employees to *cue* them mid-task, letting them know whether they are meeting their goal and if any adjustments are needed.

- *Possessed abilities.* Similar to valued abilities, these are a worker's self-perceived abilities. For example, if a worker recognizes his or her skilled abilities in math, he or she will be motivated to excel on tasks requiring math.

- *Future effects.* Employees will be motivated to excel when they feel involved in making decisions that will impact them.

- *Past success/past failure.* Employees who have succeeded in the past in a particular role or activity will expect to do well again in similar roles or activities. In the same way, past failures will set a negative expectation in the mind of a worker when similar tasks are assigned.

Q34. What is the achievement theory, and why is the need to achieve only one of three parts of the theory?

A34. David McClelland's achievement theory is also commonly called the three-needs theory and the acquired-needs theory. His studies showed that people acquire three main needs over time, and each one affects their motivations. These three needs each have their own complexities and challenges, as well as interdependencies, summarized as follows:[8]

- *The achievement motive.* Employees have a strong intrinsic need to make things better. They enjoy opportunities in which they have personal responsibility in the outcome and in which the work itself reveals their success in achieving the outcome. In consideration of this need, McClelland stated the need for a balance between motivation and the risk level of the work: High achievers may not feel sufficiently challenged by low-risk goals, but they might also feel that a very risky project does not offer a sufficiently high chance of success. Tasks that are too challenging or involve too much risk can be de-motivating.

- *The affiliative motive:* Some employees clearly are much more social than others and will be more successful on projects that meet their needs for being with other people. Some people have a strong need to avoid unpleasant situations, such as conflict with other people, and this need can be key to their motivation. McClelland calls this the *avoidance motive.*

- *The power motive.* Some people have a strong need to impact others. This can include having a negative, dominating impact, but it can also mean exercising power on behalf of others (e.g., leading a volunteer organization). Those who believe in hard work, self-sacrifice, charity, and centralized authority make good managers and use their power to positively influence others. The level of one's affiliative motive plays a strong role in determining one's use of power.

Project managers can apply McClelland's theory by first understanding each individual's unique needs and then assigning those individuals to roles that best align with those needs. For example, assign team members who have the greatest need to achieve tasks that will sufficiently challenge them; involve those with a strong need for affiliation in activities that require the most people skills; and keep staff who demonstrate a need for power in mind for tasks that offer strong leadership or influencing opportunities.

TEAM-BUILDING AND AWARDS

Q35. What are some highly effective team-building activities PMs can try?

A35. The best team-building exercise can often be as simple as just taking the extra time and effort to invite your team out to an appreciation lunch or dinner. Getting everyone away from the office for a couple of hours can often work wonders for morale and team cooperation. But the more interesting, fun, and different your team-building activity is, the better the results can be. Figure 11-5 suggests five out-of-the-box team-building activities (none involving paintball!), all of which I have seen work very well.

Q36. What are best practices for giving awards to motivate people?

A36. Everyone likes receiving awards, but they can be counterproductive to motivating your people if they are not administered the right way. Here are a few tips based on my own experience:

- *Make sure they are 100 percent fair.* When the most deserving person wins an award, everyone knows it, and it can motivate the recipient and everyone else. But when an award is given for any kind of political reason, it can demotivate other team members.

Group painting activity. A facilitator splits each team into individual groups, and each group sits at a table set up with paints and paintbrushes. Each group collaborates on a quick group painting, working from the facilitator's written instructions.
Dragon canoe racing. Ten or 20 team members sit in a long canoe decorated with Chinese dragon heads and tails and race other teams, relying on the group's collective paddle power.
Writing an article or white paper as a team. Team members work together on a piece for a website, magazine, or internal company publication. This motivates team members to exercise their creativity and brain power, and it also makes them feel special and acknowledged for what they do.
Study groups. Several people from a company take a class together, such as a PMP® course, and form study groups. The groups meet for lunch to compare notes and pool resources.
Corporate-sponsored charity events. Many companies offer opportunities, such as a community volunteer day, for employees to work together to serve others. Employees might, for example, lend their services at a soup kitchen on the eve of a holiday. These activities foster a sense of accomplishment and camaraderie that employees can't help but bring back to the office.

Figure 11-5: Team-Building Exercises

- ***Don't overdo it.*** At some small companies, practically everyone winds up getting awards because there aren't many employees. The value of awards then gets diluted—they are no longer special.

- ***Be careful about how you present the award.*** Remember the anecdote from Chapter 10 about the student whose company delivered an award to her at home on a Saturday? She thought the delivery might be a pink slip and still hasn't quite forgiven her employer. Presenting an award is like gift-wrapping a present. Determine the best way for the individual to receive it, and then take the time to do it right. Would the recipient enjoy getting the award at a ceremony with the team, or would she prefer that you present it to her one-on-one? Would he enjoy a surprise, or would he prefer a heads-up first?

- ***Don't wait until after the project is over.*** For maximum benefit, try, when possible, to give recognition *during* the project.

THE FIVE FORMS OF POWER IN PROJECT MANAGEMENT

Q37. What are the five recognized forms of power available to a PM, and which are considered the most positive?

A37. The five forms of power applicable to project management include:

1. Expert power
2. Reward power
3. Legitimate power
4. Referent power
5. Punishment power.

PMI most favors expert and reward power, respects legitimate and referent power, and especially discourages the use of punishment power. A good PM knows when it is appropriate to use each type.

Q38. What is *expert power*, and why is it considered a highly favorable form of power?

A38. The maxim "knowledge is power" defines expert power. If a PM is a technical expert on the subject of the project he or she is leading—for example, an engineer running an engineering project—team members often immediately respect the PM because of his or her knowledge. In this situation, this PM has expert power.

Expert power is considered a very positive kind of power because it has a purity that legitimate power (discussed in Q&A 40) does not have, in that team members often like to follow the lead of a respected expert and sometimes prefer this to following the lead of managers who are above them in the chain of command. Note that when a PM does *not* have expert knowledge, he or she may have trouble gaining the respect of his or her team. Even though the PM has some degree of formal power, the team may not naturally want to follow him or her.

Expert power also manifests itself in another way. When particular team members hold all the expert knowledge, they can take on expert power as well, and other team members will look to them for direction. This can be either positive or negative, depending on how the team members with expertise and the PM handle the situation. It is good for the PM to make use of these team members' expert power and knowledge and abilities, provided the team members do not abuse their expert power and compete with the PM for authority.

What can you do if you, the PM, don't hold expert power in key areas of the project?

- If you can gain expert knowledge on the project's key areas—for instance, by putting in some extra time studying the documentation, working with the system, or reading a book or taking a class—doing so may be well worth your time, because it will increase your expert power on the project.

- Align yourself with a SME on the team who does have expert power. Make the SME your right-hand person, work closely with him or her, and he or she will be there for you when expert knowledge is needed on decisions. Another benefit of forging an alliance like this is that it indirectly gives you expert power; for practical purposes, you have it when you need it.

Some PMs (not all) don't feel confident running a project if they don't have expert power. If this is true of your personality and management style, you need to be aware of that. You can try to always select projects for which you do have expert knowledge, and be ready to compensate for it in cases in which you won't.

Q39. What is *reward power*?

A39. A manager who is in the position to reward employees in various ways for their work, most obviously with money, e.g., raises and bonuses, has reward power. Employees tend to have respect for those who have the power to reward them and are not afraid to use it.

Even if staff reports to functional managers—so you as the PM don't have full reward power—you still may be able to reward employees in various ways. Consider:

- Writing a note to the employee's functional manager to let him or her know that the employee did a good job. The note may be included in the employee's permanent record.

- Nominating the employee for a company award. In addition to recognition, awards may also offer monetary compensation.

- Requesting extra time off for the employee after they have gone the extra mile for you.

- Offering to act as a reference for the employee in the future.
- Connecting to the employee on social networking sites, such as LinkedIn, and writing a recommendation for the employee, if permitted by your company and the employee.

Q40. What is meant by a PM's having *legitimate power*?

A40. Team members often follow the direction of whoever is in charge of the project by virtue of his or her legitimate power, which is also known as *formal power*. It may seem as if it should be simple for PMs to exercise their legitimate power, but sometimes it isn't.

- Sometimes the PM is not the direct manager of all of his or her team members, so employees' loyalties are divided between the PM and their functional managers.
- Sometimes the PM is a temporary consultant, but the team members are permanent. This can weaken the PM's formal power on a project.
- The geographic distance between a PM managing a virtual team and his or her team members can give rise to a "while the cat's away, the mice will play" situation, exacerbated by the fact that the "cat" is *always* away on many virtual teams.
- The PM is not always a technical expert on the subject of the project and thus lacks expert power.

Q41. What is *referent power*?

A41. There are several types of referent power. First, people generally like to follow strong, charismatic leaders. Charisma and looking the part are therefore good assets in a leader, because it helps them naturally attract and lead followers. The people who gravitate toward such leaders may feel that some of the positive qualities of the leader rub off on them.

Another type of referent power could involve a PM who is new on a project. He may not have very much power on his own, but he may be perceived as being closely aligned with the senior manager who hired him. This is referent power because he takes on some of the formal power of the senior manager by association.

A third type of referent power could is when a PM occasionally gains cooperation from the team by saying something like: "You may not see the need for doing this, but I can tell you that our sponsor sees this as a top priority." The PM is literally referring to the higher-up to trade on their power. This tactic should be used sparingly, however, because PMs can lose credibility as well as power if they appear to be *name dropping* (an illegitimate sibling of referent power!).

Q42. Is punishment power good, bad, or both?

A42. Punishment power, as you might guess from the name, is the authority to fire an employee or otherwise take punitive action with team members as you see fit. This is also called coercive power, meaning that you can force people to do things under threat of punishment. It is considered a very negative form of power by PMI; firing should be a last resort. It's a bad manager who abuses his or her position by wielding punishment power, saying such things as, "I could fire you, you know." (I have seen managers make comments like this, more to dominate than to threaten, and it's not pretty!)

But sometimes punishment power is very much needed when quick, decisive action is called for. And it can be very difficult to hold the respect of your staff when you don't have firing authority. In some situations, terminating an employee for the good of the project is the only feasible solution, and if you don't have the power to do it directly, the process can drag on or never happen at all. As you have probably seen on projects, when an employee gets away with not pulling his or her weight, it often erodes the morale of the rest of the team and can harm the project. Think of punishment power as a necessary evil: You shouldn't use it unless you absolutely have to, but you want to have it at your disposal in case you need it to do what's best for the project.

MANAGING CONFLICT

Q43. What is the single best way to manage conflict on projects?

A43. By the PMI standard, there is only one right way to handle conflict: Meet the problem head-on and come up with the solution that is best for the project, even if it doesn't please all stakeholders equally. PMI calls this problem-solving, and it may sound like the obvious way of doing things. But many managers do not do this because they don't like conflict. And as a result, many wrong decisions are made on projects, leading to unsatisfactory consequences and poor project results.

Problem-solving is also called confronting or confrontation in PM jargon. When several people on your team have their own ideas about a solution, it can be a fight trying to get one side to accept a solution that isn't their preferred choice. But it's the role of the PM to make a decision for the greater good of the project and to do his or her best to make sure that the team accepts and implements that decision. As the PM, you should, ideally, ruffle as few feathers as possible. But more important, you need to be strong enough to do what's best, even when that means making choices that are unpopular to some.

Confronting is one of five methods of conflict management, but it is the only recommended way. The four common conflict resolution methods that PMI considers to be wrong ways of dealing with conflict include compromising, forcing, withdrawal, and smoothing, discussed in Q&As 44–47.

Q44. When is compromise *not* a good thing? Shouldn't everyone be willing to compromise?

A44. We are all taught to compromise, and some compromises are necessary. But a bad compromise on an important decision on a project can do more harm than good.

For example, suppose there is a project to design a software system. The mainframe specialists on the team want the solution to use mainframe technology, but the client/server specialists want the new system to be built using client/server software and hardware only. A bad compromise (and I have seen this done in the real world!) would be to have a compromise for the sake of compromise: "Ok, we'll make it part mainframe, part client/server." The problem is that this hybrid system might not be right for your customer, and even if it works well, it might bring support problems down the line. The best solution would probably be *either* mainframe *or* client server, depending on the company's existing configuration and the needs driving the new system.

Unless a compromise is the best technical solution, it's not recommended. Many such compromises are made for the wrong reasons, usually in an attempt to keep both sides happy. But this often doesn't work anyway, because neither side gets what it wanted, so it's considered a lose-lose situation. Moreover, people may lose respect for a PM who allowed a bad compromise in trying to be a people-pleaser, when it is obvious that he or she didn't make the best decision.

Of course, not all compromises are bad. In situations in which the decision is not critical, compromises are fine. If some team members want Chinese food for a team lunch and others want pizza, it might actually be best to go with Indian food, where both sides would appreciate the compromise.

Q45. What is *forcing*, and why is it so common if it's not a recommended technique?

A45. Forcing is the term PMs use to describe a dictatorial, "my way or the highway" management style. No one likes being ordered around and allowed no input into the decisions on a project. Forcing not only feels bad, but it often doesn't make much sense—team members may know more about an issue involving their work packages than the PM does. Yet many managers like the forcing style. They may believe that because they are the manager, everyone should do what they say when under pressure to get things done. Or they may be consciously trying to look like a strong leader by over asserting their authority.

Whatever the manager's reason, there is little room in modern PM for forcing. If the building is on fire, you don't have time to hear about people's feelings as you rush them out the door. But otherwise, except when you are under severe deadlines, there is no excuse for it. People work better when they feel listened to, understood, and persuaded (as explored further in Chapter 10). And you'll foster better morale, and get better results, if you make people *want to* work for you by being fair, making good decisions for the project, and showing that you care about your staff.

Q46. Why isn't withdrawal a recommended method of conflict management?

A46. *Withdrawal* is the term for such behavior as hiding in your office, pretending to work on some important report, while the waters of conflict rage outside your door. Hoping a problem goes away is obviously not the best way to get good results or to make your best effort for your customer or manager.

There are exceptions: Withdrawal can be appropriate for minor problems or for problems that have a fair chance of resolving themselves. For instance, if one team member doesn't get along with another, but he is leaving the company in a couple of days anyway, it would be a waste of resources to spend your time and theirs trying to patch things up.

Q47. What is *smoothing*, and why is it considered uninspiring, unproductive, and uncool?

A47. Smoothing is a tactic for avoiding difficult discussions by distracting the other person and going for some kind of agreement that is irrelevant to the issue at hand; for example, "I know you wanted to discuss the rumor about no promotions this year. Hard to focus on that with those summer Olympic Games going on—have you seen some of those gymnasts up on the parallel bars? Who doesn't like watching that!" You have changed the subject with a joke, and because you're the manager, people may laugh. But even if they do, it's highly unlikely they've forgotten the problem they brought up, and now, in addition to being frustrated, they may also be angry that you evaded their issue.

A harsher type of smoothing comes closer to lying. For instance, in an answer to the same question about promotions, some managers may respond with something like: "The company is always big on promoting from within. I think we've all seen that over the years." This could be a true statement about promotions, but not one that addresses the concern that there won't be any promotions this year. This is telling people what they want to hear, not what they *need* to hear.

Smoothing also can be seen as a manipulative or bullying tactic, though it is less obvious than forcing. But it's worse in a way because it's passive aggressive (see Chapter 10 for a discussion of passive aggression). Smoothing has an insidious element of deceit; you are pretending to answer a question, but you are really avoiding the question. Like forcing, you're doing it because you can, exploiting the unfair advantage your position gives you over your team members.

TEAM ROLES

Q48. What personality traits make for positive team roles?

A48. A number of personality traits are referred to in project management as positive versus negative team roles: They are considered either helpful on a project or not helpful. The eight roles described in Figure 11-6 generally are good ones for team members to take on. The key element many of these team roles have in common is empathy—caring for and awareness of others. Empathetic team members recognize others' need for help and are motivated to step up and assist the PM or his or her fellow teammates.

When hiring staff, PMs should think about which of the positive roles listed in Figure 11-6 would benefit each position, and then screen for those personality traits. (At the same time, PMs can look for evidence of the negative roles listed in Figure 11-7.) When working with their teams, PMs should try to encourage and acknowledge the good behavior and discourage the bad. Modeling the good roles and avoiding setting an example of the bad—in other words, taking a "do as I do" approach—will help.

Encourager: The kind of employee who, whether or not he or she is the PM, likes to make an effort to praise and even motivate his or her teammates ("Good job on that app—nice!").

Harmonizer: Some people naturally like to smooth out conflict or tension and proactively work to help defuse a troubled situation when it arises.

Gatekeeper: Sometimes stakeholders or team members may be quiet types or reluctant to speak up for various reasons. Gatekeepers are those who recognize this in others and try to draw them out. For instance, on an outsourced development effort, one of the engineers at the home office might say on a conference call: "We haven't heard from our friends across the pond in a while—what do the developers think about this issue?"

Initiator: Go-getters who are highly motivated to take on new things even before you ask them to. Can't have enough of those!

Information seeker: Team members who enjoy helping the project, for instance, by doing research on their own time without even being asked.

Information giver: Some team members are very willing to share information with their coworkers. (The opposite of an information giver is an information *hoarder*, who feels it's in his or her [selfish] interest not to share, such as for job security.) When necessary to encourage more giving, PMs can make clear that team members will be evaluated in part on their willingness to share with the team.

Clarifier: Some team members automatically help out the PM by offering to help clear up a point in a meeting when they sense confusion among the team.

Summarizer: Similar to clarifiers are those who help the PM out by summarizing points in a meeting when they feel it will help others understand a complex issue or to make sure none of the steps discussed are lost in translation.

Figure 11-6: Positive Team Roles on Projects

Q49. What roles on a project are negative, and are any partially negative and partially positive?

A49. You can probably guess why each of the roles appearing in Figure 11-7 made the list. Each of these traits should be avoided if possible when hiring team members. But the last two, *devil's advocate* and *recognition seeker,* while largely negative, also have a positive side that is noted in their descriptions. I would call both of these roles "gray," meaning neither can be entirely good or bad, depending on the way the employee behaves in that role.

Topic-jumper: Stakeholders who constantly change the subject during meetings and interrupt with whatever topic comes into their head frustrate the PM and team members. If a team member is prone to this behavior, the PM needs to look out for it and nip it in the bud any time it starts. Creating a written agenda and sticking to it helps a lot—the PM can always refer to it and say that there is no time to digress from the planned action items, but additional items can be discussed offline.

Dominator: No one likes it when a team member tries to dominate him or her, team meetings, or project activities with his or her agenda. Some people may do this consciously in an effort to get ahead or gain power by looking like a manager (which, unfortunately, does work sometimes). But PMs must curtail dominators for the sake of the group, not reward bad behavior.

Aggressor: Similar to dominators, aggressors are more hostile than helpful. They intimidate others on the team not necessarily with an agenda, but because it's their way. The PM has an obligation to do whatever it takes to protect the other team members and create a safe work environment, or morale and productivity will suffer, and victims of the aggression might even quit. Meeting with an aggressor one-on-one and calling him or her on his or her bad behavior often works. It shows him or her that you're serious and won't tolerate disruptions to the project. If this doesn't work, escalating to the aggressor's functional manager often does the trick.

Blocker: This is the kind of team member who tries to stop new initiatives and does everything he or she can to obstruct the PM as well as his or her teammates whenever anyone contributes ideas. Anticipating in advance of a meeting how he or she will try to block you or your team members and deciding how you'll respond is often a good way to deal with blockers. Calling on other meeting attendees who are on your side also helps. This shows that the majority is with you. It isolates the blocker and reveals his position as an obstructionist, not someone who is sincerely trying to advance the project. Meeting a blocker for a friendly lunch may help. You may win him or her over to your side, or at the very least, you will learn where he or she is coming from and what underlying issues may be motivating him or her.

(*Continued on next page*)

Withdrawer: This is the kind of employee who does not want to speak up in group settings or feels that it's not their job to "do meetings." If the employee is extremely shy, you as the PM can initially try to coax him to participate by asking yes/no or other nonthreatening questions. But if the employee has information you need her to share, but she simply prefers not to, it's up to you to make her understand that her contributions are not optional!

Devil's advocate: The strong negative stigma associated with the term *devil's advocate* is a result of the type of person who predictably always focus on what is wrong with any idea or initiative, almost as a knee-jerk reaction. These people can undercut the PM and can even derail a project. Devil's advocates hurt themselves, too—after a while, people stop listening to their opinions. But the other side of the coin is that good PMs don't surround themselves with yes-men. They need people who are willing to be devil's advocates in the positive sense—team members who bravely speak up about potential risks or other negatives on a project, even initiatives that are favored by management.

Recognition seeker: This one also has a strong negative connotation—and everyone knows the kind of employee who tries to take all the credit for successful team efforts. They are often not fair minded about who deserves credit and mainly look out for #1. A positive type of recognition seeker, however, is the manager who ensures that his or her entire team is recognized. For instance, a manager who nominates the team for an award, or helps get an article written about the team, or passes on a kudos note from a customer. This kind of recognition seeking can help position team members for promotions or bring them exposure that leads to their working on bigger and better projects in the future. And many PMs tell me that one of the key ways to increase productivity is by building appropriate recognition into their process. PMs need to keep in mind that while the recognition seeker is considered negative overall, many staff members can be motivated by appropriate recognition.

Figure 11-7:   Negative Team Roles on Projects

TOP TEN HUMAN RESOURCES PITFALLS FOR PROJECT MANAGERS TO AVOID

1. Making someone a PM because he or she has technical expertise in the project's subject area but lacks management skills.

2. Hiring fewer or less-qualified resources to save money. This is definitely not worth the savings if you don't get the right results.

3. Keeping a team member on the project who continues to perform poorly even after you have done your best to help improve his or her performance. Whether you are doing this to avoid hurting the employee or you don't want to lose a body, retaining a poor performer can be pure poison for the rest of the team's morale.

4. Trying to manage a virtual team without making special accommodations, such as paying an on-site visit to meet the team members in person.

5. Failing to provide training or mentoring when needed. A little guidance can make a big difference in project results, but too often, PMs or higher-level managers don't want to spend the time or money, which can be short-sighted.

6. Devoting too little time to interviewing candidates for your team ("I'm going to interview three people on Friday and pick one!") or doing too little prep work for the interviews.

7. Failing to ask for references or contact the references or really look closely at what the references have to say before hiring a team member.

8. Neglecting to use best-practice documents, such as RACI charts, to plan staffing and manage HR on your project.

9. Failing to conduct performance reviews or team performance assessments.

10. Managing by memo—not meeting enough with your people and not managing conflicts face to face, in favor of sending off a lot of notes with the excuse that it's more time efficient.

Notes

1. Gerard Huizinga, *Maslow's Need Hierarchy in the Work Situation* (Groningen, Netherlands: Wolters-Noordhoff Publishing, 1970), and Abraham Maslow, Deborah Stevens, and Gary Heil, *Maslow on Management* (New York: John Wiley & Sons, 1998).

2. Abraham Maslow, *Motivation and Personality, Third Edition* (New York: Harper & Row Publishers, Inc., 1987).

3. Frederick Herzberg, Bernard Mausner, and Barbara Block Snyderman, *The Motivation To Work* (New Brunswick, NJ: Transaction Publishers, 1999).

4. Douglas McGregor, *The Human Side of Enterprise* (New York: McGraw-Hill, 2006).

5. Fred E. Fiedler, *A Theory of Leadership Effectiveness* (New York: McGraw-Hill, 1967).

6. Ibid.

7. Victor H. Vroom, *Work and Motivation* (New York: John Wiley & Sons, Inc., 1964).

8. David C. McClelland, *Human Motivation* (Glenview, IL: Scott, Foresman, and Company, 1985).

CHAPTER 12

Leadership Best Practices

Rather than ask what one can do to become an Alpha, a better approach is to ask what we can learn from the Alphas in order to improve our performance.

—Andy Crowe

This chapter is devoted to the skills managers must have to step up to a leadership role. In this chapter, I describe classic best practices for management, such as using four-color assessments, as well as modern methods like virtual teams and stand-up meetings. We'll also explore advanced concepts such as sustainability and the recently developed value triple constraint, as well as the key differences between strategic and tactical planning, mentoring versus training, and between management and leadership itself. Finally, because management missteps can cause serious problems, key "must-avoids" in leadership are also covered in detail.

SUSTAINABILITY

Q1. What is *sustainability*, and why are companies moving in this direction as part of an overall leadership strategy?

A1. Sustainability means taking the society at large, as well as the ecological environment, into consideration on strategic decisions. It has at least three meanings in the business world:

- It can apply to the deliverables your projects produce and how you create them. Ideally, you will use green processes and leave the smallest possible carbon footprint. For example, in the timber industry, responsible companies plant many new trees to replace the old ones they cut down. If enough companies treat trees as a renewable resource, the industry can last long into the future.

• Sustainability also means keeping the goals of long-term success and expansion in mind as you conduct business with your clients and other companies.

• With regard to managing staff, sustainability comprises managers' efforts to keep team members healthy, productive, and able to help their company thrive long into the future.

Sustainability is part of forward-thinking leadership, and many companies are starting to include it in their mission.

Q2. When is using green processes not the same as having a sustainability strategy?

A2. Using green processes *is* having a sustainable strategy—when it's done right. Many companies have started to embrace green initiatives, but these are not always successful. As an example, one company packaged its products in recyclable plastic bottles, but the majority of its customers wound up not recycling the bottles. In the early days when green initiatives were becoming popular, this effort, without any oversight or follow-up, might have passed as a successful sustainability strategy. But progressive companies today would see this initiative as a sustainability failure. They would try to see what could be done to make this project truly successful, by improving the recycling instructions on the package or increasing awareness of their products' recyclability through better marketing.

Q3. What is *zero environmental footprint*, and how does it apply to sustainability?

A3. Some companies prioritizing sustainability are focusing on *zero environmental footprint* (ZEF) as a goal to shoot for in their projects. This is an outgrowth of the concept of leaving a small carbon footprint popular in earlier years. ZEF means running a business without polluting the environment, depleting natural resources, impacting endangered animal species, or causing ripple effects, such as hurting local economies. Overall, companies focusing on ZEF want their project, product, and business to leave a net-zero effect on the planet.

ELEMENTS OF LEADERSHIP

Q4. What key area is often neglected when PMs communicate to stakeholders about the status of the project?

A4. Many PMs don't realize that their communications to stakeholders may require an element of *salesmanship*, and they neglect this necessary ingredient for project success. To win and keep a customer's trust:

- *Always emphasize the specific benefits your project is bringing to your customer.* This works especially well when there are individual deliverables that will be released to the customer throughout the project's life cycle. Each release can be announced with a note or meeting or even training for the customer. The announcements should detail the benefits and how the customer can best take advantage of them, not just the fact that you've hit the milestone. Remember, it's not about you, it's about the customer.

- *Remind the client of the overall value the project will bring them.* This is especially important in cases when they won't see results until a long time down the road—for example, if the deliverable is a software app that won't go live until the very end of the project.

Part of the reason that salesmanship gets neglected is that many PMs are not comfortable putting on a salesman's hat. Also, PMs often make the assumption that everyone on a project is on board with its goals, but this is not always true. Often, senior managers drive the inception of a project but do not work to sell the idea to their staff—creating a disengaged or even unwilling group of stakeholders. Stakeholders may even want to cancel a project they did not initiate if the original project champion is no longer involved due to staff turnover.

How Publicizing a Project's Benefits Helped Save It

I was once tasked with implementing a change management system for a customer base of more than 1,000 developers. The system had been installed long ago but had gone nearly unused for many months. It was in danger of being cancelled, despite a directive from senior management to use it. The application would bring many valuable benefits for the department but was being met with strong resistance from the developers, who felt inconvenienced by the new process that had been added to their routine.

To market the product, we put together a quick class on how to use it. We emphasized the features that would most benefit the developers—in particular, a feature that would automate the back-out process when bugs were found in their programs and changes had to be reversed. In our classes, we asked the developers if, the next time they received a phone call at 3:00 a.m. to back out a change, they would like to scramble around looking for all the old versions of their software components and do manual replacements (as they were currently doing)—or if they would rather just type *B* to back out and press Enter. These two keystrokes would replace all software components for them.

This developer-centered training raised compliance with the new system from 5 percent to 100 percent.

Q5. What is meant by *strategic* versus *tactical*, and how can PMs be more strategic?

A5. When the question of whether a manager is strategic or tactical is raised, it's usually to suggest that he or she has a shortcoming. It implies that he or she may be strong in the *tactical* elements of management—the specifics, or the "what and the how"—but lacking in the *strategic* elements—the big picture, or the why. For example, suppose that a junior PM is good at working with schedules in MS Project and following up on individual tasks, but he is not seasoned enough, or sufficiently creative in his thinking, to handle the challenges of a large project on which a lot of decisions will be required.

Often, the manager in question does not lack aptitude, but rather needs further training or mentoring or, in some cases, more empowerment from his or her senior managers.

- *Training/mentoring:* The right class can make a big difference. Besides the general PM classes, you can find specific offerings focusing on strategic leadership, including seminars often given at PM conferences. Participating in a mentoring program (discussed in more detail later in this chapter) is a highly recommended way of learning from someone you have chosen because you respect his or her strategic abilities.

- *Empowerment:* While you don't want to throw a PM into the coldest, deepest river you can find to see if he or she can swim, PMs are often kept from growing into strategic decision-making roles because they are good at doing specific tasks, and management needs to keep them doing those tasks. From a senior leadership perspective, planning a PM's career growth should include thinking about putting him or her into new roles where the challenges and the people the PM will be working with will stretch his or her strategic muscles. In the long run, increasing a PM's skill set will add value to the organization.

Q6. What are the key differences between management and leadership?

A6. Leadership is more strategic compared with management, which is more tactical. A PM who can do a good job executing the projects assigned to him is succeeding as a tactician, and it's very likely that he is also using some strategic thinking. But a manager who has vision and proactively comes up with innovations and new ideas for improving her organization, and maybe manages programs, not projects, has graduated into more of a leadership role.

This element of being proactive also applies to the difference between managing versus leading. In this context, you can think of a manager as someone who follows a checklist and does all the required things for getting a project done. But a *leader* is flexible and creative and comes up with all kinds of ways to bring out his people's best potential, including ways that may be out of the box.

Another way to put it is that employees *have* to do what their manager tells them. But they *want* to follow a leader because a leader has a lot of vision, passion, and creativity and thinks strategically about the entire department or organization (beyond the project at hand).

When you are perceived as a leader, not just a manager, people will gravitate to work for you. Your staff will hope that as you go farther in your career, so will they.

Q7. What are *four-color assessments,* and are they important for PMs?

A7. For many years, companies have been sending their managers and leaders (not just PMs) through leadership training, which often includes what is commonly referred to as a four-color assessment. Participants of these assessments are asked to complete a survey of some kind and, concurrently, their peers and managers are also asked to complete a similar survey about the participants. The results are then compiled and analyzed, and the participants are evaluated to determine their strengths among the four color categories. Most participants reflect all four categories to varying degrees, but each individual has a slightly different combination.

Some of the most popular assessments are the Myers-Briggs Type Indicator® (MBTI® Instrument), the Keirsey Temperament Sorter®, and the Revised NEO Personality Inventory, or NEO PI-R, developed by Paul Costa and Robert McCrae.

Based on my experience with assessments of this sort, I would encourage any PM to take part: Gaining more awareness of your personal leadership style can influence you to refine the way you manage. And as part of this kind of assessment and related training, you will learn how to blend your style to match and work with managers and other stakeholders who have different color combinations and personality types.

Q8. What kind of leadership do project teams need at the beginning of a project?

A8. As PMs, we often fall into the trap of thinking that projects belong to *us*. But it's important to remember that your team members think of a project as *theirs*, and they may judge you based on your efforts to prepare for the project. You may be focused on the greater good of the end results of the project, but your staff may lose faith in you as a leader if you don't attend to their direct needs, especially at the beginning of a project. It is very important to take care of early administrative tasks such as getting everyone's laptops, phones, badges, passwords, email accounts, and payroll paperwork in order *before* they are needed, and then distribute early planning documents, such as the project charter and org charts, to each new team member. Even if these details do not seem urgent to you when you start a project, creating a strong first impression will help you win your team's trust early on.

Q9. How does a PM's role as a leader evolve on a project, and where does flexibility come into play?

A9. During the forming and storming phases of team development, team members may test the PM's authority. Planning and preparation help, but can't always eliminate the conflict that can arise during these phases. To help alleviate this, you as the PM can come in ready on day 1 to establish your presence as a strong leader. (This is a good day to wear that power suit hanging in your closet!) Even if you're not comfortable using the forcing form of power, it's good to start off strong to make sure everyone gets off on the right foot. A little like having a pet dog or riding a horse, people actually prefer some structure and to know who is running the show. It makes for better morale when they know they have a PM who is comfortable in the role.

Later, as the project evolves through the life cycle, you will often be able to let down your guard and fall into the role of advisor or mentor, as your team graduates from the storming phase and hits their stride in the performing phase. It's good to keep watch on how the team is doing, with the goal of at least partly ceding the driver role to the team itself.

You might find that some team members don't need a strong manager, while others do. For those team members who are very motivated, you might be able to be more of an advisor from the beginning; others may need a lot more direction and supervision from you. So you should be alert to the differences in your people, and flexible enough to respond to those differences with the various management methods you are capable of.

Q10. What is the *value triple constraint*, and how can this concept help leaders improve project success?

A10. Traditional project management focuses on the metrics of turning over the deliverables on time and on budget to a customer. But to measure success from a broader leadership perspective, companies should concentrate on the value the project will ultimately yield *after* it is implemented.

Angelo Baratta, PMP, CMC, has developed what he calls the value triple constraint, or V Triple C, which he describes as an evolution of the classic triple constraint.[1] Instead of focusing on the delivery phase, which is all about creating the deliverables, this concept emphasizes the *realization phase*, which is when the goods and services created by the team will begin to be used by the customer and add real value to their organization.

V Triple C also factors in the opportunity costs of performing a project in two ways: First, the value a project brings to a company should take into account the value the customer gave up by not choosing other projects (traditional opportunity cost). Second, V Triple C also factors in the costs lost in the time it takes to select and perform the project (before benefits are realized), which Baratta calls *schedule opportunity costs*.

From a leadership perspective, part of the goal of using V Triple C is to better measure the value a project adds. But it's also intended to expedite the project selection process. Reducing schedule opportunity costs and getting to the realization phase quicker can increase the profitability of and value added by the project.

FOSTERING A POSITIVE PM ENVIRONMENT

Q11. What are ways to foster a productive work environment?

A11. A PM can do a great deal to positively influence the work environment, and consequently, the work results. Here are several effective techniques:

- *Emphasize and model doing the right work.* Unfortunately, in many companies, the *wrong* work is emphasized. For example, a company might insist that everyone follow certain processes, like consistent status reporting, but this can make team members lose sight of the quality of the deliverables. The PM must stress the importance of doing the right work according to the metrics agreed upon with the customer. And he or she needs to bring this point home by setting a good example.

- *Have a customer-service mentality.* Unfortunately, many PMs do not have a customer-service focus. For instance, they might have their own high technical standards in mind without concentrating on customer service. Customers are often dissatisfied—even when the project team completes high-quality technical work—if they perceive a PM as unresponsive. For PMs looking to develop their customer-service mentality, a number of courses, books, and coaching services are available on this exact subject. A desire to improve is key.

Q12. What can PMs do to instill a customer-service attitude in their team members?

A12. It's always best to screen for and hire employees who have a strong customer-service (CS) mindset. Having a team that is focused on customer service can pay many dividends toward the end goal of having a customer who is satisfied with the deliverables and the project.

The PM needs to keep an eye out for team members who aren't focused on customer service. Even if they otherwise do good work, those employees can cause problems on the project, such as doing things that they think is best, even if it's not what the customer, or the PM, or even the sponsor wants. This can also have a negative influence on other team members, hurting morale, or leading others away from a customer-focused attitude.

Fortunately, there is a lot you as a PM can do to foster good CS skills. You can nominate deserving employees for customer-service awards if your company supports those, or you can start a CS award program if there isn't one already. Awards can be a great motivator and can help instill a CS spirit on the project. And with status reporting, you can regularly ask employees about the CS component of each of their accomplishments. For example, when a team member gives their status, you can ask something like, "And how did the customer respond when you told her about the new feature?" These efforts should make an impression on even the most stubborn worker, who will start to realize that his or her work is being evaluated based in part on his or her CS efforts.

Q13. How can a PM foster a lessons-learned environment?

A13. Lessons learned are another often-neglected area on projects. Some PMs like to act as if they are in such a hurry to get to work that they have no time to look for relevant historical information. But from a leadership perspective, lessons learned can make a crucial difference in getting faster, better, cheaper results.

There is a lot a PM can do proactively to make lessons learned a core part of the project's environment. Here are a few specific recommendations:

- *Allocate time.* Make time at meetings to share lessons learned, even if it's just five minutes.
- *Set an example.* By sharing lessons you've learned from your own past projects, you can show that it's OK to have made a mistake as long as you learned from it.
- *Provide lessons-learned templates.* Providing a specific outline for documenting lessons learned (see Chapter 2, Q&A 4) will encourage team members to do so.
- *Set up a lessons-learned database or intranet site.* Also discussed in Chapter 2, creating a place where lessons learned can be quickly and easily

stored and located can bring many benefits to your company. Starting such a site is a great way for you as the PM to show leadership.

- *Don't wait until the end of the project to discuss lessons learned.* Teams lose a great opportunity to share information if lessons from the current project aren't discussed until the post mortem, because this kind of information can often help improve the present project, as well as future efforts.

- *Emphasize positive lessons learned.* Some of the best lessons learned are success stories, and encouraging team members to talk about positive results can be a great team-building technique. This gives some team members who might otherwise be shy or quiet a chance to shine, and it also provides a forum for team members to help each other out and bond in the process. The more team members share both positive and negative lessons, the more the stigma of discussing mistakes will disappear, resulting in more good information-sharing that can help your project.

Q14. How can I influence the PM environment to make sure my people behave ethically?

A14. Here are a couple tips:

- *Walk the walk.* It is essential for PMs to follow all the rules they ask team members to follow. Managers often think they are above the rules, but when team members see a PM breaking the rules, they no longer take his or her words seriously. "Do as I say, not as I do" never works. Everyone spots the hypocrisy and assumes that the PM isn't really serious about the rules.

- *Use your ethics board (or establish one if none already exists).* If your company has an ethics board or documented ethical policy statement, make sure your team knows that it's there and that you support it. If there is no ethics board or policy, you can help establish one. Having a good ethics board—one with teeth—is a best practice for helping foster an ethical environment.

For much more on ethics in project management, see Chapter 9.

Q15. What is meant by the term *safe-to-say environment*, and how does a safe-to-say environment work?

A15. It is a best practice to make a strong point of telling your team members that they are working in a safe-to-say environment, meaning that honesty is encouraged and there are no penalties for telling the truth. Fostering a culture of openness will benefit your project's quality, efficiency, and more.

The challenge is to make team members believe you really mean it. Many employees are afraid to speak up out of fear of retribution. You must make clear, firmly and sincerely, that whatever your people say to you will be a truly safe communication. It may take some time to build a sufficient level of trust. But as your employees begin to realize that you appreciate their feedback and that they have not been penalized for being honest, they will likely tell their coworkers about the environment you've helped create, and a safe-to-say culture can begin to take hold.

Q16. How can I implement a "bring solutions, not problems" strategy?

A16. Start by explaining to your team that you have a "bring solutions, not problems" policy, which means that while you welcome openness and the raising of problems and risks, you require whoever raises any new issues, problems, or risks to take ownership of them. This kind of strategy is a very simple yet very effective problem-management tool, and setting a policy like this is one way PMs can begin to transition from managers to leaders.

A "bring solutions, not problems" policy has a number of specific benefits:

- It forces your team members to do more critical thinking before raising issues, saving you valuable time.

- It empowers your people to think for themselves and come up with their own creative solutions, rather than just handing you raw problems. This helps your staff grow from tactical thinkers to critical thinkers, which is good for their career development in the long term. In the short term, it improves morale and encourages innovation on the project.

- It can act like a fire extinguisher, tamping down much of the venting, griping, whining, and other nonproductive behaviors that can waste a lot of time in meetings.

Q17. What are some ways to encourage creativity among my team members?

A17. Here are three methods that are often successful:

- ***Allow time for creative thinking.*** One simple yet effective method is to build some time into your meetings for allowing your people to generate creative ideas. Many employees are hungry to use their creativity on the job; they just need permission and a bit of encouragement. A specific technique for eliciting creative ideas is brainstorming (discussed in Chapter 3 as a useful strategy for requirements gathering; see Q&A 10).

- ***Offer rewards.*** Offering a reward for sharing the best creative ideas is a method many companies use as a motivator. Related to this, PMs can tell team members that creative contributions will be rewarded by the company at raise and bonus time.

- ***Make it safe to make a mistake.*** Establishing a safe environment is crucial for creativity. Team members need to be made to feel unafraid of trying and even sometimes failing. Mistakes can be part of the creative process. Remember that Post-it® notes were invented as the accidental by-product of glue that failed to hold as planned.

REVIEWING PERFORMANCE

Q18. Why are performance reviews necessary on projects?

A18. Performance reviews are an excellent way to motivate people to do better. Most PMs want to get very good results on projects, and improving their people via performance reviews is one of the best ways to do it. Yet many PMs don't do performance reviews because:

- They don't like to take the time to prepare for them
- They may find giving in-person reviews somewhat awkward
- On shorter projects or in consulting situations, reviews are not automatically built into the structure of the project (unlike annual reviews that are commonly required when managing permanent people).

Everyone on the planet can improve him- or herself, and most people like to look for ways they can improve. But if you don't let an employee know how he can improve, he most likely will not ask you, and therefore he probably won't improve.

Giving performance reviews on projects is a best practice because it often improves individual employees' productivity, and with it, the project.

If your team doesn't currently do reviews, you can recommend instituting them.

Q19. What are some tips on giving performance reviews?

A19. There are three basics:

- *The focus needs to be on future performance*, not on looking back and finding fault. You can use examples from the past, but always frame them in the context of how the employee can use the lessons learned to succeed in upcoming scheduled activities. Also, any past problems should have already been dealt with directly at the time they occurred. Your people should not feel that you are saving up a list of issues to nail them on during their review, but rather that you have put time into analyzing how best you can help them improve going forward.

- *Lead off with positives.* People want affirmation for what they've done well, and this is always the best way to start off any performance review, even when you have important corrective issues to address.

- *The purpose of reviews should not be to fix faults but to build on strengths.* One of the most common mistakes PMs make is to try to fix what they see as the deficiencies in their people. But often, what they see as faults are part of the core personality of the employee (very difficult to change), and focusing on faults often just makes the employee feel bad. As an example, suppose you have an employee who is a very capable engineer, and engineering is key for your project, but she has little aptitude for leading meetings, which is not absolutely necessary for her to do anyway. Rather than trying to train her in meeting facilitation, you might help her much more by sending her to an advanced engineering seminar, which she will find stimulating and motivating.

Q20. Do 360 reviews really add value, and what's the best way to administer them?

A20. Think of an owl spinning its head all around, taking in a 360-degree view of its environment. The purpose of a 360 review is to assess the performance of an employee by getting an all-angles view of him or her. This is done by interviewing people both above and below the employee in the reporting structure on your project, as well as some at his or her peer level.

The manager usually asks the employee to suggest five or six names of stakeholders he or she has worked with in the period under review, say in the past six months. The manager then emails each named stakeholder to announce that he or she is conducting a 360 review of the employee and that the employee suggested the stakeholder as a possible contact. The manager asks each contact the same set of questions. For example:

- How did you like working with the employee on the project?
- What specifically did you appreciate about his or her performance?
- Do you have any suggestions on where the employee might improve?

Most PMs I have talked with about this have told me they feel the 360 method makes performance reviews a more fair process, as they aren't based solely on supervisors' opinions.

But it's important to note that there are right ways and wrong ways of delivering feedback from a 360 review.

- ***Wrong way:*** Some PMs have told me they did not like the 360 review process because their supervisor kept the 360 feedback anonymous—for example, if the supervisor said, "One of your 360 contacts said such and such... but to preserve confidentiality, I can't tell you who."
- ***Right way:*** PMs liked the 360 when the feedback was delivered in the form of specific, constructive comments attributed to their sources: "Phil told me he very much appreciated your contributions on the 200 Project, and that you created very clear documentation. But he thought if you gave a hands-on demo of the system in future situations, it would be very useful for your customers."

The Team Performance Assessment

There is a PMI best practice of writing an assessment at the end of the project on how the team performed as a team. It is similar to the idea of an individual performance assessment. The PM can help his or her performing organization here by documenting such findings as:

- Which team members worked especially well together and should be paired again on future projects (or the converse—who should not be paired together next time)
- Who showed leadership and other qualities that might benefit the company on future projects
- What kind of projects this existing team might be a match for.

MANAGING LOW-PERFORMING EMPLOYEES

Q21. Why is "hire slow, fire fast" a highly recommended rule of thumb for PMs?

A21. *Hire slow* is just the commonsense idea of doing a good job of analyzing the requirements and making sure you are thorough and careful in the interviewing process. No mystery there, yet many PMs often see staffing the team as a goal in itself and rush to fill positions, only to have to live with unsatisfactory consequences.

When you hire the wrong team member, not only may he or she cause problems, but these problems often create a ripple effect: The new hire proves to be a drain on the PM and the other team members. Having to get rid of the new employee often poses quite a problem in itself, especially when a lengthy case must be made before anyone can be terminated (as in government agencies).

Once it's been determined that an employee is not the right fit, it is extremely rare for the PM to be able to turn the situation around. Yet many PMs make the mistake of going through a long, lingering process of trying to see if they can salvage the hire, while time and money bleed on the project. And sometimes they wind up keeping the employee on for the wrong reasons—for example, to avoid acknowledging to the client or senior management that they made a hiring mistake or to keep up the head count. Neither reason is honest, and neither gets the work done.

The ripple effect often morphs into a vicious cycle. The problem team member's actions build resentment among the other team members and hurts their morale, which causes the team to lose respect for the PM, which further contributes to low morale and low productivity. It is much better to terminate the employee quickly.

As a best practice, some companies take a highly proactive approach here, for instance, by a formal policy that all newly-hired employees are officially on probation for a set period, during which they can be terminated at will. Zappos Shoes even has created a bonus system specifically around firing fast![2] Zappos is very careful in choosing the best employees through their hiring process, but when the occasional new employee isn't working out, he or she is terminated after the first five weeks, but with a generous amount of extra pay. The five weeks helps the company keep only the hires they feel will be productive, while the extra pay creates good will. The terminated employee walks away with a large check and no hard feelings.

Q22. Where should I draw the line when trying to save a low-performing employee?

A22. A rule of thumb here is that if you as the PM believe the employee can truly become productive, such that the team is better with him than without, then it *is* worth putting in the extra effort. This can include mentoring or training the employee or temporarily teaming him up with someone else on the team who can help bring him up to speed.

But if you don't strongly believe that you can turn the employee around, it's a disservice to your customer and everyone else involved (including the employee) to keep him.

Q23. Is a probation period worthwhile and recommended when a PM is considering terminating an employee?

A23. It is not always the employee's fault when a position turns out not to be a fit. There are often gaps and miscommunications in the interview process, and important issues are not covered. This can make a quick termination unfair.

However, as soon as it becomes clear that a team member may not be working out, the PM must immediately address the problem by meeting with the team member and possibly putting him or her on probation. The PM needs to be very specific about the expectations the employee is not meeting, as well as the necessary benchmarks of success for the employee to meet in the near future to retain his or her role.

Whether you go the probation route or not partly depends on what rules and protocols you have at your company. Putting someone on formal probation is a drastic step that most employees will find very threatening, so it might be counterproductive. But this does often work well as a wake-up call for others, so it's a judgment call for the PM. It also might involve a lot of specific rules and red tape in some companies, so the process might take up a lot of your time. So you should try meeting with the employee one-on-one first to see if you can improve the situation without formal probation.

MEETINGS

Q24. What's the biggest danger of having too many go-around-the-room status meetings?

A24. The biggest pitfall is that having too many status meetings is a time suck. There are so many ways to share information electronically that traditional status meetings are no longer really necessary. The same results can often be accomplished in much less time by having the team send bulleted status updates to the PM or to the entire team or even by updating a project database or intranet site—whatever works best for your unique team and project.

There is more waste in status meetings than meets the eye. Traveling to meetings takes time (and may cost money) and takes time away from work (opportunity cost). Also, some team members wind up going overboard preparing for meetings so their status will sound good, while others are uncomfortable giving status in front of the group. And many people get back to their everyday tasks slowly after shifting gears for a meeting.

That said, it's still important to many people's morale to have the constancy, interpersonal connections, and validation offered by a weekly meeting, especially when they are used to them after many years of having them. And many still prefer a live meeting in a room to a virtual meeting, where everyone has to log in with special passwords just to join in and see the shared screens, and for some, it doesn't feel the same.

Q25. If status meetings are no longer considered a best practice, which meetings *are* considered necessary?

A25. Many team meetings *are* vital, especially when there is a real purpose for getting everyone into one room. These include kickoff meetings to start a project off right, quick announcements that affect a whole group, and especially emergencies for which you need everyone on the team's live presence and brainpower. Holding a meeting to address specific challenges is known as bringing stakeholders into a "war room"—a name that carries a sense of urgency and purpose.

Q26. What is a *stand-up meeting*, and is it really better than the old-school sit-down meeting?

A26. *The Sopranos* made it famous to call a meeting a sit-down. But like Tony Soprano himself, traditional meetings are now considered old school. One new way of meeting that is becoming increasingly popular among agile management practitioners is called a *stand-up meeting*. Attendees literally have to stand and give their status or other comments in one minute or less (before anyone's feet start to hurt!).

The main benefit of a stand-up meeting is increased speed and conciseness, as the format discourages long-windedness or spending time on unimportant issues. With traditional meetings, it's common for people to settle in for the allotted time slot, such as one hour, and stretch out the meeting to that length. But with stand-up meetings, there is a built-in impetus to get back to work ASAP, as fast as the meeting points can be dispensed with. This in itself helps build a feeling of efficiency and productivity into the project, which can become a self-fulfilling prophecy.

The stand-up format also eliminates red tape by encouraging direct communications and some streamlining (ok, bypassing!) through the chain of command. Because everyone is already on their feet, participants feel it's appropriate to walk directly up to whichever stakeholder in the meeting can most effectively address their issues, instead of first addressing their manager's manager and so on.

When people first hear about this kind of meeting, they are often skeptical, but you will find an increasing number of PMs, especially in agile PM environments, testifying to their effectiveness.

MENTORING AND TRAINING

Q27. What is *mentoring* in a project management context?

A27. Mentoring is a way to help team members develop. It has an added dimension beyond just teaching a skill. It involves taking a personal interest in the employees you mentor and providing individual guidance—not necessarily just immediate guidance toward the current project, but also with the mentee's long-term career goals in mind. This often helps establish a special bond between mentor and mentee and can instill feelings of loyalty, friendship, and mutual respect, which may carry forward far beyond the current project.

The Free PMI Mentoring Program

Many PMs are not aware that PMI offers mentoring as a free benefit of membership in many of its local chapters. You can request a mentor to coach you, either in the same industry you are currently in, or in a different area you may want to explore. Or you can volunteer to mentor another chapter member, usually a junior PM. Either way, the PMI mentoring experience helps you sharpen your own mentoring skills, making you a better mentor for your team members. It also pays an added dividend—participating in the PMI mentoring program provides free PDUs toward recertification for PMPs, PgMPs, PMI-SPs, and PMI-RMPs (up to five PDUs per year for *both* mentor and mentee).

Q28. What are some recommended mentoring methods?

A28. Recommended mentoring methods include:

- *A formal corporate mentor program:* Some companies offer formal mentoring programs as a best practice. These are very similar to PMI's mentoring program. A junior employee indicates that he or she would like some guidance, and a senior leader takes the employee on as a mentee. The two agree to meet on a regular basis, perhaps once per month, to discuss the employee's latest concerns and progress. The mentor and mentee document milestones along the way to track the mentee's progress and so that the mentoring itself can be evaluated later for its effectiveness.

- *On a project level:* The PM meets one-on-one with some of the less experienced team members to mentor them.

- *Peer-pairing:* Another popular approach is to pair up a junior team member with one who is more senior. The junior person learns the ropes, and the senior member shares his or her knowledge and experience. Another benefit of this is that it gives the senior member some experience that may help him or her toward a management role down the road.

Casual Mentor Program

I once worked in a company that had created a formal mentoring program, but I found my own mentor who was willing to work with me in a more casual way: We scheduled meetings on an as-needed basis, only at times when I had an issue I wanted to discuss. We both found it more convenient and time-effective not to go through the firm's formal mentoring program, which meant we could avoid documenting agendas and reporting our status up to the program office, and our arrangement worked out very well.

Formal or informal, mentoring can be highly beneficial for both parties and to the organization as a whole.

Q29. What is the key to effectively training team members?

A29. Probably the biggest secret to success in training others is having the ability to put yourself into what's known as a *beginner's mind*. This means that even though you may be an expert on what you are teaching your team members, you can still put yourself in their shoes, think about what they know and don't know, and empathize with what it would be like to learn the topic from their frame of reference.

Empathy can have both analytical and emotional components. For example, before trying to teach someone how to use an online application, you can think about what you needed to know as a prerequisite when you first learned the app. On the feelings side, it can help to try to remember how you felt going through the process of learning to use the app for the first time—what difficulties you encountered, which parts came easily, what early successes you enjoyed, and how you learned what you did.

A best practice is to try to plan early successes into your agenda when teaching your colleagues, such as having them use the product or tool very early on to create a small deliverable. This helps the learner both analytically and emotionally: They make progress learning, and they also gain confidence early on, which further helps accelerate learning.

Q30. What is a recommended approach for selecting the right training method for team members?

A30. First off, the wrong way to approach training is to try to fix team members' faults. It is understandable to want to use training as a way to improve your people's flaws, and sometimes this is necessary. But generally, throwing a class at someone to fix what you perceive to be his or her weaknesses may not work. For one thing, you can't make people into what they are not. And it also can be counterproductive or even demoralizing to be in a class in which you can't succeed because you have no aptitude for a certain skill.

A recommended way is to agree on a training plan. Sit down with your team member and decide together which training approach would work best for him or her. Of course, there must be alignment between the kind of training the employee wants and what the project and your company needs. But it's ideal if you can also tie the training to the employee's long-term goals. This creates a spirit of mentoring. By getting team members' input and especially their buy-in, you will greatly increase the likelihood that the training will be successful and have a positive effect on your project.

Q31. What's the single biggest mistake PMs make in the way they try to train their people, and what can they do to fix it?

A31. The most common mistake PMs make is to handle training sessions for the team as lectures, often delivered off the cuff. First of all, like anything else, good planning makes training sessions go better. But even more important, most people don't learn well from the "I'll talk, you'll listen" approach, where the PM tries to impart their knowledge by pouring it like water into their team members' heads. The problem with this kind of information shower is that most people learn better with discussion and hands-on practice, not just by listening to a lecture.

A best practice is to put some effort into planning an interactive session. And focus on questions—both the ones you'll ask and the ones you think your people will ask you:

- *Plan questions from you.* Spend time coming up with good questions, which will stimulate team members' thinking and help get across the concepts you'll talk about.

- *Plan time to field questions from them.* Make your team members feel comfortable about asking a lot of their own questions throughout the session. PMs, eager to get through their agenda, often say something like, "Everyone, hold your questions to the end, and I'll try to get to all of them." But that approach often fails. People want to ask questions as they think of them and are distracted when they can't. And while having Q&A time at the end of a meeting can be beneficial, it often gets cut out altogether when a PM, carried away with his or her agenda, runs out of time (and then rationalizes that he or she covered pretty much everything they could in the limited timeframe).

Figure 12-1 offers more tips for PMs about training a team.

Ask open-ended questions	Avoid yes/no questions, which don't add much to your presentation. Instead, ask open-ended questions such as, "Can anyone tell me how this skill could come in handy on our project?" These tend to get responses that help reinforce what you are trying to get across.
Make it hands on	Many people learn by doing. Planning some hands-on practice with the system or skill you're teaching will pay off.
Make it deliverable based	Choose a deliverable for the training—for example, have the participants make a production update to the system you are teaching, and build as much teaching around this task as you can.
Give homework	Coming up with some kind of follow-up activity encourages your people to review what was covered and to find and correct any gaps in their learning. Here are two different ways to accomplish this after the training session: • Ask one team member to document the skill for the rest of the team. • As a review, ask one team member to teach back the skill to the other team members.
Put together a hard copy of the materials	Take the time to come up with some kind of handout to help participants follow along. (Developing a handout also helps you better plan the key points you want to cover.)
Check in to make sure they're learning	Making sure your participants are really learning is key. Asking very specific questions is one very good way to do this. If you're teaching a software skill, walk over to each participant's PC to see if and where he or she is struggling.

Figure 12-1: Team Training Tips

Q32. When is out-of-the-box training necessary?

A32. Often the only training that makes sense for a project is in specific skills directly attached to the deliverables, such as training in advanced Java coding for the developers coding the system the project is building. While this seems like a practical approach, it sometimes pays to think outside the box on training. The goal of training is to get the best project results, not to blindly go through lists of classes the company is considering for the year.

Case Study: A Successful Out-of-the-Box Training Program

I once was managing a couple of systems support personnel who had learned English as a second language and who both struggled with communicating in English. This was a problem because both were required to write memos to our customers from time to time, and they had to perform a lot of help desk support. The miscommunications that arose were causing problems for our projects.

We proposed to our senior management that we bring in a communications coach to help both technicians improve their speaking and writing skills. The powers that be balked at first because they considered communications training not *directly* applicable to the work the team members were performing. But my manager and I prevailed, and the results the trainer delivered were truly extraordinary. Both employees became much more efficient and productive on all of the projects they did for us, especially the one who was more self-motivated to improve in this area.

PRESENTATIONS

Q33. What are the key mistakes PMs make when trying to use PowerPoint or similar tools to make presentations to the team?

A33. PowerPoint is an awesome product, but it is misused so often that books have actually been written on how *not* to use it. The most common mistakes that PMs as well as trainers make with it are:

- *Putting too many ideas on each slide.* Ideally, one main idea per slide is best.

- *Putting too many bullet points on each slide.* Less is more when it comes to bullet points.

- *Creating too many slides.* PMs often rely on PowerPoint as a crutch and put together a ton of slides to click through as a way of getting through a presentation, rather than communicating, checking in, and interacting with their stakeholders in the meeting.

- **Putting too much text on slides.** If a slide looks like a page from a book or manual, people will try to read it and may not listen to what the PM is saying. They will also wonder why they are attending the presentation at all when they could be sitting at their desks reading it.

- **Using no graphics or the wrong graphics.** The best PowerPoint slides often have one graphic and a little bit of text supporting that graphic. Many bad slides are text only; others are covered in overly glitzy graphics, which distract the viewer and hurt more than they help.

Figure 12-2 lists several rules from trainers about how many bullet points and slides are recommended for presentations.

The Rule of 6 x 6
This rule states that for best results: • No more than six bullet points per slide is best. • No more than six words per bullet is a good guideline.
The Rule of 10 x 20 x 30 (attributed to expert trainer Guy Kawasaki)
• Use no more than 10 slides. • An ideal presentation should last no longer than 20 minutes. • Use no font size smaller than 30 points.
The Rule of 7 x 20 x 21 (This idea originated in Japan for presentations by architects. It's now used when there are multiple speakers and you want to keep each speaker moving right along.)
• No more than 7 minutes long • No more than 20 slides • No more than 21 seconds per slide.

Figure 12-2: Rules of Thumb from Expert Trainers on Effective Presentations

Q34. When is PowerPoint not the best tool for a presentation?

A34. Unfortunately, PowerPoint too often dominates presentations. A few key slides can be great for bullet-pointing your agenda and for highlighting your main concepts, but it's often best to use other media and materials as well. For instance, a simple whiteboard can be used very effectively when supported by just a few slides. Too many slides force the presenter to stick to a rigid order, killing spontaneity. This can also make the presenter neglect to check in with and interact with the participants.

Also, to paraphrase U.S. Army Brigadier General H.R. McMaster, not all ideas are bullet-izable. He was specifically referring to how PowerPoint is being improperly used in military presentations, where overly elaborate slides are confusing and counterproductive. In the same article, Thomas X. Hammes, a retired Marine colonel, says that some in the military call PowerPoint bullets "dumb-dumb bullets," emphasizing how they can dumb down ideas.[3]

Finally, different people learn best from different media, so it's best if Power-Point is used in moderation, along with other vehicles such as the whiteboard, handouts, live demos, hands-on exercises, and participatory discussions and games.

Q35. What are some guidelines for using graphics in presentations?

A35. For many topics, an ideal slide contains one idea conveyed by one graphic, plus a few words of text to help communicate that idea. And the key when using graphics is choosing images that you think can best convey the ideas to your audience—not just ones that you think look cool.

Too many graphics, or very complex, busy, or over-animated graphics, are also pitfalls to watch out for. If in doubt about whether a graphic will get your concept across, the easy way to find out is to test it in advance on a couple of team members or colleagues. Ask for an honest answer (and really listen to what they tell you), and you'll find out right away if it works or not.

COLLOCATION

Q36. What is *collocation*, and what are the benefits?

A36. In more traditional work environments, groups are segregated by function, e.g., the developers are all together in one area and the testers in another. This is common in functional project environments. Collocation is a modern best practice based on the idea that improved teamwork and increased efficiency can be achieved by locating people together—in a large bullpen area, for instance, or by seating the developer and tester together in the same office so they can discuss issues face-to-face as they come up.

Collocation eliminates a lot of time-consuming email chains, and on a larger scale, also eliminates the "us versus them" attitude that is common when groups work in their own isolated silos. Collocated teams often also achieve increased camaraderie, along with a clear sense that all groups are on the same side, working toward the common goals of the project. It's a good way to get rid of the "I'm doing *my* piece" mentality.

Q37. What are the drawbacks of collocation?

A37. The biggest drawback is loss of privacy and autonomy. With the trend away from private offices and into small, shared spaces (often driven by cost-cutting more than anything else), PMs sometimes get sloppy about traditional sensitivities. For example, they may forget that they should never criticize a team member in front of the others on the team. It is the rare employee who would *not* feel embarrassed or even shamed by being given feedback such as, "I was disappointed in the way you wrote that module," in front of his or her peers.

If a team is collocated in close quarters, there is no excuse for not taking a little bit of extra time and effort to have a quick private meeting, maybe grabbing an office for a few minutes or popping down to the company cafeteria. Delivering constructive feedback is a key function of the PM's role and is not to be taken lightly. Doing it the wrong way can make things worse, not better, and can permanently alienate your employees.

VIRTUAL TEAMS

Q38. How should I decide if virtual teams are the way to go for my project?

A38. When they first became prevalent, virtual teams picked up a bad reputation in the United States and other countries because they were directly associated with outsourcing and the loss of local jobs. They also were seen as a lower-quality alternative, with the primary benefit being the cheaper rate of labor in other countries.

But virtual teams are becoming increasingly popular as people realize that they offer significant benefits beyond just cost, especially:

- *Access to a global talent pool:* When companies are not restricted to using local resources only, an entire world of talent opens up. PMs open to virtual teaming gain access to capable, skilled people across the globe.

- *Mobile management:* When your team is thousands of miles away, it becomes unnecessary for you as the PM to come into the office every day from 9 to 5. PMs leading virtual teams often communicate with staff by phone and through electronic meetings from their laptops. This enables them to do a lot of their managing from home or on the move between meetings with their customers.

We can see that virtual teaming has opened up many new possibilities for project management. The two key questions when considering virtual teams are:

- Will virtual teams improve your project (as well as your company, business model, and profitability)?

- Before you jump in, do you know enough about how to take advantage of virtual teams to make them work for your project? (If not, there are many seminars, webinars, and new books devoted to this subject; see the Bibliography.)

Q39. What special planning is needed before deciding to use a virtual team?

A39. As part of your HR planning, it is recommended that you do a cost/benefit analysis to see if virtual teaming makes business sense for your project. Also, think hard about exactly which functions you would be outsourcing to the virtual team, and try to determine if those parts truly would be best handled by an outsourcer or by your home team. If in doubt, you might want to interview some of the stakeholders who would be most affected if the work were done overseas.

The challenge is that anyone can play bean-counter and choose virtual to lower costs. Keep in mind that some virtual teams succeed, and others do not. Virtual teaming can be a mistake, financially and otherwise, because it is not right for every project.

A Best Practice for Virtual Teams

When outsourcing work to foreign countries, some U.S. companies hire a manager from the other country and collocate them here in the United States. For instance, an American-based company contracting to India for an IT development project would hire a manager from India, who would then travel to the United States, where she will interface with the developers in India. An arrangement like this can instantly eliminate language barriers, cultural differences, and staffing and other supervisory problems that have reduced the effectiveness of outsourcing on many past projects.

MANAGEMENT AND LEADERSHIP PROBLEMS

Q40. What is the danger of managing by memo?

A40. A manager who sits in his office all day sending out emails and instant messages, neglecting the face-to-face interactions that would likely be more effective, is guilty of managing by memo. Emailing and IM-ing are not only addictive, but they also allow people to avoid conflict (always tempting!). But though they can seem time-efficient, they also lead to a great deal of communication errors and often hurt productivity as much as they help it.

The biggest problem with managing by memo is that it weakens the human relationships that used to be forged by in-person dialogue. Having a work discussion over coffee with a stakeholder connects the PM and the stakeholder. It's a social experience, which helps with team-building. Face-to-face meetings also allow the time and proper forum to generate new ideas for the project. An email might contain the same words you would say in person, but because it is a one-way-only communication, it does not have the relationship-building potential that even a brief get-together provides. And it doesn't provide the instant reality check that a face-to-face meeting offers, to make sure you and your stakeholder are on the same page.

Q41. What is *shunning* in the PM world, and how can it be handled?

A41. For a variety of reasons, team members sometimes shun other staff. In the PM world, this can take many forms, from not including certain team members for lunch to forming cliques on the project—some people are in and others are out (reminiscent of the movie *Mean Girls*).

Some PMs take a passive approach to how the interpersonal dynamics will shake out and feel that team members are on their own in this regard. But good PMs and functional managers know they bear responsibility to correct this kind of situation, for the sake of the customer and project, as well as for the team members. In extreme cases, this can lead to what I call the red-ink mentality, discussed in the next Q&A.

Q42. What is the *red-ink mentality,* and what can be done to prevent employees from engaging in red-ink behavior?

A42. "Red ink" is a name for a kind of behavior I have observed that is like shunning on steroids. Sometimes two team members believe themselves to be in competition. Let's say a layoff may be on the horizon, and one of the team members thinks that only one of the two will survive. So he may start treating his competitor like "red ink," meaning an employee who is not worthy of his paycheck and who deserves to be fired, in the hope that wishing will make it so. It's even worse when an entire group treats a rival team in this way.

Red-ink behavior is the opposite of teamwork and cooperation, and it is very destructive to morale. The PM must address it proactively and not just look the other way, hoping it will work itself out. (Directly confronting such behavior is one way that true leaders separate themselves from managers.) Well-planned team-building activities with an emphasis on mutually shared goals can sometimes help. But if the PM feels that this behavior is beyond his or her control or that there are serious underlying causes or conflicts, it's necessary to bring senior management into the loop to correct the situation. A red-ink mentality can lead to red ink for your project.

Q43. What is the "who gets it next" attitude on a project team?

A43. Some groups seem to always have one bad apple who is next in line to be fired. There's the constant feeling in the air among the managers that if only they could get rid of that one underperforming employee, then the project would be golden! But then the minute they do terminate that worker, someone else immediately pops up on the radar as the next bad worker, again as the only thing preventing the team from being all it can be.

Part of the root cause is the need to scapegoat—it's convenient to always have someone to blame for low productivity. But it's up to the PM to guard against this attitude. It's a double failure of leadership if a particular individual is constantly being blamed for a team's problems and the PM does nothing about it.

A solution is applying Goldratt's bottleneck concept, discussed in the next Q&A.

Q44. What is a *bottleneck*, and how can a PM handle bottlenecks from a leadership perspective?

A44. Eliyahu Goldratt describes in his book *The Goal* that on any team, there will always be one slowest worker, or a particular part of a system will require the most attention from the manager. He calls this a bottleneck. But a bottleneck is not always as negative as it might sound. Instead of demonizing the slow employee or considering him or her to be a bad apple who must be removed from the team, the PM can approach a situation like this in a positive way. He or she can proactively identify the current bottleneck and develop a strategy for improving the employee or speeding up the slowest part of the production chain.

In many cases, meeting with the employee to talk about what's causing his or her slowness will help. A meeting like this often reveals underlying problems the PM was not aware of, and the employee has a chance to offer his or her own perspective on what might improve things. Sometimes the solution might be training or mentoring the employee. Other times, temporarily adding staff to an activity or creatively reordering tasks on the schedule might break up a logjam and increase performance.

As with many PM techniques, hunting for the bottleneck and correcting it is not a one-shot fix but, rather, is an iterative process. Once one bottleneck gets handled, sooner or later, a new bottleneck will appear, though it may not be as significant. The PM's work of looking for and correcting bottlenecks is never done until the project is completed.

Q45. What can the PM do if he or she is assigned a team member who doesn't want to work hard?

A45. PMs are sometimes assigned low-performing employees, presumably because the employees are being protected by someone in senior management.

The textbook answer might be to get rid of the employee, but that is not possible when the employee is being shielded by upper management. Based on my experience, the best thing to do is to assign such employees plenty of work (not so much that they can't do it, but probably more than they want you to give them). You might want to choose to give them tasks that are not on the critical path if you feel you can't trust them fully. But you need to make every effort to make them productive, or else you will set a bad example for the rest of the team by tolerating slacking, and morale will suffer.

I have personally succeeded in managing employees with this strategy. In one case in particular, an employee truly did have a protector who was very high up and feared by some managers. But it worked out well: The employee became very productive (and nothing bad happened to me!). No senior manager wants to appear to be coddling someone who isn't working. So you should always be on safe ground here, as long as you are fair. Assign work you know the problem employee can perform, and don't go overboard or try to set him or her up to fail. When you do succeed at getting good work out of an employee like this, it will be win-win for the project, the employee, and for you as a leader.

Q46. How can a PM try to avoid what is called a void of leadership?

A46. It's said that nature abhors a vacuum, and this is true in project management. If a PM is too remote from the team, or appears weak, or spends too much time polishing up the old MS Project plan instead of actually managing, the team *will* perceive a lack of leadership (there's no maybe about it). This can lead to chaos, anarchy, rebellion, and other bad stuff, so it's imperative that you as the PM avoid this situation by being the team leader you are getting paid to be.

The key is to remember to get out there and, as they say in politics, press the flesh. Walk around, visit each team member's cube, schedule one-on-one meetings or informal coffee breaks, and at times ask your team members if there is anything you can help them with. When you give this a try and ask like you mean it, you will definitely get some responses, giving you opportunities to add a little oil to the machine. Just making an effort and showing that you're there for the team can make a big difference.

Q47. How can I combat the dreaded "not invented here" (NIH) philosophy?

A47.   One of the worst things a project team can do is waste time reinventing the wheel by ignoring best practices that others have developed or refusing to use products that have been successful in other companies. But in many PM environments, the NIH mentality is heavily imbedded in the corporate culture. The assumption at these companies is that any method not developed there can't possibly be any good and is not even worth exploring. This often leads to tremendous resistance to new ideas; stakeholders are overly invested in showing the value of the methods they have used in the past, rather than aggressively pursuing the best of all possible solutions for their client and project.

   The best way to handle NIH is to address it when it comes up on a specific issue. You as the PM should make the strongest case you can for what you believe is the best tool or technique. It's best to make an argument that is very objective and fact-based; focus like a laser on how the new method will benefit the customer. By staying firmly on message and keeping the NIH factor out of the equation, you can help the new method bubble to the surface as the obvious solution.

Q48. When is consensus-driven management a bad thing?

A48.   Consensus is great when everyone on the team finds themselves truly in agreement. True consensus helps generate cooperation from your team and

A Gigantic Case of NIH: East Meets West, West Ignores East

Sometimes NIH rears its head on an industry level, spanning countries and even continents. NIH is extremely prevalent in the auto industry. For example, Japan forged ahead of the United States with lean production, while the West stubbornly stuck to mass production, which had been the key to its earlier supremacy and industry dominance. Long after the Japanese car companies surpassed them, the American giants were still very slow to react. Chrysler and GM, once industry leaders, have in recent years filed for bankruptcy and required government bailouts to stay in business.

stakeholders. However, too much emphasis on going for consensus is a bad thing. PMs that are overly worried about consensus are often ineffective for several reasons:

- *The PM needs to lead, not follow.* Striving for consensus too often implies that the PM is weak. Team members will be less willing to follow him or her, making the PM seem even weaker (a vicious cycle!).

- *The PM needs to do what truly is best for the customer, project, and company*, which is not always the decision a consensus approach will produce.

Trying to achieve consensus can eat up a lot of valuable time that you often can't spare on a project. Even in cases where you *might* win consensus, it could still be counterproductive, time-wise, to put a lot of effort into seeking it. In many cases, you can implement the same decision earlier—and stay ahead of schedule—by simply directing your team to what you consider to be the clear solution.

Q49. When is bureaucracy a double pitfall for leaders?

A49. Bureaucracy truly is a two-headed monster—either too much or too little can harm the work environment. It's always popular to complain about too much bureaucracy, but it's necessary to have the right number of procedures and controls. In organizations with too little bureaucracy, such as small consulting firms or dot-coms, people often waste time reinventing the wheel because the company doesn't have sufficient systems or best practices to draw from on its projects. And managers in these environments may not treat their employees well because small companies often lack the bureaucratic checks and balances that protect employees in larger firms (e.g., required annual reviews, ethics boards, strong HR departments).

But too much bureaucracy is probably worse and is well deserving of its bad reputation. Too many procedures that are too rigidly enforced definitely stifle creativity and can harm productivity. For example, some organizations require employees to fill out two time sheets (one for paycheck purposes, one for back-billing purposes). The company may have a good reason for needing both time sheets, but the wasted time and redundancy hurts morale and may produce an impression that the extra documentation is just the tip of the bureaucratic iceberg. For this reason, it's worth going easy on implementing bureaucratic ideas that are not really needed.

Q50. What can happen if there is too much corporate message?

A50. Sometimes very large companies have so many groups putting out communications that they bombard their employees with emails, directives, requirements, announcements, surveys, mandatory classes, town hall meetings, and more. Productivity can suffer if every day people come into work wanting to work but get derailed by the latest urgent requirement that must be grafted onto their current project.

For instance, let's say that a team is in the middle of working on a very valuable project that will bring many benefits for a company. One day, a directive comes down from senior management stating that all projects must suddenly undergo a cost-cutting study or incorporate a new software tool or methodology. A sudden requirement like this can slow things down, or far worse, lead to the failure of a project that would have helped the company.

Only top management can keep corporate messaging in check, but they might not always be aware of the problem. Sometimes lower-level employees need to bring this issue to the forefront for the benefit of their projects and the company as a whole.

Q51. What are *bright spots*, and how can leaders use this concept to improve a project team or work environment?

A51. Bright spots refers to a best practice for bringing about change and is described in detail with several successful case studies in *Switch: How To Change Things When Change Is Hard*, by Chip and Dan Heath. The idea is that instead of a leader imposing his or her ideas from the outside, that he or she should instead look for bright spots—methods that individuals within the particular environment are already using successfully.

The formula for success here is to take these methods that have already proven successful and slowly bring around other individuals in the organization to help implement them. Because they were already proven effective, developed internally, and utilized by the company's own people, there is no NIH factor. So these methods will stand a much better chance of succeeding than those a leader brings in from the outside.

Q52. What is an *inflection point*, and how can leaders use this concept to their advantage?

A52. You can think of the inflection point as the moment in the middle when you switch from reverse to forward while backing up your car. You are moving backwards, you brake, slow down . . . and there's that split second where you are not moving at all. As your car shifts into gear, you commit to and begin the change.

The concept of an inflection point has significance on a company level as well as on a project level.

- *On a company level:* Sometimes there is a moment when an organization realizes that it must make a significant change, and implements that change. One dramatic example: when Dell Computers decided to adopt a just-in-time model (see Q&A 15 in Chapter 6). This allowed customers for the first time to easily custom order their own PCs from home, which led to Dell's capturing great market share and bringing in large profits.

- *On a project level:* It's always tough for a team leader to decide that a current method isn't working and to choose a new method. PMs often are met with strong opposition to change in this situation. But making the necessary decision, coming up with a winning game plan, and being firm about the new direction can give a struggling or even failing project a chance to succeed. For example, suppose a project was not on track to meet its deadline. The PM and key stakeholders were considering whether to try agile project management on this project. Such a large change was a risk, but the project seemed like an ideal candidate for agile PM, and the team believed the switch might turn things around. And so they took the plunge.

TOP TEN PITFALLS TO AVOID IN LEADERSHIP

1. Not investing sufficiently in training for your people.
2. Senior leaders not being honest with their direct reports about issues such as the health of the company or upcoming raises or bonuses.
3. Rushing and cutting corners to meet milestone dates and budgets but sacrificing quality and long-term results.
4. Not sufficiently supporting the employees or managers under you.
5. Not doing what's necessary to retain your top people.

6. Not giving performance reviews, or not requiring the supervisors under you to do them for all team members.

7. Accomplishing the technical work of the project, but failing to sell the stakeholders on the benefits and value the deliverables will bring to them.

8. Going along with directives from senior management that you disagree with because you are putting your own career ahead of the project and your team.

9. Making the mistake of thinking that your team will follow you because of your awesome charisma without figuring out how to best motivate them.

10. Not intervening when you see bad behavior, such as team members behaving unethically or mistreating coworkers.

Notes

1. Angelo Baratta, "Value Triple Constraint: How To Evaluate Project Value Delivered," *Executive Brief, Technology Management Resource for Business Leaders* (February 2010).

2. Tony Hsieh *Delivering Happiness: A Path To Profits, Passion, and Purpose.* (New York: Hachette Book Group, 2010).

3. Elisabeth Bumiller, "We Have Met the Enemy and He Is PowerPoint," *New York Times,* April 27, 2010.

CHAPTER 13

How to Become PMP® Certified

Tips for Applying for, Preparing for, and Passing the PMP® and Related Certification Exams

The current certification trend among project managers continues to increase in the United States and around the world, both in private industry and in government. PMP® certification used to be considered nice to have; now it has become a rigid requirement for offering job interviews in many organizations. Some companies are even starting to hire PMs conditionally; they must attain the certification within a certain time period after being hired to retain the position.

From the hiring side, the certification is frequently used as a screening tool, useful to recruiters because it validates candidates on several levels. By acquiring the certification, candidates show that they have:

- Managed projects for a certain number of years
- Met certain educational requirements
- Mastered the extensive and challenging material in the *PMBOK® Guide* and passed a comprehensive and fast-paced test.

By maintaining the certification, PMs demonstrate that they are keeping up with their PM knowledge by continuing to take courses, attending PMI meetings, and attending project management conferences, seminars, and webinars.

From the PM's perspective, certifications such as the PMP® can open many career doors. The skill set and the certification can help applicants get interviews they wouldn't otherwise be eligible for, give them an edge on the job market over competing PMs, and also make them more promotable at their current companies, eligible to manage more people and more and larger projects.

This chapter answers a lot of the many questions candidates frequently bring to my classes about the PMP® certification from PMI. Some applicants find the application process, especially documenting their projects, intimidating before they jump into it, so visual examples are provided here to help simplify the steps. The other primary area of concern for candidates starting the process is, of course, the exam. To demystify it, the key logistics of the test are covered here in detail, and I provide many tips.

The good news for PMs is that in addition to the PMP®, there are four more certifications from PMI that they may be eligible for. Also, other vendors offer a number of valuable PM certifications as well, some which are also largely based on PMI's *PMBOK® Guide*. So once PMs master the material in this book, much of which is directly in line with the *PMBOK® Guide*, they can quickly pursue the PMP® certification, as well as several more credentials, to boost their profile.

THE BASICS

Q1. What exactly is PMP® certification, and why is it considered so valuable today?

A1. The PMP®, or Project Management Professional, certification is the world's leading certification for project managers across many industries. It is issued by PMI, the Project Management Institute, the world's largest certifying body for PMs, and is considered the gold standard for certification. At the time of this writing, the organization has over 300,000 members worldwide, and membership is trending upward.

Attaining the PMP® certification proves that a PM has mastered the subject matter of PMI's *PMBOK® Guide*, meaning that he or she is fluent in the most current skills, concepts, and best practices currently in use among PMs worldwide. It also means that he or she has passed a long, challenging, and comprehensive exam on this material. It requires preparation and experience—before applicants are accepted to take the exam, they must pass PMI's prequalification requirements, which include project management education. And to maintain the credential after they pass the exam, certified PMPs must continue their learning process, validated through PMI's Continuing Certification Requirements (CCR) program.

Q2. What are the prequalifications required for the PMP® certification?

A2. To apply for the PMP® certification, candidates must meet three main criteria:

- *Education level:* Candidates must have a high school diploma or the equivalent.

- *Documented PM experience:* Candidates must have a specific number of hours of experience managing projects, which they are required to document and sign off on as part of their application. The hours required vary based on education level, as follows:

  o With a high school diploma, the required experience managing projects is five years, covering at least 7,500 hours. All hours of experience must fall within the eight years prior to the application date.

  o With a four-year college degree (or global equivalent, such as a three-year bachelor's degree, as is the norm in India), the PM work experience required is three years, covering at least 4,500 hours. Again, these hours must have been worked within the last eight years).

- *Formal PM training:* Candidates are required to have completed at least 35 hours in PM education before being accepted to take the exam. Many take a PMP® project management class, geared toward helping PMs learn the concepts required for the test and also satisfying the requirement in one shot.

But note that the 35 hours do not have to come from a specific PMP® prep course. PMI also will credit many other classes toward the certification, such as project management courses taken toward an MBA or other classes that help PMs do their job effectively, such as business writing, presentation skills, conflict management, and many others (if in doubt, check with PMI).

Disclaimer

Please note that for the latest and complete prequalification details for the PMP® and other PMI certifications, candidates need to review the current handbooks for each certification, available for free download at PMI's website, www.pmi.org. All information is subject to updates and changes by PMI.

APPLYING TO TAKE THE PMP® CERTIFICATION EXAM

Q3. How long does the application process take, and how long does it take to hear back from PMI that a candidate has been accepted to take the exam?

A3. From my own experience and from that of many of my students, the application typically takes four to six hours to complete, between documenting your background information, describing the projects you've managed, and verifying all the names, dates, and contact numbers. Note that it doesn't have to be done all in one sitting; you can begin the process, log out of the PMI website, and then come back later and pick up where you left off. TIP: Do *not* go overboard by laboring over the application. It just needs to be short and sweet, as well as accurate.

For those who apply electronically (the vast majority of applicants), PMI officially pledges to reply to each applicant within five business days after the applicant submits his or her application. This process takes longer for those in special circumstances who apply by paper and for applicants who are selected for a random audit by PMI, discussed in the next Q&A.

Q4. Does PMI do a detailed review of every applicant's background, references, and projects?

A4. When a candidate applies for any of the PMI certifications, he or she electronically signs off to verify that all the information he or she is submitting is true to the best of his or her knowledge. All of the information in the application is fair game for PMI to verify as it sees fit. PMI states that it conducts a random audit—a full, in-depth review—on one out of every ten applications. This can include a request for additional documentation to be mailed in by the applicant, such as copies of diplomas or course-completion materials from the PM class he or she may have taken. PMI may also request signatures from the applicant's work supervisors to confirm that the applicant led the projects he or she documented on the application. The good news is that the audits keep the quality level of applicants high, making the certification more valuable for all involved. This differentiates PMI's certifications from others.

A good approach for applicants to take is to aim for complete honesty, with the awareness that any candidate may or may not be audited. In keeping with

PMI's strong emphasis on ethics, candidates are required to submit their applications with a sign-off attesting to two things:

- The documented information they are submitting is all true.
- They pledge to uphold the PMI Code of Ethics and Professional Conduct in all their future dealings as a PMP (discussed in Chapter 9).

Q5. What are the main parts of the PMP® certification application process?

A5. The PMP® application process is actually very straightforward and can go very quickly once you plunge in. Figure 13-1 outlines the ten sequential steps for applying for the PMP®. Steps 4 and 5, which involve documenting your project experience, are the most challenging and are detailed in the next two Q&As.

---

1. Go to www.pmi.org and select "New user? Register now."

2. After obtaining an ID and password, select "Get Certified."

3. Log in with your ID and password and select "Apply for PMP® Credential."

In steps 4 and 5 you will document several of the projects you have managed.

4. On the screens provided, document the number of hours you spent on each project, by process, for each PM process group (e.g., initiating, planning).

5. In the box provided on the screen, write a brief description of each project (only 500 characters maximum allowed per project).

6. Document your PM education hours (they must add up to at least 35 hours).

7. Click submit, and wait for PMI to approve your application. It will take up to five business days to hear back.

8. Once your application is approved, join PMI. Click on "Become a member." As a member, you are eligible for a $150 discount on the PMP® exam, plus many other benefits.

9. Go to www.prometric.com and sign up for the PMP® test.

10. Study and take the test.

Figure 13-1:   The Ten-Step Process for Applying for and Earning the PMP® Certification

Q6. What is involved in documenting your project hours?

A6. Documenting project hours online is much easier than most people think (Figure 13-2). The screens will walk you through each of the five project management process groups for each project you enter. All you need to do is fill in the number of hours you spent on the different processes for each project. For example, when the initiating panel comes up for a project, you might

---

- Some PMs work from their resume, documenting projects in order, then estimating and filling in the hours spent on each process.

- Some PMs like to create a quick spreadsheet in Excel or Word to estimate the hours spent on each process per project. From there, it's a simple matter to transfer the numbers into the application. Alternatively, you can use one of the blank templates available online to draft your hours; just make sure that the process names are correct before using it.

- It *is* OK to document zero hours for some of the processes. PMs are not expected to have managed every process on every project. Your distribution of hours should be your best estimate for each process.

- For each project, you will document the time you spent working on each of the five process groups on the appropriate screen of the application. Your breakdown may look something like the grid excerpted below:

Process Group
Number of Hours Spent

INITIATING
Identify key stakeholders and perform analysis to gain buy-in and gather requirements.
| 40 |

PLANNING
Create the work breakdown structure with the team to develop the cost, schedule, resource, quality, and procurement plans.
| 20 |

EXECUTING
Execute the tasks defined in the project plan in order to achieve the project goals.
| 550 |

Figure 13-2: Tips for Filling out Your Project Hours on Your PMP® Certification Application

fill in 40 hours for one initiating task, 20 hours for another, and so on, until you have filled in a numeric value for every initiating process, summarizing how you spent your time on that project.

Q7. What are some suggestions for documenting the projects you've worked on in the application?

A7. Describing your projects is the part of the application that takes the most thought and effort. But it's not that tough, because each description must be very short—you are allowed to write a maximum of 500 characters for each project. This is only about 100 words, which works out to four or five sentences. There is no set format for writing these descriptions. Figure 13-3 shows a recommended format that has worked well as a basic, generic style for hundreds of my students.

- Start with one sentence describing the purpose of the project. For example, "Project was to build an interactive online application to handle payroll for all employees of our web design company."
- Then pick several deliverables (these can be internal deliverables, such as project schedule or WBS, or external deliverables, such as web pages built for your client) and describe each in one sentence, including your role in managing the creation of each. Some examples follow:

Project to Design Online Payroll App

  o *Project schedule:* As the PM, I created the schedule in MS Project, led weekly status meetings, and used critical path method to help bring in the project on deadline.

  o *Risk register:* I facilitated a brainstorming session early on. The team identified key risks for this project, which I documented and monitored in the risk register.

  o *System implementation:* Our team created and implemented a software system, which we designed to fit our customer's needs, and we integrated the app into their environment.

Note: The PMP® application screen keeps an automatic character count for you; it won't let you submit your application if you have typed more than 500 characters for any project (but a handy feature is that you *can* save it as a draft with more than 500 characters).

Figure 13-3:   Tips for Describing Projects on Your PMP®
Certification Application

Q8. Should the emphasis be on how successful the project was or on its size, cost, or some other factor?

A8. A lot of students ask this question. The point of the documentation is to show how much project managing you did, and PMI verifies this through your descriptions of how well you followed the PMI processes and managed the creation of the project artifacts, such as the WBS and schedule, and the deliverables of the project itself. Giving a little flavor of the size or scope of your project is fine as part of your one-sentence descriptor of the project, but this is not strictly required. Adding too many details about the size of the budget, for instance, is distracting and wastes space that you could better use to write about your specific *duties* leading the project, which is primarily what PMI will be evaluating your candidacy on.

Q9. What if a project is still ongoing or ended without ever being completed?

A9. Here are some suggestions:

- *For ongoing projects:* Many candidates include current, ongoing projects in their PMI project documentation, and that is perfectly acceptable. For ongoing projects, it is appropriate to document "zero hours" spent on the closeout processes.

- *For projects that never completed:* It is a well-known fact that projects do not always run to successful completion. Sometimes budgets are cut, and there are many other reasons for a project to be cancelled or terminated. Candidates should not feel that they cannot use such projects in their applications. If you write about a project that did not complete, the point still is to document what your duties were in leading it—*not* to focus on why it did not finish (or worse, to try to set the record straight on why it wasn't your fault—definitely not a good idea, but I have seen people do this!).

Q10. What is the total cost of the application and certification process?

A10. First of all, it is free to submit the application. The PMP® exam fee, at the time of this writing, is $555 for those taking the test electronically. But there is a $150 discount for PMI members, so almost all applicants join PMI before paying for the exam. This brings the exam fee down to $405. The exam fee is lower for those taking the test on paper, but the process takes much longer, and the paper exam is not available in many geographic locations (it's primarily for locations that don't have online testing centers). Contact PMI or see the *PMP® Handbook* for full details. Joining PMI is $119 for annual membership, plus a $10 one-time sign-up fee, adding up to $129. Total costs, then, are $129 (membership) + $405 (exam if a member) = $534.

Note that after being approved to take the test, applicants have one year to pass the exam, which they can take up to three times in that year. The charge for each attempt is lowered after the first time. If a candidate does not pass by the third try, he or she would need to wait one year before he or she could reapply and retake the exam.

OTHER PROJECT MANAGEMENT CERTIFICATIONS

Q11. What are the other kinds of PM certification from PMI, and how does an applicant choose the one that's best for him or her?

A11. PMI currently grants five certifications: PMP®, CAPM, PgMP, PMI-SP, and PMI-RMP. Table 13-1 summarizes these five PM and PM-related certifications from PMI. For complete, current details on each certification's requirements, candidates should consult the specific handbook for that certification, e.g., the *PMP® Handbook* or *CAPM® Handbook*.

All handbooks are available via free download from www.pmi.org.

Table 13-1: Project Management Certifications from PMI

Certification	Description
PMP® (Project Management Professional)	PMI's primary certification for experienced PMs, detailed throughout this chapter.
CAPM (Certified Associate in Project Management)	For less experienced (or beginning) PMs. • Candidates need either 1,500 hours of PM experience *or* 35 hours of PM education but, contrary to a common misconception, do *not* need both. • Similar exam to the PMP® (also based on material from the *PMBOK® Guide*) but shorter and with fewer questions based on experience.

(Continued)

Certification	Description
PgMP (Program Management Professional)	Has a dual requirement (both project and program management experience), as follows: • With a high school diploma, candidates must have 6,000 hours (4 years) PM experience, plus 10,500 hours (7 years) PgM experience. • With a college degree (or global equivalent), candidate must have 6,000 hours PM experience, plus 6,000 hours PgM experience. • The written test is also largely based on the Standard for Program Management, plus questions based on experience managing programs. • Application includes a peer review process (like a 360 review). • Also requires the candidate to write a number of essays.
PMI-RMP (Risk Management Professional)	For specialists in the risk management (RM) knowledge area. • With a high school diploma, requires minimum 4,500 hours of risk management experience in the last five years, plus 40 contact hours of specific education in RM. • With a college degree (or equivalent), 3,000 hours experience in the last five years, plus 30 contact hours RM education. (See the *PMI-RMP® Handbook* for current specifications.)
PMI-SP (Scheduling Professional)	For specialists in scheduling (time management knowledge area). • With a high school diploma, requires minimum 5,000 hours of schedule management experience in the last five years, plus 40 contact hours of specific education in SM. • With a college degree (or equivalent), 3,500 hours experience in the last five years, plus 30 contact hours SM education. (See the *PMI-SP® Handbook* for current specifications.)

Q12. Which are the most valuable certifications for PMs from other certifying bodies?

A12. In addition, or as an alternative, to the PMP® certification, you may be eligible for one or more of the certifications from other organizations listed in Table 13-2. You may find that it enhances your profile to pick up one or two

Name of Certification	Acronym/ Short Name	Certifying Organization	Key Facts about the Certification
Project+	Project+	CompTIA	• Officially based on the *PMBOK® Guide*, Project+ has a shorter exam than the PMI exams (90 minutes and 95 questions). • Does not require a set amount of project work or educational experience. • Some PMP® candidates take this test first as a steppingstone to the PMI tests. • Some certified CAPMs also go for this certification, giving them two certifications as a PM (CAPM and Project+). For those not yet eligible for the PMP® certification, this is a good combination on a resume.
Microsoft Certified Technology Specialist	MCTS	Microsoft	One variation of this certification from Microsoft combines two disciplines: PMI's *PMBOK® Guide* and MS Project 2007.
Microsoft Certified IT Professional	MCITP	Microsoft	More IT focused, but like the MCTS, it also combines knowledge of the *PMBOK® Guide* and MS Project 2007.
Prince2 Foundation Level or Prince 2 Practitioner Level	Prince	OGC (Office of Government Commerce in the U.K.)	Popular in Europe. Similar to the PMI credentialing process, candidates take exams based on the proprietary Prince2 (Projects IN Controlled Environments) process-driven methodology (not the *PMBOK® Guide*).

(*Continued on next page*)

Name of Certification	Acronym/ Short Name	Certifying Organization	Key Facts about the Certification
Yellow Belt, Red Belt, Black Belt, etc.	Six Sigma	Six Sigma	For specialists in quality management. Originated and still popular in the manufacturing industry.
ITIL Foundation, Intermediate, Expert, and Master	ITIL	ITIL (Information Technology Infrastructure Library)	For PMs in IT who are specialists in ITIL's proprietary library of infrastructure utilities and best practices.
Certified Business Analysis Professional	CBAP	IIBA (International Institute of Business Analysts)	For business analysts/PMs specializing in the business side of project management, a certification based on the *BABOK®* (the Business Analysis Body of Knowledge).
Certified Management Consultant	CMC	Canadian Association of Management Consultants	Issued in Canada, this certification is for management consultants and is recognized as a global credential in all countries that that are part of the ICMCI (International Council of Management Consulting Institutes).
Certified Scrum Master, Scrum Product Owner, Scrum Professional, Scrum Trainer, and Scrum Coach	CSM	Scrum Alliance	A project management certification in the specialization of Scrum, an agile PM method that concentrates on short, focused activities called sprints.

(Continued on next page)

Name of Certification	Acronym/ Short Name	Certifying Organization	Key Facts about the Certification
Qualified Project Practitioner, Registered PM, Master PM	QPP RPP MPP	AIMP (Australian Institute of Project Management)	Similar to the PMI credentialing process, QPP is a popular certification for PMs in Australia.
Professional (also Senior Professional) in Human Resources	PHR/SPHR	Society of Human Resources	For senior managers in human resources. The material for this exam shares some overlap with the HR discipline discussed in *PMBOK® Guide*.
Certified in Production and Inventory Management	CPIM	APICS	For managers in operations and production, includes knowledge of demand management, performance management, procurement, capacity planning, and more.
Certified in Risk and Information Systems Control, Certified Information Security Manager, Certified Information Systems Auditor, Certified in the Governance of Enterprise IT	CRISC™ CISM™ CISA™ CGEIT™	ISACA (Information Systems Audit and Control Association)	Several new security- and risk-related certifications from this large organization for auditors.

Table 13-2: Certifications

additional certifications. (One of my students once told me that in London, where she is from, they call this "badge collecting.") British humor aside, in today's economy and highly competitive job market, the more certifications a PM has (within reason), the more demonstrable skills he or she has, and the more valuable many employers will consider him or her.

A little-known tip is that Project+ is fully based on PMI's *PMBOK® Guide*, even though it is issued by CompTIA and not PMI. So while studying for the PMP®, you might consider it worthwhile to pay for one more test and quickly get Project+ under your belt first. Project+ is a much shorter test than the PMP® exam and has no PM experience prerequisite. So for some, it is not as well-known or as highly regarded as the PMI certifications, but it's a quick way to get certified on information given in the *PMBOK® Guide* and can also be a stepping stone to the PMP® or CAPM. You can study toward the PMP® exam, take the Project+ test, get feedback in your scoring on the areas you might need to study more, and then keep going and get your PMP®.

Other certifications, like the Six Sigma certifications or the Microsoft MCTS, share *some* overlap with the PMP®, but also have a particular in-depth focus (quality management for Six Sigma or, for the MCTS and MCITP, Microsoft Project). Picking up a Six Sigma "karate belt" or one of the Microsoft certifications enhances your resume as a PM and also lets you claim an added specialization that can differentiate you from competing PMs.

Other certifications like Prince2 or those issued by the Australian Institute of Project Management are somewhat similar to PMI certifications but not officially based on PMI's knowledge areas. And some companies pursue certification on an organizational level. Table 13-3 lists several examples.

ABOUT THE PMP® EXAM: LOGISTICS AND TIPS

Q13. How long is the PMP® exam, and what is the format?

A13. The logistics of the PMP® exam are very precise:

- Four hours are allotted for answering the test's 200 questions.
- All items are multiple choice, in the same A, B, C, D format.
- The percentage of exam questions based on each *process group* is given in the *PMP® Handbook*.

Table 13-3: PM-Related Certifications for Companies

Name of Certification	Acronym/ Short Name	Certifying Organization	Key Facts about the Certification
Capability Maturity Model® Integration	CMMI® or CMM	Carnegie Mellon SEI (Software Engineering Integration)	Companies bring on-site an SEI-authorized lead appraiser to conduct an evaluation of one of their ongoing projects. Based on that appraisal, the appraiser rates the organization on its quality level on a scale of 1 to 5 (1 lowest, 5 highest).
ISO-9001 Certified	ISO	International Organization for Standardization	Companies bring in an independent auditor to verify that they are sufficiently in conformance with quality standards. They are evaluated on how well they monitor their internal processes, on their effectiveness at capturing and correcting defects, on their level of documenting procedures, and for the degree of their efforts toward continuous improvement.
Organizational Project Management Maturity Model	OPM3®	PMI	Measures an organization's capabilities in PM in preparation for improvement and helps develop the roadmap the company will follow to improve its performance.
Individual certifications on a large-scale level	N/A	Various agencies, including PMI	Another way to raise an organization's overall quality level (besides pursuing the ISO/CMM/OPM3˚ certifications) is to train an entire team or department on any of the individual certification disciplines (e.g., PMP®, Six Sigma, ITIL). This helps all staff focus on process improvement and encourages them to apply the techniques in concert.

- Scoring is broken down by knowledge area. In each knowledge area, test takers are rated:

  o Proficient (above average)

  o Moderately proficient (average)

  o Below proficient (below average).

Scoring is pass/fail, and candidates *can* pass even if they score below proficient on individual sub-areas, as long as their overall score is passing. Note that PMI does not publish the exact grade it uses for a passing score. Like many certifying bodies, the way it scores the exam, such as how it weights answers, is proprietary and not publicly available.

Q14. Is my score kept in a PMI database?

A14. Yes, it is retained in two places. You will have access to your score and breakdown through your personal PMI account. This information is available only to you when you log in to your password-protected account. Also, PMI maintains a database called the PMI Online Credential Registry through which people can find your name and your active PMI certifications (visit http://www.pmi.org/CertApp/Registry.aspx). But your score is kept confidential by PMI. Note that the registry list does not include all certified PMs; most certified PMs prefer to be listed, but for confidentiality/security reasons, some individuals opt out, and their names are not publicly viewable.

Q15. Is it true that not all 200 questions on the exam are counted?

A15. Yes, but not for any devious purpose! PMI maintains high standards of quality for the exam by continuously trying out new questions to see how people do on them. Every PMP® candidate tests out 25 trial questions on the exam (15 for the CAPM® exam). This means that each question is vetted before it makes it into the real test. If too many people get it wrong, or too many get it right, that means the question needs to be thrown out, or at least tweaked, before it can be accepted into the pool of questions. So your PMP® exam score is based on only the 175 questions that will be counted on your exam, and your CAPM® exam on 135 questions.

Q16. Are candidates allowed to take breaks while taking the test?

A16. Yes and no. Breaks *are* allowed, but the clock keeps running while you're on the break. Even though breaks will come out of your allotted four hours, most PMP® experts and authors highly recommend taking at least two breaks. Most test-takers tend to do better if they plan in breaks, rather than trying to keep their head down for four hours nonstop. Breaks not only let you relax and regroup but also give your brain a chance to work some more in the background on some of the questions you might not have been sure of when you first read them.

Q17. Can you bring snacks or beverages to the test?

A17. Again, yes and no. It's important to note that none of the Prometric test centers allow food or drinks in the testing room. But some (not all) allow you to store food and drinks in the locker they provide for your personal belongings. At sites that do allow test-takers to bring and store snacks, you are allowed to go to the locker on breaks, leave the test area, and take a stretch or snack break.

It is highly recommended that you verify the snack policy with potential test centers in advance before committing to that test site. (For the time and money you are investing in the certification, why not maximize your test experience and possibly boost your score by bringing a good old iced coffee and power bars?)

Q18. Can I bring my own calculator?

A18. Bringing a calculator used to be allowed before many calculators became sophisticated enough to do neat tricks like store formulas in memory. Nowadays, outside calculators are not allowed, but all candidates are permitted and encouraged to use the calculator function on the PCs provided for the test. It is highly recommended that you try out the PC calculator provided at the test center *before* your exam begins, during the practice time before the clock starts.

Also, practice using a PC calculator in advance of taking the test. Try doing some calculations with the PM formulas using your own laptop's calculator. Part of the challenge of the test is the speed and stamina required, and boosting your speed and accuracy with a little extra home practice will be well worth it.

Q19. Are translations of the test offered in other languages?

A19. A little-known tip is that PMI offers what it calls *language aids*, which can be very helpful if English is not your first language. The PMI exams are given in English, but if a test-taker arranges for a language aid in advance, he or she will be able to click on any individual test question one at a time and instantly bring up a translation of that question in his or her language of choice. Figure 13-4 shows the list of languages PMI currently supports.

Arabic	Hebrew
Brazilian Portuguese	Italian
Chinese (*simplified*)	Japanese
Chinese (*traditional*)	Korean
French	Russian
German	Spanish

Figure 13-4: Languages Supported by Language Aids for the PMI Exams

Q20. Do you have any advice on scheduling the test?

A20. A few suggestions:

- *Schedule the test for a day off or a Saturday.* It is not recommended to take a long test like this after a long workday.

- *Pick your most productive time of day.* A number of time slots are available. If you are a morning person, schedule the exam for the best time of the morning for you.

- *Put it on your calendar.* If you think you might be ready in a couple of weeks, schedule the test for that time. Getting it on your calendar will help you gear up for it. WARNING: You *are* allowed to reschedule the test at no cost, but be aware that you can only reschedule for free up to 48 hours before the test, after which you would be charged the full cost of the test. Most candidates are not permitted to take the test on paper, but those who are taking it on paper should note that they must notify PMI 35 calendar days in advance of the test to reschedule.

Q21. Is guessing on the test recommended?

A21. You are not penalized for giving wrong answers on the PMP® test, so when you're not sure of an answer, follow the two suggestions below. It can mean the difference between passing and failing.

- *Take your best guess.* You have a 1 in 4 chance of choosing the right answer, and higher than that if you've narrowed your answer down to a couple of choices.
- *Mark items for later.* With just a couple of clicks, you can mark any question to return to later when you have time. This modern feature offers several benefits:
  o You don't have to scramble to write down the question numbers on your scrap paper or worry about keeping track of them—the test software does it for you.
  o When you're ready to take another look at questions you've marked for later, you can instantly bring *just those* questions back up on your screen by clicking a button clearly designated for that purpose.
  o The original answers you gave for all questions marked for further review *will* be counted the way you marked them if you don't have time to go back and change them (if you marked "B," it will be counted as "B").

Q22. Are there any other tips about the logistics of the test?

A22. You might want to quickly take (or at least skim through) the optional tutorial and survey given before your test starts. These don't count toward your score in any way, but it will help you get comfortable with the keyboard and make sure all of the equipment is working properly and that the test is set up correctly for you. If there are any problems, speak to the proctor immediately, and he or she should be able to quickly remedy the situation. The test (and countdown) won't start until you tell the proctor that you're ready.

Q23. What is a *brain dump*, and how does it help a test taker?

A23. In the 15 minutes before the test begins, you are allowed to write down anything you want on the scrap paper that is provided for you at the beginning of the test. This is called a brain dump. Many successful test-takers have used this method. It is particularly helpful to write down the PM formulas from memory on your scrap paper, so I recommend that you learn the formulas well enough to be able to do so. This way, each time you come to a math-oriented question, your mind will be freed to focus on the question being asked, not trying to remember the formulas.

In addition to the formulas, many candidates memorize the nine PM knowledge areas, the five process groups, and the planning processes. This information is easy to find in most PMP® books, including the *PMBOK® Guide*, where it is listed in a table called "Project Management Process Groups and Knowledge Areas Mapping." Memorizing this one-page grid will make it easier to handle questions such as, "If a PM is engaged in [this activity], which process would she likely do next?"

Here are a few suggestions for preparing for a brain dump:

- Appendix B of this book provides a list of all the key PM formulas, followed by a fill-in-the-blanks table to help you self-test and gauge how your memorization of the formulas is going.

- Appendix C provides a grid of the knowledge areas, process groups, and processes. You don't have to memorize *all* of the project management processes, but I do recommend that you memorize the planning processes. The planning steps are largely sequential, so it is fairly easy and makes the most sense to memorize as many key planning steps as you can along with the knowledge areas and process groups.

- Another approach that works well is to memorize the general order of the project document flow (see Figures 2-1 and 3-1). Memorizing the key documents also helps you learn the sequence of the processes during which those documents are created.

Q24. Are there any other strategies for the test?

A24. It is worth planning two things in advance:

- **The timing of your breaks.** If you plan to take the recommended two or three breaks, it's good to decide in advance roughly when you'll take them. For example, you might plan a ten-minute break after one and a half hours and another ten-minute break after two and a half hours. Being able to look forward to a break, pacing yourself accordingly, and then resting your mind during the break can be very helpful.

- **Test strategy—which questions should you skip?** Deciding in advance which types of questions they plan to guess on and mark for later helps improve some people's confidence, speed, and efficiency. For some, a good strategy might be to take a best guess on and mark the math questions for later, then come back and focus on them all in one shot at the end. Thinking about your areas of strength and weakness can help you plan how to best manage your time on the test.

Q25. Are there any special recommendations regarding the ethics-based questions?

A25. As expressly stated in the *PMP® Handbook*, 9 percent (or 18 out of 200) of the questions an applicant faces on the PMP® test are ethics-oriented. The percentage is high because PMI encourages strong ethics toward making the best business decisions on the job.

Here are several tips to help you answer these questions:

- The key to making the best decisions as a PM and to correctly answering the ethics questions on the test is to think, "Which one is truly the most ethical choice here?" As discussed in Chapter 9, a helpful way to decide this is to try to equally weigh three competing interests: (a) the customer, (b) the project, and (c) your company. Satisfying all three while remaining true to your own ethics and values is a formula for success, both in the real world and on the test. (And remember, the customer is not always right—beware of trick questions along these lines.)

- Studying the PMI Code of Ethics and Professional Conduct, which spells out what PMI considers to be ethical behavior for PMs, is recommended. The code of conduct is not in the *PMBOK® Guide* (though I would suggest that it should be), but it *is* now part of the *PMP® Handbook*, which is available via free download from www.pmi.org.

- A common mistake when answering questions is to think, "My company does this, so it must be OK." Of course, that is not necessarily true.

- Don't try to second guess the test by thinking, "I wouldn't really do this in the real world, but I think the test is looking for this answer." This is counterproductive. Based on my teaching experience, students get the wrong answer more times than not when they try to approach questions this way. Pick the answer *you* think is the best choice!

- Map each of the ten pitfalls at the end of Chapter 9 to a specific clause or two in the code of conduct. This is good a good way to learn the code by applying it to the real world.

PREPARING FOR THE PMP® CERTIFICATION EXAM: PREP CLASSES AND OTHER RESOURCES

Q26. Is a class necessary for preparing for the test?

A26. Yes, it is strongly recommended that students take a PMP® prep class to help them prepare for PMI tests, which are known to be pretty challenging.

Of the many hundreds of certified PMPs and CAPMs I have met through PMI, I can count on one hand those who have passed without taking a PMP® prep class of some kind.

Even if you learn very well on your own, PMI requires 35 hours of PM education to apply for certification. So unless you have already taken 35 hours of courses, you will need to take some PM classes anyway to qualify. The best way for most people to meet the education requirement, learn PM current best practices, *and* gear up for the test is to take a PMP® class, ideally one recommended by a friend who has taken the class and attained his or her certification.

An approach for strong self-learners in lieu of a PMP® prep class would be to take the best 35 hour mix of PM-related courses that you feel would most help you in your current job or job search, and study the PMP® material on your own for the test. This can be very educational and broadening, and it offers targeted learning. Just be aware that this approach has three possible drawbacks:

- A lot of material you'll need to known for the PMP® exam may not be covered in those courses. You'll need to be sure to study this material on your own.

- If you are in any hurry to get certified, it might be hard to schedule and complete 35 hours of courses in a short period.

- You'll want to verify in advance with PMI that each of the classes you take will be accepted toward the 35 hours, and find out how many hours will be granted for each course.

Q27. How do students decide what kind of PMP® class to take?

A27. As with any class, it's always best to choose a class and instructor recommended by a friend who has successfully completed the class and attained certification. Ask your friend (or other educational consultant) these questions:

- Is the instructor PMP®-certified? It's important that he or she not only knows the material well but also can guide students properly through the certification process.

- Was there sufficient student participation? Many PMs bring a lot of strong experience and can share their own best practices with classmates.

- Did the class offer opportunities for networking among participants?
- Did the class cover information just to prepare participants for the test, or to teach skills, or to offer a good mix of both? For many PMs, both are equally important.

Another key decision is choosing the format you prefer as a learner. Most PMP® classes are classroom style, with an instructor and students all in the same room. Virtual classes are another option; participants may listen to the audio over the phone and follow the instructor's slides over the Internet. And there are some guided study-at-home classes, with direction, assignments, and due dates provided by the facilitator.

Q28. Does the duration of PMP® prep courses vary?

A28. Yes, and students have to take the length of the course into consideration. PMI requires that PMP® candidates attend a minimum of 35 hours of PM training. But some courses billed as PMP® prep are less than 35 hours long for various reasons, so they would not be sufficient by themselves to meet the PMI requirement. Students who took a prep class lasting less than 35 hours must document additional classes that they have taken to add up to the required 35 hours. (PMI has the right to approve or deny any course submitted for approval toward the 35 hours.)

Q29. Is there a standard structure for PMP® prep courses?

A29. There are three main formats for 35-hour PMP® classes:

- *Over a number of weeks (long):* A long course might consist of one class per week over 12 weeks; two a week over five to six weeks; or three a week over three weeks. The long format gives students ample time to study and absorb the material between classes. Typically, each class lasts three to four hours.

- *A one-week course comprising five 7-hour classes (medium):* This is a popular format and is usually the structure of the course I teach. Students like this format because they can take a week off from work and get the course done in five normal seven-hour workdays. The pace is moderately fast (neither too fast nor too slow). Each day builds on the previous day, so there is strong continuity, helping students learn quickly and retain key information.

- *A four-day course, followed by the exam on day 5 (short):* Considered a cram course, this is ideal for some, but not for everybody. The biggest benefit is getting it done quickly. But there are several drawbacks:
  - o A great deal of material is covered in a short time, including a lot of memorization.
  - o Cramming is not the way many people prefer to learn.
  - o Some say that retention of information after the test is low.
  - o There is a heavy emphasis on the test, leaving less time for practical application of the *PMBOK® Guide* or for student participation and discussion.

Q30. Can PMP® study groups substitute for a class?

A30. Many PMI chapters help coordinate the offering of local PMP® study groups. The participants get together, usually once or twice a week, and each week, one member learns a knowledge area and then presents it to his or her groupmates. Hours from group study sessions *do* satisfy PMI's educational requirement for the application.

There are two primary benefits to preparing for the PMP® exam this way. Number one, it's free. And number two, it's a pretty cool networking experience (when it works) because everyone is in the same boat, and there is a very strong "we're all in this together" kind of camaraderie. I do know one study group participant who humorously referred to this method as the blind leading the blind. But I also have met several PMPs who learned well enough from their study groups to pass the test.

The obvious downside of a study group is that it may function like a very long class without a good teacher. The participants not be well versed in the material, or they may not feel comfortable teaching (or both). Another drawback is that the test can become the entire focus of the group, at the expense of the practical skills and concepts of the PMP® credential.

But study groups can also be high quality, depending largely on who runs the group and how much the participants put into it. Sometimes groups invite a charming, bon vivant PMP® instructor to volunteer to help the group (yes, I have done this!) by leading the kickoff session and maybe teaching one of the tougher topics. This helps lay a strong foundation and models effective teaching methods the participants can use later when teaching the material to each other.

Q31. What books can help me prepare for the PMP® test?

A31. The bibliography at the end of this book cites several excellent PMP® prep books that I used to study for the test myself, especially Andy Crowe's *The PMP: How to Pass on Your First Try* and Rita Mulcahy's *The PMP Exam—Rita's Course in a Book*. I also highly recommend *Head First PMP* by Jennifer Greene and Andrew Stellman, which I find a bit less comprehensive than Crowe's and Mulcahy's books, but it is very strong on the concepts and quite a fun read—plus it has creative graphics and exercises, such as PM crossword puzzles, to help drive home the ideas. All three books provide a lot of practice test questions and explanations for all the correct answers.

PMI's *PMBOK® Guide* is also excellent, but it is more a desk reference by design than a cover-to-cover read. Also, it is *not* geared toward the test the way the PMP® prep books are, and it offers no practice questions at all.

And while the PMP® exam is not the primary focus of *The Project Management Answer Book*, many of the key concepts the exam covers are discussed here in detail (as well as this entire chapter in particular) based on my experiences helping many students prep for the CAPM® and PMP® exams.

STUDYING FOR THE PMP® CERTIFICATION EXAM

Q32. How much study time is recommended between completing a PMP® prep class and taking the exam?

A32. This can vary greatly, based on the learning habits of the individual and his or her current work situation, which can affect his or her ability to study. I gear my students toward submitting their application as soon as they're eligible per PMI's standard, which is on the morning of the fifth and final day of class. Students hear back by the following Friday (or sooner) and are ready to schedule their test as soon as their local Prometric center has an opening, which is often within the next day or two. Students who are working full time sometimes give themselves an extra week or two to review and do some more practice questions on the weekends.

Q33. Is it recommended to drill on practice questions, and if so, which quiz sources are best?

A33. For a test this long and this comprehensive, I definitely think it's helpful for students to drill on practice questions. The three PMP® books

I recommend in Q&A 31 all include practice questions. And each of the three provides explanations for the suggested answers (a good study resource in itself). The authors of these books are all certified PMPs, known and respected in the field, so the reader can assume a degree of professionalism about the research that went into the questions and answers and the explanations behind them, and the books have been published by established publishers. For additional sources for sample test questions and other materials, see Appendix A.

Two words of caution about sample test questions: First, always be sure that they are compatible with the current version of the *PMBOK® Guide* on which your test will be based. Second, I would be leery of questions obtained from websites that do not credit their sources. You have no way of knowing if the questions are good, if the answers are right, or how the questions were developed.

Q34. How will I know when I'm ready for the PMP® certification exam?

A34. There are two indicators that students are ready for the test:

- They have memorized everything they want to memorize, including the formulas, PM process names, and other key concepts and facts they have been studying.

- They are consistently scoring in the 85 percent or higher range on practice tests. Most students will not score that high the first time through. Going over the questions you got wrong, rereading the rationales for the suggested answers, and redoing the quizzes is a way of building up your score, speed, and test-taking muscles.

Q35. Any more tips about studying for the ethics-based questions on the PMI exams, which are known to be tricky?

A35. Because the ethics questions make up almost 10 percent of the test and can be nuanced and tricky (like ethical situations in the PM world), I always recommend that my students start reading the ethics column in their local newspaper as they're preparing for the test. The letters present scenarios to an ethics expert, who responds with opinions and suggestions. If you'd like to try this, first read each letter, think about what you would advise, and then read the response. This may sound like an unorthodox way to prepare for the PMP® test, but my students tell me it helps them.

If your local paper does not have an ethics column, I recommend Randy Cohen's "The Ethicist," which appears in the *New York Times Magazine* and is available at www.nytimes.com. It is also available as a podcast, with New York-based actors performing the letters and Randy Cohen himself reading his responses (who says studying for the PMP® can't be fun?).

Q36. What are some tips for learning the formulas for the test?

A36. There are 11 main earned value (EV) formulas, which is quite a few. But six of them are the core formulas of the topic, and once you've memorized those, you've got the gist. These main six formulas break down into three easy pairs, where:

- In each pair, the two names of the formulas *sound* almost the same.
- In each pair, the two formulas *look* almost the same.
- In the four formulas in which EV appears as a variable, EV comes first each time.
- In each pair, the two formulas logically go together. That is, in pair 1, the first formula is planned, and the second is its *earned* counterpart; and in pairs 2 and 3, the first is schedule and the second is its *cost* counterpart.

Figure 13-5 shows the six core Earned Value formulas broken down into three logical pairs.

Appendix B of this book provides a complete list of all the key formulas tested on the PMP® and other PM certification exams. The 11 earned value formulas are grouped together and highlighted as a subset.

Pair 1: Planned value (PV) and earned value (EV)	PV = Planned percentage complete * BAC (budget at completion) EV = Actual percentage complete * BAC
Pair 2: Schedule performance index (SPI) and cost performance index (CPI)	SPI = EV / PV CPI = EV / AC (actual cost)
Pair 3: Schedule variance (SV) and cost variance (CV)	SV = EV − PV CV = EV − AC

Figure 13-5:   Paired Earned Value Formulas

Memorizing all 11 earned value formulas for the test is great, but that's a lot to remember. You might start by memorizing the six shown in Figure 13-5, so you'll know going into the test that you have at least these burned into your brain. You can write them down on your scrap paper before your test begins (*brain dump*, see Q23).

Q37. How about tips for memorizing the processes?

A37. There are 42 PMI processes in the current Version 4 *PMBOK® Guide*, and memorizing does help, especially when you have to answer questions like, "If you're performing [this activity], what comes next?" But 42 processes is a lot for most people to comfortably memorize. Plus, they are not all sequential, making it that much harder.

I recommend memorizing the 22 sequential steps: the two initiating processes, plus the 20 planning processes. For most of my students, it's very easy to memorize the two initiating processes—(1) developing the project charter, and (2) identifying stakeholders—because they are essential to starting off most projects. So that leaves just 20.

Chunking is a great way to memorize a list like the 20 planning processes. *Chunking* means breaking a long list up into small, logical groups and memorizing one group at a time. Because the planning processes are already grouped by knowledge area, it's easiest to memorize one group at a time. For example, memorize the three scope-management planning steps as one small group. Practice writing them down from memory a couple of times, then move on to memorizing the five time-management planning steps, and so on.

Remember that the PM certification exams are 100 percent multiple choice. You don't have to memorize all 20 processes in exact order, nor do you have to remember their exact names. Memorizing as many of the planning processes as you can (it doesn't have to be all 20), still may be very helpful.

Q38. How about tips for memorizing the process groups and knowledge areas?

A38. To make it very easy to memorize the five process groups and nine knowledge areas, here are two mnemonics that my students have found very easy to learn and use:

- *For the process groups:* **IP EMC** (for **i**ntegration, **p**lanning, **e**xecuting, **m**onitoring and controlling, and **c**losing). Many IT PMs are familiar with

IP addresses, and "EMC" is reminiscent of the well-known energy/mass formula.

- *For the knowledge areas:* Did you ever learn a nonsense sentence as a child for memorizing the planets in order from the sun? Here is a sentence to help you remember the knowledge areas: "**IS t**he **c**ost of **q**uality **h**igh **c**ompared to **r**isk and **p**rocurement?" (for **i**ntegration, **s**cope, **t**ime, **c**ost, **q**uality, **HR**, **c**ommunications, **r**isk and **p**rocurement).

When you arrive at the test site, write the five process groups horizontally across the top of your scrap paper, and write the nine knowledge areas vertically down the page. This gives you a quick summary grid of the *PMBOK® Guide* as well as a rough sequence of the steps on a project, and you'll be able to refer back to this list throughout the exam. You can also write in as many individual process names that quickly come to mind, too (see Q&A 37).

Q39. How can I learn the many inputs, tools, and outputs of the PMI processes?

A39. It is important to have a solid understanding of each of the PMI processes for the exams. But with 42 processes, each having many inputs, tools, and outputs, there are roughly 700 key facts total about all the processes, too many for most people to memorize. And even if you *could* memorize them all, there is no real point in putting time and effort into doing so because the exams test your overall understanding.

So, I recommend that you start by memorizing the chief outputs for each process. Most processes create one key artifact (or sometimes a couple), and by associating the process with its primary artifacts, you will remember its main purpose. For example, the main output of the process of defining the scope is the scope statement and for the process of developing the schedule, it's the schedule.

Memorizing the outputs in this manner not only prepares you for direct questions about them, but will also help you figure out many other questions about the purpose of the processes in the grand scheme of things on the project. If you are faced with a test question about the key inputs needed for defining the scope, simply imagine yourself as a PM sitting down to create the scope statement. Then calmly and logically think about what inputs you would need to do it, such as the requirements doc in this case, and then select the best answer from the choices.

Q40. How about advice for remembering all of the documents and artifacts?

A40. This is much easier than it may seem. Start by looking at Figures 2-1 and 3-1 to learn the document flow. Because there are so many documents, the trick is to memorize just the key documents, and in the order in which they are created. For example, charter → stakeholder register → requirements doc → scope statement → WBS→ (and so on). This will not only help you remember the documents, but will help you learn key content from the *PMBOK® Guide* by reinforcing the logical order of the process flow.

Q41. Any final advice for preparing for the test?

A41. A great way to get maximum benefit out of drilling on practice tests is to put particular emphasis on any questions you got wrong. People tend to remember their mistakes, so these questions are ideal learning opportunities. Look at every question you missed, and ask yourself, "Why do renowned PMP® experts disagree with me? They must be wrong! No, wait a minute... let me see what they're trying to teach me with this question."

The more open you are to understanding the answers from trusted sources, the more you will be able to learn lessons and apply them on the test and back in the work world.

Q42. How can I stay sharp in between my PMP® prep class and the time I take the test?

A42. A couple of tips:

- ***Do five practice questions every day.*** Even after a long, busy workday, tired as you may be, it's not hard to do five or 10 sample questions. Pretend you are still in your class, and you have to do just one more drill to get done. Regular practice keeps you focused on the *PMBOK® Guide* and on retaining all the material.

- ***Don't do the questions cold.*** Review your notes first, or read a little from one of your PM books before tackling the questions. This brings the material back and puts you in a test mindset.

- ***Study from a second PM resource.*** Many learners benefit from a little variety. A second book can make all the material fresh, and you'll pick up new insights and perspectives. In my classes, I call this *new and review*; you are going over the same material, but adding new ideas, further solidifying your knowledge.

Q43. Are there any tips for job hunting if I haven't taken the test yet?

A43. Many people don't realize that after you have taken a class toward one of the certifications, it is legitimate to put on your resume that you are a *candidate* for that certification (meaning you have learned a lot of the material and are gearing toward the test). Noting on your resume that you are a PMP® or Six Sigma or ITIL candidate can help recruiters find you electronically. You can also add the dates of your class and the training company that offered it.

TOP TEN PITFALLS TO AVOID IN THE PMP® CERTIFICATION PROCESS AND ON THE EXAM

1. Not finding the right PMP® course for your needs and learning style. For example, if you don't like or do particularly well in cram courses, don't take a cram course just because it might sound like the fastest path to certification.

2. Taking the test before you're ready. Rushing the test before you've studied and drilled sufficiently on practice questions can lead to your having to pay twice for an expensive exam. A rule of thumb is to take the test after you are averaging 85 percent or higher on the practice questions.

3   Putting off the test too long and forgetting what you've learned—or worse, until a new version of the *PMBOK® Guide* has come out. You would need to learn everything that has changed from the old version to the new to answer some of the test questions.

4. Trying to go for the wrong certification. Choose the one that best fits your background and will most help you on the job, in your job search, and in making progress toward your long term career goals.

5. Misrepresenting your background on the certification application. Not only is this unethical, but for PMI certifications, anyone who suspects you did so can easily report the violation to PMI, which has a system in place for handling such cases.

6. Not preparing for the pacing of the test. It's recommended that you keep a close watch on your timing as you drill on practice questions. Training for a brisk pace will help you on the exam.

7. Not taking breaks on the test, ideally with snacks and beverages (at testing sites that permit them).

8. Using unauthorized test questions to practice, such as anonymous resources you might find on the Internet. A much better idea is to study from one of the many high-quality authorized materials available. These are tried and true and will probably do you more good anyway.

9. Not requesting the language aid for your primary language if English is not your strongest language (this single tip can make a *huge* difference!).

10. Having a this-answer-is-just-for-the-test attitude. A common beginner's mistake is to try to guess the answer you think the test "wants" you to choose, instead of giving your most honest, best answer. This approach may hurt more than help on the test, and it can also get in the way of learning the concepts while you're studying.

Final Words

I hope this book helps make you more efficient and productive on your projects, as well as more successful in your career.

A great many of my PM students have sent me thank you notes after passing their CAPM®, PMP®, and Project+ exams (sometimes within seconds of passing, thanks to smartphones!). This always makes me feel a little like Jimmy Stewart in *It's a Wonderful Life*—very lucky to be able to help so many people become certified and often find high-paying new jobs as a direct result. (Every time someone passes their PMP® exam, an angel gets its wings?) In fact, as I'm writing these final words, I just received a note from a student who did both: he passed his PMP® exam today and got a new PM job this week, too.

With *The Project Management Answer Book,* I look forward to helping many more PM students and practitioners. I hope to have answered in one handy reference guide all the questions I have ever been asked by the many PMs who have attended my classes.

—Jeff Furman

Networking Tips and Social Media for PMs

Networking and making use of social media are critical for today's PM. This appendix provides links to the most helpful networking resources for PMs. A more complete list is available at www.jeff-furman.com; click on "Jeff's List."

Most of the organizations cited offer live networking events and leading-edge seminars for members. Some offer excellent webinars for those who like to learn and network from the comfort of their home or on a lunch break at the office. Many of the seminars and webinars are free and also offer professional development units (PDUs), which help attendees keep up their PMP® certifications. Most offer PMs chances to help their peers by sharing advice or information—a way of networking which can help forge especially strong long-term relationships.

Some of the events are directly geared toward job seeking, including some audio conferences. Others, including local chapters of PMI, offer job boards exclusively for PMs.

Some of these groups also allow participants the chance to give their own presentations or webinars (an exceptionally good networking move!). And PMI also offers members opportunities to manage volunteer projects, mentor less-experienced PMs, or be mentored themselves. PMs often sign up for such events with networking and resume boosting primarily in mind, but then they discover that these activities are also highly rewarding for them.

TOP TEN NETWORKING PITFALLS

1. It's not all about you! While you *are* networking primarily to help yourself, it usually works out better if you take a "How can I help *you*?" approach. Ways of networking by helping others include offering good resources you've found, writing online recommendations for coworkers you admire, and sharing an announcement about an upcoming event that you think will help your contacts. Remember that everyone else is busy trying to help their own careers, too, so people will remember you for helping them and will want to help you in return.

2. Don't just offer help for the sake of offering. Most people can easily detect insincerity. Making an obviously phony offer if you're clearly only looking for help yourself is not going to get you very far.

3. Don't blindly contact a lot of people. Planning and strategizing are key here (just as they are in project management). Instead of taking a scattershot approach, think about what kind of networking help you want, and who best can help you get it, and network in a strategic, organized way. Work smart, not hard.

4. Don't send out a mass mailing when you can send personal notes. Taking a little extra time to send individual, personalized notes to your contacts is a much more effective way to engage people than is sending a generic message to a list. Sending personal notes allows you to remind each contact about who you are and what your relationship to him or her is.

5. Don't bombard contacts. Try not to contact anyone too many times, and allow people enough time to get back to you before you follow up. On the Internet, as well as at in-person networking events, you should always be courteous and respectful of others' space and time. Otherwise, you can easily push people away.

6. Don't let virtual networking replace making in-person contacts. As powerful as the Internet can be, it still is not a replacement for in-person networking. Go to seminars and meet real, live people (not avatars!). Then, go back home and invite them to connect virtually to reinforce your relationship. Meeting people first makes for a much stronger virtual connection, one that is more likely to lead to meaningful additional connections.

   There are a great many in-person networking events. The organizations in the list provided below can connect you to many free events in your local area and give you ideas for where to find more.

7. Don't ask people you don't know at all for favors. You wouldn't expect walking up to total strangers and asking them for career guidance to work. The same is true online. It's always better to take the time to cultivate relationships before asking for contacts, job leads, information, or advice.

8. Resist Internet addiction! This is no joke. Studies now show that interaction on the Internet causes a rush of endorphins in your brain. But you shouldn't spend too much time online or let it interfere with your other networking efforts, such as going to in-person events. Remember why you're spending time on the Internet, and save a quick email break for a reward after you get some other good work done.

9. Don't do networking moves you don't believe in. There's a tendency to go overboard with Internet networking because it's so easy to hit the Send button. Don't jeopardize good relationships you have with friends and associates by being overly willing to send casual contacts their way, or providing recommendations that you don't really stand behind, in the hope that your contacts will do the same for you in return. People still expect the old-fashioned values of honesty and integrity, even when using the most modern networking methods.

10. Networking should be fun, not forced. Try to have as much fun with social networking as you can, and don't force it—you'll get better results. It's very easy for people to tell if you are genuinely enjoying the interaction or if you are only using networking as a means to an end. Try modeling after people you observe who obviously *do* like it, and who do it well. The better you become at helping others, the better you'll start to feel about networking for yourself and the more others will want to help you meet your networking goals.

PM-SPECIFIC SOCIAL NETWORKING AND EDUCATIONAL SITES

An up-to-date list is available at www.jeff-furman.com. Click on "Jeff's List."

ASTD: American Society for Training & Development. www.astd.org.

ASTD/NY: The New York City chapter of ASTD. Offers monthly seminars, plus many special interest groups (SIGS), including Coaching SIG, e-Learning

SIG, Training Directors' SIG, Book Group SIG, Consultants' SIG, and more. www.astdny.org.

Cairn Consulting LLC: Dr. Carol Mase, president/organizational consultant/executive coach/speaker. www.cairnconsultants.com, www. organizationsasorganisms.com (blog).

Careers for NYC: New York City offers its citizens a whole portfolio of free career services, ranging from assistance with resumes and career counseling to job placements through Mayor Bloomberg's Workforce1 Career Centers. For more information, visit www.nyc.gov/workforce1.

CompTIA: Computing Technical Industry Association. Offers many technical certifications, including Project+, Security+, Network+, A+, Project+, Certified Technical Trainer (CTT+). www.comptia.org.

CompTIA SmartBrief: News for the IT industry, including leading-edge articles and a daily digest. http://smartbrief.com/comptia.

Cornell University Library Guides Home: Many good articles, webinars, videos on leading-edge topics. http://guides.library.cornell.edu

Deloitte Insights (podcasts): Cutting-edge podcasts on a great variety of business topics from Big 4 auditing corporation Deloitte. http://www. deloitte.com/view/en-us/us/insights/index.htm.

The Ethicist: Randy Cohen, author and speaker, is best known for his popular weekly column "The Ethicist" for the *New York Times Magazine*, also available via podcast at http://www.nytimes.com/ref/multimedia/ podcasts.html. Also see Cohen's blog, "Moral of the Story," offering the Ethicist's take on weekly news items. Email the Ethicist at ethicist@ nytimes.com.

Gantt Head: "The online community for IT project managers." www.gantt head.com.

GovLoop: A social network for government. www.govloop.com.

HR/NY: Human Resources Association of New York. www.hrny.org.

IIBA: International Institute of Business Analysis. Offers a certification in business analysis with a knowledge area somewhat modeled after PMI's. www. theiiba.org.

InfraGard: Nationwide, FBI-affiliated organization offering live meetings and seminars in many cities around the United States, with a focus on security and guarding the U.S. infrastructure (infrastructure + guard = InfraGard). www.infragard.net

International Institute for Learning, Inc.: Educational webinars, many offering PDUs, some for free. www.iil.com.

LinkedIn: The number-one social networking site in the world for many categories of business professionals; very valuable for PMs. You can use LinkedIn to post a professional profile and contact and connect with other business professionals. Basic LinkedIn services are free; additional services are available for paying members. www.linkedin.com.

Net MBA: Source of quality business knowledge resources, including key business terms and more. www.netmba.com.

NYC SPIN: New York Software Process Improvement Network, offering free, high-quality software and project seminars in Manhattan. The seminars also provide PDUs. www.nycspin.org.

PmHUB forums: Information, recommendations, and a forum for PMs to post questions and give and receive feedback. http://forums.pmhub.net.

PgMP instructor: Dr. Ginger Levin, PhD, PMP, PgMP, PgMP instructor and coach, author of many books on PM and PgMP, and dynamic guest speaker. ginlevin@aol.com.

PMConnection: Links to industry articles and more. www.pmconnection. com.

PM Daily Digest/Project Management Excellence Center. Free PMP® exam question of the day, other resources for purchase. www.pmexam.com.

PM HUT: PM-focused articles, resources, and news. www.pmhut.com.

PM Lessons Learned: A phone-based project management networking organization; three free teleconferences on PM topics each month. www.pmlessonslearned.com.

PM Link: Links to articles, blogs, books, jobs, and more. www.pmlink.org.

PM Webinars: Free webinars on software best practices. http://www.itmpi.org/webinars.

PM411: Free audio podcasts, blog posts, links to test-prep resources, and more. http://pm411.org.

PM Fastrack: Books, courses, webinars, and presentations from PM expert Rita Mulcahy. http://www.rmcproject.com.

PM Podcast: Free and premium audio podcasts. www.project-management-podcast.com.

The Project Management Institute: International organization for project managers and the issuing body of the CAPM, PMP®, PgMP, and other certifications. Offers local chapters, lectures, conferences, volunteer programs, mentoring, and other resources for members. www.pmi.org.

Process Fusion: Resources on project management and process improvement, including free white papers, articles, and podcasts. www.process-fusion.net; information@process-fusion.net.

Project Leadership Podcast: Free podcasts on PM and business topics. www.projectleadershippodcast.com.

ProjectManagers.net: "The Social Network for Project Managers." www.projectmanagers.net.

Project Smart: PM templates (some free), white papers, articles, guidance on methods, and more. http://www.projectsmart.co.uk.

Risk Doctor: Internationally recognized risk expert David Hillson offers risk consulting, risk management white papers, and speaking services. www.risk-doctor.com.

Toastmasters: Forum for giving presentations and receiving critiques from peers; also an excellent networking organization. www.toastmasters.org.

Max Wideman: Comparative glossary of project management terms. http://www.maxwideman.com/pmglossary/index.htm.

Using LinkedIn Groups

LinkedIn users can join groups of people with similar interests, such as the 14 PMP®-related groups below. Groups link you to people with similar professional interests. One benefit of joining groups is that you can participate and start discussions in which members share information and ask for and offer advice. Some PM-related LinkedIn groups include:

- ASTD: The American Society for Training and Development.
- CAPM: Certified Associate Project Management (CAPM's) official group
- Global Program and Project Networking Group
- PgMP Credentialed Networking Group
- PM Lessons Learned
- PMI Certified PMPs
- PMI PgMP Certified
- PM Job Shop
- PMP® Credentialed Holders
- Project Management Group
- Project Management Link—www.pmlink.org
- Project Manager Alliance!
- Project Manager Networking Group
- Smart Leaders.

How to Send a Personalized LinkedIn Invitation

A common mistake people make with LinkedIn is to simply give an email address and send a generic "would like to connect" invitation without taking a few minutes to include a personal note reminding the person they are contacting who they are and how they know him or her. You are much more likely to get an acceptance if you personalize your invitation.

To personalize an invitation:

1. Use the people search box in LinkedIn to find your contact, and pull up his or her profile. (Sometimes you'll need to go through a mutual contact to be introduced to a contact, but this is often not necessary because many LinkedIn users have publicly available profiles.)

2. After pulling up the profile, click on "Add [name] to your network."

3. Write a brief personal note in the box labeled "Include a personal note: (optional)."

4. Optionally, where the screen asks: *How do you know this person?* you can also select one of the choices, such as "colleague" or "classmate" or "group," and then specify the company, school, or LinkedIn group you have in common. This further personalizes your invitation, making your contact more interested in connecting with you (and takes all of about two seconds!)

The Formulas PMs Need to Know for Certification Exams

FORMULAS, KNOWLEDGE AREAS, AND PROCESSES

Name	Formula	Knowledge Area	PMI Process
PERT estimate/ three-point estimate	PERT = (P + 4M + O)/6	Time (and cost)	Estimate activity duration
SD (standard deviation)	SD = (P − 0)/6	Time (and cost)	Estimate activity duration
Float (slack)	Late finish − early finish *or* late start − early start	Time	Control schedule
Free float	(ES of successor − EF of predecessor) − 1	Time	Control schedule
Duration	(Early finish − early start) + 1 *or* (Late finish − late start) + 1	Time	Control schedule
BAC (budget at completion)	No formula—just the estimated budget amount (used with formulas below)	Cost	Control costs

Name	Formula	Knowledge Area	PMI Process
AC (actual cost)	No formula; the amount of money actually spent so far on the project (used with formulas below)	Cost	Control costs
PV (planned value)	PV = Planned percent complete * BAC	Cost	Control costs
EV (earned value)	EV = Actual percent complete * BAC	Cost	Control costs
SPI (schedule performance index)	SPI = EV/PV	Cost	Control costs
CPI (cost performance index)	CPI = EV/AC	Cost	Control costs
Cumulative CPI	$CPI^c = EV^c/AC^c$	Cost	Control costs
SV (schedule variance)	SV = EV – PV	Cost	Control costs
CV (cost variance)	CV = EV – AC	Cost	Control costs
EAC (estimate at completion)	EAC = BAC/CPI or EAC = BAC/CPI^c	Cost	Control costs
ETC (estimate to complete)	ETC = EAC – AC	Cost	Control costs
VAC (variance at completion)	VAC = BAC – EAC	Cost	Control costs
TCPI (to-complete performance index)	TCPI = (BAC – EV)/ funds remaining	Cost	Control costs

Name	Formula	Knowledge Area	PMI Process
COQ (cost of quality)	COQ = Prevention costs + appraisal costs + failure costs	Quality	Plan quality, quality assurance, quality control
Communication channels	Communication channels = (N(N − 1))/2	Communications	Plan communications
PI (probability and impact)	PI = P * I	Risk	Perform *qualitative* risk analysis
EMV (expected monetary value)	EMV = P (as a percentage) * I (as a dollar amount)	Risk	Perform *quantitative* risk analysis
PTA (point of total assumption)	PTA = Target cost + (ceiling price − target price)/buyer's % share of cost overrun	Procurement	Plan procurements

FORMULAS, KNOWLEDGE AREAS, AND PROCESSES: FILL-IN-THE-BLANKS VERSION

You can use this as a practice worksheet or study aid.

Name	Formula?	Part of which knowledge area?	Used in which specific process?
PERT estimate/ three-point estimate	PERT estimate =	Time (and cost)	
SD (standard deviation)	SD =	Time (and cost)	
Float (slack)	Float =	Time	
Free float	Free float =	Time	
Duration	Duration =	Time	

Name	Formula?	Part of which knowledge area?	Used in which specific process?
BAC (budget at completion)	No formula; just the estimated budget amount (used with formulas below)	Cost	
AC (actual cost)	No formula; just the amount of money spent (used with formulas below)	Cost	
PV (planned value)	PV =	Cost	
EV (earned value)	EV =	Cost	
SPI (schedule performance index)	SPI =	Cost	
CPI (cost performance index)	CPI =	Cost	
Cumulative CPI	CPI^c		
SV (schedule variance)	SV =	Cost	
CV (cost variance)	CV =	Cost	
EAC (estimate at completion)	EAC =	Cost	
ETC (estimate to complete)	ETC =	Cost	
VAC (variance at completion)	VAC =	Cost	

Name	Formula?	Part of which knowledge area?	Used in which specific process?
TCPI (to-complete performance index)	TCPI =	Cost	
COQ (cost of quality)	COQ =	Quality	
Communication channels	Communication channels =	Communications	
PI (probability and impact)	PI =	Risk	
EMV (expected monetary value)	EMV =	Risk	
PTA (point of total assumption)	PTA =	Procurement	Which process? Which contract types?

Quick Study Sheet for the Processes Covered on the PMP® Exam

PMP® PROCESSES GRID

Knowledge Area	Initiating Process Group	Planning Process Group	Executing Process Group	Monitoring and Controlling Process Group	Closing Process Group
Integration Management	Develop project charter	Develop project management plan	Direct and manage project execution	Monitor and control project work	Close project or phase
				Perform integrated change control	
Scope Management		Collect requirements		Verify scope	
		Define scope		Control scope	
		Create WBS			
Time Management		Define activities		Control schedule	
		Sequence activities			
		Estimate activity resources			
		Estimate activity durations			
		Develop schedule			

(Continued on next page)

	Initiating	Planning	Executing	Monitoring & Controlling	
Cost Management		Estimate costs Determine budget		Control costs	
Quality Management		Plan quality	Perform quality assurance	Perform quality control	
Human Resource Management		Develop human resource plan	Acquire project team Develop project team Manage project team		
Communications Management	Identify stakeholders	Plan communications	Distribute information Manage stakeholder expectations	Report performance	

(Continued on next page)

Knowledge Area	Initiating Process Group	Planning Process Group	Executing Process Group	Monitoring and Controlling Process Group	Closing Process Group
Risk Management		Plan risk management		Monitor and control risks	
		Identify risks			
		Perform qualitative risk analysis			
		Perform quantitative risk analysis			
		Plan risk responses			
Procurement Management		Plan procurements	Conduct procurements	Administer procurements	Close procurements

PMP® PROCESSES GRID: FILL-IN-THE-BLANKS VERSION

	Process Group #1	Process Group #2	Process Group #3	Process Group #4	Process Group #5
Knowledge Area #1					
Knowledge Area #2					
Knowledge Area #3					
Knowledge Area #4					
Knowledge Area #5					
Knowledge Area #6					
Knowledge Area #7					
Knowledge Area #8					
Knowledge Area #9					

Bibliography

Baratta, Angelo. "Value Triple Constraint: How To Evaluate Project Value Delivered." *Executive Brief, Technology Management Resource for Business Leaders* (February 2010).

Beck, Kent, et al. "Manifesto for Agile Software Development." 2001. http://agilealliance.org/show/2.

Berkun, Scott. *The Art of Project Management (Theory In Practice).* Sebastopol, CA: O'Reilly, 2004.

Buckingham, Marcus, and Curt Coffman. *First, Break All the Rules.* New York: Simon & Schuster, 1999.

Bumiller, Elisabeth. "We Have Met the Enemy and He Is PowerPoint." *New York Times,* April 27, 2010.

Carnegie, Dale. *How To Win Friends and Influence People.* New York: Simon & Schuster, 2009.

Covey, Stephen R. *The 7 Habits of Highly Effective People.* New York: Free Press, 2004.

Coy, Peter, Michelle Conlin, and Moira Herbst. "The Disposable Worker." *Bloomberg BusinessWeek*, January 18, 2010.

Crosby, Philip B. *Quality Is Free: The Art of Making Quality Certain.* New York: McGraw-Hill, 1979.

Crowe, Andy. *Alpha Project Managers: What the Top 2% Know That Everyone Else Does Not.* Kennesaw, GA: Velociteach Press, 2008.

Crowe, Andy. *The PMP Exam—How To Pass on Your First Try.* Kennesaw, GA: Velociteach Press, 2009.

DeBord, Mathew. "Toyota's Blind Spot." *New York Times*, February 5, 2010.

Fiedler, Fred E. *A Theory of Leadership Effectiveness.* New York: McGraw-Hill, 1967.

Friedman, Thomas L. "Who's Sleeping Now?" *New York Times*, January 10, 2010.

Furman, Jeff. "Advance Disaster Planning: A Q&A with Three Senior Risk Managers on How Preparedness is Changing after the Hurricanes of 2005." *Technical Support Magazine*, March 2006.

———. "Data-Aging Tools: Key Evaluation Criteria." *Year 2000 Journal*, July/August 1998.

———. "PMP: Is It the Certification or the Knowledge That Matters Most?" *NaSPA,* December 2007. http://naspa.com.

Furman, Jeff, Cliff Candiotti, and Albert Marotta. "Party When It's 1999." *Software Magazine*, April 1995.

———. "The Year 2000: Not Just An Applications Issue." *Technical Support Magazine*, July 1995.

Furman, Jeff, and Albert Marotta. "Year 2000 Denial." *ComputerWorld*, October 24, 1994.

Greene, Jennifer, and Andy Stellman. *Head First PMP.* Sebastopol, CA: O'Reilly, 2007.

Goldratt, Eliyahu M. *Critical Chain.* Great Barrington, MA: North River Press, 1997.

———. *The Goal: A Process of Ongoing Improvement.* Great Barrington, MA: North River Press, 1984.

———. *Theory of Constraints.* Great Barrington, MA: North River Press, 1990.

Heath, Chip, and Dan Heath. *SWITCH: How To Change Things When Change Is Hard.* New York: Broadway Books, 2010.

Herzberg, Frederick, Bernard Mausner, and Barbara Block Snyderman. *The Motivation To Work.* New Brunswick, NJ: Transaction Publishers, 1999.

Hillson, David. "Working Backwards To Opportunities." *Risk Doctor Briefings*, no. 33 (October 2007). http://www.risk-doctor.com/pdf-briefings/riskdoctor-33e.pdf.

———. "Does Opportunity Management Mean Scope Creep?" *Risk Doctor Briefings*, no. 20 (January 2006). http://www.risk-doctor.com/pdf-briefings/risk-doctor20e.pdf.

Hsieh, Tony. *Delivering Happiness: A Path To Profits, Passion, and Purpose.* New York: Hachette Book Group, 2010.

Huizinga, Gerard. *Maslow's Need Hierarchy in the Work Situation.* Groningen, Netherlands: Wolters-Noordhoff Publishing, 1970.

Kolata, Gina. "In Cancer Fight, Unclear Tests Confuse Therapy." *New York Times*, April 20, 2010.

Langfitt, Frank. Introduction by series host Ira Glass. "This American Life Tells the NUMMI Story." National Public Radio's *This American Life*, March 26, 2010.

Lillycrop, Mark. "The Millennium Bug." *ServiceTalk the Journal*, January 2010.

Mah, Michael. "The World May Not Be So Flat (Making Tom Friedman Grumpy)." White paper presented at the NYC SPIN (Software Process Improvement Network) meeting. New York, NY, February 13, 2007.

Management Concepts. *The 77 Deadly Sins of Project Management.* Vienna, VA: Management Concepts, 2009.

Maslow, Abraham. *Motivation and Personality, Third Edition.* New York: Harper & Row, Publishers, Inc., 1987.

Maslow, Abraham, Deborah Stevens, and Gary Heil. *Maslow on Management.* New York: John Wiley & Sons, 1998.

McGregor, Douglas. *The Human Side of Enterprise.* New York: McGraw-Hill, 2006.

————. "The Human Side of Enterprise." Chapter 1 in *Leadership and Motivation: Essays of Douglas McGregor*, edited by Warren G. Bennis and Edgar H. Shein, 3–20. Cambridge, MA: The MIT Press, 1966.

McClelland, David C. *Human Motivation.* Glenview, IL: Scott, Foresman, and Company, 1985.

Mulcahy, Rita. *PMP® Exam Prep, Sixth Edition: Rita's Course in a Book for Passing the PMP® Exam.* Minnetonka, MN: RMC Publications, 2009.

Phillips, Joseph. *CAPM®/PMP® Project Management Certification All-in-One Exam Guide.* New York: McGraw Hill, 2007.

Project Management. *A Guide to the Project Management Body of Knowledge (PMBOK® Guide).* Newtown Square, PA: Project Management Institute, 2009.

Project Management Institute. *Project Management Institute Code of Ethics and Professional Conduct.* 2006. http://www.pmi.org/en/About-Us/ Ethics/~/media/PDF/Ethics/ap_pmicodeofethics.ashx.

Rad, Parvis F., and Ginger Levin. *Achieving Project Management Success Using Virtual Teams.* Fort Lauderdale: J. Ross Publishing, 2003.

Stolovitch, Harold D., and Erica J. Keeps. *Telling Ain't Training.* Alexandria, VA: ASTD Press, 2002.

Sutton, Robert I. *The No Asshole Rule: Building a Civilized Workplace and Surviving One That Isn't.* New York: Hachette Book Group, 2007.

Toyoda, Akio. President and CEO, Toyota Motor Corporation. Testimony to the House Committee on Oversight and Government Reform. 111th Cong., 2nd sess., February 24, 2010.

Vroom, Victor H. *Work and Motivation.* New York: John Wiley & Sons, Inc., 1964.

Wayne, Leslie. "A Promise To Be Ethical in an Era of Temptation." *New York Times*, May 30, 2009.

Wikipedia. "Parkinson's Law." http://en.wikipedia.org/wiki/Parkinson%27s_ law.

Wolfe, Tom. "One Giant Leap To Nowhere." *New York Times*, July 19, 2009.

Womack, James, Daniel Jones, Daniel Roos, and Donna Sammons Carpenter. *The Machine That Changed the World.* New York: Macmillan, 1990.

Index

Certified Information Security Manager
(CISM), 361
Certified Information Systems Auditor
(CISA), 361
Certified Management Consultant
(CMC), 360
Certified Scrum Master (CSM), 360
CGEIT. *See* Certified in the Governance of
Enterprise IT
change control system, 29
change management plan, 30
charter
definition, 2–3
elements of, 3–4
need for, 4
preliminary documents, 34
chief information officer (CIO), 9
CISA. *See* Certified Information Systems
Auditor
CISM. *See* Certified Information Security
Manager
closeout, 219–221
closing processes, 5
CMC. *See* Certified Management
Consultant
CMMI. *See* Capability Maturity Model
Integration
Code of Ethics and Professional Conduct,
228–229
collocation, 337–338
communication skills
active listening, 252–253
alpha project managers, 265
arguing in bad faith, 274
being agreeable, 268–269
commit-to listening, 253
communication channels formula,
264–265
diplomacy, 269
distributing information, 259
effective listening, 252
electronic communications, 265–266
emotional intelligence, 256–257
empathetic listening, 254
false balance, 273–274
false parallels, 274
formal communications *versus* informal
communications, 263
importance of, 251

managing customer expectations, 261
managing stakeholder expectations,
260–262
marking emails, 266
message *versus* medium, 262
multitasking, 266
no blame, no shame, 270
noise, 253–254
paralingual vocal qualities, 254–256
passive-aggressive behavior, 272–273
performance reports, 260
personal mistakes, 270
pitfalls, 275–276
pointing out mistakes, 267–268
proxemics, 263–264
sharing secrets, 273
spin, 271
stakeholder identification process,
257–258
teleconferencing, 267
triangulation, 272
videoconferencing, 267
white lies, 271
win-win results, 270
communications management plan, 31,
258–259
computer-aided design (CAD), 11
conceptual estimates, 96
configuration management plan, 30
conflict
compromise, 305–306
forcing, 306
managing, 304–305
smoothing, 307
withdrawal, 306
consensus-driven management, 344–345
contingency reserves, 79–80, 170
Continuing Certification Requirements
(CCR), 350
contracts. *See also* procurement
boilerplate, 198
concessions, 197
cost plus, 199–200
cost plus award fee, 200
cost plus fixed price, 200
cost plus percentage of costs, 200
cost reimbursable, 200
definition, 196–197
firm fixed price, 198–199

Guerrilla Project Management
Kenneth T. Hanley, M. Eng. (Project Management)

To manage effectively in today's complex project environment, you need a framework of project management (PM) competencies, processes, and tools that can be put to use immediately and that flexes and scales to meet the needs of any project. In this book, Ken Hanley emphasizes key project management competencies, including managing stakeholders effectively, assessing risk accurately, and getting agreement on the objective measures of project success. Hanley presents an alternative approach to project management that is light, fast, and flexible—and adapts readily to the many changes every project manager faces. This is *the* go-to guide for today's nimble project manager!

ISBN 978-1-56726-294-0 ▪ Product Code B940 ▪ 236 pages

Integrated Cost and Schedule Control in Project Management, Second Edition
Ursula Kuehn, PMP

Building on the solid foundation of the first edition, this updated second edition includes new material on project planning in the federal government, integrated baseline reviews (IBRs), federal requirements for an ANSI/EIA-748 compliant earned value management system, and federal requirements for contract performance reports (CPRs). This book continues to offer a practical approach that is accessible to project managers at all levels. The step-by-step presentation, numerous case studies, and instructive examples give practitioners relevant material they can put to use immediately.

ISBN 978-1-56726-296-4 ▪ Product Code B964 ▪ 319 pages

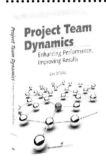

Project Team Dynamics: Enhancing Performance, Improving Results
Lisa DiTullio

Companies that embrace the power of collaboration realize that the best way to solve complex problems is to build cohesive teams made up of members with different skills and expertise. Getting teams to work productively is at the heart of project management. Developing the structure for teams to work at a high level of efficiency and effectiveness is at the heart of this book. With examples drawn from contemporary project management, she demonstrates the effectiveness of this straightforward approach and the risks of not building a strong team culture.

ISBN 978-1-56726-290-2 ▪ Product Code B902 ▪ 179 pages

Project Management Fundamentals: Key Concepts and Methodology, Second Edition
Gregory Haugan, PhD, PMP

To achieve success in any endeavor, you need to understand the fundamental aspects of that endeavor. To achieve success in project management, you should start with this completely revised edition that offers new project managers a solid foundation in the basics of the discipline. Using a step-by-step approach and conventional project management terminology, this book is a commonsense guide that focuses on how essential project management methods, tools, and techniques can be put into practice immediately.

ISBN 978-1-56726-281-0 ▪ Product Code B810 ▪ 380 pages

Interpersonal Skills for Portfolio, Program, and Project Managers
Ginger Levin, DPA, PMP, PgMP

Any formula for management success must include a high level of interpersonal skills. The growing complexity of portfolios, programs, and projects, as well as the increasing number and geographic dispersion of stakeholders, makes a manager's interpersonal skills critical. The frequency and variety of interpersonal interactions and the pressure to execute portfolios, programs, and projects successfully while ensuring customer satisfaction have never been greater. This book offers practical and proven tools and methods you can use to develop your interpersonal skills and meet the challenges of today's competitive professional environment.

ISBN 978-1-56726-288-9 ■ Product Code B889 ■ 286 pages

Organizational Project Management: Linking Strategy and Projects
Edited by Rosemary Hossenlopp, PMP

Organizational project management (OPM) aligns project deliverables with strategy. Understanding this emerging process is essential for all stakeholders, from the corporate sponsor to project team members. OPM is a valuable new tool that can enhance your organization's successful execution of projects in alignment with strategic priorities. Under the editorship of Rosemary Hossenlopp, PMP, ten contributors from around the globe, representing a wide variety of industries, offer valuable insights on how OPM can give any organization the competitive edge.

ISBN 978-1-56726-282-7 ■ Product Code B827 ■ 193 pages

Achieving Project Management Success in the Federal Government
Jonathan Weinstein, PMP, and Timothy Jaques, PMP

The authors offer a realistic cross section of the project management discipline in the largest single enterprise in the world—the U.S. federal government. Based on research and interviews with a wide variety of project managers who shared their lessons learned and advice, this book offers practical guidance and insights to federal leaders, project team members, and others involved with project management in the government.

ISBN 978-1-56726-275-9 ■ Product Code B759 ■ 304 pages

The 77 Deadly Sins of Project Management
Management Concepts

Projects can be negatively impacted by common "sins" that hinder, stall, or throw the project off track. This book helps you better understand how to execute projects by providing individual anecdotes and case studies of the project management sins described by experts in the field.

ISBN 978-1-56726-246-9 ■ Product Code B777 ■ 357 pages

CPSIA information can be obtained at www.ICGtesting.com
Printed in the USA
BVOW06s0401110913

330826BV00003B/3/P